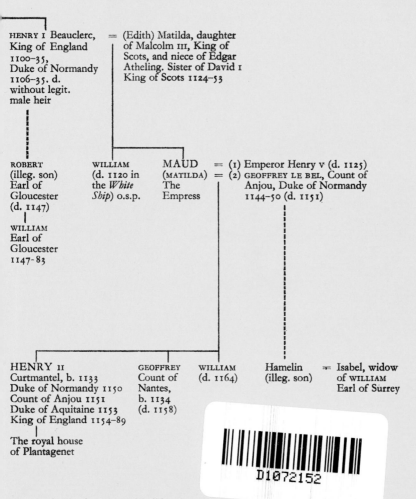

HENRY I Beauclerc, = (Edith) Matilda, daughter
King of England   of Malcolm III, King of
1100–35,   Scots, and niece of Edgar
Duke of Normandy   Atheling. Sister of David I
1106–35. d.   King of Scots 1124–53
without legit.
male heir

ROBERT   WILLIAM   MAUD   = (1) Emperor Henry V (d. 1125)
(illeg. son)   (d. 1120 in   (MATILDA)   = (2) GEOFFREY LE BEL, Count of
Earl of   the *White*   The   Anjou, Duke of Normandy
Gloucester   *Ship*) o.s.p. Empress   1144–50 (d. 1151)
(d. 1147)

WILLIAM
Earl of
Gloucester
1147–83

HENRY II   GEOFFREY   WILLIAM   Hamelin   = Isabel, widow
Curtmantel, b. 1133   Count of   (d. 1164)   (illeg. son)   of WILLIAM
Duke of Normandy 1150 Nantes,   Earl of Surrey
Count of Anjou 1151   b. 1134
Duke of Aquitaine 1153 (d. 1158)
King of England 1154–89

The royal house
of Plantagenet

Note 1. Stephen's consort, Matilda of Boulogne, was the daughter of ...
Count of Boulogne (who was descended from Charlemagne) and his wife Mary, a
sister of David I, King of Scots. She was a niece (by marriage) of Henry I, and also
neice of Godfrey de Bouillon the Crusader and of Baldwin I, King of Jerusalem
1100–08.

Note 2. Of Henry I's numerous illegitimate offspring, those who are mentioned
in this book are: Robert, Earl of Gloucester, b. before 1100, d. 1147; Reginald de
Dunstanville, Earl of Cornwall, d. 1173; and Maud (Matilda), wife of Rotrou, Count
of Perche. She died in the *White Ship*, as did another illegitimate son, Richard.

The Reign of Stephen
1135–54
Anarchy in England

Studies in Medieval History
Edited by R. H. Hilton

'Here is Hell and the angel is shutting the door'. From the *Winchester Psalter* made for Henry of Blois, Bishop of Winchester, 1129–71 (British Museum, Cotton MS Nero c. IV fo. 39r.)

The Reign of Stephen
1135–54
Anarchy in England

H. A. Cronne
Professor of Medieval History in the
University of Birmingham

Weidenfeld and Nicolson
5 Winsley Street London W1

SBN 297 00015 2
Printed in Great Britain
by Ebenezer Baylis and Son, Ltd.
The Trinity Press, Worcester, and London

To Ann and Sally

Contents

Tables

Map

1*

Preface

This book is based upon evidence with which I have long been familiar. It has been written during a time when illness has made it very difficult to work in libraries and record offices. This has restricted my studies and imposed certain disadvantages, such as the necessity of using a quite well-known translation of Ordericus Vitalis instead of the almost unobtainable edition of Le Prévost and Delisle.

Any study of Stephen's reign is necessarily limited by the kind of source material that is available. There are of course contemporary histories, chronicles and annals, though there are very few that adequately cover the reign as a whole. Our interpretation of it might have been different if the great works of William of Malmesbury and Ordericus Vitalis had not ended so early; it would certainly have been very much less satisfactory had not Sir Roger Mynors rediscovered the long-lost ending of *Gesta Stephani*. There are numbers of royal charters and writs and of episcopal, monastic and baronial *acta*. There are also some contemporary letters, precious collections such as those of St Bernard of Clairvaux and Gilbert Foliot. Beyond these sources there is very little – no great financial record such as the single but invaluable pipe roll that has survived from the reign of Henry I, no Chancery enrolments, no wardrobe books or other records of the royal household save the tantalising *Constitutio Domus Regis*, no court rolls, no ministers' or manorial accounts, no episcopal registers. It is therefore a distorted view of the period that we get from our sources because of their limited range. I have perhaps relied too much upon royal charters and writs, with which my work has made me most familiar, and far too little on private deeds. Some aspects of Stephen's reign will always remain obscure unless some quite miraculous hoard of documents should ever come to light. This is especially the case in the study of the peasantry and of agrarian history specifically during the years 1135–54, and much research still remains to be done on clergy, aristocracy and towns before anything approaching a moderately satisfactory social history of the period can be written. It should be clear why a full history of Stephen's reign has not even been contemplated here. Rather, I have tried, by approaching it from as many different aspects as I could manage, to give some semblance of stereoscopic quality to the picture. In so far as any choice has been open to me, I have tried to concentrate upon those aspects which seemed likely to contribute most to an understanding of the reign as a whole. Thus, for example, in dealing with the aristocracy, I have concentrated upon a few family groups which were most prominent in the 'politics' of the time. I have argued that continued disputation about the meaning and significance of feudalism has caused a great deal of unnecessary confusion, and I have emphasised the family connections of the aristocracy far more than their feudal relationships. This does not mean that I underestimate the importance of the latter, but rather that I think the time is not yet ripe for another discussion of this very important subject, except at the most technical level of research. There is every reason to hope that the scholars now working in this field will soon carry forward the work of their distinguished predecessors to new heights.

I have to thank the Librarian, Dr K.W. Humphreys, and the staff of Birmingham University Library for their unfailing helpfulness and indulgence to a borrower who has sometimes strained their regulations. It will be very obvious to anyone who is familiar with work in this field that I am deeply indebted to Ralph Davis, my friend and collaborator for many years. Our views and interpretations of events and characters do not agree in every particular, but I think we have far more in common than at variance. Mr Davis has contributed more to this subject than any living historian. His deep knowledge and insight have shed light for me, as for others, in many dark places. There is a much older debt of gratitude, which I gratefully acknowledge, and that is to his father, the late Professor H.W.C. Davis, under whose eagle eye and strict guidance I first began to work on the subject. Also, I was most fortunate in a very long association and collaboration with the late Charles Johnson, that venerable sage, whose historical knowledge was fathomless, far beyond my plummet's sounding, and whose meticulous scholarship set a standard worth striving after. I have been happy, too, ever since a memorable evening in Balliol more than forty years ago, in my opportunities of drawing inspiration and encouragement from Vivian Galbraith's generous interest, passionate devotion to medieval history and erudition, which has ever flowed with distinctive vivacity and scintillation. To Rodney Hilton, general editor of this series, my colleague for twenty-two years past, I offer my very grateful thanks for the help he has given me with this book despite his heavy commitments, for many stimulating discussions and for his cheerful undertaking of so many academic burdens which, more than anything else, has given me an opportunity of writing. I am indebted also to another colleague, Margaret Archer, for reading some of my chapters in manuscript. My latest debt is to those whose care made it possible for this book to be written at all. Beyond all others I am indebted to my wife, and not least for her valuable historical criticism.

   The errors and shortcomings of the book are entirely my own work.

H. A. CRONNE

The Old House
Mucklow Hill
Halesowen
January 1969

I

'The Anarchy of Stephen's Reign'

It has long been the habit of historians to talk in over-simplified terms of 'The Anarchy of Stephen's Reign', thereby singling out two decades of England's far from tranquil medieval history as outstandingly the period of violence, confusion and lack of governance. There has even been a temptation to treat this condition almost as though it were susceptible of measurement at different times and places in ergons of anarchical output. This is not a very profitable historical exercise. In the broad frames of reference of world history and of twelfth-century European history, the conditions in Stephen's England are not uncommon; seen in the long perspective of English medieval history, they are not unexampled. In fact it is in its stark contrast with the stern, though far from peaceful, rule of the three Norman kings who preceded him and the firm dominion of the first Plantagenet who followed him that Stephen's disturbed reign appears exceptional.

There were habitually lawless and ruthless men, denounced by contemporary historians as tyrant lords of castles, and we are told most about those whose sins brought down upon them the more spectacular manifestations of divine retribution. It is very much more difficult to learn anything of the lives of men who sought only life, liberty and the pursuit of happiness. There were violent outbreaks of rebellion. Civil war was carried on between Stephen and the empress; private wars were waged between magnates with conflicting territorial claims and family ambitions, and these led at times to their espousing, for as long as it suited them and without any strong conviction, the side of the king or the empress. There were exceptions, men whose conduct was determined by genuine loyalty and not solely by self-interest, but they were not relatively numerous. Private feuds tended to be put to an end, not by the exercise of royal authority, but by private treaties. There were regions, such as that surrounding Wallingford, strategically situated in the Thames valley, whose lord, Brian fitz Count, held out valiantly and successfully for the empress, that were the scenes of constant raiding and siege warfare. The prevalence of what may be called 'castle warfare' inevitably brought pillage and destruction, making the maintenance of public order well nigh impossible during a great part of Stephen's reign.

In John of Salisbury's well-known list of public enemies, all have one thing in common.[1] These men were, whatever their other crimes, violators of churches. Geoffrey de Mandeville, William of Salisbury and Robert Marmion were notorious as such and they suffered prompt and dramatic retribution for their evil deeds, to the edification of the righteous and the warning of sinners. John of Salisbury's list was far from comprehensive, since he was merely singling out the best known examples. Every soldier in fact ran the risk of sinning in this way, not necessarily from malice or wickedness or complete disregard for the consequences: without attempting to condone on the ground of military necessity the appalling atrocities committed by ferocious and ruthless men, it is well to remember that military considerations were involved in all the examples we know. In an age of timber and wattle-and-daub building, when stone houses were still uncommon and a great many castles were of the motte-and bailey type, a stone-built church with its tower was always a potential and sometimes an actual strongpoint. A military commander neglected it at his peril in the course of any operations in its neighbourhood. A church was also a natural sanctuary for refugees and a storehouse for their belongings. These two uses of churches were not easily reconcilable and the refugees often suffered a grim fate. We are told in *Gesta Stephani* how, among other fortifications erected by the empress in the Oxford region in 1142, one was built in the village of Bampton 'right on the church tower, an ancient structure of marvellous design, built with astonishing skill and ingenious labour'.[2] In Hereford in 1140, when the royalist garrison was besieged in the castle there, the cathedral graveyard was dug up to make a gruesome earthwork and siege engines were mounted on the top of the church tower. Few soldiers hesitated for a moment when confronted with the military desirability of using or destroying a church, or of plundering and devastating its lands in order to deny their use to the enemy or to feed and reward their own troops.

These men trusted in being able eventually to make atonement with handsome reparations. The 'movent' clause of a charter of earl Roger of Hereford granting the manor of Broadward to Leominster, a dependent house of Reading Abbey, *c.* 1148–55, is quite typical. It includes the words 'as reparation for the injuries which were inflicted upon the men and the property of the aforesaid monks by me and my men during the war'.[3] If churches sometimes suffered severely, they were likely to gain considerably in the long run in land and worldly wealth. That was probably the view of most barons and knights in Stephen's reign. Some, like Mandeville and Marmion, were unfortunate enough to be slain before they could make fitting atonement for their sacrilegious acts and so were held up to obloquy, while others hardly less guilty became the 'pious and noble benefactors' of many a bidding prayer.

Anarchical conditions, however, were neither universal nor continuous in England as a whole and there were even some regions, such as Kent, which saw little fighting and suffered, relatively speaking, very lightly. There was not such a complete breakdown of government as the word 'anarchy' might imply. One of the most impressive and significant aspects of Stephen's reign is the survival, despite all the turmoil, of the Anglo-Norman governmental machine, very severely tried, but nevertheless in some sort of working order. To examine the functioning of this machine in a period of severe stress is a main purpose of this book.

'The Anarchy' in England has commonly been regarded as an essentially feudal phenomenon, the nemesis of an aristocratic society organised for war. In so far as anarchy did undoubtedly raise its sinister head in England, not for the first nor for the last time, between 1135 and 1154, was this because a tendency towards anarchy is inherent in every feudal society? Or was it because turbulence was an inborn characteristic of the Normans, as Ordericus Vitalis suggests in the deathbed speech he attributes to William the Conqueror?

The Normans, when ruled by a kind but firm master, are a most courageous people, surpassing all others in the invincible bravery with which they meet difficulties and strive to overcome every foe; but in other conditions they bring destruction upon themselves by rending others. They are eager for rebellion, ready for tumults and for every kind of crime. Consequently, they must be held in check by the strong hand of justice and made to walk in the right way by the reins of justice. But if they are allowed their own way without a yoke, like an untamed colt, they and their princes will be overwhelmed with poverty, shame and confusion.[4]

Did anarchy arise in England under Stephen because Anglo-Norman society and the state it had evolved were not yet stable enough, three-quarters of a century after the coming of the Normans, to withstand successfully the stresses of a disputed succession to the throne? Did it result from yet other causes at work in western Christendom in the twelfth century? It is as difficult to answer these historical questions as to discern the causes of unrest and violence in our own contemporary world, unless one is satisfied with superficial answers.

It is very questionable whether the value of the concept of 'feudalism' as a means towards an understanding of medieval European society, or any other society, has outweighed the confusion and the odium it has caused.[5] To make such a suggestion may seem an impertinence, since so many eminently distinguished historians have devoted whole lifetimes to the study of 'feudalism', but it ought not to be regarded in that light. If a technical concept, such as that of 'feudalism', is to be used, sufficient criteria must first be formulated. New technical terms may be used with different prescriptive meanings by different persons. To begin with, there is no question of right and wrong usage but, when the concept becomes part of the established stock of a particular realm of thought and discussion, questions begin to be asked about its correct use. Disputes may arise about the facts involved, or about the criteria, or about both: so it has been in the case of 'feudalism'. New instances and the exposure of anomalies may affect the criteria in several ways. They may make it necessary to alter the concept and so to modify the criteria. They may reveal aspects of the concept previously unnoticed so that, again, the criteria may have to be modified. They may show that the concept is lacking in precision because it does not provide the means of answering some of the questions that now arise, and so the criteria must be revised. In process of time, technical concepts filter into the vocabulary of ordinary language, giving rise to misunderstandings and conflicts between the technical and the ordinary meaning. What are we to do about the concept of 'feudalism', which has undergone all these processes and continues to do so? Ought historians to extend or to restrict its use? Obviously, if complications and lack of precision are to be avoided, we ought to maintain rigorously a tight set of formulae. But, if we insist upon such restriction, we may risk the danger of losing some of the explanatory potential of the concept. Are historians to take the view that since certain societies differ in some respects from those they have been accustomed to call 'feudal', they must not regard them as feudal? Or might they, on the contrary, say that since certain societies resemble in some, but not all, important respects those they have been accustomed to call 'feudal', they ought to – or might as well – call them feudal too?

The adjective *feodalis* and the adverb *feodaliter*, denoting the tenure of land or other things as a fief, especially as distinct from, and indeed as the antithesis of, allodial land, are of considerable antiquity. They are probably as old as the time when in common usage the word *feodum* replaced the word *beneficium* for such a holding, but this does not mean that 'feudalism' was a medieval concept. We begin to approach such a concept when, in 1639, the legally trained antiquarian and glossarist, Sir Henry Spelman, wrote his treatise *Of Feuds and Tenures by Knight Service*.[6] He defined a 'feud' as:

a right which a vassal hath in land or in some immovable thing of his lord's, to use the same and take the profits hereditarily, rendering unto his lord such feodal duties and services as belong to military tenure; the mere propriety of the soil remaining to the lord.

This would not now pass as an adequate definition of a fief: but the important thing is that Spelman was using the word 'feodal' in a legal sense, and the essence of the institution, as he saw it, lay in the duties and services to which it gave rise. These had financial implications for lord and vassal, which were still of practical importance when Spelman wrote his treatise, since feudal tenures, together with the Court of Wards and Liveries, were not abolished in England till 1660. The concept of 'feudalism', as distinct from the fact of feudal tenures, arose only after that abolition. In the Age of Reason and in that of the French Revolution the concept of feudalism became as much a part of the common stock of political thought, economics and history as of law. Montesquieu, Voltaire, Blackstone, Burke, Adam Smith and others all used it with varying emphasis and in the nineteenth century and thereafter Karl Marx and his disciples gave a new significance to the historical rôle of 'feudalism'. In so far as the word became part of the vocabulary of everyday language, it seems to have acquired a Gothick, romantic meaning, but, very much more, a pejorative sense. It became, and it has remained, part of the armoury of political and social vituperation: imperialist, bolshie, fascist, colonialist, racialist, feudalist – these tend to speak to the emotions rather than to the intellect. Here is confusion enough, but it does not end the tale. For some three centuries, different groups of scholars – lawyers, political thinkers, economists, historians and archaeologists – have used the terms 'feudal' and 'feudalism' with somewhat different prescriptive meanings and this has added greatly to the confusion. Not only so, but different historical approaches – those of legal, constitutional, ecclesiastical, military, economic, social and political historians – emphasising different aspects of the concept of 'feudalism', have resulted in conflicts of opinion both as to facts and as to criteria. In the absence of any general agreement, or the slightest likelihood of one in the foreseeable future, as to how the criteria must be modified in the light of research, the confusion about 'feudalism' continues to be aggravated.

Finally, the use by individual scholars and groups of historians of different types of source material has affected the concept and its criteria. Too exclusive a reliance upon, for example, early law codes, or Carolingian capitularies, or twelfth-and thirteenth-century legal treatises tends to encourage stereotyped views about the rights and obligations of the upper ranks of society and the degree of subjection of the peasantry. Such sources are themselves somewhat of the nature of stereotypes, often too formalised to represent correctly the complexity of the society that produced them. Such studies have tended to concentrate attention far too much upon two things: the early origins of 'feudalism' and what, from a legalistic viewpoint, might be regarded as its fully developed form in the twelfth or even the thirteenth century. The temptation is to project late and supposedly fully developed forms back, as criteria, into earlier ages. It is obviously a disastrous mistake to judge the development of feudal society in the Carolingian dominions in the ninth century by the standards of feudal perfection figured fourth in the *Assizes of Jerusalem*. It is also, in fact, a mistake to judge simply by these standards the society of the Latin Kingdom of Jerusalem itself before its fall. The society of Stephen's England and its legal system are not properly to be understood by a perusal of Glanvill's treatise, though these are near to each other in time, and in fact Glanvill is much better appreciated if one knows what directly preceded the situation there depicted. Equally, a too exclusive use of manorial court rolls, surveys and accounts of the thirteenth century and later has often resulted in the placing of excessive emphasis upon the (admittedly important) servile sub-structure of society, unjustifiably projecting this back into earlier times, when we cannot be sure that it existed in quite the same form. Modern research probably tends to show that the full process of enserfment was a relatively late phenomenon. Other kinds of source material, such as charters, writs, deeds, wills and the like also give their characteristic point of view and, taken alone, can be very misleading. Even archaeology has, to some extent, bedevilled the situation and, if medieval literature, both Latin and vernacular, has not done so to an embarrassing degree, perhaps that is only because historians and others have paid far less attention to it than they ought. All the facts relevant to the concept of 'feudalism' have not been established and it is unlikely that all ever will be established beyond dispute. It is, therefore, exceptionally difficult to determine the criteria of this concept and general agreement about it is unlikely to be achieved, for a long time.

These are formidable difficulties. There is another, which was long ago pointed out by F.W.Maitland: 'the impossible task that is set before the word "feudalism" is that of making a single idea represent a very large piece of the world's history; represent the France, Italy, Germany, England of every century from the eighth or ninth to the fourteenth or fifteenth'. We might add to these, as some scholars in the various fields have done, the Egyptian and Mycenaean civilisations, the late Roman Empire, Byzantium, medieval 'Russia', Persia, Ethiopia, Japan – or, nowadays, almost anywhere else. Feudal cowboys and Indians or feudal gangsters would be in no way surprising; they might even, speaking seriously, be illuminating.

It seems questionable whether the concept of 'feudalism' is being elucidated by such extensions; perhaps it is becoming less and less meaningful and correspondingly valueless. The late Sir Frank Stenton, whose views on 'feudalism' were clear-cut and comprehensible, attempting to clarify a situation which, even in English history alone, was becoming obfuscated, expressed the following opinion:

It is turning a useful term into a mere abstraction to apply the adjective 'feudal' to a society which never adopted the private fortress nor developed the art of fighting on horseback, which had no real idea of the specialisation of service, and allowed innumerable landowners of position to go with their lands to whatever lords they would.

This opinion as a whole and each constituent clause of it, except perhaps the last, has been argued about and rejected by some scholars. That is no reflection upon the distinguished scholar who put it forward. The whole situation emphasises the vital importance of a question that has already been asked: is it really necessary to continue the process of modifying the criteria of 'feudalism'? There is little hope that we shall ever find criteria which shall be universally applicable in time and space, applicable to many different societies in the same age, in different geographical and climatic conditions and different economic circumstances, or applicable to the same people in different ages. It is neither possible nor profitable to consider whether a tendency towards anarchy is inherent in 'feudal society' when we cannot say, without contradiction, in what such a society consists.

The term 'feudal' is hallowed by centuries of usage and in spite of all the confusion about its meaning it is still very difficult to avoid using it, so habituated are we. Let us, at least, not be obsessed by the concept. Let us rather study the characteristics of society as we find it revealed in the available sources of information, without bothering too much about the exact shade of meaning to be attached to the term 'feudal' in relation to it.

Sources are indeed scanty for any detailed study of agrarian conditions and peasant life specifically in Stephen's reign, though there are a few estate surveys, such as those of the abbey of Burton-on-Trent, which are sufficiently close to it. Material for an investigation of urban life and trade, outside London, is equally meagre. We are best provided with evidence relating to land-tenure and the relationships of lord and vassal. When it appears that the tenure of fiefs by military service, the possession of manorial estates, and the relationships involved therein between lord and vassal, manorial magnate and peasant, exercised a determining influence upon the structure of English society between 1135 and 1154, as of course they did, this state of affairs will be called 'feudal', without pejorative implications or other value judgments. It means no more than that society depended to a great extent upon obligations and rights connected with fief and manor. Reference is sometimes made to 'the feudalisation of public authority', which may have more than one meaning. It may mean simply the exercise of administrative and judicial powers by lords in virtue of their relationship with vassals who hold their fiefs or with the peasant population of their manors. It may mean the exercise by such lords, in virtue of a royal grant, of a franchisal jurisdiction of a public kind as, for example, when a hundred court came into private hands. Finally, it may mean the tenure, often hereditary, of offices such as those of justice or sheriff on the same basis as fiefs. A very natural tendency for men who held important, prestigious and lucrative public offices was to try to assimilate these to their private positions and to make them similarly hereditary. Such a tendency does not, however, seem to be confined to men whose lives were regulated by feudal tenures. The ambition is natural in a family man, as the church so well understood when it insisted, never with complete success, upon the celibacy of its clergy. The dynast is no less important a figure than the feudatory, if we understand by dynasticism the building up of an hereditary position of wealth and authority. This was perhaps easier of achievement in a society depending upon feudal tenures than in any other. The striving of great and lesser aristocratic families to amass lands and scale the heights of nobility and power is very obvious in twelfth-century England, though its effects are not always fully appreciated. Ambitions of a similar kind can be observed among the burgesses in their different environment and if we could learn more about them a great deal of light would be shed upon urban history and trading relations. It may be that the lowest ranks of the peasantry were too repressed and too dull to harbour any such dreams, but at least the rent-paying peasant tenants, and there were a good many such on some estates, might engage in dynastic striving no less than Robert Marmion, earl Miles of Hereford, bishop Roger of Salisbury or king Stephen himself. Stephen, though he played his dynastic game out to the end, had none of the success of his Angevin rivals or his Capetian contemporaries. Relatively, he was less successful than were, in the long run, the peasant Pepizes of Cottenham on the estates of Crowland Abbey.[7] I shall venture, in a later chapter, to employ the term 'feudo-dynastic' in relation to the activities of men who pursued their family ambitions and built up their dynastic alliances upon the basis of estates held by feudal tenure. The explanation of much that happened in Stephen's reign is to be found in such activities.

A study of the nineteen winters when 'Christ and his saints slept', as the Peterborough chronicle put it, is not inappropriate at the present time. Although in the twelfth century events which seemed cataclysmic moved at horseman's pace and not at supersonic speed, it may be that the fundamental causes of turmoil then and now differ in degree rather than in kind. The present-day reaction to unsettled and frightening conditions and the preoccupation with violence and the more sordid aspects of life are nothing new. They can be discerned in the literature and art of the twelfth century, 'age of faith' though it was, with the utmost clarity. The opening quatrain of the German Archpoet's 'Confession' (he died *c.* 1165) reveals to us the angry young man, if not the hippie or the junkie, of the twelfth century:

Estuans intrinsecus	Anger seethes within me
Ira vehementi	A madly raging wind;
In amaritudine	In bitterness of spirit
Loquar mee menti	Let me speak my mind.

. . . .

Implico me vitiis	I clasp my vices to me tight
Immemor virtutis	Virtue's mere negation;
Voluptatis avidus	Avid ever for delight
Magis quam salutis	What care I for salvation
Mortuus in anima	My soul is stricken with a blight
Curam gero cutis.	The flesh is compensation

These sentiments are echoed and the vices unblushingly detailed in many a verse; and that is not to condemn the twelfth-century Latin lyric which, at its best, was a noble contribution to European literature.

Still more symptomatic of the age are the great intellectuals of the so-called 'twelfth-century renaissance'. It is in times of economic, social and political confusion that men call in question the dogmas and beliefs which in quiet times tend to be taken very much for granted; and this questioning becomes a potent cause both of further confusion and of new development. 'The first key to wisdom', said Peter Abelard, the most brilliant intellect of the age, 'is questioning, diligent and unceasing . . . By doubting we are led to inquiry and by inquiry we may perceive the truth'. Abelard's intellectual honesty in pursuit of this ideal, as well as his intellectual pride, contributed largely to his personal tragedy. Dialectic, that is formal logic, was the great driving force behind the intellectual movements of the twelfth century. What may now appear as hair-splitting arguments in the philosophical controversy between Realists and Nominalists meant to them all the difference between heaven and hell, for they led, like every branch of scholarship and every conceivable line of investigation, straight to what mattered most to thinking men: their religion and the mysteries of the faith. Already in the eleventh century the doctrine of transubstantiation had been questioned by Berengar of Tours (who died in 1088). Soon after the forces of orthodoxy had compelled his retraction, the even more redoubtable Roscelin of Compiègne (c. 1050–1122) caused the very foundations of the church to quiver by bringing his formidable intellect to bear upon the doctrine of the Holy Trinity. These men had their opposites in great figures such as, and so different from one another, St Anselm and St Bernard. England herself produced none of quite such calibre (St Anselm, though archbishop of Canterbury, was not English by birth or education), but she had her John of Salisbury, who never strayed from the paths of correctitude. She had, too, a whole plethora of Roberts, men of note in their time: Robert of Mélun, who taught philosophy in Paris and Mélun and wrote a *Summa Theologie* before he returned to his home country as bishop of Hereford in 1163; Robert Pullen, cardinal and papal chancellor; Robert Ketene 'the Englishman', first translator of the Koran. There was also that interesting personage, Adelard of Bath, for a time the tutor of the future Henry II, who travelled in Europe, Asia and Africa and wrote works on Arabic science. Twelfth-century England participated with some distinctiveness in the great intellectual movements of the time. She felt the impact of the revolutionary developments in the study of law, with which the names of Peter Lombard and Gratian are so closely associated, no less keenly than the force of philosophical and dialectical studies. Gratian applied the dialectical method to canon law with outstanding success in his *Concordantia Discordantium Canonum*, commonly known as the *Decretum*, while the study of civil law likewise experienced a widespread revival. In Stephen's England the jurisdiction and litigation of the courts christian greatly expanded. About 1145 both to meet the need for professional assistance in legal work and to assist him in maintaining his authority vis-à-vis Henry, bishop of Winchester, Theobald, archbishop of Canterbury, imported the Mantuan jurist, Master Vacarius, civilian as well as canon lawyer. So successful was Vacarius as a teacher and so formidable a champion of the archiepiscopal cause that he was silenced by Stephen, who was at odds with his archbishop. Perhaps, too, the feudal outlook of Stephen's baronial advisers made for suspicion of foreign law and jurisprudence. In the sphere of secular laws English jurists were still groping for principles but the crown continued, as under Stephen's Norman predecessors, to act in a practical and empirical manner, striving to extend the scope and the profits of royal justice. In many respects the legal studies and the legal developments of twelfth-century Christendom were of far more practical importance than the dialectical interests to which, in the past, classically educated historians probably attached disproportionate weight.

There is no need to spend much time on the horror stories of the anarchy. Our knowledge of it is derived to a great extent from contemporary historical writers, for whom history was the progressive revelation of the divine plan for the world. Government, even when tyrannical or ineffective, was partly the divine remedy for men's sins and partly the punishment for them. Historians with any pretensions to scholarship regarded their subject as a branch of ethics. The words of William of Malmesbury, perhaps the greatest English historian of his day, are typical: 'What more concerns the advancement of virtue, what more conduces to justice, than to recognise the divine favour towards good men and God's vengeance upon the wicked?' Again, 'it is valuable to know the changeability of fortune and the mutability of human affairs, God alone permitting and ordaining them'. Here, then, was the true purpose of the clerical or monastic historian's work and it largely guided the selection of events to be recorded, as well as his comments upon them. Seldom was he happily engaged in the elucidation of causes, other than the sinfulness of man and the vast providence of God, nor would it ordinarily have occurred to him, as it immediately does to us, to seek explanations in political, constitutional and economic developments and social change. These, regarded *sub specie aeternitatis*, were to him both superficial and ephemeral. The best known description of the anarchy, that of the Peterborough chronicler, ought to be read after one has studied a picture in the *Winchester Psalter* made for Henry of Blois, bishop of Winchester, king Stephen's brother (see frontispiece).[8] It bears the inscription ICI EST ENFER S E LI ANGELS KI ENFERME LES PORTES, and the tortures of the damned depicted there are only a little less gruesome than the tortures which the chronicler attributes to the castle-men:

... When the castles were built, they filled them with devils and wicked men. Then ... they took those people that had any goods ... and put them in prison and tortured them ... to extort gold and silver ... They were hung by the thumbs or by the head and mail shirts were hung on their feet. Knotted ropes were put round their heads and twisted till they penetrated the brain. They put them in prisons where there were adders and snakes and toads and killed them like that. Some they put in a 'torture chamber', that is, a chest that was short, narrow and shallow, and they put sharp stones in it and pressed the man in it, so that all his limbs were broken ... (I omit further details of a similar kind) ... They levied taxes on the villages every so often, calling it 'tenserie'. When the wretched people had no more to give, they robbed and burned all the villages, so that you could easily go a whole day's journey and never find anyone occupying a village, nor land tilled. Then corn was dear, and butter and cheese, because there was none in the country. Wretched people died of starvation ... the heathens (i.e. the Danes) had never done worse than they did. For, contrary to custom, they respected neither church nor churchyard, but took all that was inside and burned the church ... neither did they respect bishops' land, nor abbots', nor priests' ... the bishops were constantly excommunicating them, but they thought nothing of it, because they were all utterly accursed ... it was openly said that Christ and his saints slept. Such things ... we suffered nineteen winters for our sins.

Which came first, the pictures of hell or the monkish literary descriptions of atrocities? Perhaps both owed their origin to the horrors of contemporary life.

Quotations from this well-thumbed passage in the Peterborough chronicle usually end at the point indicated above. It is worth continuing a little further for, even though what immediately follows is a later insertion in the chronicle, there is no need to doubt its substantial truth. The later writer perceived that his predecessor (who obviously derived a certain masochistic enjoyment from recounting horrors and disasters), carried away by his dramatic theme, had neglected the very substantial manifestations of divine mercy:

> In all this evil time, abbot Martin held his abbacy for twenty years and a half and six days with great energy, and provided for the monks and guests everything they needed, and held great commemoration feasts in the house, and nevertheless worked at the church and appointed lands and income for it and endowed it richly and had it roofed, and brought them into the new monastery on St Peter's Day with great ceremony – that was AD 1140, twenty-three years since the fire . . . And he got back lands that powerful men were holding by force . . . and he made many monks, and planted a vinyard, and did much building and made the village better than it had been before . . .

There can be no doubt that lawlessness and extreme violence. cruelty and oppression were common at this time, but we are left with a strong impression that the chronicler's account of it conformed to a standard pattern used for centuries, with appropriate variations, by every medieval historian writing in similar circumstances, and tinctured by folk memories of the 'fury of the Northmen'.

The main manifestations of the strains and stresses in the unsettled world of the twelfth century are not difficult to enumerate, which is not to say that they can be explained simply. First, there are the great movements in the church, monastic and papal movements for reform, and the resulting crises in the relations between the spiritual and the secular powers, which might be described as a series of political conflicts within the framework of an ideological agreement. That phase of the conflict which is generally known as the 'investiture struggle' ended early in the third decade of the twelfth century, and a new phase was beginning. In England, significantly, it had ended in 1107, fifteen years earlier than in the Empire, because Henry I was strong enough to make concessions to the church, secure in the knowledge that he could continue to exercise his authority effectively in other ways. Stephen, on the other hand, was in no such happy position. Accused, as he was, of perjury and usurpation, the benevolence of the church was of vital importance to him; but political circumstances involved him in conflict with certain of the church's ministers. The Roman church itself, however, was far from united: it was in fact torn and distracted by the schism of Anacletus (or Pierlone) and the great dominating figure of St Bernard of Clairvaux, who overshadowed the papacy itself, aroused not only the enthusiastic support of the Cistercian Order and the champions of reform, but also the determined opposition of a considerable body of cardinals and others both in the curia and in various parts of Christendom. The bitterness of these conflicts, their manifestations in England and the extent of St Bernard's intervention there are not always appreciated. No one has yet fully worked out in detail the effects of these on the political situation in Stephen's reign and on the affiliations of individuals and groups. The best example so far is Dom David Knowles's study of the disputed elections to the see of York, which will be considered in a later chapter.

Next, one must consider the development of kingship, which was regarded as no less divinely ordained than the papacy itself. Till the twelfth century the consecration of a king was still a sacrament, which gave him a peculiarly sacrosanct character and was even held by some to bestow upon him certain rights of control over the church. Even though Henry I had abandoned some of the claims which were most offensive in the eyes of the church, still 'all the water in the rough, rude sea cannot wash the balm from an anointed king'. The capture and imprisonment of king Stephen in 1141 and his temporary replacement by Maud as 'Lady of England' (she was never crowned) was a profoundly disturbing event, even for his most determined enemies, as witness Robert, earl of Gloucester, taking his tender conscience to the pope, and Brian fitz Count, the most devoted adherent of the empress anxiously consulting Gilbert Foliot about his allegiance and about the perjury of which he feared he had been guilty.[9] All the circumstances – Stephen's oath to accept Maud as Henry I's successor, his obtaining the crown in despite of his oath, the perjury of which he was consequently accused, his capture, imprisonment and restoration – shook England to its foundations, just as his arrest of the bishops in 1139 shook the church, and had profoundly disturbing consequences. The greatest weaknesses of early kingship usually lay in the lack of adequate material resources and the absence of effective means of administration, and in the continuance of the ancient tradition that the kingly dignity was elective within the circle of the royal family. The eleventh and twelfth centuries witnessed a steady, persistent and varyingly successful attempt on the part of kings everywhere in Christendom to build up their material and financial resources, found their dynasties on a permanent basis, whittle away the power of the nobility and establish the royal authority throughout their realms. Even where kings were relatively successful, as in Norman England, their position was precarious and its maintenance depended upon ruthless determination and a very firm hand. The slightest relaxing of authority, a disputed succession to the crown, as after the death of Henry i, or a serious defeat, like Stephen's debacle at Lincoln, could bring swift disaster.

A further symptom of disorder, and a very significant one, is to be seen in the structure of feudal society and, more specifically, in the changes which were taking place in it. If in its earlier phases the organisation of feudal society was relatively uncomplicated, by the twelfth century it had become exceedingly involved. One of the reasons for this was simply that land in the form of fiefs could be obtained by a man's becoming a vassal, and lords had need of vassals. Many tenants-in-chief became mesne-tenants of other tenants-in-chief and vassals soon came to hold fiefs from more than one lord, thus introducing into the lord-vassal relationship extraordinary complications and a disturbing element of conflicting allegiance. In fact, the process of sub-infeudation went so fast and so far, as consequently did the sub-division of knights' fees and services, that the whole system of services and aids, upon which feudal contracts were based, became very difficult to operate. Furthermore when, as was not uncommon, a tenant-in-chief and three or four or half-a-dozen other individuals and bodies, not to mention the king at the top of the scale and the peasants at the bottom, had an interest in the same piece of land, confusion and difficulties were bound to arise. There were, inevitably, disputes and legal complications and if there were no governmental authority capable of coping effectively with the situation open strife could very easily ensue. Twelfth-century feudal society existed on the crust of a volcano.

Given a small population rooted and grounded in the soil, a feudal order of society might have achieved some degree of stability on a rather low level. But, at least by the middle of the eleventh century, evidence can be discerned of a marked expansion of population which was not merely an English phenomenon. This was one of the basic forces which helped to determine the trend of economic and social evolution. Its consequences were far-reaching. They included the great movements of expansion and colonisation – both internal colonisation, involving the clearing of forest, scrub land and marsh land to bring them under the plough, for the growing population had to be fed, and external colonisation, eastwards from Germany for example. Thus a new era of movement and vigorous enterprise was inaugurated, bringing opportunities of profit-farming in place of mere subsistence-farming, of growing trade and an expanding money economy. Wealth was no longer the virtual monopoly of a landed aristocracy; it was coming into the hands of a rising merchant class. Towns were growing and their burgesses were aspiring to a measure of freedom and control over their own affairs, which was essential for their continuing prosperity but which a restrictive and reactionary feudal order would have denied them. Their striving for this objective often took a more or less violent form, as in many of the urban communes of northern France and Flanders, or in the great cities of northern Italy which were soon able to participate in and profit from the wars between emperors and popes. In England the rise of the bourgeoisie was not a violent one, but its effects on society and the state were profound and even revolutionary.

To the powerful forces which have been mentioned may be added another – the invaders who had been attacking Christendom from the eighth century till the eleventh, especially the forces of Islam and the Northmen. The contributions of both, direct and indirect, to European development and culture were enormous, and in particular the absorption of the Normans into European society had tremendous consequences. They brought to civilisations higher in achievement, if not in promise, than their own, remarkable qualities of character and genius, an urgent spirit of adventure, insatiable land-hunger, militant churchmanship and an astonishing ability to adapt themselves to varying environments. These qualities made them a dynamic force in Christendom and beyond it. All these developments were coming to a head in the late eleventh and early twelfth centuries and west European society was in a state of flux. The whole atmosphere of the age was, inevitably, one of unrest, uncertainty, turbulence and violence.

To appreciate the underlying causes of turmoil in England it is necessary to know at least a little about the nature of the Norman settlement, the settlement of a relatively small military aristocracy and ecclesiastical hierarchy. Orderic's view of the Normans has already been quoted; the equally outspoken opinion of William of Malmesbury is also worth quoting:

The Normans ... (are) exceedingly particular in their dress and delicate in their food, but not to excess. They are a race inured to war and can hardly live without it; fierce in attacking their enemies and, when force fails, ready to use stratagem or corrupt by bribery ... they live with economy in large houses; they envy their equals; they wish to vie with their superiors; and they plunder their subjects, though they defend them from others. They are faithful to their lords unless a slight offence gives them an excuse for treachery. They weigh treachery by its chance of success and change their sentiments for money. They are the most polite of people, they consider strangers to deserve the courtesy they show one another, and they intermarry with their subjects ... you might see churches rise in every village and monasteries built after a style unknown before ... every wealthy man counted the day lost in which he neglected to make some outstanding benefaction.

The last remark is interesting. England, like Normandy, participated to the full in the great monastic movements of the age. Despite the conditions which existed during Stephen's reign, more religious houses were founded during that time than in the previous century. Monasteries and churches suffered, and grievously, yet as we have seen in the case of Peterborough Abbey they prospered nonetheless and their endowments were increased. A passage in the chronicle of the Holy Cross, Waltham Abbey, gives a laudatory account of Geoffrey de Mandeville, whom we are accustomed to hear of as a violent disturber of the peace and the desecrator of Ramsey Abbey. This good opinion of him is surprising, considering that Geoffrey burned Waltham in the course of his vendetta with William d'Aubigny, earl of Arundel. The Waltham chronicler was, nonetheless, ready not merely to forgive him in a becoming spirit of Christian charity, but positively to find excuses for him. This suggests a depth of understanding between feudal lords and ecclesiastics which was often proof against the effects of violence. Things like this throw a lot of light on the character of the age and the habits of mind of twelfth-century people, and we do not pay half enough attention to them. There is always a temptation to say of ages other than our own that men cannot possibly have acted as they are recorded as having done, but, more often than not, they probably did. If the Norman aristocracy really resembled the pictures that Orderic, the monk of St Evroul, and William, the monk of Malmesbury, have given us, it is not surprising that the death of Henry I was followed by an outburst of violence, especially when a disputed succession fatally impaired the authority of the crown. This outbreak was all the more violent because the reins of power had been drawn in so tightly by the Conqueror and his two sons, while Stephen had not the hands to control the still 'untamed colt'.

The first half of the eleventh century had witnessed the rise in Normandy of a new nobility, many of whose members were related to the ducal house. Great houses emerged, like those of Beaumont, Ferrières, Grentemaisnil, Mandeville, Montfort, Montgomery, Tosny. The relationships between these families, the intermarriages, the alliances and the feuds were already very complex in 1066. The same period saw the full development of a feudal order of society among the Normans. At the beginning of the eleventh century the duke was not yet in firm control of the situation and the prevalence in Normandy of private warfare had encouraged the practice of sub-infeudation, whereby retinues of knights were settled on the lands of tenants-in-chief. Thus, under the aegis of the great families lesser vassal houses grew and flourished: Harcourt, Curzon, Martel, Chandos, Say, Muschegros and many more. Warfare was the profession and the delight of them all, greater and lesser feudatories alike. The *Consuetudines et Justicie* of William the Conqueror (compiled in 1091, after his death, as the result of an inquest held at Caen) shows how the duke attempted to limit, though he could not completely abolish, the blood feud and private war, and the sort of thing he had to cope with in this endeavour.[10] 'It was unlawful for anyone in Normandy, on the pretext of a claim concerning land, to burn a house or a mill or to wreak any devastation or to take booty. It

2

was unlawful, likewise, to attack a man or lay an ambush for him in the duke's forests. It was unlawful for anyone seeking his enemy or levying distraint to bear a banner (the formal sign of warlike intent) or wear armour or to sound a horn or ring a bell after which he would lie in ambush . . .' At least it seems that the warlike Norman barons did not pursue their vendettas in any mean and underhand way, but rode with banners displayed, and sounded a horn or rang a bell by way of fair warning. They enjoyed a good fight. Brutality was second nature to them. The same code lays it down that they must not take matters into their own hands so far as to deprive a man of his members without judgment, unless he is caught in an act for which that is the penalty, and, even then, only by the decision of the duke's court in cases which pertain to him, or by the decision of barons' courts in cases which pertain to them. 'It was unlawful for anyone in Normandy to commit a breach of the peace in a house (*hamfare*) or arson or rape, or to make distraint without having lodged a claim with him who ought to receive it.' If these represent the kind of crimes that the Conqueror was attempting to suppress among the Normans, it is not altogether surprising that violence was widespread when things got out of hand in England under his grandson. The first half of the eleventh century had also seen an enormous development of church influence in Normandy, the vigorous growth of monasticism and the rise of a race of extremely able bishops related by family ties to the nobility and to the ducal house itself.

All these varied relationships were transplanted into England in 1066 and, with them, rivalries and feuds. It is not known exactly how the Norman feudal settlement in England was effected, or how lands were allotted to the Conqueror's followers: we only see the results set out in Domesday. To what extent individuals managed to retain lands which they overran in the course of the campaigns of 1066 and the following years, we simply do not know. The Normans being what they were, we may be sure that the settlement was not achieved without a good deal of dispute and recrimination. The settlement of alien landlords in a country with its own distinctive laws, which William 1 was pledged to maintain, was bound to give rise to a good deal of confusion and litigation. However definitive the Norman settlement may appear in Domesday, it was not entirely stable. The whole situation could very easily get out of control if the stern authority exercised by the crown were relaxed for a moment.

The nature of the Norman settlement can best be appreciated at the local level. There are a good many problems and obscurities connected with, for example, Nottinghamshire but, having regard to what happened in Stephen's reign, it has a number of interesting features. The royal demesne in the shire was extensive, including some sixty vills extending across it. By far the largest fief held in chief of the crown was that of Roger de Bully, who was a tenant-in-chief in many other shires. He died about the end of the reign of Rufus and, as his only son predeceased him, his honour (known as the honour of Tickhill, or of Blyth) escheated to the crown. Henry 1 included a good many of the lands of which that honour was composed in his grant of the honour of Lancaster to his nephew, Stephen, count of Boulogne and Mortain, who already had a small fief in Nottinghamshire. Consequently Stephen, when he became king, had extensive estates in this county. But, in the fabulous grant which he made to Rannulf, earl of Chester in 1146, he included those of his lands which had formerly belonged to the honour of Roger de Bully.[11] The earl of Chester, whose tentacles already spread far and wide over the Midlands from Chester to Lincoln and down to Coventry, was given a large stake and a strong footing in Nottinghamshire, where his Domesday predecessor had possessed only a single fief.[12] When earl Rannulf was in rebellion against Stephen from Christmas 1140 till the end of the reign, except for very short periods in 1141 and 1146, he had considerable scope for his activities in Nottinghamshire. Here Stephen's cause was maintained by William Peverel, descendant of the Domesday tenant-in-chief of the same name, whose possessions in the shire were comparable in extent with those of Roger de Bully. His power was further strengthened locally by his constableship of the royal castle of Nottingham and possession of considerable estates in the Peak region, which had come into Peverel hands in the reign of Henry 1. The other lay tenants-in-chief shown in the Nottinghamshire Domesday held relatively small fiefs, but this does not mean that they were relatively unimportant men. They included members of some of the greatest Norman families, whose resources in respect of holdings elsewhere were enormous and probably gave them a degree of influence in Nottinghamshire out of all proportion to the amount of land they held there. Among them were Hugh de Grentemaisnil, Berengar de Tosny, Henry de Ferrers, whose descendant was created earl of Derbyshire by Stephen in 1138, Robert Malet and others. The lands of Roger the Poitevin, forfeited in 1102, should not be forgotten. The Conqueror's considerable non-Norman contingent was represented in Nottinghamshire by the Fleming, Gilbert de Gant, and the Bretons, count Alan, lord of the honour of Richmond (Yorks) and Geoffrey de Wirce (from La Guerche, near Rennes), who was rewarded with extensive English fiefs.

The other notable Nottinghamshire tenants-in-chief were prelates, the archbishop of York and the bishop of Lincoln. The latter's lands lay in the east of the shire, dominated by Newark, where bishop Alexander the Magnificent built a splendid castle. The lands of both these prelates have a special interest and importance in Stephen's reign, since the temporalities of both sees came, at different times, into the hands of the crown. Those of the see of Lincoln were taken over in 1139 upon the arrest of the members of that great administrative family who held the bishoprics of Salisbury, Lincoln and Ely. A process of this kind caused a good deal of disturbance not only for the tenants but for neighbouring landlords and, in the case of the temporalities of the see of York, this was especially serious and protracted because of the prolonged dispute over the York elections after the death of archbishop Thurstan, and the bitter and often violent conflicts between the adherents of William fitz Herbert and his opponents.

It must be remembered that even where the lands of a tenant-in-chief were concentrated in one part of a shire, as in the case of the Nottinghamshire lands of the see of Lincoln, they consisted not of solid blocks but of manors mingled in an intricate mosaic with those of other landholders. It was by no means unusual for two or more manors to divide a single vill between them. Such conditions in any circumstances, and especially in a newly-conquered land, inevitably give rise to innumerable petty squabbles and territorial and other disputes between neighbours. These were liable to be magnified out of all proportion to their real importance. Such incidents of feudal life as escheats (reversion of lands to the overlord) and forfeitures and the replacement of one landholding family by another, as well as the bewilderingly rapid development of the process of subinfeudation, tended to have this effect. Every sub-tenant naturally looked to his lord for warranty, support and protection when he became involved in disputes and feuds with his neighbours. What began as a small-arms affair was liable quickly to involve the heavy artillery. Bitter indeed were the disputes that arose over inheritances, not least when a feudatory was succeeded by co-heiresses (and it is surprising how many instances there were in the first half of the twelfth century) who married into different families. Thus, to the other quarrels of a quick-tempered and litigious race like the Normans was added the force of family alliances and feuds. Family relationships were very complex, for intermarriage between the members of an aristocracy relatively small in numbers was bound, within the space of a very few generations, to produce an extraordinarily intricate web of family connections, intrigues and feuds. A number of examples will be examined in a later chapter and an effort will be made to show how great a determining influence they exercised on the course of events in Stephen's reign. In addition to this, great magnates and lesser men, too, vied with one another not merely in amassing estates but in attempting to obtain for themselves, hereditarily if possible, offices under the crown, such as sheriffdoms, shire justiceships and constableships of castles, forest offices and the like, which augmented their wealth and, no less important, enhanced their social prestige and their local authority. In all these ways local rivalries reached alarming proportions, and the pattern is repeated in every English shire.

The fact of William I's personal conquest of England and his acquisition of the crown gave the Norman dynasty an initial advantage in the struggle to control its followers. It was possible here to impose upon them more stringent conditions of tenure and to enforce obedience more firmly than was practicable in Normandy itself. With this advantage, the resources which the crown controlled and the ruthlessness and determination of the Conqueror and his two sons enabled them to prevent the situation in England from ever getting seriously out of control. Henry I in particular seems instinctively to have understood the trends of his time. With remarkable subtlety, combined with a relentless concentration upon the advancement of his own interests, he exploited every resource of royal power for his own advantage. No king ever made more effective use as royal servants of men who came from families of modest fortune. He bound them to his service by the opportunities he gave them of operating in association with the work of royal administration to their own advantage as well as his. He enabled them to profit from the difficulties and misfortunes of baronial families, obtaining advantageous marriages, wardships and the like, but he saw to it that they worked hard, and paid for every opportunity they got. This highly successful manipulation of royal patronage required, as Professor R.W. Southern has pointed out, 'a sophisticated machinery of government, a highly developed system of royal courts and royal justice, a tenurial system at once complicated and yet subject to a unitary control, at once hereditary and yet full of doubtful points of law'.[13] It required, in addition, a financial machine geared to these conditions. As a result of Henry I's relentless activities there emerged a social order which differed a great deal from that of the Norman settlement and a governmental machine that, for its day, was highly developed, efficiently staffed and firmly established. The harshness of the king and his ministers and their unscrupulous use of this new machine of government left many barons with bitter grievances because they had been deprived of what they regarded as their rightful inheritances, their just dues and their proper rights. These formed a large section of 'the disinherited' in the next reign. Such men were very ready to take advantage of the circumstances of a disputed succession to recover all they could and to pay off old scores, so that Stephen, at the very outset of his reign, was faced by a whole crop of violent outbreaks and rebellions.

One of the most interesting investigations for an historian of Stephen's reign is concerned with the survival of Henry I's governmental machine. Was it strong enough to survive a period of extreme stress and, if so, how effectively did it function and in what shape was it taken over by Stephen's successor? Again, the development of law, the administration of justice and especially the maintenance and extension, or otherwise, of royal justice provides a wide and interesting field of study. What is the relation of Henry II's reforms to the conditions resulting from Stephen's reign? Another investigation of special interest relates to the social order. What effect had the stresses of Stephen's reign upon the social order that was emerging under Henry I and how did they affect the further development of English society under the Angevin kings? Finally, what of the church? How far was its rôle in society affected by the circumstances of Stephen's reign and were the seeds of future conflict planted during that time? These are some of the main questions with which a study of Stephen's reign should be concerned.

A Chronicle of Events 1135-54

A brief account of Stephen's reign as a whole is needful as a frame of reference for discussion of the problems of the period. This chapter will therefore consist of a bare chronological record of events. There are still some unsolved problems of chronology connected with the reign and in some cases, where solutions have been proposed which depend upon the balance of probabilities, we cannot be certain that these are correct. It is nonetheless possible to set out the sequence of events in a coherent and reasonably satisfactory fashion.[1]

King Henry I, great monarch though he was, never sat carefree on his English throne and he was even less secure on his Norman ducal seat. Royal succession was not yet determined by primogeniture – had it been so, Henry would not have sat on either, nor would Rufus before him. The claims of their elder brother, Robert Curthose, duke of Normandy, were supported by an important section of the nobility both in England and in Normandy. Henry I was successful like Rufus, but by other means, in dealing with the situation and early found ways of getting rid of the most dangerous of Robert's supporters. His complete ascendancy over his elder brother was clinched by the battle of Tinchebrai on 28 September 1106, forty years to the day after the landing of William the Conqueror at Pevensey. Robert was imprisoned for the rest of his life, but his son and heir, William Clito (the atheling or prince), then only six years old, remained at large, an exile and a wanderer, the centre of constant plots by king Henry's enemies. In the circumstances, Norman affairs and relations with the king of France, the counts of Flanders and Anjou and the emperor occupied a very great deal of Henry's time and care. Both in Normandy and in England his personal safety, his government and the ultimate succession of his heir depended entirely on his efficient, firm and relentless control and his reliance for administrative purposes upon a loyal, quasi-professional body of royal servants, dependent upon royal favour, rather than on the uncertain support of the feudal nobility, whose power must at all costs be curbed. This is the key to an understanding of Henry 1's reign. Rule or ruin were the alternatives that confronted him. The danger represented by William Clito was not finally removed until more than a score of years after the crowning mercy of Tinchebrai. Surmounting a series of crises from 1111 onwards and defeating his enemies both in war and in diplomacy, Henry was stronger in 1120 than ever before and he was free to return from Normandy to England with an easy mind.

Henry sailed from Barfleur on Thursday 25 November 1120. In the gathering dark of the same evening the *White Ship*, latest masterpiece of the shipwright's art, put to sea to overtake the king's fleet. On board were prince William, the king's only legitimate son and heir, aged seventeen, with his half-brother, Richard, and his half-sister, Maud countess of Perche (both illegitimate), also a young man who was a relative of the emperor Henry v, several earls and barons and quite a few members of the royal household. Crew and passengers had royally celebrated the embarkation for this maiden voyage. Whether owing to an inexcusable error of pilotage or to the frantic rowing of a crapulous crew, or both, the new vessel ran hard on a reef, was stove in and foundered. It was said that prince William got away safely in a boat, but ordered it back to take off his sister, whereupon so many desperate people leaped into it that it was swamped and lost with all hands. Only one man, a butcher of Rouen, it was said, escaped to tell of the shipwreck. It was a titanic disaster – 'a kind of judgment upon a delicate and luxurious society'. King Henry, a widower since the death of queen Matilda in 1118, was bereft of his sole legitimate male heir. There remained in the direct line only his legitimate daughter, Maud, wife of the emperor Henry v.[2] The precarious stability of Henry's dynastic position, and with it the very fabric of his power, was menaced. He promptly set about restoring it, marrying a second wife, Adeliza, daughter of Godfrey of Louvain, duke of Lower Lorraine, in the hope (vain, as it turned out) of having a new male heir. Henry did everything in his power to frustrate the designs of, and the designs on behalf of, William Clito. The emperor Henry v died in 1125 and the widowed Maud

2*

returned home in September 1126, to become a pawn, though a formidable one, in her father's dynastic game. On Christmas Day, 1126, a very reluctant baronage, including the king's favourite nephew, Stephen, with many misgivings took an oath to recognise her as heiress to the throne. The danger with a royal heiress was that she might marry someone unacceptable to the tenants-in-chief, bringing the kingdom under her husband's authority: the barons therefore stipulated that Maud should not marry outside the kingdom without their advice and consent which, feudally speaking, they had a right as well as a duty to tender to the crown. From their point of view, the worst happened and their stipulation was ignored. That, in itself, was a snub which they took very ill. Within six months Maud was secretly betrothed to Geoffrey, the son and heir of Fulk, count of Anjou, whom she married on 17 June 1128. The Angevins, it must be remembered, were hereditary enemies of the Normans and count Fulk had been an active supporter of William Clito. Whatever the feelings of the barons of England and Normandy, the political reasons for such a marriage alliance were, from Henry I's point of view, strong. In the sequel, he must have had many uneasy and choleric moments. There was a ten-year disparity of age between the contracting parties, and the temper of the fourteen-year-old bridegroom was as combustible as that of the bride, distinguished by her hubris. Maud was shortly sent packing back to Normandy by her husband, but second thoughts and probably winged words from king Henry prevailed. Maud returned to Anjou. On 5 March 1133 the future Henry II was born and, in the following year, Geoffrey. It may now have seemed to the king that any uncertainty about the succession, apart from the unlikely event of the birth of a son to queen Adeliza, was settled, and the barons were bound by the reaffirmation of their oath. Bound they might be, but many under duress, for they had not dared to refuse the lion's command. But there were numbers of Normans who had already preferred to join William Clito when he became a candidate for the countship of Flanders after the murder of count Charles the Good in 1127, rather than accept Maud. William Clito was mortally wounded in July 1128, and so the whole question of the succession to Henry I was once again in the melting-pot as far as numbers of English and Norman barons were concerned. There were possible rivals to Maud, notably count Theobald of Blois and his brother,

Stephen, lord of great fiefs in England and Normandy and count of Boulogne in the right of his wife, another Matilda. These were the sons of Adela, the sister of Henry I, and in their veins ran the blood of the Conqueror. Either might prove more acceptable in England and Normandy than the empress. Stephen was popular with the barons, but he had taken the oath to recognise Maud as Henri I's heiress. Not only so, but he had also striven successfully with Robert, earl of Gloucester, for precedence in taking the oath. Robert, though illegitimate, was a possible candidate, for a bar sinister was not, surely, a bar absolute among the descendants of William, known to fame as 'the Bastard' before he became 'the Conqueror'. The outcome would only be known when the old king died. Most men seemed content, or deemed it safer, to await the event, but clearly two men had laid their plans – Stephen and his younger brother, Henry of Blois, now bishop of Winchester. They carried them out when the moment came with admirable nerve and smooth efficiency, which ought to have augured well for their future collaboration.

The crisis, so long expected, arrived on 1 December 1135, with one of the cyclostomata as the silent persuader of destiny. Six days earlier, at Lyons la Forêt, the king had enjoyed a favourite, but strictly forbidden, dish of lampreys, so it was said, and suffered the extreme penalty for flouting his physician's directions. As soon as Henry's death was known, there was an outbreak of violence in Normandy and England, and a paying off of old scores, such as invariably occurred between the death of a ruler and the formal assumption of power by his successor. The interregnum might be more or less lengthy and while it lasted there was no authority to enforce law and order. The Norman barons discussed the succession problems and seriously considered the election of Theobald of Blois as duke, but the matter was taken out of their hands by his younger brother's action. Stephen, as soon as he heard of his uncle's death, dashed straight over to London, where he was welcomed by the citizens, who elected him king, a privilege which they claimed as their right.[3] This, no doubt, carried some weight, but it did not settle the matter. Stephen hurried to Winchester, the seat of the treasury, where he was welcomed by his brother, bishop Henry, and recognised by Roger, bishop of Salisbury, Henry I's chief justiciar and head of the administration, and also by William de Pontdelarche, the chamberlain in charge of the treasury, who handed over Henry I's treasure to him. These events were much more decisive, since they resulted in Stephen's securing control of the most vital parts of the governmental machine.

There was still one major obstacle, which had to be overcome if Stephen were to be not merely recognised but consecrated and crowned by the archbishop of Canterbury, whose right it was to do so. Stephen had taken the oath to recognise Maud and so had archbishop William of Corbeil. Both had to be freed from the obligations of that oath, for otherwise Stephen's coronation would have been a blatant act of perjury by both of them. Happily for Stephen – and it is hard to believe that this had not been arranged, so opportune was it – Hugh Bigod, a great Norfolk feudatory and a royal steward, arrived with two knights from Lyons la Forêt, where they had been on duty in the royal household when king Henry died. They took an oath publicly in the presence of the archbishop that Henry, on his deathbed, had disinherited his daughter and designated Stephen as his successor. The archbishop's mind was set at rest and Stephen's coronation duly took place, probably on 22 December 1135, just over three weeks after Henry's death. This, in the circumstances, was extraordinarily good going. There is no doubt that the influence of the bishop of Winchester and the guarantee he gave of his brother's good behaviour and high-minded intentions towards the church did more than any other single thing to ensure Stephen's coronation. He was now the Lord's Anointed and pope Innocent II confirmed the action of his legate, the archbishop of Canterbury, in conferring that indelible unction upon him. Thus the papacy's hands were to a great extent tied when Maud appealed to the curia against Stephen. Although the Roman curia was loath to condemn Stephen outright, it would never again pronounce positively in his favour. If a wrong had been committed by Stephen's snatching the English throne from Maud, it was considered by the curia that even if an anointed king were not to be deposed he must not be allowed to establish his dynasty; so that, at least when he died, the situation might right itself. Stephen had gained a position from which, as time was to show, neither temporarily successful foes nor even the successors of St Peter could easily dislodge him. Nonetheless there clung to him throughout his reign an aura of disrepute, as one who was never quite cleared of the accusation of perjury and usurpation. The monarchy was consequently placed in an equivocal position, and sincere men on both sides were a good deal concerned about their allegiance.

The first external threat to Stephen that materialised was from Scotland. King David I, maternal uncle of the empress, who had taken the oath to her in his capacity as an English earl (by marriage), crossed the border in her support as soon as he heard of Stephen's accession. He was not entirely disinterested; he had his own designs in the north of England. He quickly took Carlisle, Wark, Alnwick, Norham and Newcastle. Stephen lost no time in marching north to Durham, where he arrived by 5 February. David was probably a good deal disconcerted by this unexpectedly quick reaction on Stephen's part, his prospects of a military victory were slender and he was ready to negotiate. Stephen, whose position in England was not yet secure, was willing to meet him. David drove a hard bargain and Stephen's concessions were unnecessarily lavish. Here Stephen made a cardinal error both in exposing to the Scots a weakness which invited further aggression, and in buying them off with concessions at the expense of others, whom he ought never to have risked antagonising. Since David himself would on no account do homage to Stephen, it was agreed that the English earldom of Huntingdon should be held by David's son, Henry, who did homage for this and the other lands at York. Wark, Norham, Alnwick and Newcastle were relinquished by the Scots but, in addition to the earldom of Huntingdon, Henry was given Doncaster and Carlisle, with the large area of land in Westmorland and Cumberland that went with the latter. In addition, Stephen promised to give first consideration to the Scottish claim to the earldom of Northumbria. David had done very well for his son and heir without very much effort or risk: Stephen, on the other hand, had made an enemy who was to prove implacable. Carlisle had formerly belonged to Rannulf I le Meschin (died 1129), earl of Chester, father of earl Rannulf II de Gernon (or *aux Gernons*). Henry I had found means of depriving Rannulf I of this honour when, but not ostensibly because, he succeeded to the palatine earldom and the honour of Chester in 1120. Rannulf and his son felt very strongly that they had been unjustly deprived of the honour of Carlisle and earl Rannulf II nourished the hope of recovering it from the soft and generous Stephen. The latter's alienation of it to the Scots was an insult and a bitter disappointment to one of the most powerful of English magnates and an error of the first magnitude. Its long-term results were to be momentous.

On the short view, all seemed well. Stephen was enabled to appear at his splendid Easter court at Westminster on 22 March as a king who had promptly and successfully dealt with Scottish aggression: he had even brought the heir of the king of Scots with him, almost, it may have seemed, as a hostage. Henry, however, left the court, insulted by the archbishop of Canterbury and the earl of Chester, who in turn felt themselves insulted when Stephen placed the prince at his right hand. Stephen would probably have enhanced his reputation immeasurably and strengthened his position if, with the great military force at his disposal, he had put his fortune to the touch and fought and defeated the king of Scots in 1136. 'Ifs' of history are unprofitable for historians; they serve best when they mark errors committed and opportunities lost.

The attendance at Stephen's Easter court demonstrated to the sight of all the extensive support that he had won. The missing man of consequence was Robert, earl of Gloucester, who was still in Normandy and had not yet proffered his allegiance. The question was, would he do so? Important matters must have been discussed at the Easter court, including the settlement to be made with the church and the liberties to be announced for the realm. Stephen's coronation charter of liberties had been brief and none too explicit.[4] The court was adjourned to Oxford, where it met about a month later. To Oxford came earl Robert of Gloucester, who had at last, in all probability, reached the conclusion that for the time being nothing much was to be gained by holding aloof: he might far better serve his sister's cause by making his peace with Stephen, establishing himself in England again and keeping in touch with men and events there in her interest. 'Therefore,' William of Malmesbury tells us, 'he did homage to the king conditionally, namely, for as long as he maintained his dignity unimpaired and kept the agreement.'[5] Knowing Stephen, Robert must have felt pretty sure that the king's conduct would provide him with sufficient excuse to renounce his allegiance when it suited the cause of the empress. The second event of significance on the occasion was the issue of what is usually called 'The Oxford charter of liberties'.[6] This embodies the details of the agreement which through the instrumentality of his brother, the bishop of Winchester Stephen had made with the church. This has often been represented as a complete surrender by the crown, but at least there was embodied in the superscription an unequivocal recognition by the papacy of Stephen's regal position. This charter will be considered in more detail in the chapter on the church: Stephen was paying an extremely reasonable price for the crown, which would have been quite beyond the reach of a man who was vulnerable to the accusation of perjury because he had not been accepted by the church.

Troubles soon beset the king, the troubles that beset a man who is 'soft'. In 1136 a report of Stephen's death led Hugh Bigod to seize Norwich castle, which he refused to hand over till the king arrived. This episode was followed by the rebellion of Robert of Bampton resulting from the enforcement of the king's justice upon him in respect of a land plea. Robert is an early example of the 'castleman'. Much more serious was the insurrection of Baldwin de Redvers, castellan of Exeter, a descendant of an illegitimate branch of the Norman ducal house.[7] He had been a staunch henchman of Henry I and might have been expected to give his allegiance to the empress. He had at first refused to recognize Stephen and now, when he thought better of it and proffered his allegiance on condition that his lands should be confirmed, the king, with every justification, refused. There followed a three months' siege of Exeter castle but when the rebel garrison had been reduced to the utmost extremity by drought, Stephen again showed his fatal weakness: instead of making an example of the rebels, as the bishop of Winchester urged, he allowed himself to be persuaded by earl Robert and others who favoured their cause to allow the garrison not merely to go free but to march out with all the honours of war and go to any lord they would. Baldwin de Redvers departed to his lands in the Isle of Wight (pursued by the king) and there he organised a pirate fleet which preyed upon the commerce of Southampton and Portsmouth. Forced at last to abjure the realm, he joined the Angevins. Here was a pretty example for the numerous potential rebels and the discontented who had been disinherited by Henry I. Next, characteristically alternating leniency and severity, Stephen held a forest assize at the royal hunting lodge at Brampton in Huntingdonshire where, to their unconcealed annoyance, he impleaded numbers of barons for forest offences, thus, as Henry of Huntingdon, no admirer of his, remarked (not quite correctly), 'breaking his oath to God and to the people'.

Normandy now claimed Stephen's urgent attention. The count of Anjou was raiding in the south and venting his Angevin hatred of the Normans in the most barbarous fashion. It was time for Stephen to show himself in the duchy to be acclaimed as duke and to undertake the defence of the land against his rival. Circumstances should have been in his favour: there was the old Norman hatred of the Angevins and the strong probability that the king of France would never permit an Angevin occupation of Normandy. Rebels like Rabel de Tancarville, chamberlain of Normandy, and Roger de Tosny might be reduced with the powerful aid of Waleran, count of Meulan and his brother Robert, earl of Leicester.

The king crossed over to Normandy in mid-March 1137 and remained there until the end of November. It was his only visit to the duchy during his reign and it was a disastrous failure. In May, it is true, he received investiture as duke at the hands of the suzerain, the king of France. It was fortunate also for Stephen that the earl of Gloucester, who was now in Caen, did not join the invading forces of the count of Anjou. There Stephen's good fortune ended. He had been tactless enough to bring a large force of Flemish mercenaries, commanded by William of Ypres, into the duchy. A fracas developed between these and Stephen's baronial supporters, who left the royal camp without first taking leave of the king. This was constructed as *lèse-majesté* and Stephen pursued and arrested some of them. This unfortunate affair effectively put an end to the projected campaign against the Count of Anjou. Furthermore, the earl of Gloucester professed to have discovered an ambush laid for him by Stephen. He was preparing to renounce his allegiance. Stephen, instead of settling himself resolutely to the task of subduing Normandy and scotching the Angevin threat of invasion and conquest, fiddled about half-heartedly, trying to patch up relations with the barons.

Stephen was, in fact, facing the kind of dilemma with which he was to become increasingly familiar throughout his reign. David, king of Scots, had again gathered his forces for an invasion of Northumbria after Easter, 1137. His advance was blocked by an army of English barons at Newcastle. By the mediation of

Thurstan, archbishop of York, a truce was arranged to last till Advent (28 November). As this date approached, the Norman situation had become no easier. What was Stephen to do: confront his Norman difficulties and seek a military decision against count Geoffrey, or, leaving his lieutenants to undertake the defence of Normandy, return across the Channel to meet the Scottish threat? His appreciation of the situation proved to be disastrously wrong, for he decided that the Scottish menace was the more serious of the two, probably because it more immediately threatened his security in England, which was the centre and source of his royal power. The barons of northern England could not be trusted on their own to put up an effective resistance to renewed Scottish invasion. A number of them held Scottish fiefs, which they would be very loath to sacrifice, and were bound by ties of friendship and self-interest to the king of Scots and his son. The presence of king Stephen in person seemed essential to deal with this admittedly dangerous situation. On the other hand, the conquest of Normandy, or even of a substantial part of it, by the Angevins would raise the problem of fiefs in two territories and a consequent divided allegiance on a very much larger scale and in an even more acute form than in the case of Scotland. Normandy was absolutely vital, as both Rufus and Henry 1 had fully understood. If the duchy of Normandy and the kingdom of England were subject to different rulers, the adherents of the one were likely to be the rebels of the other. For the numerous baronial families, and for their mesne-tenants, too, whose families held fiefs on both sides of the Channel, a very difficult situation would arise if Normandy were conquered by the Angevins. Unwilling to relinquish their connections on either side, what were they to do? If once the Angevins conquered Normandy, as they did by 1144, and if they got a footing in England as well, as they did in 1139, they would stand a good chance of attracting increasing support from English barons. Normandy, in fact, presented by far the gravest danger and the king's own presence was needed to deal with it firmly: this counted for much while lieutenants like the Beaumonts, upon whom Stephen very greatly depended, were prone to wage their private wars rather than to concentrate their efforts single-mindedly against the king's most dangerous enemies.

Since Stephen had elected to deal with the Scottish threat, the only realistic policy would have been to concentrate every effort upon a decisive military victory, which would have secured his position in the north and would probably have enabled him to conciliate the earl of Chester. To begin with, the king was distracted by the rebellion of Miles de Beauchamp and the necessity of besieging Bedford castle, after Christmas 1137.[8] Tidings then reached him of renewed Scottish invasion before he had received Bedford's surrender, and he hastened to Northumberland at the beginning of February 1138. A thoroughly ill-organised and ill-conducted offensive, with reprisals in south-east Scotland, petered out within a fortnight, for there were traitors in Stephen's unenthusiastic army. An outright victory would not have been at all agreeable to barons with Scottish as well as English interests. The expedition was abandoned and the initiative was now lost on the Scottish border as well as in Normandy. After Easter Stephen's attention was fully occupied by widespread rebellions, especially in the south and west. Some of these were the outcome rather of private grievances, as Miles de Beauchamp's had been, than of devotion to the Angevin cause, but private interests served the Angevin turn well enough. Shrewsbury and Hereford, Bristol, Dunster and Castle Cary, Dorchester, Wareham and Corfe saw uprisings and warlike activities and by mid-April bonnets were over the border again. Stephen was on the run, desperately trying to beat out the fires of insurrection without plan or method or firmness of purpose.

In this emergency the north had to be left to fend for itself. King David made the mistake of going too far and thereby alienating many of his friends among the English barons. They were content that Henry of Scots should have Northumbria, to which he had a colourable, hereditary claim, but when David pushed down into Yorkshire, allowing his barbarian Galwegians a free hand to ravage and plunder the countryside, the northern barons were no longer prepared to stand aside. The Scottish fury aroused the nearest thing to national resistance that twelfth-century England saw – the old fighting spirit of the Anglo-Scandinavian north. Under the leadership of that old royal servant, archbishop Thurstan of York, the local forces, fyrd as well as baronial retinues, were rallied at Northallerton under the banners of the patron saints of York, Beverley and Ripon placed on a wagon. There on 22 August in the 'battle of the Standard' this army met and defeated the Scots, though its success was not completed by an effective pursuit, so that a considerable Scottish force remained in being and active on the soil of northern England. Nonetheless it was clear that the Scots could be beaten. In the autumn of 1138 the papal legate, Alberic, bishop of Ostia, was actively concerned together with Stephen's queen in negotiating terms of peace with the king of the Scots. A good many English barons were opposed to this,[9] but terms were eventually agreed at Durham on 9 April 1139, which gave the Scots what they had gained in 1136 with the addition of Northumbria for Henry, but with the exception of Newcastle and Bamborough, for which compensation was provided in the south.

Meanwhile, Stephen had made the disastrous mistake of allowing the close alliance between himself and his brother, the bishop of Winchester, to break down. William of Corbeil, archbishop of Canterbury, died on 21 November 1136 and the see was kept vacant for more than two years. Something had gone badly wrong, for the obvious successor, as far as Stephen was concerned, ought to have been his brother, who was the dominant personality in the English church and who had brought about and guaranteed Stephen's agreement with it. He undoubtedly expected to be promoted from the see of Winchester. Perhaps by the influence of Stephen's Beaumont advisers, Henry was balked of his ambition. On Christmas Eve 1138, while bishop Henry was conducting an ordination of deacons at St Paul's, the electors, at the council of Westminster in the presence of the king and the papal legate, chose Theobald, abbot of Bec, as archbishop of Canterbury. Henry cannot have been fully consoled by receiving from pope Innocent II the office of papal legate in England on 1 March 1139, whereby an anomalous position was created. The archbishop of Canterbury, traditionally the head of the church in England was now subordinated to one of his own suffragans. This was not, however, appreciated for some months, for Henry did not publish his legatine commission till the council of Winchester was summoned.

Henry was by no means fully reconciled with his brother. The original compact and alliance between them which had secured Stephen's succession to the throne had been strained to breaking-point. On 22 June 1139 in Oxford an incident was provoked which gave the king a flimsy pretext for the arrest of Roger, bishop of Salisbury, his nephew Alexander, bishop of Lincoln and his son Roger, the chancellor. Bishop Roger's other nephew, Nigel, bishop of Ely, managed to escape to Devizes castle, which he prepared to hold against the king. Under Henry I bishop Roger had been chief justiciar and head of the administration, an office which he continued to occupy till the time of his arrest. Bishop Nigel had been Henry I's treasurer, a man with a flair for financial administration and had taken a leading part in building up the exchequer machine. Bishop Roger and his family had, in fact, until June 1139, a firm grip upon the country's central administration. The bishops, too, had strong stone castles at Sherborne, Devizes, Malmesbury and Newark, which they had recently been munitioning. Their loyalty to Stephen was suspect: an Angevin attempt on England was widely expected in 1139 (it occurred at the end of September), and Stephen's supporters feared that bishop Roger and his family were planning to assist the daughter of their old master. There may have been good grounds for the suspicion which attached to the members of this distinguished clerical family of royal servants and administrators, and their defection to the empress would have been a very serious matter for Stephen. There was every justification for some action to prevent such a defection or at least to minimise its effect, but the action taken was clumsy and brutal. Not only were sacrilegious hands laid upon the persons of two bishops, but Stephen pursued the third to his lair and in order to secure the surrender of Devizes castle threatened to hang his ex-chancellor, the son of bishop Roger. This unfortunate business had two major results. One was that the administrative structure so painstakingly built up under Henry I was severely jarred and the effective government of the country put in jeopardy. The other result was the alienation of the church, led by Stephen's brother. Stephen had flagrantly broken the promises he had made to the church in his Oxford charter of liberties. The bishop of Winchester cited his brother to appear before a legatine council at Winchester on 29 August 1139. Stephen, after consultation with his advisers, allowed his case to be presented before the court by Aubrey de Vere, the chamberlain, and since the argument was acceptable to Hugh, archbishop of Rouen (a Cluniac), he probably hoped that there would be an end of the matter. Since, however, there was some talk of appealing to Rome against him, Stephen himself appealed to Rome against any sentence that the council might dare to pronounce upon him. There was no decision, no settlement, no reconciliation.

This was the situation when movements began in anticipation of the arrival of the empress. The exiled Baldwin de Redvers landed at Wareham and took Corfe castle; William de Mohun, castellan of Dunster, declared for Maud; and John, the king's marshal and castellan of Marlborough, did likewise – and both were burning and pillaging. While Stephen was trying ineffectively to deal with these outbreaks, the empress and Robert, earl of Gloucester, landed at Arundel with 140 knights, probably on 30 September. Earl Robert hastened to his stronghold in Bristol, leaving the empress in Arundel castle under the protection of the dowager queen Adeliza and her new husband, William d'Aubigny. Stephen marched to Arundel from Marlborough, and he might have captured the empress; but by the advice of the bishop of Winchester, so it was said, he allowed her to go free and gave her an escort to her brother at Bristol. Henry's reason for giving such advice was said to be that it would be wiser to allow the king's rivals to concentrate in one place, where they might be dealt with in a single operation, rather than risk several outbreaks in different places. He well knew his brother's hopeless inability to cope with such a situation but, nonetheless, he was strongly suspected of bad faith. Meanwhile Angevin power was indeed concentrating in the west and Miles of Gloucester, an old servant of Henry I, a constable in the royal household and a power in Gloucestershire and Herefordshire and in Brecknock, was won over to the side of the empress. Brian fitz Count, lord of Wallingford, likewise proclaimed his loyalty to the empress and put at her disposal his castle, strategically placed in the Thames valley, an eastern outpost for the Angevins, a threat to Oxford, and a menace to its communications with the capital for any royalist force operating in the upper Thames region and beyond.

Stephen's military ineptitude was now to be demonstrated but, before we condemn him on that score, let us remind ourselves of the difficulties that confronted medieval commanders. Intelligence was rudimentary; problems of location and consequent dependence on local guides were a severe handicap; timing and therefore co-ordination were matters of extreme difficulty. Where fortifications were concerned, even in rudimentary motte-and-bailey castles and certainly in those that were built of stone, defenders enjoyed considerable advantages over attackers, at least in the short-term, while food and water held out. This was hardly less of a problem for a besieger, since armies lived off the country. A common tactic was to devastate the countryside surrounding a castle, so as to deprive the garrison of food supplies. Sieges were liable to be very protracted affairs and in a country with as many castles as there were in England any campaign could easily degenerate into a series of sieges, with small forces detached to pursue them, thereby progressively weakening the field force and fatally impairing its mobility. Stephen's first move from Arundel was against Wallingford. Failing to carry it speedily, he left a besieging force there and moved westwards, confident in his large army, to come to grips with the Angevins. While he was taking the castles of South Cerney and Malmesbury and sitting down before Trowbridge, Miles of Gloucester got round his flank and relieved Wallingford. Stephen whipped round like an animal whose tail had been trodden upon and returned to London. If, in fact, the forces that the Londoners could raise were even a fraction of what they were said to be, and if they were at all reliable, Stephen might have left Miles to break his teeth on that nut, while he himself pursued his western offensive. Miles returned to the west and sacked Worcester, drawing Stephen off in that direction, but avoiding any major action. After some minor successes, Stephen heard of the death of Roger, bishop of Salisbury on 11 December 1139, and immediately went to secure the see.

Scarcely had the new year dawned[10] than Stephen was again rushing frantically across the length and breadth of the country – to Ely to deal with the serious rebellion of bishop Nigel, to Cornwall to deal with Richard fitz Turold and Reginald, illegitimate son of Henry i. The earl of Gloucester was not in a strong enough position to bring Stephen to battle when he had stuck his neck out so far into the remote south-west. After returning as far as Winchester, Stephen set off on another offensive in the Worcester region and had the satisfaction, if such it was, of sacking the earl of Gloucester's mansion at Tewkesbury. That was about all he accomplished. By June he was again on the other side of England, in East Anglia, where Hugh Bigod was in rebellion. Stephen succeeded in taking Bungay castle and in patching up relations with him. We hear of the king subsequently in other eastern parts, but the chronology of this period is so obscure and complicated that it is impossible to trace his movements in any detail.

Meanwhile a series of events was in train which after beginning in a small way soon expanded into widespread and serious strife. On 6 February 1140 Thurstan, archbishop of York, died. The finding of his successor proved an extremely difficult and controversial business. In this case the traditional procedure, whereby a royally approved candidate was elected and consecrated, did not work smoothly. This was not primarily because of the rift which had occurred between Stephen and his brother, the legate, but because a group of Cistercian and Augustinian zealots, backed by the formidable St Bernard, interested themselves in the electoral proceedings. A favourite candidate of the reformers and of the party of the empress was Waldef, prior of the Augustinian house of Kirkham, step-son of king David and brother of Simon of Senlis, earl of Northampton. Stephen vetoed Waldef and Henry de Sully, abbot of Fécamp, son of Stephen's sister Agnes, was put forward with the support of the legate. Henry was unwilling to surrender his abbacy, hoping to hold it in plurality with the archiepiscopal see of York, just as his uncle, the legate, held the abbacy of Glastonbury and the see of Winchester. He was vetoed on this account by pope Innocent II. Then William of Aumâle, earl of York, intimated to the electors on the king's behalf that William fitz Herbert, another nephew of Stephen (son of his half-sister, by Herbert the chamberlain) and treasurer of York, was to be elected. A majority of the chapter elected him in January 1141, but a minority, supported by Cistercian influence, opposed this. William was sent to the king, who was then besieging Lincoln castle, and received the temporalities of the see. Both parties in the York chapter sent representatives to the papal curia and the elect himself went there to seek papal approval. Meanwhile the whole situation in England was completely altered by the defeat and capture of the king.

In 1140 the supporters of the empress had continued their military efforts. Hereford was attacked by Miles of Gloucester and Geoffrey Talbot. In August the earl of Gloucester made an unsuccessful attempt on Bath and in September he sacked Nottingham. The whole military situation was extremely fluid, not to say chaotic, and mercenary captains, like the notorious Robert fitz Hubert, who was first employed by the earl of Gloucester, were getting quite out of control. Neither side was achieving anything in the least bit decisive. In such circumstances the legate made an attempt at Whitsuntide to negotiate some kind of compromise. A meeting was arranged near Bath, the king being represented by the queen, the legate and the archbishop of Canterbury, the empress by Robert, earl of Gloucester and others. William of Malmesbury's view is that they 'wasted both words and time', but that the empress showed herself the more willing to submit to the judgment of the church. In September the legate crossed the Channel for discussions with Louis VII, king of France, and Stephen's elder brother Theobald, count of Blois. He returned near the end of November, bringing proposals for the good of the country, 'if there had been anyone to turn words into deeds'. According to William of Malmesbury, the empress and the earl of Gloucester promptly agreed to accept them, 'but the king postponed the matter from day to day and finally frustrated the whole plan'. There is no clear indication of the nature of the proposals but since the king of France was consulted, they may have included the cession of Normandy to the empress or her son Henry. The king of France had a double interest in any settlement which involved the inheritance of Stephen's eldest son and heir, Eustace. Not only was Louis VII the suzerain of the duke of Normandy, but his sister Constance was betrothed to Eustace in February 1140, and the marriage took place by the end of the year. If the cession of Normandy was involved in the proposals that the legate brought to England, there must have been some very substantial compensation but, even so, it would have been very foolish of Stephen to accept such a settlement.

The next crisis was already approaching, but from another quarter. The earl of Chester, nursing his grievances, made trouble for Stephen in the latter part of 1140. The details are not known, for unfortunately there is a lacuna at this point in the manuscript of *Gesta Stephani* and other contemporary authors do not supply the missing information. Stephen, as had become his habit, tried to buy off the troublemaker. He met the earl of Chester and his half-brother, William de Roumare, earl of Lincoln, in Lincolnshire before Christmas and, according to William of Malmesbury, he had 'loaded them with honours'. (*Comitemque Cestrensem et eius fratrem honoribus auxerat.*)[11] Whatever the agreement, *Gesta Stephani* indicates that the earl did not honour it. He and his brother got possession of the keep of Lincoln castle by a trick, expelling the royal warders, and began to oppress the citizens of Lincoln. An urgent call for help from these citizens and from bishop Alexander brought the king to Lincoln in the Christmas holidays to besiege the castle. The rebel earls were taken by surprise, for they had not expected such a quick reaction, but earl Rannulf made a daring escape to seek the aid of his father-in-law Robert, earl of Gloucester, and to raise troops in his earldom of Chester and from among the Welsh. Earls Robert and Rannulf returned to relieve Lincoln castle on 2 February 1141 with an army which included numbers of 'the disinherited'. These were men of whom some, or whose forebears, had incurred forfeiture of their lands under Henry I and had failed to get them back from Stephen, and also a few who had been disinherited by Stephen himself.[12] In the pitched battle that ensued before the walls of Lincoln, Stephen's baronial followers let him down badly and several of the most important fled at the first onset. The outcome was a crushing defeat of the royal army and the capture of Stephen himself. This had every appearance of irretrievable disaster for Stephen's cause. Stephen was sent captive to the empress at Gloucester and then to Bristol, where he was imprisoned, at first honourably and later in irons.

The bishop of Winchester, as papal legate, now held the key to the whole situation for if Stephen were to be deposed and Maud consecrated and elevated to sit in his place, this would have to be done by the judgment, and with the support, of the church. The empress was slow to react and it was not till 2 March, a full month after the victory at Lincoln, that she and her chief supporters met the legate at Wherwell, near Winchester. It was a wet and cloudy day, 'as though', says William of Malmesbury, 'the fates portended the intrusion of ill-fortune in the cause'. The empress undertook upon oath, as did her leading adherents, 'that all major affairs in England, especially the bestowal of bishoprics and abbeys, should be subject to his (the legate's) authority, if he would receive her in holy church as lady and remain ever faithful to her'. The legate, in turn, gave an assurance of his loyalty, provided that the empress kept faith with him. The following day Maud was given possession of the king's crown, the castle and the royal treasure and she was received in Winchester cathedral by the legate and a number of bishops and abbots. The archbishop of

Canterbury only put in an appearance a few days later, when he and most of the bishops insisted on personally obtaining the king's permission to change their allegiance. Maud was now recognised as 'Lady of England', the correct title for an heir to the throne before consecration and coronation. Already the dictator's strut began to be observed: 'she at once put on a most supercilious manner instead of the modest demeanour proper to a woman, and she began to walk and speak and do everything more stiffly and arrogantly than she had been wont'.[13]

The empress spent Easter at Oxford and a legatine council was summoned to meet at Winchester on 7 April. We have a very full account of its proceedings from William of Malmesbury, who was present at it. The proceedings were significant, for they were intended by the legate not merely to pronounce judgment on Stephen and settle the succession but to confirm and emphasise the supreme authority of the church in this vital matter:

That same day, after the reading of the letters of apology by which some excused their absence, the legate called to him the bishops and held a private discussion with them; shortly the abbots were summoned and finally the archdeacons. Nothing was made public about their deliberations, but the minds and mouths of all were busy with what had to be done.

On the following day the legate made a speech in which he denounced the wickednesses of his brother Stephen in his treatment of the church and his failure as a prince, excused his own part in bringing about Stephen's elevation and concluded thus:

Therefore, since God has executed his judgment upon my brother, allowing him without my knowledge to fall into the power of the strong, lest the kingdom should totter without a ruler, I have invited you all, by my legatine authority, to meet me here. The case was stated yesterday in private before the greater part of the clergy of England, whose right it particularly is to elect and ordain a prince. Therefore, first, calling God to our aid, as is fitting, we elect as Lady of England and Normandy the daughter of a pacific king, a glorious king, a rich king, a good king incomparable in our time, and we promise her fealty and support..

Here the claim of the church to a decisive voice in the choice of a monarch is stated in the strongest terms, even more explicitly than in the superscription of Stephen's Oxford charter of liberties.

This legatine council cleared the way for Maud's acceptance as far as the church was concerned, but her recognition by the people and her coronation must take place in the capital. From that point of view, all was not well, as two ominous events now emphasised. Representatives of the Londoners had been summoned to the council since, as William of Malmesbury says, they were virtually nobles because of the greatness of their city, though he does not mention any claim on their part to a say in the election of a king. These burgesses arrived late and they made no demonstrative manifestations of joy at the success of the empress. On the contrary, they announced that they had been sent from 'the commune of London, as they call it', to ask for the release of their lord the king, and 'all the barons who had long since been admitted to their commune were urgent in demanding this of the lord legate, the archbishop and the clergy who were present'. Such a demand from the wealthy and powerful capital city must have been disconcerting for Maud's advisers. The representatives of the Londoners entered into no binding agreement; they merely promised rather glumly to explain the council's decision to their fellow citizens and give it what support they could. The Londoners, in fact, were in a position of considerable strength and capable of disrupting very seriously the plans of the empress for her coronation.

The other ominous event was the arrival at the council of a clerk of Stephen's queen, Matilda, with a letter demanding the king's release. This he insisted on reading out 'with admirable assurance' in spite of the legate's attempt to prevent him. This was no empty gesture. The queen's position, too, was strong enough to threaten the success of the empress. As lady of Boulogne, she controlled the English lands which belonged to it, mainly in Essex in the region of Colchester. Furthermore, with the aid of William of Ypres she was in firm control of Kent. Thus she was probably in a position to control the river approach to London and, if necessary, to exercise considerable pressure upon the city by blockade. Furthermore, control of Kent secured her cross-Channel communications with Boulogne, which was a relatively important sea-power, and reinforcements of mercenaries could easily be brought in from Flanders. The queen was not altogether lacking in baronial support; there were on her side the count of Meulan, the earl of Warenne, the earl of Northampton, William

Martel and others. The queen, in fact, was in a strong strategic position and commanded considerable military strength; she was still a very formidable opponent for the empress. The outlook for the empress after the council of Winchester was by no means as bright as might have been expected and, if we are to believe the *Gesta*, Maud's behaviour did nothing to improve it. She was haughty with her own most devoted adherents, choleric and abusive with those of the king who came to make their submission and exceedingly arbitrary in her conduct of affairs. Stephen had incurred the bitter hostility of 'the disinherited', who fought so effectively against him at Lincoln; Maud proceeded to disinherit a great many more. Her most loyal supporters had cause for concern and the bishop of Winchester had strong reasons for reconsidering his attitude. Maud showed no disposition to listen to his advice and as regards the bestowal of bishoprics and abbeys, which she had promised that the legate should control, she blatantly disregarded her undertaking. She favoured the pretensions of William Cumin, formerly chancellor of the king of Scots, who was endeavouring forcibly to obtain the see of Durham. The legate upheld the strong objections of the Durham chapter, but Maud was determined not only to recognise Curmin but to invest him with the ring and the staff, the symbols of the episcopal office. A proposal so unbelievably reactionary shocked and alarmed the clergy and was a calculated insult to the legate and a flouting of his authority. Unless this virago could be restrained, the position of the church seemed likely to be far worse than it had been under Stephen, who might at least be open to persuasion.

The empress was slow in moving to the capital. It was not till a few days before 24 June that the Londoners were finally persuaded to admit her to the city. A good deal of the time which had elapsed since the dispersal of the council of Winchester must have been spent in negotiation with them and with Geoffrey de Mandeville, whom Stephen had created earl of Essex in 1140. Geoffrey had already been guilty of an action which had aroused the hostility of queen Matilda and which was destined two years later to cost him very dear. After the battle of Lincoln it would seem (for the precise date is uncertain) he had refused to allow the princess Constance of France, bride of Stephen's son and heir Eustace, to accompany the queen from London. He retained her in the Tower as, in some sort, a hostage, though he may have hoped if occasion should arise to represent this as a measure for her protection. If Geoffrey were won over by the empress, his control of the tower should enable him to overawe the Londoners; his power in Essex should enable him to attack the lands of the honour of Boulogne in that shire. At the same time, the adherence of Hugh Bigod to the empress after the battle of Lincoln (probably secured by a grant from her of the earldom of Norfolk) was important. As a great Norfolk magnate he would be expected to cope with the earl of Warenne and other royal adherents in the region of East Anglia. Bishop Nigel in the Isle of Ely also represented a formidable military power favourable to the empress which would help to dominate the whole eastern region on her behalf.

Probably Geoffrey de Mandeville's adherence to the cause of the empress in the summer of 1141 was largely responsible for bringing the Londoners into a mood sufficiently submissive to receive her in the city, but she had to make enormous concessions to win him over. Her first charter in Geoffrey's favour, issued about midsummer, did not entirely satisfy him and within a few weeks, when her cause had already suffered a serious setback, she had to augment and reinforce it with another in the last week of July.[14] Geoffrey was fully confirmed in his earldom of Essex and in addition he was made hereditary sheriff and justice of that shire. He also obtained the hereditary constableship of the Tower of London and many territorial concessions besides. The second charter added the shrievalty of London and Middlesex at the old ferm of £300, the amount at which his grandfather had held it, for by the time this charter was issued the Londoners had forfeited, as far as the empress was concerned, any right to the *firma burgi* which they had obtained from her father. Geoffrey was also given the hereditary justiceships of London, Middlesex and Hertfordshire in addition to that of Essex. These were only the most outstanding of the concessions which made earl Geoffrey the most formidable feudal magnate in this very important region and brought about on a very large scale the feudalisation of public authority in his hands. Fortified by the alliance with Geoffrey, even though its terms were not yet embodied in a charter, Maud arrived in London. She sent for the wealthiest citizens and demanded from them a very large sum of money. When they asked for some consideration and respite, she turned upon them with blazing fury and virulent recrimination, refusing 'to spare them in any respect or make the slightest abatement of her demands'. It was a chastened and gloomy delegation that returned home. It would be difficult to say how much intelligence of events in London reached queen Matilda in Kent – probably a good deal. She chose this psychological moment to send her army to ravage the district around London. The author of *Gesta Stephani* explains the effect that this had:

The Londoners, then, were in dire distress. On the one hand, the country was being stripped before their eyes and reduced by hostile ravages to the habitation of the hedgehog and there was no one to afford them present help. On the other hand, that new Lady was going beyond the bounds of moderation and oppressing them grievously. They had no hope that she would have bowels of mercy for them in the future, since at the very beginning of her rule she had no pity on her people and demanded of them what was intolerable. Consequently they judged it worth considering a renewal of the pact of peace and alliance with the queen and uniting, all of them, to rescue their king and lord from his chains.[15]

On 24 June the bells were rung and the Londoners swarmed out like angry wasps to attack the empress at Westminster, where she was just sitting down to a banquet. They were a very formidable force and, taken completely by surprise, the only course open to Maud was precipitate flight. She rode to Oxford. The tide had turned and already men were quietly leaving her court. The queen and William of Ypres promptly took possession of London in the name of Stephen. Earl Geoffrey was in danger of losing everything he had gained and the price of his continued adherence to the empress was high, as the second of her charters in his favour clearly shows. The earl did not long remain loyal, and the concessions made by the empress gave him a very useful bargaining counter for his negotiations with the other side: they need not try to palm him off with anything less.

The legate was incensed against the empress because of her reactionary attitude to church affairs and the arrogant treatment he had experienced at her hands. Furthermore, his family feeling was outraged because Maud refused to allow Henry's nephew, prince Eustace, to have the lands which belonged personally to his father. He therefore met the queen at Guildford, reached an agreement with her and released Stephen's supporters from the sentence of excommunication that had been pronounced upon them. The legate then returned to Winchester and the empress went there at the end of July to deal with this contumacious prelate of the house of Blois. She arrived at the royal castle and sent for him. The bishop fled, leaving a garrison in his castle of Wolvesey, in the south-east of the city. He appealed to the queen for help. Queen Matilda promptly sent an army to Winchester, with William of Ypres and the Flemish mercenaries, the formidable military forces of the city of London, and Geoffrey, earl of Essex, who had taken good care to catch the tide of his affairs at the flood. With the empress at Winchester were David, king of Scots, the earls of Gloucester and Hereford and several other earls, including Rannulf, earl of Chester, whose attempt to join the queen's band-wagon had been rebuffed, and who arrived too late to be of any use to the Angevins. William of Ypres, the queen's commander, almost succeeded in closing the net round the forces of the empress and on 14 September their retreat began. Brian fitz Count and Reginald, earl of Cornwall, were detailed to get the empress away safely to Devizes and Gloucester, which they did, while earl Robert and the others covered the operation by trying to cut their way out. The king of Scots was thrice captured and thrice succeeded in bribing his captors to release him (they must have been ignorant of the value of their prisoner). Miles of Gloucester threw away his armour and barely escaped with his life. The archbishop of Canterbury, with other bishops, was a sorry fugitive. Some barons and knights who fell into the hands of rustics were severely beaten, which throws a very interesting light upon the peasants' feeling of desperation at this time. This should be compared with the fate of king Stephen's son-in-law, earl Hervé, who according to *Gesta* was besieged in Devizes castle by a mob of peasants leagued together under oath against him (*Simplici rusticorum plebe in unum se globum in malum illius coniurante*). The retreat of the army of the empress soon became a fantastic rout, such as minstrels loved to celebrate in song, and the author of *Gesta Stephani* all but bursts into verse in his description of it. Fugitives, riderless destriers, abandoned arms and armour were scattered far and wide in that lush countryside. The earl of Gloucester, commanding the rearguard, was taken as he attempted to ford the river Test at Stockbridge – a record catch for the end of the season on a famous beat. Winchester was, naturally, sacked by its liberators.

It was an obvious suggestion that the earl should be exchanged for the king. Robert of Gloucester, however, took the line that he and Stephen were not of equal consequence and he would only consent to the proposal if he himself and all who were captured with him were exchanged for the king. This suggestion was not at all acceptable on the king's side, because a good many of his adherents had taken valuable captives: William of Ypres, for example, had taken Humphrey de Bohun and Gilbert de Clare, earl of Hertford, had taken William of Salisbury, and they were eager for the ransoms. An effort was made to bribe earl Robert with 'lordship over the whole land' under the king, if he would abandon his sister, which he refused to do. Eventually he was made to realise his own importance as the effective leader of the Angevin party in England and to agree to an exchange for the king on equal terms. On 1 November Stephen was released, leaving the queen, his son and two magnates as sureties for the release of the earl of Gloucester. Two days later the earl was released, leaving his son as surety for the release of the queen and her fellow hostages, and when these reached Winchester the earl's son was set free.

A legatine council was held at Westminster on 7 December, where the bishop of Winchester explained away as best he could the proceedings of the past nine months. Stephen declined any gesture of restoration or reconsecration, insisting that he had never been deposed and the situation was restored to what it had been before the council of Winchester in April. There had been some notable deserters from Stephen's cause after the battle of Lincoln and the greatest of them was Waleran, count of Meulan, upon whom, together with his twin brother Robert, earl of Leicester, Stephen had so greatly relied both in Normandy and in England from the beginning of his reign. There is little doubt that their advice and support had led to the arrest of the bishops in June 1139, and Stephen's dependence upon these Beaumont earls had been a main cause of the rift between him and his brother, the bishop of Winchester. Waleran did not immediately desert the king after the debacle of 2 February 1141. He joined the queen in Kent. In March 1141, Waleran's brother Robert, earl of Leicester, who had been maintaining Stephen's cause in Normandy, secured a truce for his brother and himself from the count of Anjou so that he might return to England for consultations. The situation seemed hopeless and Waleran, who had inherited his father's Norman and French fiefs, decided that if he were to retain these he must make his peace with the Angevins. This he did before the autumn.

There would be a new government in England now. The old influence of the Beaumonts was gone. Perhaps both Stephen and his brother Henry had learned enough from recent disasters to realise that their best hope lay in a firm fraternal alliance and a sincere renewal of the old compact that had secured the throne for Stephen. Perhaps an atmosphere of complete mutual trust could never again be established, but with the exercise of some forbearance on both sides the king and the bishop of Winchester should be able to work together reasonably well. The royal household, which must to a great extent have disintegrated as an effective administrative body after the battle of Lincoln, would have to be reorganised, and since the loyalty of the baronage had, with some exceptions, been shown to be a broken reed Stephen would have to rely more than ever before upon a small group of intimates comprising William of Ypres and a number of household officers like William Martel the steward and Robert de Vere the constable, such loyalists as Richard de Lucy and Richard de Camville and, for the rest, such earls and barons as proved reliable – and that reliability depended very much on self-interest.

We have no information about the king's movements until after the middle of April, when he was in York, perhaps to raise an army for he had loyal supporters there. He prevented a tournament between William of Aumâle, earl of York, and count Alan of Richmond. A mid-twelfth-century tournament was not the courtly affair of two or three centuries later, but a fierce mêlée, very apt to degenerate into a serious battle, which would have done the royal cause no good. Moving southwards Stephen was taken ill at Northampton, so very ill that his death was widely reported and he was unable to move till the end of June. This was fortunate for the empress, whose position had been dangerously weak since the rout of Winchester. In March envoys had been sent to her husband, count Geoffrey, urgently asking for help which, occupied as he was with the war in Normandy, he was not at all anxious to give. He indicated that the earl of Gloucester, the responsible leader of Maud's party, should go to Normandy to discuss the situation, and this the earl did at the very time when

Stephen recovered from his illness. He sailed from Poole Harbour, the most convenient place of embarkation for Normandy from the West Country, an area which was commanded by Wareham castle. Stephen hurried there, seized the castle and left a garrison to deny the earl of Gloucester a convenient landing if he returned with reinforcements. Thence he marched to Cirencester, which he burned, and so via Bampton and Radcot to Oxford, which he carried by assault on 16 September and where he set siege to the castle in which the empress had taken refuge. When Robert of Gloucester heard news of this he persuaded the count of Anjou to allow his young son and heir, Henry, to accompany him to England. It was a risky undertaking but the effect on the morale of those whose sympathies were with the empress justified it. Geoffrey showed no desire to go to the rescue of his wife and perhaps it was just as well that he did not, for the English barons would certainly have regarded him as an unwelcome intruder. Robert returned with a fleet of fifty-two ships and more than 300 knights, landing and setting siege to Wareham castle. Stephen this time refused to be distracted from the siege of Oxford castle, for here the empress was trapped, and her capture would be decisive, at least in England. The empress was a courageous woman, as she had already shown on more than one occasion. In the snows of December she made a night escape from the castle to Abingdon and Wallingford. Stephen's only consolation was that he won this key position in the Thames valley, commanding the main routes from London to Gloucester and from Southampton to the Midlands. This put a stop to any effective movement by the armies of the empress eastward from the upper Thames valley, and Wallingford, defended by Brian fitz Count, remained an isolated outpost.

There ensued a chess-like war of castles and sieges accompanied by local devastation which it would be otiose to follow in detail. The main military event of 1143 was the battle of Wilton.[16] Here Stephen was surprised by the earl of Gloucester and narrowly escaped capture, mainly because his faithful steward, William Martel (who was taken prisoner), fought a dogged rearguard action which enabled the king to get away. The ultimate outcome of this passage of arms was that the whole region between the Bristol Channel and the south coast came under the control of the earl of Gloucester, who created there a 'certain semblance of peace' (*umbra quaedam pacis sed pax necdum perfecta*).[17]

The year 1143 in ecclesiastical affairs was marked by further developments in the disputed York election. The parties were summoned to appear before the pope on 7 March. Innocent II then decided to refer the case to the bishops of Winchester and Hereford as judges delegate, with precise instructions. If the dean of York, William of Ste Barbe (consecrated bishop of Durham on 20 June 1143), would swear that the election of William fitz Herbert had been free, it should stand. When the elect returned to England or very soon after, he had in his possession a papal letter (fabricated undoubtedly) purporting to allow an alternative oath to be substituted for that of William of Ste Barbe.[18] William's attention was fully occupied by the struggle to eject the intruder William Cumin from the see of Durham and he did not take the required oath (nor indeed was he willing). The legate, convinced by the supposed papal letter and by the oaths of other witnesses, consecrated William fitz Herbert as archbishop of York on 26 September. Two days earlier pope Innocent II had died and on the very day of William fitz Herbert's consecration his successor Celestine II had been elected. The bishop of Winchester's legatine authority automatically lapsed as soon as this news reached England. St Bernard wrote to the new pope and to the cardinals denouncing William fitz Herbert in the most forceful terms. The old and feeble Celestine (who lived only till 8 March 1144) took no action but although William was not deposed, he did not receive his pallium, the symbol of a metropolitan's authority. With St Bernard and the English Cistercians working relentlessly against him, archbishop William's position was indeed precarious. The real struggle over the see of York was just beginning.

The year 1143 was also marked by strong action against two important men upon whose loyalty Stephen could by no means rely. Nigel, bishop of Ely, who had tried to defy Stephen at Devizes after the arrest of his relatives in June 1139, who had raised a rebellion against the king in the Isle of Ely in 1140 after the death of his uncle, the bishop of Salisbury, and who preferred the daughter to the nephew of king Henry, remained something of a menace to Stephen's position in eastern England. It has to be remembered that the earl of Chester was still in possession of Lincoln and that Hugh Bigod was a power in Norfolk. The time had come when, if Stephen could not make very much progress in the west, he might at least try to strengthen his position in the east. Bishop Nigel was attacked with the weapons of the church. At a legatine council held by bishop Henry of Winchester in Lent 1143, he was accused of various ecclesiastical offences as well as stirring up sedition in the country. To clear himself he had to journey to Rome, and partly owing to the obstacles put in his way he was out of the country till 1145.[19]

The more dramatic and notorious case is that of Geoffrey de Mandeville, earl of Essex, whom Stephen suddenly seized at his court at St Albans, about Michaelmas, charged with treason and threatened to hang unless he surrendered the tower of London and his other castles.[20] Having surrendered his castles, Geoffrey was released and promptly flew into frantic rebellion. He occupied Ely, seized Ramsey abbey, expelled the monks, and turned it into a fortress. He sacked Cambridge and ravaged the countryside for miles around with dreadful barbarity, which probably provided the Peterborough chronicler with first-hand material for his description of the anarchical conditions in Stephen's reign. It is not true, though it has sometimes been suggested, that these atrocities were mainly confined to the time and the area of Geoffrey's rebellion. There is plenty of evidence of similar occurrences in other regions at various times, especially when mercenary captains broke loose. These outbreaks too were local affairs. The king was quite unable to bring Geoffrey to battle, for he could always find secure refuge in the fens. The result might have been interminable and inconclusive swamp warfare, had not Geoffrey been mortally wounded by an arrow during an attack on Burwell in August 1144. He died excommunicate and unshriven on 16 September. In this rebellion Geoffrey was abetted by Hugh Bigod, earl of Norfolk. The episode occupied Stephen long enough in 1144 to allow his enemies to take the initiative in the west and attack Oxford and Malmesbury. Stephen had made an unsuccessful attempt on Lincoln about May and he then turned to the west to counter the enemy threats in that region. He relieved Malmesbury and had some limited successes in Gloucestershire when Geoffrey de Mandeville's death brought the fenland rising to an end. It also brought to an end the dangerous Mandeville domination in London, Middlesex, Essex and Hertfordshire. Stephen meanwhile returned to East Anglia to deal with Hugh Bigod and built castles to restrain his raiding.

In Normandy, in 1144, things had gone from bad to worse for

Stephen. Since 1141 count Geoffrey had been steadily extending his conquests in Normandy to the west bank of the Seine and throughout the Contentin. In January 1144 he crossed the Seine and was received in Rouen, though its castle held out till 23 April. Geoffrey then, by means of territorial concessions, easier perhaps for an Angevin than for a Norman to make, won recognition as duke of Normandy from Louis VII. When the castle of Arques finally capitulated in 1145, Stephen had lost his very last hold in Normandy and the chances of his ever recovering the duchy were obviously remote. This was a very grave set-back to his cause and ominous for the future, because it revived once again the old problems of divided allegiance for the feudatories with connections and lands on both sides of the Channel, which Rufus and Henry I had striven so hard and so successfully to avoid. A very difficult choice was involved for many barons, both great and lesser men. Would it be wise to recognise Stephen, thereby hoping to safeguard their English lands, but almost certainly sacrificing their Norman lands, interests or family connections? Might it, on the other hand, be wiser to support the empress, who still had a strong footing in England, hoping that she might win and that the ultimate succession of her son Henry, an acceptable heir, would resolve their difficulties by reuniting Normandy with England? Considerations and calculations of this kind were probably among the strongest reasons for the increasing support that the young Henry obtained, especially after his arrogant mother left England early in 1148 and after he himself became duke of Normandy in place of his alien father in 1150. At least it may be said in favour of duke Geoffrey that he was careful not to interfere in England even after Normandy had submitted to him. He was astute enough to understand the situation.

The year 1145 is in some respects obscure and certain events appear rather mysterious because we lack adequate factual information. There was the peculiar behaviour of Turgis of Avranches, a man of undistinguished family, whom Stephen had raised to a position of some importance. He was given custody of the castle of Saffron Walden with the surrounding district when it was surrendered by Geoffrey de Mandeville. Turgis refused Stephen admittance to the castle because, it was said, he feared that he might be deprived of the constableship. All this seemed as the author of *Gesta Stephani* says, 'absurd and incredible', but it gives a very clear indication of the state of insecurity and uncertainty in this region following the rebellion of Geoffrey de Mandeville and Hugh Bigod. Stephen caught Turgis out hunting, 'joyfully sounding his horn', threatened to hang him and received the surrender of the castle. It was not a serious revolt, but might very easily have developed into just such an episode as those of Robert fitz Hubert and Robert fitz Hildebrand, which, occurring on any widespread scale, spelled anarchy. In the west the main military effort of the forces of the empress was concentrated in the attempt to take Malmesbury castle. In his efforts to counter the move Stephen succeeded, with the aid of the Londoners, in taking the castle of Faringdon, built by the earl of Gloucester at the request of his son Philip to cut communications between Oxford and Malmesbury. Then we learn that Philip, who was the castellan for the empress at Cricklade, deserted to Stephen. There is no satisfactory explanation of this astonishing event, for it is difficult to believe the simple story in *Gesta Stephani* that he was bribed by grants of lands which his father had forfeited. There must have been more than mere bribery behind Philip's action, but there is no means of knowing whether it was the outcome of a purely personal quarrel between father and son or of a disagreement about military policy and the failure of earl Robert to relieve Faringdon.[21] Attempts were made at this time to bring about peace between the king and the empress, and when Reginald, earl of Cornwall, who was engaged in an embassy for this purpose on behalf of the empress, was captured by Philip of Gloucester, Philip was obliged to give him up. The king and the empress did actually meet, but 'since an overweening spirit prevailed on each side' and neither was prepared to make the slightest concession, the negotiations quickly broke down. These negotiations may have been brought about by the influence of men anxious for a compromise that would safeguard their possessions and interests in both England and Normandy. They were frustrated because the principals were confident of the strength of their positions and blind to the need for compromise. The situation did not in fact become amenable to compromise till the firm attitude of the church and the death of his elder son and heir, Eustace, brought it home to Stephen that his dynastic ambitions were incapable of fulfilment.

The year 1146 was dominated by the temporary adherence of the earl of Chester to Stephen's cause and his subsequent arrest and rebellion. Since the date of Stephen's astonishingly large grant of lands to the earl is almost certainly 1146 (though it might have been as early as 1144), it seems likely that this represents the implementation of the king's side of a bargain between them.[22] The earl's support meant for Stephen a great strengthening of his position in the north, the Midlands and Lincolnshire and a considerable military reinforcement. The earl was to be left in possession of the royal castle of Lincoln, which he had seized at the end of 1140, till his Norman lands were recovered. Earl Rannulf helped Stephen to capture Bedford from Miles de Beauchamp and assisted him with a substantial force of three hundred knights in yet another attempt upon Wallingford. Stephen's grants and concessions to the earl of Chester were very largely at the expense of other people, who along with others who disliked the earl and had suffered at his hands, suspected his loyalty and used all their influence with the king against him. The outcome was an angry scene in the king's court at Northampton, the sudden arrest of the earl and his release on condition that he should restore all the royal lands and castles which he had unjustly seized, give hostages for his good behaviour and take an oath not to resist the king any more. Stephen spent Christmas 1146 in triumph in Lincoln castle and earl Rannulf of course rebelled as soon as he was released. For Stephen to have accepted this arch-rebel, the cause of his disaster in 1141, as a friend and ally and loaded him with honours was certain to arouse the fury of many of his supporters, whom he could not afford to alienate. Then to have treated the earl of Chester as he did, whatever the excuse or justification offered, was to discourage any others who had contemplated defection from the empress. When Rannulf rebelled and made attacks, unsuccessful though they were, on his former strongholds of Lincoln and Coventry, Stephen seized his hostages, of whom the most important was Gilbert, earl of Hertford, who was obliged to surrender his castles. He, too, rebelled. Stephen alienated Gilbert's paternal uncle, the earl of Pembroke, by refusing him custody of his nephew's castles, seizing three of the earl's own strongholds and besieging him in Pevensey. It is difficult to understand how Stephen could have been so crassly stupid as thus to alienate the powerful house of Clare, whose members had not been supporters of the empress. Neither, indeed, had the earl of Chester been such a supporter: he had fought always for his own hand.

The year 1147 saw Henry, the fourteen-year-old son and heir of
the empress and duke Geoffrey, in England on an escapade of his
own. He managed to persuade a few mercenaries to accompany
him across the Channel and he attempted to mount a campaign in
the region of Cricklade. Very soon the mercenaries were demanding their pay, which Henry was totally unable to produce. Appeals
to his mother and his uncle, earl Robert, for help met with no
response; probably they hoped that this would bring the truant to
heel. Not so: Henry had another idea. He appealed to king
Stephen, as his kinsman, for money and, surprisingly, got it, so
that he was able to return to Normandy with something of a
swagger before the end of May. It had been rather a lark. The
young man would be back again and would have to be taken rather
more seriously. The other notable event on the Angevin side was
the death on 31 October 1147 of Robert earl of Gloucester, the
effective leader of the party in England. This was a severe blow to
the empress, who withdrew to Normandy at the beginning of
1148. The future would now depend very much upon her son,
Henry.

This year was also a critical one in Stephen's relations with the
church. We last saw the feeble and short-lived Celestine II failing
to respond to the stimulus of St Bernard's invective against archbishop William fitz Herbert and the bishop of Winchester. The
new pope, Lucius II, was positively resistant to the exhortations
of the formidable abbot of Clairvaux. He gave the bishop of
Winchester a friendly reception in the curia, though he stopped
short of renewing his legateship, but he sent Imar, bishop of
Tusculum (a Cluniac), to England as legate, bearing with him the
pallium for the archbishop of York. For a number of reasons, including the opposition of St Bernard and the refusal of the bishop
of Durham to swear that the election had been canonical, this
important symbol was never delivered to William. In any case,
bishop Imar's legateship lapsed very soon after his arrival in England, for Lucius died on 25 February 1145. His successor Eugenius
III was a Cistercian who had been a fellow monk with Henry
Murdac, now abbot of Fountains, and a disciple of St Bernard;
people were soon saying that the abbot of Clairvaux was the real
pope. In the matter of the York election the new pope was in a very
difficult position. On the one hand, his revered master was demanding the deposition of 'that idol of York, on the other, a

majority of the cardinals, less disposed to bow to Bernardine authority, favoured William fitz Herbert, and the deposition of a consecrated archbishop was rather a tricky affair. Towards the end of 1145 William went to Rome in person to ask for his pallium. The case was again considered and although many of the cardinals favoured William, the pope decided that, since the required oath had not been taken, his consecration was illegal, and suspended him till such time as the bishop of Durham should have sworn the oath. William seems now to have abandoned hope and he went to the court of his relative, king Roger of Sicily. His supporters in Yorkshire were not, however, disposed to accept defeat and, attributing it (rightly enough) to Cistercian influence, especially (with less justification) to the machinations of Henry Murdac, attacked and partially burned his abbey of Fountains and mutilated Walter the archdeacon. These outrages brought another fierce appeal from St Bernard for the deposition of archbishop William and the pope pronounced this sentence early in 1147. A new election was held on 24 July at Richmond, since York was barred by the hostility of earl William of Aumâle. A party of the electors led by Stephen's chancellor, Robert de Gant, dean of York, and the king's nephew, Hugh du Puiset, treasurer of York, proposed the election of master Hilary (later bishop of Chichester) a canon lawyer and a papal chaplain. The choice of candidate is interesting. He might, from Stephen's point of view, prove a less satisfactory archbishop than William fitz Herbert, but there was a chance that he might win the support of those who were hostile to the influence of St Bernard and the Cistercians in the church. The other party, led by the bishops of Durham and Carlisle, the precentor of York and the archdeacons, and supported by Cistercian influence, put forward Henry Murdac, abbot of Fountains. Pope Eugenius cut the matter short by consecrating Henry Murdac at Trèves on 7 December 1147. Stephen, of course, had no right to require the acceptance of his candidate, but it had long been traditional for royal nominees to be accepted by English cathedral chapters. In his indignation at being thus overridden by the pope, he absolutely refused to accept Henry Murdac as archbishop of York and took the temporalities into his hands. The stage was set for an embittered conflict when Murdac returned to England in 1148.

This clash with the church developed at an embarrassing time

3*

for Stephen. It is true that the death of earl Robert and the subsequent withdrawal of the empress from England early in 1148 must have greatly increased his confidence and, it might seem, strengthened his position. His elder son and heir, Eustace, had now reached (according to twelfth-century ideas) an age of maturity, when he should assume the privileges and the obligations of manhood. At the end of 1146 or early in 1147 (very probably at the great Christmas celebrations in Lincoln) Stephen knighted Eustace, gave him a splendid retinue of knights and created him a count (i.e. of Boulogne). Few contemporary sources have much good to say of Eustace, except *Gesta Stephani*, but even at this early age he was a most active and vigorous soldier, determined to defend his heritage. It was within Stephen's competence to proclaim Eustace count of Boulogne, but to ensure his succession to the throne of the English was another matter. This became Stephen's principal aim, but if it were to be achieved the recognition of the church would be indispensible. If Eustace were to be crowned during his father's lifetime, in the manner of Capetian heirs, the rite would have to be performed by the archbishop of Canterbury. Stephen's intransigence over the see of York went far towards ruining such very slender chances as he ever had of securing the recognition of his son and establishing the dynasty of Blois on the English throne. The bishop of Winchester did all in his power to assist his brother by undertaking a mission to Rome, foredoomed, in the circumstances, to failure. Henry had long ceased to enjoy legatine authority in England and Theobald, archbishop of Canterbury, the rightful leader of the English church and no friend of Henry's, would never lend his support to the policy that Stephen was pursuing. His visit to pope Eugenius III in Paris in May 1147 coincided with one from Geoffrey, count of Anjou and duke of Normandy. As far as Stephen and his brother were concerned, Theobald was not to be trusted.

The pope summoned a general council of the church to meet at Rheims on 2 March 1148. Stephen forbade the English bishops to attend, but appointed a small delegation of his own choosing, consisting of bishops Hilary of Chichester, Robert de Bethune of Hereford and William de Turbe of Norwich, to go and apologise for the absence of the archbishop and the other bishops. The only prelate to defy the royal prohibition was archbishop Theobald, who slipped across in a fishing boat to attend the council. The pope intended to excommunicate Stephen forthwith, but Theobald begged a three months' respite in the hope that the king would mend his ways. Stephen refused to allow the archbishop to return to England and on 12 September the kingdom was laid under an interdict. This was singularly ineffective. Nothing is more striking at this time than the reluctance of the English episcopate, as a body, to join the archbishop of Canterbury in resisting the king. Nonetheless, the real initiative in English ecclesiastical affairs was beginning to be firmly taken by the pope and the archbishop of Canterbury. In 1148, after the death of Robert de Bethune, Gilbert Foliot was chosen to fill the see of Hereford without any reference to Stephen and he was consecrated by archbishop Theobald at St Ouen at the pope's command.

The northern province, meanwhile, remained in a state of schism; not that there was an anti-archbishop, for William fitz Herbert had accepted his deposition with humility and dignity and Stephen, too, had acquiesced in the papal judgment, though not in the elevation of Henry Murdac to the see of York. The citizens of York refused Murdac admission to his metropolitan city and he replied with an excommunication. Hugh du Puiset, the treasurer of York, riposted with a counter-excommunication. The archbishop sought support elsewhere in his province and received it not only from the bishops of Durham and Carlisle but, it would seem, from the king of Scots. While conditions in the north continued thus in 1149, the young Henry Plantagenet arrived at Carlisle at the very time (Whitsuntide, 22 May) when archbishop Murdac was to be received there by the king of Scots and bishop Adelulf. Ostensibly Henry came (accompanied by earl Roger of Hereford) to receive knighthood at the hands of his royal kinsman – really to take part in a political and military move against Stephen, and if it should appear that this was done under the aegis of the church all the better. There also came to Carlisle the earl of Chester, with whom the king of Scots had succeeded in making an agreement. Rannulf was to recognise David as lord of Carlisle, to which formerly the earl had so persistently laid claim, and do him homage. In return there was conceded to him the whole honour of Lancaster and a marriage alliance was arranged between one of Rannulf's sons and a granddaughter of the king of Scots. With these matters so satisfactorily arranged, the three allies could now undertake the military part of the plan. They marched to attack York, but Stephen had intelligence of this from the citizens of York and forestalled them by hastening there himself with a large army in August. The Angevin offensive quickly collapsed. Henry, fleeing south-westwards, pursued by a body of Stephen's troops and beset by those of Eustace from his base in Oxford, narrowly escaped capture. Eustace undertook a ravaging campaign to harass the Angevin garrisons in Marlborough, Devizes and Salisbury and deny Henry a refuge, and late in September Stephen went down to join in the hunt. Henry was saved by diversions in the eastern part of the country where Rannulf earl of Chester attacked Lincoln while Payn de Beauchamp attacked Bedford and Hugh Bigod operated in East Anglia. Thus both Stephen and Eustace were diverted from their major purpose of cornering Henry in the south-west. He was now able to take the offensive in Devon and Dorset, and he captured Bridport but failed to make further headway. Towards the end of 1149, Eustace was able to return to the south-west and almost succeeded in a surprise attack on Devizes. Now about the beginning of 1150, as the author of *Gesta Stephani* explains:

Henry, the lawful heir to England, was advised to go speedily to Normandy, and augmenting his strength and resources with the assistance not only of the Normans but also of his father to return with greater and more enduring force to overcome king Stephen.[23]

The sixteen-year-old prince returned to Normandy not, it is true, as a conqueror, but with very considerable credit as a soldier, and his father marked this 'coming of age' by handing over to him the duchy of Normandy. Henry's arch-enemy, the youthful Eustace, also emerged from the operations of 1149 with great credit, to all appearance a better general than his father and a more ruthless soldier. As the *Gesta* says of him two years earlier, 'what he did as a mere stripling (for he had not yet sprouted his first down) was admired by men inured to war'.

Stephen, with his position greatly strengthened, as he supposed, by the events of 1149, seems to have been confident as well as foolish enough to give further provocation to the pope. In 1150 he made a very ill-advised demonstration. Cardinal Paperone, papal legate to Ireland, was refused safe conduct through England unless he would give a solemn undertaking not to engage in any intrigue against the king. It is difficult to see any sense in

offering such an insult to the papacy at this stage. In the same year
a reconciliation was brought about between Hugh du Puiset and
archbishop Murdac, with whom Eustace had an interview. The
archbishop was solemnly received at last in his metropolitan seat
on 25 January 1151 and then journeyed to Rome, where he
celebrated Easter. The reconciliation with Stephen is said to have
been based upon an undertaking by Murdac to put to the pope the
case for the recognition of Eustace as heir to the throne.[24] He cannot
have been a very ardent or convincing advocate and Stephen had
given offence too often. At the instigation of archbishop Theobald,
Eugenius forbade the hallowing of Eustace, expressly basing his
prohibition on the ground that Stephen had usurped the crown
in violation of his oath. Rome at last had spoken unequivocally.
Here was encouragement for duke Henry, who had been engaged
in not unsuccessful warfare with the king of France and Eustace
of England. Peace was made at Paris early in August 1151 and
Henry was formally invested with the duchy of Normandy.

The way now seemed clear for the renewal of Henry's attack on
England, but this was delayed, first by the death of his father,
count Geoffrey, on 7 September and by the consequent need to
establish his own position in Anjou; then further delay was caused
by the annulment of the marriage between Louis VII of France
and Queen Eleanor, the heiress of the duchy of Aquitaine, on 21
March 1152. Henry conducted a whirlwind courtship of this
notorious divorcée (if indeed he had not begun it in Paris in the
previous autumn) and married her in May, thus adding the whole
duchy of Aquitaine to his rapidly expanding dominions. Next he
had to face a rebellion in Anjou on behalf of his younger brother
Geoffrey, whom he had cheated of that inheritance, and a renewed
invasion of Normandy by the enraged king of France. Henry
dealt with both these threats successfully. Now for England!

Henry sailed from Barfleur with a force of one hundred and
forty knights and three thousand infantry and landed at Wareham
about 13 January. It seems a small force for such an undertaking,
but it proved quite adequate. He could count upon the support of
the old hard core of opposition to Stephen and, besides, the
atmosphere in England had changed considerably since he had
left the country early in 1150. During the intervening years
Stephen had done nothing to consolidate his position, though
Eustace had striven to weaken his rival by an active alliance with

his brother-in-law, the king of France, against Henry. Stephen was widely recognised as king and there was no serious question of deposing him, but it was equally well understood that Eustace could not be recognised as his successor. Henry was generally regarded as the legitimate heir even by such previously staunch supporters of Stephen as the author of *Gesta Stephani*.[25] Many barons undoubtedly had a sense of loyalty to the king but they were not prepared to sacrifice themselves in a war *à outrance* with Henry. The death of Stephen's queen, Matilda, on 3 May 1152 must have been a great blow to him for she had sustained his cause in the face of disaster in 1141 and had always been one of the wiser of his counsellors and prominent in every move for the promotion of peace. Stephen may have sought an anodyne in renewed military activity, or he may simply have been moved by Henry's impending invasion. Soon after the queen's death he attacked and captured Newbury castle, held by John, the marshal, and made yet another attempt on Wallingford (whose lord, Brian fitz Count, was now dead) and he built a castle against it at Crowmarsh on the opposite side of the river. It was a determined siege and the capture of this fortress would greatly have strengthened Stephen's defensive position in the Thames valley. The besieged urgently sought aid from duke Henry towards the end of 1152. The duke, when he landed, marched not to Wallingford but to Malmesbury, taking the town but not the castle. Stephen arrived to relieve it, but avoided battle, ostensibly because the river Avon was in spate, actually because he saw that some of his leading barons were 'slack and very remiss in their military service and had sent envoys secretly to make a compact with the duke'.[26] In the circumstances Stephen agreed to a truce and to the demolition of Malmesbury castle, but Jordan, the castellan, surrendered it intact to Henry. The duke now went by way of Bristol and Gloucester to conduct a successful campaign in the Midlands and it was not until well on in the summer that he marched to the relief of Wallingford, laying siege to Crowmarsh. Stephen and Eustace advanced to offer battle and, once again, only a river separated the armies. The barons on both sides insisted upon the opening of negotiations. Stephen and Henry had a colloquy (if such it can be called) across the river in which they must have agreed, much against their will, to negotiate, each complaining bitterly that he had been let down by his barons.[27] While the detailed negotiations went on, Henry went off northwards and took Stamford and sacked Nottingham, while Stephen took Hugh Bigod's castle of Ipswich, but no clash occurred between the king and the duke. Eustace, furious at the negotiations, went rampaging into Cambridgeshire and died suddenly on 17 August 1153, struck down, it was believed, by divine vengeance for his depradations upon the lands of St Edmund's Abbey. This considerably eased the situation, and Stephen was now content to recognise Henry as heir to the throne provided that all his own personal lands should pass to his second son William, who had married the heiress of the house of Warenne. A meeting was arranged between Stephen and Henry at Winchester on 6 November 1153, when the terms of peace, which had been negotiated by Theobald, archbishop of Canterbury and Henry, bishop of Winchester, were agreed. These were finally embodied in a royal charter issued at Westminster shortly afterwards.[28]

Mr Davis has strongly emphasised the significance of the stress that was placed upon hereditary right in the treaty of Westminster. Henry was recognised as the lawful heir to the kingdom by hereditary right and Stephen took an oath to maintain him as his 'son and heir'. Further, according to Robert of Torigni, it was agreed in principle that all lands should be restored to those who held them in the reign of Henry I, a recognition, that is, 'that the barons held their lands, not by pleasure of the king, but by hereditary right; and as such it marked an important step in the creation of the English nobility'.[29] This is a point of great importance. True, it would be difficult to unscramble the egg and restore lands to the right people, but the old actors, many of those most closely involved in the problem, were departing from the stage in a manner that would have delighted the dramatist John Webster.

The year 1153 saw the deaths of St Bernard of Clairvaux; pope Eugenius III; Henry Murdac, archbishop of York; David, king of Scots (his son Henry had died in the previous year); Eustace, Stephen's son; Rannulf, earl of Chester; Simon of Senlis, earl of Northampton and Huntingdon; and Roger earl of Warwick. Earl Rannulf's death was attributed to poison at the hands of William Peverel, whose fief had been included (conditionally) in duke Henry's big grant to him in the spring of 1153.[30] William fitz Herbert, the ex-archbishop of York, when he learned that pope

Eugenius had died on 8 July 1153, went to Rome to plead his own cause before the new pope Anastasius IV, and while he was there, news came of archbishop Murdac's death on 14 October. William was therefore restored to the see of York. He returned to England and was received there on 11 April 1154. On 8 June he was dead, as a result, it was rumoured, of poison administered in the chalice, a story which William of Newburgh strenuously denied on what he believed to be reliable first-hand evidence.[31]

King Stephen ended his days on 25 October 1154 at Dover, where he was suddenly stricken by some severe abdominal illness. Gervase of Canterbury describes it as a sudden and violent attack of pain in the intestines and 'the old flux of haemorrhoids'. Whatever the illness, it was swiftly fatal. He was carried into the Augustinian Priory, where he expired.

3
The King and the Empress

I. The King

History has never treated Stephen kindly, for his was the calamitous sin of failure which could neither be concealed nor forgotten. In the eyes of his opponents he was a perjurer and a usurper, whose lot should be with the damned; yet the Roman church, deeply embarrassed by the situation and distracted by other conflicts and dangers, never pronounced upon him such a sentence, though he came perilously near to incurring it in 1148. Stephen has never really ranked with the bad kings, the tyrannical and the infamous, for nature had not cast him for such a rôle. Few of his actions for good or ill were spectacularly impressive, perhaps only three: his dash to England, immediately after Henry I's death, to secure the treasury and the throne; his arrest of the bishops in June 1139; and his Horation stand at Lincoln on 2 February 1141. The latter, at least, ought to endear him to the English people. It is plain that his was in no way an impressive or memorable character; he was far more often the victim than the moulder of circumstances. Seldom did he seem capable, even after a good beginning, of carrying matters relentlessly to a desired conclusion and, too often, his beginnings were not good.

Through his mother, Adela, there flowed in Stephen's veins the potent blood of the Conqueror, her father; and, it might be added, the blood of that remarkable woman, Herleva, the tanner's daughter of Falaise, who was William's mother.[1] But there were weaknesses of character, too, in the Norman royal house. Rufus and Henry, however unpleasant their faults, had in full measure the determination and ruthless drive of their father and so, beyond a doubt, had their sister, Adela. The Conqueror's eldest son, however, duke Robert II (Curthose) of Normandy, lacked this quality. He was superbly courageous, he was adventurous and he was reckless. He had the charm and captivating manner that distinguished the Norman princes, when they chose to exercise it, and he was extravagant. 'Wishing', in the words of Orderic Vitalis, 'to please everyone, he was too ready to accede light-heartedly to any request' and, utterly lacking in judgment, he was constantly the victim of schemers, not least his two younger brothers. His fate was to lose his duchy and suffer imprisonment from 1106 till the day he died in 1134. His survival into the next reign would have greatly complicated the situation. In many of the traits of his character Stephen closely resembled Robert and he was fortunate to escape the same fate; he had a very bitter taste of it in 1141, when his thoughts may well have turned to the uncle whom he could hardly have remembered except in the same circumstances as his own then were.

Such characteristics as Stephen inherited from his father, Stephen count of Blois and Chartres, may have been no great asset to him, though perhaps this is an unfair judgment on the elder Stephen, who was one of the leaders in the first Crusade. His record in that extraordinary campaign was irreparably blotted when, after he had been elected to the chief command, he appears to have lost his head during the siege of Antioch in 1098, ignominiously leaving the army with two companions. It would be very interesting indeed, since such peculiar incidents happened at Antioch, if the real motive for count Stephen's departure were ever discovered. The story of the *funambuli* or 'rope walkers' who let themselves down from the walls may not be true – it smacks of propaganda – but it was with this unenviable and rather clownish reputation that count Stephen returned home. His formidable wife sent him back to complete the Jerusalem pilgrimage – that, at least, must be achieved if the faith of a crusader were to be kept and his hopes of Heaven realised – and he fell in the disastrous battle of Ramleh in 1101.

The son of the Norman princess Adela and the seemingly weak-willed count Stephen must have had a difficult inheritance both temperamentally and in his public relations. People must often have wondered, and king Stephen must have been well aware of it, whether he might not panic like his father in some crisis. It is not at all surprising that we have evidence, at one critical moment at least, of an agitated mind. At high mass on the morning of the battle of Lincoln, when Stephen was probably aware that he could not depend upon the loyalty of all his supporters, the consecrated wax taper broke in his hand, though he held on to it – an omen, of course, to most contemporaries. Henry of Huntingdon adds that the pyx fell from the high altar, indicating agitation in a more exalted quarter.

There is one anecdote coming from a later date which, if true (and the story is not an improbable one), sheds a kindly light on Stephen's character. It is told by the writer of the metrical *L'Histoire de Guillaume le Maréchal*[2] about the early childhood of his hero, William Marshal, earl of Pembroke, one of the paladins of Christendom and regent (*rector regis et regni*) during the early years of Henry III's minority. John fitz Gilbert, hereditary master marshal in the royal household, early deserted Stephen for the empress and, apparently at the time of the siege of Newbury in May 1152,[3] was compelled to give his little son William, aged about five or six, to the king as hostage. By deliberate default he left the child at the king's mercy saying, with cheerful callousness, that Stephen might hang him if he pleased, for he himself had a fruitful wife and 'the hammers and anvils to forge still better sons'. Stephen reluctantly told his men to lead William to a convenient tree. The little boy had no idea what the preparations portended and, seeing William d'Aubigny, earl of Arundel, the king's master butler, nonchalantly twirling a spear in his fingers, asked to have a try. The kindly Stephen was quite overcome and carried the child away to his tent, which was strewn with many-coloured flowers. There, some time later, the two were discovered playing at 'knights' with plantain-stalks – a game analogous to 'conkers'. The barons' original idea about how to remonstrate with the recalcitrant John, the marshal, was said to have been to set the little William in a siege engine, in place of the ordinary missile, and lob him over the castle wall. It can be said at least that this vivid, circumstantial story is not incompatible with what we know of Stephen's character both from contemporary writers and from his own actions and *acta*. Kindness and goodness of heart were his by nature. William of Malmesbury refers to him as a very gentle man who, if he had obtained the kingdom legitimately, would have lacked little that adorns the character of a king. One gains the impression from many of his charters – though formal official documents may not seem an obviously reliable source of psychological information – that genuine feeling for his parents, his wife, his children and kin was strong in Stephen. Concern for their souls' health is stressed in numbers of his charters, and his mother, for whom he obviously had a profound respect, and his younger children – not merely Eustace, the heir – are found mentioned by name, not simply in the general terms in which ancestors and progeny are commonly referred to in a formal 'movent', setting out the reasons for a pious benefaction. Some of his scribes, perhaps echoing their master's voice, use the more affectionate term 'boys' (*pueri*) instead of the more formal 'sons' (*filii*). In his treaty with duke Henry in November-December, 1153, when his eldest son Eustace was dead and when he had abandoned the hope of perpetuating his dynasty on the throne, it is obvious that Stephen was concerned, above all, to provide handsomely for and to safeguard the future of his younger son, William, who had married the heiress of the earl of Warenne. Care in furthering the careers of several of his kin, on both sides of the blanket (e.g. Henry de Sully, Hugh du Puiset and William fitz Herbert), can also be observed, but that was no more than was expected of any great man.

Courteous and affable, it was agreed on all sides, beyond, perhaps, what was entirely fitting in a prince, neither proud nor haughty, chivalrous, it seemed, and with all the splendid physical courage of his race and class and kin, Stephen is completely overshadowed by the domineering personalities of the grandfather and the two uncles, whom he succeeded, and the cousin who followed him, upon the throne of the English. No contemporary writer, whether favourable to him or hostile, took the trouble to limn a detailed portrait of him: such a portrait could hardly have compared with those of the leaders in an age whose great men were apt to appear more than life-sized. Even his obituaries, in which, if anywhere, twelfth-century historians might have been expected to spread themselves, are perfunctory to a degree. Verses such as those in which Orderic lamented the death of Henry I, are conspicuously absent – though Orderic, it must be said, excellent historian though he was, enjoyed but little reputation in the Middle Ages and his example was unlikely to have inspired anyone in the Anglo-Norman lands. Henry of Huntingdon reserved his verses for a dramatic address by England to her new Angevin sovereign. The contemporary recorders of *memorabilia*, in fact, faithfully reflecting the feelings of churchmen and feudal nobility in 1154, were obviously delighted to have finished with Stephen's dismal reign and men were all agog for the new age. To peasants, suffering grievously from the cumulative effect of nineteen seasons of civil war, it may have brought a ray of hope, though for them at the best of times hope brought very modified rapture. Burgesses may have felt a little differently, for even though they must have suffered very severely at times, as in the sack of Lincoln after the battle on 2 February 1141, Stephen found some of his staunchest support in cities like York, Lincoln and especially London. To them he probably was, as far as in him lay, a good lord; and this, as Mr R.H.C.Davis has rightly emphasised in his recent book, has a significance that goes much beyond an easy and affable way with the citizenry.[4]

If Nemesis (to borrow a metaphor dear to Mr P.G.Wodehouse) often lay in wait for Stephen 'with a stuffed eel-skin', her weapon was sometimes a fool's bauble. Stephen, according to Orderic Vitalis,[5] did not sail on board the *White Ship* on 25 November 1120 because he was suffering from an attack of diarrhoea and did not like the look of the drunken passengers and crew. So on that day a trivial circumstance as well as a maritime tragedy determined the fate of England and Normandy. Stephen hardly qualifies for inclusion in that select list of rulers who, from Ethelred the Redeless to James II (or whom you will), exhibited ineptitude as monumental as it was varied; his talents did not extend to the larger lunacy. Nor, on the other hand, can it be truly said that he did nothing in particular and did it very well, though that was the view which, in all matters of government, his successor chose to adopt. In his considered opinion the nineteen winters between one Henry and the next were best forgotten. It is of course true that Henry I's achievement survived and provided the basis of that of Henry II. Stephen's reign, however, cannot be ignored, for not only did it constitute a grim warning to English feudal society but it conditioned a great deal of what was done by Henry II.

The best of the slight sketches of Stephen's character by contemporary historians is that of William of Malmesbury.[6] It is an unfavourable assessment but not a malicious one; it gives the impression of a balanced judgment.

He was a man of less judgment than energy, an active soldier, of remarkable spirit in difficult undertakings, lenient to his enemies and easily placated, courteous to all. Though you admired his kindness in

making promises, you doubted the truth of his words and the reliability of what he promised. This was why after a short time he put aside
the counsel of his brother, by whose aid, as I have said, he had pushed
aside his adversaries and ascended the throne.

This emphasis upon the importance of the part played by Stephen's
brother, Henry, bishop of Winchester, is very significant.

The picture of king Stephen most commonly drawn by historians all through the ages, and it does contain some tincture
of truth, has been derived from the spineless figure in that classical
account of the anarchy in the E. version of the Anglo-Saxon
Chronicle, commonly called the Peterborough Chronicle.[7] This
is a set piece in conventionally dramatic terms, closely comparable
with accounts of Viking and Scottish atrocities which set a high,
but far from unsurpassable, standard. The age was as intensely
preoccupied with violence as is the present one; witness the lurid
story of Robert fitz Hubert, 'cruellest of all men within the recollection of our time'[8] and the revolting atrocities perpetuated by
that monster, Thomas of Laon,[9] to mention only two examples.
The 'mild man, soft and good, who did no justice', or as it has
been better but less dramatically translated 'who did not exact the
full penalties of the law', is a figure over-simplified for the purpose
of this passage, where he provides a striking contrast with the
'Lion of Justice' of other recent annals of the Chronicle and a foil
for the 'traitors' who committed the all-too-real atrocities.
Interestingly enough, no names are mentioned in this passage in
the way that they are mentioned by other historians who denounce
evil deeds. Some, like John of Salisbury, merely list the offenders
and hold them up to the obloquy of history (*infamia celebris*):
'Where are Geoffrey, Miles, Rannulf, Alan, Simon, Gilbert, not so
much earls as public enemies of the realm? Where is William of
Salisbury? Where is Marmion whom the Blessed Virgin caused to
fall into the ditch he prepared?' The pious reader needed no
prompting to give the answer in words like Dante's: 'ove i bolliti
facean alte strida'. [10]

Recently Stephen has been set in a more disreputable, even
sinister, light as a vain, sly and shifty character in whom a veneer
of chivalry and good feeling concealed a nasty venom and a fundamental disregard for the laws, the conventions and the ordinary,
common decencies of feudal society.[11] He is shown as a man who
nourishes a grievance, bides his time and then suddenly and

'without lawful judgment' (as the contemporary phrase goes) lays violent hands upon men who guilelessly attend his royal court. The affable approach, the unstinted grant of lands, castles and offices, the 'loading with honours'; then, the incident crudely provoked or the accusations and insults hurled by jealous rivals, who could always be counted upon, and the prison-house till castles and lands were surrendered; finally, the release of an infuriated and disillusioned vassal, followed by frantic rebellion, completes the cycle of mean, perverse stupidity. It is not a pretty picture of a king, but that does not necessarily make it untrue and it is one that some contemporaries would certainly have accepted as lifelike. Vain Stephen probably was not, by all accounts, but the other traits must be examined and judged by the standards that men expected of a king in the twelfth century.

It is worthwhile, in the first place, to consider Stephen as an exponent of the chivalric virtues which princes, nobles and knights were expected to display. Warfare being the feudal lord's peculiar *raison d'être*, it was natural that above all personal bravery, physical strength and skill in arms should be admired. Indomitability to the point of recklessness won the highest approval. Stephen's personal courage cannot be called in question. It was typical of him that at the battle of Lincoln 'mindful of the brave deeds of his ancestors, he fought with great courage; and as long as three of his knights stood by him he never ceased dealing great blows with his sword and (then) with a Norwegian battle-axe which a young man handed him'[12] till he was finally overwhelmed and captured. At this time Stephen was a man of some forty-five years, just a little elderly by medieval standards, but still every inch a fighting soldier. Even so hostile a witness as Henry of Huntingdon does not deny that he possessed 'great resolution and audacity' and he adds the interesting information that Baldwin fitz Gilbert made the pre-battle oration to the royal troops at Lincoln because Stephen 'lacked a hearty voice' (*festiva carebat voce*). Early in *Gesta Stephani* he is described as 'judicious and patient' (*discretus et longanimis*) and also 'bold and brave in all warlike engagements or in any siege of his enemies'. That this was an optimistic exaggeration is very evident from Stephen's lack of success in defending his continental lands against William Clito when that aggressive cousin attacked them in 1127, and equally clear from the endless, frustrating warfare in England that marked his whole reign. Routed and taken prisoner in the only 'set piece' battle in which he commanded (where it must be said there were many disgraceful desertions from his side) Stephen showed up poorly as a general. Neither strategist nor tactician, he failed disastrously to find any way out of the war of endless sieges and skirmishes. Indeed few commanders on either side (there were angry exceptions as for example at Lincoln and Wilton) showed very much relish for decisive action, which did not really suit the interests of the feudal baronage from a family, a political, or any other point of view. Stephen behaved like a bull in the ring, escaping disaster sometimes very narrowly, as in the large-scale skirmish at Wilton in 1143 (where he showed his incompetence in handling cavalry and was saved by William Martel's dogged, self-sacrificing rearguard action), mainly because there was no 'matador' on the Angevin side till duke Henry took the field in 1153, if even then, who was able and willing to bring him to 'the moment of truth'. Stephen unquestionably possessed the feudal virtue of reckless personal bravery but, as a soldier, he was conventional and unimaginative, if not downright stupid. For courage of another kind, for dignity and fortitude in adversity and captivity, Stephen must be given credit. We must not forget that he struggled on against innumerable difficulties both in ecclesiastical and secular affairs so long as it was possible to continue the fight. The death of his wife on 3 May 1152, and that of his eldest son Eustace in August 1153, and the collapse of all his dynastic ambitions, must have taken the heart out of him.

Second only to prowess in the calendar of chivalric virtues came loyalty: loyalty to that personal bond of mutual responsibility between lord and vassal which was the very mortar of a feudal aristocracy. 'The lord owes as much to the man as the man to the Lord, saving only reverence', as the great lawyer Ivo, bishop of Chartres, had put it long ago. This bond could be, and all too frequently was broken, but it was generally felt that homage and allegiance ought only to be renounced in the most formal and legal manner, and even then only as the result of an intolerable wrong impenitently done by one of the parties. For a king the position was complicated, for not only was he a feudal suzerain but he possessed royal rights and royal duties, one of which undoubtedly was to put down rebellion and treason whenever they occurred. Stephen's conduct in these respects will be examined later. Even where the feudal bond established by the act of homage and the oath of fealty was not involved directly, a high standard of conduct was still expected in the best aristocratic and knightly circles. It is not customary to regard William Rufus as a model of propriety but in a feudal sense his conduct was generally correct, if exceedingly stiff, by the standards of his day and he expected and saw to it that his vassals and lieges, however eminent or even saintly, like archbishop Anselm, should conform. He has been quoted as saying: 'far be it from me to believe that an honest knight would break his parole. If he did, he would be for ever an object of contempt as a man outside the law' – and men 'outside the law' had very short shrift. Rufus was praised for never holding noble prisoners in chains, a courtesy by no means universally observed. Such treatment, it must be emphasised, was not accorded to those of his ordinary subjects who broke the law or otherwise incurred the Red King's displeasure. In a feudal society the non-noble, the common soldier, the merchant, the Jew, the infidel and the heretic were treated in accordance with a different standard, as we say 'cavalierly'. Stephen was, of course, fully aware of these standards, but he was, if anything, a little lax, as many feudal magnates might have thought, in his affable treatment of burgesses. Could such a man, many contemporaries might have asked, be quite sound in other respects? There were at least two occasions when he behaved with a high, indeed fantastic, chivalrous courtesy which many of his adherents regarded as superlatively foolish.

The first of these occasions was in early October 1139, when the empress Maud and her half-brother Robert, earl of Gloucester, landed to press her claim to the crown. Maud was received in Arundel castle by her step-mother, the dowager queen Adeliza, who had married William d'Aubigny.[13] Earl Robert quickly got away to his stronghold in Bristol and some people suspected the king's brother, Henry, bishop of Winchester, of conniving at this. Stephen blockaded Arundel castle with good prospects, if not of capturing the empress, at least of immobilising her. She was not a person easily immobilised, as her escape from Oxford castle in the snow in 1142 demonstrated. Stephen, as we have seen, allowed her to go free.

The second occasion upon which Stephen behaved with outstanding generosity was in 1147 when the youthful Henry fitz

Empress came to England on an independent and forlorn small-scale expedition. He soon found himself in hopeless difficulties about paying his mercenaries, from which his mother could not and his uncle Robert, 'sitting tight on his money-bags' would not, relieve him. The sequel is related in *Gesta Stephani*:

> At this critical juncture he finally, it was reported, sent envoys in secret to the king, as to a kinsman, and begged him in friendly and imploring terms to regard with pity the poverty that weighed upon him and to listen compassionately to one who was bound to him by close ties of kinsmanship and was well-disposed towards him as far as he was personally concerned. On receiving this message, the king, who was always full of compassion and had a sense of family obligation (*pietas*), harkened to the young man and, by sending him money, as had been asked, he greatly helped one whom, as his rival for the kingdom and utterly opposed to him, he ought to have deprived of every kind of assistance. And although the king was blamed by some for acting not only unwisely, but positively childishly, in giving money and such support to one to whom he should have been implacably hostile, I think that his action was more profound and prudent, because the more kindly and humanely a man behaves towards an adversary, the feebler he makes him and the more he weakens him.[14]

The comment is that of a churchman, perhaps the bishop of Bath,[15] who was consistently favourable to Stephen until, towards the end of the reign, he clearly became convinced of the urgent need for a peace settlement based upon the acceptance of Henry as the legitimate heir to the throne. As an absolutely contemporary view of this event it is significant. It may be said, somewhat cynically perhaps, that Stephen thought it worthwhile to pay to get Henry out of the country. If so, it was just about as effective as the payment of Danegeld ever was; the invader returned. Stephen's behaviour in the two cases that have been cited, whatever the motives that inspired it, comes within any formal definition of 'chivalrous'. How formal is a matter of opinion.

It is, incidentally, worth remarking that in 1147 Stephen does not seem to have needed to count his pennies. This brings us to another feudal and chivalric virtue: generosity, *largesse*, that is the lavish, unstinted generosity which a lord ought to display towards his vassals and servants and other deserving people. It was a virtue, naturally, that was very highly extolled by minstrels, who composed and declaimed tales of prowess and depended for their living upon the generosity of their flattered patrons. 'If *largesse* dies' as Hugh de Mery starkly put it, 'we shall die in poverty and misery.' Lavish hospitality and costly gifts obtained for the noble who gave them honour inferior only to that which prowess could win him; prowess without the additional virtue of *largesse* was scarcely conceivable. There were those, and they were not always at the receiving end, who considered that reasonable generosity according to a man's means was a parsimonious thing, that real *largesse* should be reckless and boundless. Such, of course, were the views of secular men. Worldly generosity did not bear much merit in the eyes of strict churchmen and, like military prowess, could bring only vainglory. True glory came from devotion to God and generosity to his church, which gained enormously, not least in Stephen's England, from the lavish benefactions which were so characteristic of the Normans and, often enough, from the considerable reparations made by repentant feudatories of all ranks for wrongs and damage inflicted.

It may be wrong to allege that Stephen held the more exaggerated kind of view about the virtue of *largesse* in a prince, though he does seem to have been generous by nature. It would not be unfair to say that compared with his three predecessors on the throne he probably had little idea of 'the value of money', provided that we understand this to include the lands, the towns, the dues, the diverse rights over all kinds of people that brought in the revenue of a prince or lord. Stephen was a younger son of the princely house of Blois, Chartres (and Champagne), whose riches must have derived, to some extent, from the early growth of trade in those regions. He married into another distinguished family, that of Eustace, count of Boulogne, and in the right of his wife, Matilda, who was the heiress, he acquired that considerable fief, which was also relatively advanced in the development of commerce. Further, as count of Mortain, Stephen held extensive estates in Normandy and in England, the latter greatly augmented by grants from Henry I, especially the wide lands than known as the Honour of Lancaster. These great possessions on both sides of the Channel made Stephen, before he became king, probably the wealthiest of all the magnates of the Anglo-Norman dominions. Living throughout his earlier life in an atmosphere of enormous wealth, until he succeeded at the age of about thirty-nine to the still vaster resources of the kingdom of England and, for the few short years he held it, the duchy of Normandy, it would indeed have been surprising if Stephen had not taken riches for granted and even grown a little irresponsible in the disposal of his resources. In this he differed profoundly from Henry I, who as a young man had received from his father only a legacy of £5,000 of silver and a recommendation, for what that was worth, to the benevolence of his elder brothers. Henry emphatically did understand 'the value of money'.

An examination of the grants, admittedly bribes, and the most notorious of such, which Stephen made to Rannulf, earl of Chester, probably in 1146[16] and to Geoffrey de Mandeville, earl of Essex, at Christmas 1141[17] seems to indicate that the king was not at all disposed to haggle parsimoniously over an honour more or less, a town or two, a few castles, scores of knights' fees or the hereditary tenure of offices of great power and profit. The former of these grants we know only from an abstract of the charter made in 1325 which is preserved among the Duchy of Lancaster records. It reads as follows:

Charter of Stephen, king of England, whereby he gave and conceded to Rannulf, earl of Chester, the castle of Lincoln and the city until such time as the king (should be able to) cause him to have his Norman lands and all his castles. This being done, the king allows him to fortify one of his towers in Lincoln castle, of which the earl shall have control until the king hands over to him the castle of Tickhill, when the castle and city of Lincoln shall revert to the king and the earl shall retain the tower which his mother fortified, together with the constableship of Lincoln castle and Lincolnshire by hereditary right.[18] And, in addition to this, the king gave the earl Belvoir castle and the whole honour belonging to it and all the lands of William d'Aubigny (*Brito*) of whomsoever held and Greetham with its soke; and if it happen that the heirs of Greetham reach an agreement with the king, the said honour shall remain hereditarily in the possession of earl Rannulf and the king will give them an exchange for it. The king also gave the earl the New Castle of Staffordshire with all its appurtenances and Rowley with its soke and Torksey with its appurtenances and the town of Derby with its appurtenances and Mansfield with its appurtenances and Stanley with its appurtenances and Oswarbec wapentake with its appurtenances and all the land of Roger de Bully with the whole honour of Blyth, as it was devised, and all the land of Roger the Poitevin from Northampton to Scotland, except the land of Roger de Montbegon in Lincolnshire. The king gave the earl hereditarily the honour of

Lancaster with its appurtenances and all the land between Ribble and Mersey, and the land which he had in demesne in the manor of Grimsby, and the land which the earl of Gloucester had in demesne in the manor of Grimsby with its appurtenances. And furthermore, for love of the earl the king gave to Alice de Condet Horncaster,[19] as she fined for it, when the castle there was destroyed. And the king gave him (i.e. confirmed) all his other lands.

All this was in addition to the already very extensive possessions of earl Rannulf in his palatine earldom of Chester, in the Midlands and in Lincolnshire and elsewhere.[20] The grant included an element of compensation for the loss of the earl's Norman lands with the vicomtés of Bessin and Avranchin which his adherence to Stephen must cost him now that Geoffrey of Anjou reigned as duke in Normandy. The result of this grant was to give the earl of Chester an enormous feudal principality in the Midlands and the North, comparable with the greatest of the pre-Conquest English earldoms.

The grant to Geoffrey, earl of Essex, is too long to quote in full. It included five hundred pounds worth of land, a considerable amount in those days; the hereditary constableship of the Tower of London (which dominated the capital); the offices, hereditarily, of justice and sheriff of London and Middlesex at the old ferm of £300 a year which his grandfather had paid (thus depriving the Londoners of the valuable right of farming their own revenues, though, at least, the ferm was not increased). Likewise Geoffrey was given the justiceships of Essex and Hertfordshire. He was given the right to build a castle anywhere in his land and he received the service of sixty enfeoffed knights. This represents territorial, financial, judicial, administrative and military power and the status and emoluments of vitally important offices on a very big scale. Here is a compact, entrenched position in the country's capital and in the three shires of Middlesex, Essex and Hertford which it would be very difficult for the crown to overthrow by ordinary methods. The empress had already bid very highly for the adherence of Geoffrey de Mandeville [21] and her ideas of generosity in the interests of securing political and military strength in this region were lavish in the extreme. Stephen had to equal her offer for the same vital reason. Both series of grants represent a squandering of royal resources and, what was worse, power, on a scale that would have horrified and enraged Henry I.

That monarch certainly did much towards the enrichment of the 'new men', whom he is said to have 'raised from the dust', and towards the augmentation of their power, both by giving them offices and by enabling them to profit from the difficulties, misfortunes and miscalculations of baronial families, from the acquisition of rights of marriage, wardship and so forth. It might even be argued with some cogency that, in this way, Henry I started the rot, but at least he saw to it that these favoured men worked exceedingly hard for and fully earned the rewards they got.[22] The same cannot be said of Stephen.

Stephen was in no way a clever man or a cunning one. No contemporary writer, favourable or hostile, seriously credits him with such characteristics, though he is occasionally accused of guile rather in the sense of dissimulation or tergiversation than cleverness. Cunning combined with truculence was a quality of evil men and likely to bring divine retribution, if not visibly in this world to the satisfaction of the faithful, then certainly in the next. The arts of an Odysseus seem to have been taken as not unbecoming in a king. Stephen never appears in that rôle and he is placed in the former category only by his most embittered opponents. An example may be taken from William of Malmesbury. He relates how Robert earl of Gloucester got safely away to Normandy on 11 April 1137, having eluded the treacherous attempts of Stephen, instigated by William of Ypres, to intercept him. The earl, warned by one of the accomplices, avoided the trap by staying away from the king's court, where he was constantly being invited. This may seem the forerunner of similar plots on Stephen's part which will be discussed later. 'The king', William tells us,

chagrined by the lack of success which his artifices had, and hoping to achieve his end by cunning, tried by putting a good face on it and by spontaneous confession, to extenuate the enormity of what he had attempted. He swore, in words intended to please the earl, never again to countenance such an outrage.

Further, to regain Robert's good will Stephen confirmed his oath, by Hugh, archbishop of Rouen, giving his hand to Robert; 'but never', says William, 'did he give his real friendship to the earl, whose power he always feared. He would speak affably and

ingratiatingly to the earl, but vilify him behind his back and deprive
him in an underhand way of portions of his lands. Robert, too,
artfully disguised his feelings'.[23] This is the evidence of a hostile
witness and it contains such inconsistencies that it might not stand
up to cross-examination. The book in which it appears is dedicated by William, the librarian of Malmesbury Abbey, to 'his most
loving lord, Robert, son of king Henry and earl of Gloucester', so
there is at least the possibility that he was representing the situation in the light in which his patron would have liked it to be
viewed. Robert had belatedly taken a conditional oath to Stephen
(which underhand deprivation of lands, such as William mentions,
would have justified him in breaking) and his behaviour had
seemed decidedly equivocal. William's story, however, must not be
denied its appropriate weight for he was, after all, one of the best
historians that twelfth-century England produced. Stephen would
undoubtedly have liked to be able to scotch the threat to his position that earl Robert represented; quite likely he engaged in some
manœuvres to that end, urged on by his personal supporters. 'By
the birth of God', he is reported to have said, 'I will never be
called a dethroned king.'[24]

Stephen is not usually credited with sagacity; on the contrary,
he is more usually shown as naïve, easily led astray by bad advice,
easily deceived by schemers. So Henry of Huntingdon, referring
to mischiefmakers who were trying to sow dissension between
Stephen and duke Henry after their treaty, says that 'the king was
scarcely able to resist their persuasions and, after a while, as some
think, he was not even trying'; and he goes on to suggest that the
king listened not unwillingly to the counsels of evil men. This
was indeed a grave weakness in Stephen; he was too easily
persuaded. The author of *Gesta Stephani*, early in his book, writes
of Stephen as 'conceiving in his mind a great thing, like the famous
Saul'. What, one asks, is this that has come unto the son of Kish?
An answer will be suggested later. This was the great moment in
Stephen's life, at the death of Henry I and the arrival of the long-
anticipated crisis in the affairs of England and Normandy and of
the royal house. He rose to it unhesitatingly and temporarily,
with complete success, for the speed of his action paralysed all
potential opponents and he had the good luck that seldom
attended him in the future. The same author says that Stephen
'was eminent for many conspicuous virtues' (as every new ruler

is wont to be till people have taken his measure). Those that he singles out for explicit mention are the military prowess, which we have already examined, and his being 'what is acknowledged as unusual among the rich nowadays, wealthy and at the same time unassuming, generous and courteous'. The culminative impression one gets from Stephen's actions, as time goes on and in critical moments, is that he was unsure of himself and prone to believe that any other heads were wiser than his own; that he was liable to incline naturally towards the views of the more conservative and even reactionary section of his supporters. Clearly something went wrong soon after his initial success. But still, when all was said, and even reluctantly done, Stephen was quite likely to have second thoughts, prompted by good feeling or even good sense, but usually only when matters had already gone so far that to act upon them merely made a bad situation worse. Stephen was unstable; he lacked dependability and this was probably his greatest and most disastrous weakness.

Stephen, as Henry 1's favourite nephew, had intimate experience of his uncle's court for a score of years before he succeeded to the throne and, even on a prince of his limited abilities, the long apprenticeship cannot have been wholly wasted. He had the opportunity of a training unexcelled in western Christendom in all the arts of government, diplomacy and war. He could hardly have failed to gain some insight into the motives, policies and actions of the cleverest and most ruthless of the Norman kings of England. Stephen saw his other uncle, Robert duke of Normandy, kept relentlessly in detention by Henry 1 for over a quarter of a century until he died. He took some part, though it does not seem to have been a very distinguished one, in the war with Robert's heir, William Clito. He must have well understood the significance of the marriage alliances and diplomatic moves that followed the loss of Henry 1's only legitimate son and heir in the *White Ship*. All this must have helped Stephen to act with as much assurance as he did in the dynastic crisis that involved him when Henry 1 died. Stephen was bound to have observed his uncle's firm handling of assumptive prelate and recalcitrant feudatory (although the fall of the house of Montgomery was before Stephen's time, he probably heard about it), Henry's conduct in the administration of justice in rapidly changing conditions, and the profits that accrued therefrom to the crown. In the administration of justice Stephen showed himself by no means unintelligent, as we shall see. He must also have known something about the elaborate and relatively advanced financial machinery controlled by the exchequer. He could hardly have failed to be aware, for it was notorious, of the use that king Henry made of his 'new men', the firmness with which he controlled their relations with the crown and the advantages and the degree of licence he allowed them in their dealings with others. These men did not in the main stay in Stephen's service. It would indeed have been a dull-witted prince who had failed to learn valuable lessons at the court of Henry I, and Stephen, though he did not have a quick intelligence, was not altogether lacking in perceptiveness. It would also have been possible to draw wrong conclusions from what he saw at his uncle's court, and in some respects he may have done so. Himself a great feudal magnate, he must have been aware of the ambitions, the claims, the feuds, alliances and family connections of his fellow feudatories and aware, too, of the restlessness and resentment which many of them felt under the rule of the 'Lion of Justice'. His later conduct, however, does not suggest that he fully appreciated the significance of these feelings.

Stephen, then, came to the throne with a good deal of knowledge and experience of the government and affairs of England and Normandy. It was confidently expected, as we are told in *Gesta Stephani*, 'that, if we accept the man and help him with all our efforts, he will be of the greatest service to the kingdom'.[25] Whatever might be said of him later in the light of the events of his reign, it is idle to suppose that at the critical juncture in December 1135 the English magnates, or the Londoners either, who played a considerable part in his elevation, considered that they were choosing a foolish man to fill the shoes of the dead king. If Stephen's conduct in the great crises of his reign is disinterestedly examined, whether he was dealing with an extremely powerful family group of prelatical administrators, or with an archiepiscopal election in which the mighty St Bernard chose to intervene, or with the dangerous aggressiveness of a great earl, it is clear that he viewed the situation with the eye of a Norman king. Precedents from his predecessors' reigns probably occurred to him. He saw the need to take a firm line and he even had a good idea of what that line ought to be. What he lacked was the flair, the self-confidence, the clear-sighted concentration upon the most urgent and vital things, the stark realism and ruthless determination of his Norman predecessors in formulating and implementing a policy. In the circumstances of a disputed succession to the throne and because of the accusation of perjury that was levelled at him, Stephen's freedom of action and manœuvre was severely hampered. His grandfather and uncles had had rebellions to face, and difficulties with the church, and the Conqueror and Henry had each seized the throne and could have been accused of usurpation just as Stephen was; but neither of them failed to surmount and triumph over these difficulties, whereas Stephen just barely survived those that confronted him. In a reign of constant civil war (not only were there his own campaigns against the empress and her supporters but there were also rebellious outbreaks and the private wars of magnate with magnate) Stephen had to rely militarily upon two forces. One was the reputedly vast mercenary array of horse and foot that he retained in his service. There were also, as William of Malmesbury tells us, many independent soldiers of fortune who flocked to the scene of strife.[26] The mercenary is a species of carnivore which has seldom in human history been successfully domesticated. In England during Stephen's reign there were many, and very bitter, complaints about the atrocious behaviour of mercenaries and their extreme rapacity and savagery. Stephen at least did not fall a victim of his mercenaries and, while there were revolts like that of Turgis of Avranches in 1145, these revolts were relatively small-scale, local affairs: there was never a large-scale, concerted mercenary uprising. This may have been simply because they did best for themselves as local gangsters, but perhaps a good deal was owing to Stephen's old comrade-in-arms and firm adherent, William of Ypres. The other military (and, of course, political) support upon which Stephen, to a considerable extent, had to rely was that of a fluctuating and not very cohesive, stable or reliable body of earls and barons, whose ideas and advice, often brutal and reactionary, he could not afford to ignore. This is not to say that without such advice he would have acted with consistent wisdom. Stephen was generous and impulsive and prone to act a little irresponsibly. He himself confessed this fault in one formal charter in which he restored to Worcester cathedral priory the church of Wolverhampton, which he had given wrongfully and without advice (*inconsulte*) to Roger, bishop of Chester.[27]

This was not the kind of fault which many kings have ever acknowledged.

Stephen as a man, taken all in all, is unlikely to appear a wholly antipathetic character to an historian with any of that sympathy for erring and straying men by which bishop Stubbs set so much store.[28] As a king he was not a success, but let it be remembered that 'success' is a relative term, especially as applied to medieval kings. It will now be appropriate to examine Stephen's actions in a number of critical affairs in which he is usually said to have behaved badly. The sins, the crimes, in matters spiritual and temporal that are usually attributed to him fall within the categories of perjury and usurpation, sacrilege and simony and breach of the bond between lord and vassal which was constituted by homage and the oath of allegiance, and faithlessness to his plighted word. There were other faults and errors but the major sins fell within these categories.

The first and fundamental sin, from which the others followed almost inevitably, whether he was technically guilty of it or not, was that of perjury. We cannot now hope to discern the whole truth of the matter, but certain facts are indisputable. On Christmas Day 1126 the magnates, both clerical and lay, took a formal oath recognising the empress Maud as Henry I's heir, should he die without legitimate male issue. The first of the clergy to take the oath was William of Corbeil, archbishop of Canterbury, and the first of the laity was David, king of Scots, in his capacity as an English earl. Next came Stephen, striving for and achieving precedence in the oathtaking over king Henry's illegitimate son Robert, earl of Gloucester;[29] and his insistence upon such precedence shows that already he saw himself as standing very near the throne. There was no bar sinister to his ambitions (not that such was insuperable) and it was wise to ensure an early advantage over earl Robert, as a possible rival, should Maud's exclusion ever become a practical issue. The oath to Maud, repeated in 1131 and 1133, was bitterly disliked by a large part of the Anglo-Norman baronage. The problems connected with the succession of heiresses much excercised the contemporary feudal world at all levels. They had not previously arisen at the highest level in England and Normandy, where there had never been a female sovereign who might carry the inheritance to an alien husband; the prospect of having one was widely regarded with alarm and despondency when in accordance with her father's dynastic arrangements Maud was betrothed to Geoffrey, the son and heir of Fulk, count of Anjou, whom she married in 1128. A number of Normans had preferred to follow what still seemed up to August 1127 the ascendant fortunes of William Clito in Flanders, rather than to take risks with Maud. No doubt from the very beginning many of those who took the oath to Maud were prepared, if need be, to renounce it on the ground that it was taken under duress and was therefore void. As the author of *Gesta Stephani* puts it, king Henry 'in that thunderous voice that none could resist rather compelled than invited men to take the oath'.[30] Could Stephen, who insisted on the highest precedence in taking it, claim that he acted under duress? Unquestionably he could. It would readily have been understood by contemporaries that, even in acting under compulsion, this claim to precedence in the royal circle was of vital importance to a prince in Stephen's position, something for which he must strive. It was all the more important if he already had the succession to the crown in his mind's eye. It may here be observed that the prosperous fortunes of the younger brothers of the house of Blois took a further upward turn when on 4 October 1129, Henry, abbot of Glastonbury, was elected, and on 17 November consecrated, bishop of Winchester – a position from which a man might rise.

There is a case, which will be considered in more detail in another context, for the view that from the very beginning Stephen had in mind the possibility of renouncing his oath. His remarkable promptitude (which has always needlessly surprised historians) in crossing to England as soon as he had news of Henry I's death to make his bid for the throne suggests that he was acting, not upon impulse, but in accordance with a prearranged plan. Things went very much too smoothly to have been the outcome of pure chance or brilliant improvisation. How, for example, had William de Pontdelarche, the chamberlain in charge of the treasury, been worked upon to hand over the royal treasure in Winchester with so little fuss? It is difficult to believe that this was due to the instantaneously intoxicating effect of Stephen's charm. In view of the widespread antipathy to Maud's succession, Stephen may have been persuaded, if persuasion was needed, that he was the prince best fitted by descent from the Conqueror, by long training and experience at the court of Henry I and by his

personal popularity to step forward as the saviour of the Anglo-
Norman lands from the 'monstrous regiment' of Maud and her
Angevin husband. Behind the events of December 1135 one may
suspect the existence of a grand design in which Stephen's brother
Henry, bishop of Winchester, perhaps played the leading part.[31] If
this was the case, the basic terms upon which such a plan was
founded are likely to have been those which are embodied in
Stephen's so-called 'Oxford charter of liberties' of April 1136.[32]

Stephen's action in December 1135 left him wide open to the
accusation by his rivals of perjury. This was a risk which had to be
taken and undoubtedly had been anticipated. Provided that
Stephen secured the crown, means could be found of smothering
such a charge. For Stephen to be crowned, and therefore consecrated, was the vital step, and it was essential to ensure the proper
canonical celebration of the rite by the archbishop of Canterbury, whose traditional right it was to crown the king. Archbishop William of Corbeil, however, had taken the oath to Maud
and his crowning of another would be tantamount to the most
blatant perjury on his part, unless it could be demonstrated
publicly in the presence of the English church that his oath was
invalid. The argument of duress alone would not serve a churchman, who ought not to have submitted to it. How exceedingly
opportune, then, was the arrival of Hugh Bigod, accompanied by
two knights, who stated publicly on oath before the archbishop
that the late king on his deathbed had disinherited his daughter
and designated Stephen as his successor. Consequently the archbishop agreed to perform the coronation, and on 22 December
1135 Stephen became the Lord's Anointed.[33] Already the balm
was indelible. It would be exceedingly difficult, not to say embarrassing, for pope Innocent II to disavow the action of the archbishop
of Canterbury, who was also papal legate in England. Needless to
say, no pope ever attempted to deal with the situation in any such
clumsy way. On the contrary, the archbishop's action was ratified
by pope Innocent II, and Stephen was able to claim in his Oxford
charter of liberties not only that he was elected by the clergy and
people and crowned by archbishop William, but that he had been
confirmed by the pope. Innocent, striving to maintain his position
against the anti-pope Anacletus, was glad enough thus to gain
recognition in his turn. Even in 1141, when Stephen was a
prisoner, with no hope at that time of release, and when Maud as

lady of England was demanding the allegiance of all, Theobald, archbishop of Canterbury since the beginning of 1139, insisted upon visiting the captive king and formally asking his permission (which was granted) before swearing allegiance to the empress.

As for Hugh Bigod, whose oath ensured Stephen's coronation, it must be said that as far as we can judge from his career his was not a stable or reliable character. He was not included in John of Salisbury's short list of public enemies, but this negative fact is no evidence of positive virtue. Bigod was one of the three greatest territorial magnates of East Anglia, with wide lands in south and east Norfolk and also some in Essex. In the 'cartel' which he returned in 1166 he acknowledged one hundred and twenty five knights' fees of the old feoffment, that is, created before the death of Henry I. Like his father Roger, and his half-brother William, whom he succeeded, Hugh held the office of a *dapifer*, or steward, in the royal household, which may well have kept him in attendance on king Henry during his last hours. His territorial strength in East Anglia and his castles of Framlingham, Bungay and Walton gave him a formidable position in that region whether as a supporter or an opponent of the crown. In April 1136, following a report of Stephen's death, he seized Norwich castle and refused to surrender till the king arrived in person.[34] Perhaps he thought that, in the circumstances, the possession of Norwich castle would strengthen his bargaining position. Hugh was in attendance on Stephen both in England and in Normandy in 1137. In 1140 he was in rebellion, but came to terms when Bungay castle fell to Stephen.[35] Next, not without considerable surprise, we see him referred to as earl of East Anglia by Henry of Huntingdon in his account of the battle of Lincoln.[36] The probability is that Henry, writing some time after the event, anticipated the title Hugh later acquired. All the evidence of his attestations of Stephen's charters, which were fairly numerous before 1141, indicates that he was not an earl before that date.[37] At the battle of Lincoln he was one of those who deserted Stephen at the very first onset and went over to the empress. With what mixed feelings this black sheep was received may be judged from part of the oration before the battle which Henry of Huntingdon put into the mouth of the earl of Gloucester. The earl did not waste many words on Bigod but denounced him in blistering terms for his 'premeditated perjury'. Nonetheless, Hugh Bigod's reward was in all probability the grant by the empress of the earldom of Norfolk. In 1144 Bigod joined forces with Geoffrey de Mandeville, earl of Essex, his near neighbour, and took part in the devastation of eastern England so that in 1145 Stephen had to mount operations against him. When in 1148, in defiance of Stephen's prohibition, archbishop Theobald returned to England and landed in East Anglia, Hugh Bigod entertained him and gave him a headquarters in Framlingham Castle.[38] This may have resulted from simple hostility to Stephen, for he remained the king's implacable enemy, or from an exceedingly astute appreciation of the situation at that time. During duke Henry's campaign of 1153 Bigod seized Ipswich castle but was unable to hold it. In the treaty between Stephen and Henry, towards the end of the year, a clause reserving to him 'the third penny of Norfolk, of which he is earl' shows him safe home and dry, his position explicitly recognised by both the high contracting parties.[39] Hugh Bigod went on to show himself just as undependable in the next reign. This was the man upon whose oath Stephen's integrity, to a great extent, depended.

In 1136 Stephen's position seemed safe. The confirmation of his title by Innocent II must have occurred before April 1136, when the Oxford charter was issued, whether or not the pope heard the case between Stephen and the empress or merely confirmed the action of his legate. J.H.Round believed that the case was first heard in 1136, but R.L.Poole has argued for 1139. There may, though it is unlikely, have been two hearings, which might account for the statement by Gilbert Foliot that the allegation of the illegitimacy of the empress was not immediately answered. It obviously took her adherents completely by surprise.[40]

We have two fairly detailed accounts of the hearing of the case in the papal curia. One is given by John of Salisbury in his *Historia Pontificalis*; the other in a letter written by Gilbert Foliot about 1143, when he was abbot of St Peter's, Gloucester. Neither writer favoured Stephen's cause. John of Salisbury's account reads, in part, as follows:

An argument had frequently been raised against the king about his usurpation of the kingdom, which it was well known he had seized contrary to the oath sworn to king Henry. For he had sworn fealty to the empress Matilda, king Henry's daughter, and had undertaken to aid her against all men to obtain and hold England and Normandy after her father's death. The venerable bishop of Angers laid her complaint before pope Innocent, arguing that the king was perjured and had unlawfully seized the kingdom. Opposing him were representatives of the king, Roger, bishop of Chester, and Lupellus, a clerk of the late William, archbishop of Canterbury, and, as leading counsel in the case (*qui eis in causa patrocinabatur*), Arnulf, archdeacon of Séez, who later became bishop of Lisieux. In answer to the bishop he publicly alleged that the empress was not a fit person to succeed her father, because she was born of an incestuous union[41] and was the daughter of a nun whom Henry had dragged away from Romsey Abbey and deprived of the veil. He admitted the oath but maintained that it was forcibly exacted and that it was conditional, namely, that he (Stephen) would support the succession of the empress after her father with all his might, unless her father should change his mind and name another heir; for it was possible that he might have a son by his wife.[42] Finally, he submitted that king Henry had changed his mind and, acting *in extremis*, had designated his sister's son, Stephen, as his heir. And he said that this was publicly proven by the oath of earl Hugh and two knights before the English church, to William, archbishop of Canterbury, the papal legate, who on receiving this proof had raised Stephen to the kingship by the unanimous desire of the bishops and magnates: so, what had been done in such solemn fashion could not, he submitted, be undone.

Thus Stephen's leading counsel put forward his arguments in the papal curia in a clear and uncompromising fashion. He has often been blamed for bringing forward the allegation of Maud's illegitimacy, both on the ground that there was such a decisive answer to it and because it was an unpleasant thing, a thoroughly dirty piece of work. Arnold, as an advocate, undoubtedly knew very well what he was about and perhaps he ought to be given credit for perceiving quite clearly that the question of Maud's right of inheritance was really the crux of the whole case. Maud's representative was Ulger, bishop of Angers. John of Salisbury describes him as 'the leading bishop in Gaul both because of his age and his learning and his good repute and because of the inexorable rigour of his justice and his freedom of mind'. There were, indeed, other opinions about Ulger and malicious anecdotes were circulated about his prolonged stay at the curia where he was pursuing a vendetta with Petronilla, abbess of Fontevraud, about a mill.[43] It would be difficult to say whether Ulger was more exasperated by popes Innocent II, Celestine II and Lucius II than they by him; or, conceivably, the situation had become something of a joke with them all. Hearing the scandalous and probably unexpected aspersion on Maud's legitimacy, Ulger, not unnaturally, flared up. His immediate reply to archdeacon Arnulf was a bitter and insulting personal attack:

> I am astonished, Arnulf, by your temerity in attacking, now that he is dead, the man whom you adored, and your father and brothers and whole connection too, when he was alive, and who raised your whole family from ordure (*stercore* is the word used). It is marvellous with what impudence you lie, but, then, your whole kindred is incontinent of words (*loquax*) and deserves to be shown up for evil living and skill and audacity in lying. In these arts you are outstanding even among the Normans . . .[44]

There speaks the Angevin of the hereditary enemies of his people, a man who has thoroughly lost his temper and his head. It is easy to believe that bishop Ulger was taken by surprise and not sharp-witted enough to make the right reply to Arnulf's allegation. According to John of Salisbury's story, the right answer *was* given by Ulger, namely, that the church had blessed the union of Maud's parents and that pope Pascal had anointed her as empress, which could not have been done had she really been a nun's daughter. Gilbert Foliot, whose account we shall examine, denies that any effective answer was given at the time. It is possible that John of Salisbury attributes this answer to Ulger simply for the sake of completing his record of the case for the empress. As to Hugh Bigod's oath, Ulger denied that Hugh was present at Henry's 1 death-bed. This, surely, was a matter that could have been settled by the evidence of others who were present, but we are left with Hugh's word against Ulger's. The bishop, after his unfortunate exhibition of *odium forensicum*, produced a peroration which shows his advocacy in a better light:

> The proof that you claim was accepted cannot be held against the empress for, since she was neither present nor cited to appear, she could not lawfully be condemned, least of all by those who were not her judges but her subjects and bound to her by an oath of fealty.

The personal attack on Arnulf and his family traduced a learned and distinguished prelate, who together with his uncle, John, bishop of Lisieux, and his brother, John, archdeacon and later bishop of Séez, formed a Norman clerical family group almost as

4*

distinguished as that of Roger, bishop of Salisbury, and his nephews and son in England.[45]

Gilbert Foliot's account of this famous case in the papal curia is that of an eye witness, and it amounts also to an analysis of the legal arguments. This account is contained in a letter to Brian fitz Count, lord of Wallingford, whom he congratulates on the very sharp and pithy reply he had sent to the bishop of Winchester, who had taken him to task for not returning to his allegiance to Stephen.[46] In encouraging Brian to remain loyal to the empress, he reviews her claim very much more acutely than bishop Ulger did in John of Salisbury's account. In general terms he supports the succession of heiresses, because this is in conformity with *Divine Law* (Numbers, ch.xxxvi); with *Natural Law* (children's claims over-riding those of other relatives); and with *Human Law*, i.e. *Jus civile* and *Jus gentium* (Maud, a most dutiful daughter, had done nothing which could have justified her father in disinheriting her). Gilbert excuses Brian's action in renouncing allegiance to Stephen and remaining loyal to the empress because, although perjury is certainly a sin, a double perjury could only make a bad situation worse. He then recalls how he was present with the abbot of Cluny at the papal curia when the issue between Stephen and the empress was heard there. He says that Maud's case was stated by the bishop of Angers and depended on hereditary right and the oath that had been sworn to her. But, clearly, everything must turn upon the first of these, for if this fails, the claim on the basis of the oath fails with it. If Maud was not entitled to inherit, then the oath sworn to her could not be binding. Maud's opponents, therefore, argued that she was not of legitimate birth and her mother was alleged to have taken vows as a nun before she married Henry I. This, says Gilbert, was not effectively answered at the time, but the answer is this: the marriage of Henry I and Edith (Matilda) was solemnised by the saintly archbishop Anselm, who would certainly not have done so had there been any canonical impediment to their union. He expresses the hope (not destined to be realised) that pope Celestine (26th September 1143 – 9th March 1144, which is the best clue to the date of the letter) will soon pronounce in Maud's favour.

This is an admirably lucid statement of the cases of the rivals. By this time the question of Hugh Bigod's oath seems to have lost the importance that once was attached to it, because it had really served its purpose when archbishop William of Corbeil was persuaded by it to crown Stephen. The whole emphasis in Gilbert's account is upon the strict legality of the claim made by the empress, and it is this which provides such justification as there is for the weight which Stephen's counsel, Arnulf, placed upon legitimacy in his submissions in 1139. He was not on very safe ground in relying upon Hugh Bigod's evidence, nor indeed was the alleged illegitimacy of the empress a safe ground either. But whether Arnulf produced the allegation himself, or whether he simply followed the brief he had been given, it does seem that it disconcerted the representative of the empress. The case was suspended; whatever his views may have been, the embarrassed pontiff could hardly have done otherwise. Such was the dirty linen that neither party, nor the Roman curia itself, could emerge with an untarnished reputation. What seems to have been lost to view in Foliot's statement is the argument that the oath to Maud was forced and therefore void. The argument that it was conditional virtually collapsed with the vindication of Maud's legitimacy. Stephen was not left in a very strong position *vis-à-vis* the papacy when later circumstances forced him to try to take a strong line. His own position was safe enough but that of his heirs was not.

Was Stephen a brazen, impenitent and unscrupulous perjurer? That he broke his oath is beyond question, but on precisely what grounds he personally considered himself justified, as distinct from those that were put forward formally on his behalf, we really cannot say. Was he the willing but not very clear-sighted accomplice of a far abler and more ambitious brother? This may indeed be the key to an understanding of his reign. For both brothers dire consequences flowed from their early loss of mutual confidence (long before June 1139), whatever its causes.

It is a more difficult task to isolate the other crucial actions of king Stephen and examine them without becoming enmeshed in the details of political history, and this is not the purpose here. These several series of events are very well known and it will best serve our purpose to quote, where possible, the opinions of contemporary or nearly contemporary writers, some those of men favourable to Stephen and some from hostile sources.

The first of the sacrilegious acts generally held against Stephen occurred at his Oxford court on 24 June 1139, when after an affray he arrested Roger, bishop of Salisbury, his son, Roger the chancellor and his nephew, Alexander, called the Magnificent, bishop of Lincoln. Roger's nephew, Nigel, bishop of Ely, escaped to Devizes castle; and the subsequent harsh treatment of these eminent churchmen added to the heinousness of the offence already committed. The details of this notorious episode need not detain us; it is the opinions of contemporaries about it that are our concern. What had occurred was not merely the arrest of important men summoned to attend the king's court, but the laying of impious hands upon the sacrosanct persons of higher clergy. This was a grievous breach, both in the letter and in the spirit, of Stephen's Oxford charter of liberties, which was bound to alienate the sympathies of the English church, upon which he still so greatly depended for support, and to antagonise still further his brother Henry, bishop of Winchester, the papal legate, who, if our view is correct, had been the brain behind and the mainstay of the plan to place and maintain Stephen on the throne. Henry's loyalty to his brother had already been severely strained by his disappointment over the see of Canterbury after the death of archbishop William on 21 November 1136[47] and probably by Stephen's tendency to rely upon the advice of other people, especially Waleran, count of Meulan, and his brother Robert, earl of Leicester.

First, let us consider the reaction to these events of the author of *Gesta Stephani*, probably Robert, bishop of Bath. As an historian he was consistently favourable to Stephen during a great part of his reign, but as a cleric he gave the utmost emphasis to the sacrosanctity of the persons of the clergy and took a very stern view of offences against them. He himself had a very unpleasant experience in 1138, when the garrison of Bath had captured the marauder, Geoffrey Talbot, whose friends contrived by specious promises to entice the Bishop to meet them. He tells how:

At once they laid sacrilegious hands upon the preacher of the gospel, the minister of God's holy table, the reverend sower of all peoples' faith and religion, the dispenser of the grain in the Lord's granary, who bears in his breast the ark of God and the divine manna, and they showered him with indecent insults and threatened to hang him unless he handed Geoffrey back to them.[48]

This, clearly, is not a man to view lightly the arrest of his fellow bishops by the king and the threat to hang the demoted chancellor. In his account of the affair of the bishops[49] he stresses the great importance of the position that bishop Roger held at court and brands him as a traitor to Stephen. The bishops of Ely and Lincoln are also described as traitors, showy (*pompatici*) and given over to warlike habits and the vanities of this world. Our author goes on to describe the hostile reactions to these prelates of the count of Meulan and others of the king's intimates. If the king, they said, followed their advice as he relied upon their valour and wisdom, he would arrest these men and put them in custody, not as bishops but as offenders against the episcopal office and suspected enemies of the king's peace, and he would oblige them to hand over their castles. The author obviously did not greatly respect the king's advisers, nor could he approve their advice. He describes Stephen as yielding to very foolish, indeed mad, advice in allowing his advisers to do to the bishops as they wished. This attack upon bishops was indeed a monstrous sin against God. Clearly he deeply deplores the treatment meted out to them, though he is glad to see them stripped of their ostentatious splendour. He is surprised and a little pained that Stephen succeeded in making away with their wealth, though he is prepared to admit that there may have been an element of justice in this, since what had been stored up in their castles had been intended for use against the king. As far as this author is concerned, 'all's well that ends well'. The king excused himself and his followers on what he believed to be strong grounds. 'But, because it was justly decided and discreetly determined by all the clergy that he might not on any grounds lay hands on the Lord's anointed, he softened the harshness of ecclesiastical severity by humble submission and, putting aside his royal robes, groaning in spirit and with a contrite heart, he humbly accepted the penances imposed for his fault.' This does not entirely agree with other accounts, which deny the king's submission.

Let us turn to the narrative by a firm adherent of one of the victims of the outrage of 1139. Henry, archdeacon of Huntingdon in the diocese of Lincoln, moved in the highest circles of the English ecclesiastical establishment and was a cleric important enough to accompany archbishop Treobald to Rome in 1139. His *Historia Anglorum* was undertaken at the suggestion of Alexander, bishop of Lincoln, and is dedicated to him.[50] Henry was an intelligent man with some literary pretensions, but not a very good historian. It does not seem that he took a great deal of trouble in collecting his source material, nor is he as fully informed about the affairs of his own day as we could have wished.[51] The arrest of his own diocesan and patron was a matter which touched him intimately and he is deeply indignant:[52] it is 'a truly shocking and unheard-of outrage' (*res infamia notabilis et ab omni consuetudine remota*). The king is pilloried for his ingratitude to these bishops for the great services they had rendered him, surpassing all others, at the time of his entry into the kingdom; and, not only this, but also because he confiscated their wealth, obtaining therewith Constance, sister of Louis king of the French, as a bride for his son Eustace. Finally, Stephen is denounced for his refusal at the council of Winchester to accede to the request of his brother, the legate, and the archbishop of Canterbury and all the bishops present to restore their possessions to the injured bishops. This is attributed not to the iniquity of Stephen, but to the counsel of evil men. Such conduct, in Henry's opinion, inevitably brought divine retribution upon the house of Stephen and brought also all the ills which subsequently afflicted the kingdom. In that he may have spoken more truly than he knew, for if Stephen and his brother had never been alienated from each other and if they had continued their early co-operation, the history of the reign might have been very different.

The two authors whose opinions we have consulted differ a good deal in their presentation of the details connected with the bishops' arrest and the interpretations they offer are not in agreement. They are, however, agreed upon two things: the iniquity of Stephen's action and the suggestion that it arose, not from the king's evil nature, but from the advice of evil counsellors. A third contemporary historian, William of Malmesbury, whose patron was Robert, earl of Gloucester, takes a different view. The second book of his *Historia Novella* opens with a reference to the 'venom of malice' that had long been nurtured in Stephen's breast, breaking out openly in the affair of the bishops.[53] The king is represented as fearing the imminent arrival in England of earl Robert and lashing out in panic at all and sundry on the merest suspicion of hostility to him. The bishops' castle-building and munitioning are given here, as in other accounts, as the reasons or pretexts for the advice given to the king by his lay supporters to arrest them.

Stephen is represented as pretending to ignore this advice, much as he would have liked to follow it, for fear of the odium it would cause. He eagerly seized the pretext of an affray within the purlieus of the court in which the bishops' retainers were involved. We are told that Hugh, archbishop of Rouen (a Cluniac), supported the king's action but that the bishop of Winchester, 'whom no fraternal affection, no fear of danger, could turn aside from the path of truth', opposed it. If so eminent a prelate as the archbishop of Rouen could support the king, was there not something to be said in justification of his action? That is a very relevant question, which William of Malmesbury did not ask. Had the bishop of Winchester any ulterior motives in opposing his brother? That is also a question which every student of the affair must ask and answer. Many modern historians have answered it in Henry's favour, making him out a devoted champion of the freedom of the church, who would make any sacrifice in that cause,[54] but it is possible to represent him in a very much less flattering light if one leans to the view of St Bernard and pope Eugenius III rather than to that of William of Malmesbury.[55] William does, however, give by far the most detailed account of the council of Winchester, where the case was considered, with all the arguments on both sides. The arguments on behalf of the king are given their full weight, though William never conceals his ardent partisanship. He ends by saying that Stephen, prevented by bad advice, did not carry out his fair promises to the church. So even the historian who begins with an assertion of Stephen's malice, ends, as do most other contemporary writers, by blaming everything on evil counsellors.

To hold the balance even, we may consult another monkish historian as prejudiced in Stephen's favour as William of Malmesbury was against him. The malice which the latter attributes to Stephen is matched by the arrogance which Orderic, on the other side, imputes to the bishops.[56] He says that the bishop of Salisbury had a bad reputation above all the great men of the realm for disloyalty to Stephen, his lord and king, and for favouring the children of Henry I. He and his nephews and son, emboldened by their wealth and power, are said to have presumed to harrass the lords of the neighbourhood, with the result that a league was formed against them and from this, Orderic's opinion seems to be, resulted the affray at Oxford on 24 June 1139. Nigel, bishop of

Ely, is represented as a man of evil conscience and great determination; a malignant rebel. No attempt is made in this narrative
to blame Stephen's actions upon evil counsellors. On the contrary,
he appears as justly incensed by the arrogant and traitorous conduct of the bishops. Perhaps it is significant that, writing in
Normandy, Orderic adhered to the view of the Norman prelate,
Hugh, archbishop of Rouen. William of Newburgh, writing towards the end of the century, takes the view that bishop Roger
had been guilty of perjury since, having taken the oath to Maud,
he accepted Stephen as king. This being so, Stephen's action was a
well-deserved retribution, even though it was an inexpiable fault
(*inexpiabilem naevum*).[57]

It is interesting that the more extreme opinions – those concerning the malice of Stephen and the arrogance of the bishops –
should emanate from monastic cloisters. It may be that the
seculars, that is the bishop of Bath and the archdeacon of Huntingdon, who wrote the other accounts, had a more sensitive feeling
for the 'establishment' than had the monks. They were directly
involved in the practical affairs of the world. To accuse the Lord's
Anointed of malice would be, to say the least of it, very unwise on
the part of such men. Quite apart from any personal trouble in
which it might involve them, it would tend to undermine the
established state of society. Rightly considered, an anointed king
was God's vice-gerent and as such could truly will only what was
righteous and just. To state otherwise was as heinous as sacrilege
and, of course, the attribution of arrogance and treason to consecrated bishops, the shepherds of God's flock, was no less repre-
hensible. The authority of a prince, a bishop or an archdeacon,
they were undoubtedly convinced, ought not to be exposed to
such subversive attacks. An historical writer might allow his feelings, his prejudices, to show, but good sense required that the
blame for evil deeds should rest upon the shoulders of evil counsellors. William of Malmesbury, in effect, makes a related point in
his account of the council of Winchester in 1139. What is to be
done with a king who refuses to accept ecclesiastical censure? To
excommunicate him without the knowledge of the pope would be
dangerous indeed. To send representatives to complain to the
pope would also invite trouble, for Stephen intimated (as kings
did before and after him) that such men might find it much more
difficult to return home than to leave the country. The opinion of

most contemporary historians was that Stephen's conduct in this affair of the bishops was, from first to last, thoroughly ill-conceived and indeed sacrilegious but, formally at least, they laid the blame on evil counsellors. The only proper conclusion to be drawn from all this is probably that the roots of the doctrine that the king can do no wrong are very deeply embedded in history. The grounds for Stephen's conduct, which he himself undoubtedly regarded as very strong grounds, are most fully stated by the bitterest of his contemporary critics. How far they really believed in the fact, as distinct from the necessary fiction, of evil counsel, it would be difficult to say in most cases. John of Salisbury and Henry of Huntingdon frankly did not.

Stephen has commonly been accused of infringing the freedom of the English church, which he had explicitly guaranteed, especially in the matter of abbatial and episcopal elections. Accusations of simony and intrusion by royal authority were made. They were not, as a rule, levelled directly at the king himself, but they inevitably tarnished his reputation and affected his position. It is important to remember that freedom in ecclesiastical elections had been but recently achieved in principle. In England these matters were regulated by the terms of the agreement which Henry 1 had made with pope Pascal 11 in 1107.[58] The king had renounced the objectionable claim of the crown to exercise rights of investiture with the *spiritualia*, with all that this symbolism represented in terms of royal control over ecclesiastical appointments and functions. Freedom of canonical election by the appropriate capitular bodies had been proclaimed. The moral victory certainly lay with the church, but could it be turned into a practical victory? The investiture of English bishops and abbots was, in future, to be performed by the hands of the appropriate ecclesiastical authority. But when a see or abbacy fell vacant, the temporal rights of the crown were safeguarded by its holding the temporalities during the vacancy and, of course, drawing their revenues. Although the election was made by the canonically constituted body, this could not take place without royal licence and royal representatives might be present (who might stimulate the zeal of the electors for an appropriate candidate). The bishop elect was required to take an oath of allegiance to the crown before receiving the temporalities and before his consecration. In fact a strong and determined king had every opportunity of intervening and of putting forward a candidate of his own. Such pressure a capitular body would find it difficult to resist, especially as so very few chapters were distinguished for their unity and solidarity. As Dom David Knowles has pointed out, a chapter nominally free to elect had its freedom much circumscribed in practice.[59] Cathedral chapters often included members of influential families and clergy with powerful patrons, and this was very liable to bring outside considerations and influence to bear on capitular proceedings. The 'larger and wiser part' of the chapter was supposed to prevail but a minority was very apt to consider itself the 'wiser part' and often felt itself strong enough to appeal to Rome. Furthermore, as often as not, a chapter about to elect a bishop found that the king had put forward as a candidate a kinsman or a royal servant, such as Philip de Harcourt, the royal chancellor, who was nominated for, but failed to obtain, the see of Salisbury after the death of bishop Roger, though in this case the nomination was opposed by bishop Henry.

Such attempts to dictate elections led Stephen and his brother into very serious trouble. By far the most notorious case occurred in the disputed election to the see of York after the resignation and death, almost immediately after, of archbishop Thurstan on 6 February 1140. The history of this celebrated case has been most fully and authoritatively treated by Dom Knowles[60] and since an outline of events has already been given, it is unnecessary to cover the ground again here. Stephen, it must be emphasised, in vetoing Waldef, step-son of the king of Scotland, and putting forward his successive nominees, Henry de Sully, abbot of Fécamp, a nephew and William fitz Herbert, another nephew, and seeking to exercise his influence on their behalf, was not attempting anything new. In fact, acting as he did in close collusion with his brother, bishop Henry, the papal legate, he must have regarded himself, with some complacency, as working in far closer harmony with the church than his predecessors had usually done. This was just the kind of situation in which an agreement between Stephen and his brother could work to the best advantage of church, kingdom and dynasty. In attempting to deal with the vacancy in the see of York, Stephen had the misfortune to arouse the determined opposition of a group of Cistercian and Augustinian leaders. Supporting them was the formidable figure of St Bernard of Clairvaux, the mightiest champion of righteousness, as that Puritan of heroic stature understood it, in this age. It is true that his partisanship almost automatically ensured a not inconsiderable body of support at all levels in the church for his opponents in any contest; but for a king whose position was as vulnerable as Stephen's he was an overwhelmingly powerful antagonist.

St Bernard did not, in fact, take up his stand formally as an opponent of Stephen, but all that he stood for meant inexorable opposition to the achievement of Stephen's desires. In the course of the prolonged dispute over the archiepiscopal succession in York obloquy fell not so much upon Stephen as upon his nominee, William fitz Herbert. To pope after short-lived pope from Innocent II to the Cistercian, Eugenius III, St Bernard continually denounced that 'idol of York', that 'common pest' who 'trusts not in God's help but in his own riches'. He is a simoniac, a man intruded by the crown in the see of York. Let the pope, at one blow, destroy Annanias and Simon Magus. When at last, in 1147, pope Eugenius removed William from the see and when, in spite of capitular differences and violent local opposition, Henry Murdac, abbot of the Cistercian house of Fountains, was chosen in his place and consecrated by the pope himself, Stephen absolutely refused to recognise the new archbishop, who had been set up without respect for the rights of the crown. He thereby engaged in open defiance of the papacy, aggravating the situation in various ways, notably by forbidding any English prelates other than his own appointed representatives to attend the council over which the pope presided at Rheims in 1148. This, in turn, involved a clash with Theobald, archbishop of Canterbury, who defied the royal order and attended the council. Stephen thereupon carried out the threat that he had uttered in 1139 and forbade him to return to England. The archbishop returned good for ill by interceding for the king and saving him from the excommunication which he would otherwise have incurred, for already candles had been lit. Again, in 1150, Stephen made another ill-advised demonstration, refusing to give a safe conduct through English territory to cardinal Paperone, a papal legate travelling to Ireland, unless he would swear not to engage in any intrigue against the crown. This insult Stephen was foolish enough to offer at a time when he was wholly dependent upon papal favour to secure the recognition and coronation of his son Eustace as successor to the throne. The whole future of his dynasty depended upon this, but his offences had by now so completely antagonised the pope that even the king's significant gesture of reconciliation with Henry Murdac could not retrieve the situation. Pope Eugenius, repeating the prohibition of his predecessors, forbade the coronation of Eustace on the ground that Stephen had seized the crown in violation of his oath. Rome did not seek to depose Stephen, but the papal pronouncement debarred his heirs so that, with Stephen's death, the true line of succession to the English throne might be restored.

After his release from captivity and his crown-wearing at Canterbury at Christmas 1141 Stephen seems to have worked in close collaboration with his brother, bishop Henry, just as he had before 1139, in dealing with ecclesiastical affairs. Probably the course that the relations of king and church took was due at least as much to the policy and actions of bishop Henry as to those of king Stephen. Denunciations of Stephen were few, for reasons which have already been referred to. There is the occasional story, such as that told by John of Salisbury about an election to the abbacy of St Augustine's, Canterbury in 1151:

Hugh, abbot of St Augustine's, Canterbury, died and was succeeded by Silvester, prior of that house. But his election caused many to suspect simony, because the king accepted five hundred marks to allow the monks freely to elect whom they would to succeed the late abbot and to control the property of the vacant monastery. And, because the prior made the agreement and paid up and was elected, he came under this suspicion. Because no one would publicly accuse him of the crime (which it was not safe to do, since it touched the king himself and the chief officers of his household) the archbishop of Canterbury confirmed the election.[61]

Gervase of Canterbury corroborates this story only as to the freedom of election and makes no reference to a simoniacal transaction.[62] There is indeed no universal outcry against Stephen on such a score among contemporary annalists and historians although there was much ground for it. It was the simoniacal appointees who were denounced, especially William fitz Herbert (canonised, however, in 1227). But denunciations of these paled into insignificance in comparison with St Bernard's denunciation of the bishop of Winchester as the foe, that old seducer of Winchester, the herald of Satan, the enemy of right. John of Salisbury also records an alleged conversation between pope Eugenius and bishop Henry,

who was believed to be instigating his brother, the king, against
the church, though John says Stephen 'took no advice from him
or any other wise counsellor (as his works manifestly declare)'.[63]

It happened meanwhile that the king afflicted the church with fresh
tumults and, when the news was brought to the pope, the bishop of
Winchester, who was present, said 'I am glad that I am not there now,
because this disturbance would be blamed on me'. Smiling, the pope
propounded this parable: The devil and his mother were having a
friendly chat and, while she was trying to restrain her son's evil-doing
by rebuking him for his wicked deeds, a gale blew up and many ships
were sunk as they watched. 'See', said the devil, 'if I had been there you
would have blamed it all on me'. And she said, 'If you were not actually there you obviously trailed your tail there beforehand'. And, turning the moral against the bishop, he said, 'think, brother, whether you
have not trailed your tail in the English sea'.[64]

Eugenius, a Cistercian, was no doubt biased against this Cluniac
prince-bishop[65] and thought of him as 'the man who could mislead two kingdoms with his tongue'.[66] In the context of ecclesiastical policy the ambitions, the ideas and the devious ways of Henry
of Blois, bishop of Winchester, must be examined as closely as
those of Stephen. How far did Stephen really trust him after his
bitter experiences of his conduct in 1139 and 1141?

It remains to consider briefly Stephen's dealings with Rannulf
de Gernon, earl of Chester, and Geoffrey de Mandeville, earl of
Essex.[67] Both these men presented Stephen with one of the gravest
dilemmas that could confront a feudal monarch. These episodes
and the arrest of the bishops in 1139 had an important element in
common; they posed the problem of how a ruler should deal with
potential traitors. But dealing with churchmen and dealing with
laymen were very different matters, though it once suited the
Conqueror to announce that he was arresting 'not the bishop of
Bayeux, but the earl of Kent', and Stephen attempted to put the
same principle into operation in 1139. His confrontations with the
earls of Chester and Essex raised in a very acute form the conflicting obligations of the king in his capacities as sovereign and as
feudal suzerain – *rex* and *dominus*. In the former capacity, the king
had a direct relationship with every one of his subjects. They all
owed him allegiance and certain duties. The king, in turn, was
bound by his coronation oath and owed certain obligations to his

subjects. He was constituted the guardian of true peace, the suppressor of rapacity and iniquity, the just and merciful judge of his people and the maintainer of their ancient laws. As *Dominus Anglorum*, the king was the supreme landlord and in a feudal society he was bound in a relationship of mutual obligation with his tenants-in-chief. According to custom and theory this relationship could only be broken in the most formal way. If an intolerable wrong were committed by lord or vassal and if redress were refused, it was possible for the injured party formally to renounce the relationship that had been entered into by the vassal's act of homage and oath of fealty. This was called variously *diffidatio, diffiduciatio, diffidentia.* The consequence for the vassal was the loss of his fief but, the parties being no longer lord and man but on an equal footing, the dispute could be carried further by recourse to arms. Whether the lord or the vassal considered himself the injured party, breach of the feudal bond and resort to arms was not to be done in a hole-and-corner way. It was a public affair of intimate concern to the lord's other vassals, who had the duty and also the right of advising him and of acting as judgment-finders in all suits in the lord's court between vassal and vassal or between vassal and lord. For a feudal lord to act without the 'counsel and consent' of his vassals or to deprive a vassal of life, limb, land, property or honour 'unjustly and without judgment' was a grievous offence. Therefore, in any consideration of Stephen's treatment of the earls of Chester and Essex attention must be given to the formality or irregularity of his actions. But it is not quite so simple as this: the dilemma remains.

Late in 1140 the earl of Chester, whom Stephen had recently 'loaded with honours', seized the royal castle of Lincoln, ejecting its custodians, and began to oppress the citizens of Lincoln, who enjoyed a large measure of royal favour. The citizens, and also bishop Alexander (whom Stephen had arrested in 1139), complained bitterly to the king, asked for his intervention and promised to help to the best of their ability. What was Stephen to do? As king he was bound to protect his subjects from oppression and to take drastic action against one who had seized a royal fortress. As the earl's feudal lord, he ought to require him to 'stand to right' in his court. Then, with the counsel and consent of his other tenants-in-chief he might renounce the earl's fealty, and defy and attack him. This would have meant considerable delay, whereas in the circumstances firm and speedy royal action was highly desirable. Such was the course that Stephen chose. The lack of enthusiasm among his earls and barons at the siege of Lincoln and the desertion of so many prominent among them at the first clash in the battle of 2 February 1141 seems to show clearly that some were not at all happy about the situation or convinced of the justice of Stephen's action against the earl of Chester.

Henry of Huntingdon, in his account of the battle,[68] puts a brief speech into the mouth of the earl of Chester. He thanks his father-in-law, the earl of Gloucester, and the others for coming to his aid, and says it is only right that he should make the first attack upon the army of the most faithless king, who after agreeing to a cessation of hostilities (*datis induciis*) broke the peace. This same historian says that the earl had 'fraudulently taken' Lincoln castle. On the other side, Baldwin fitz Gilbert in his speech strongly emphasises the justice of the king's cause: his opponents are false to their oaths.

William of Malmesbury[69] conveys the impression that the earl of Chester and his half-brother, William de Roumare, were conscious of rectitude, for even when they had seized Lincoln castle they did not at all expect the king's arrival, certainly not so quickly, since he besieged them 'in the Christmas holidays'. By implication, the king's action within the twelve days of Christmas was an ill deed. 'This step', says William, 'seemed unjustifiable to many, because as I have said, he had left them before the festival without any suspicion of enmity; nor had he, even now, according to ancient usage, abjured his friendship with them, which is called "defying".' He goes on to say that the citizens of Lincoln (who had complained to Stephen) were slaughtered on all sides by the just indignation of the victors, and without commiseration on the part of the defeated, as they had been the origin and fomentors of this calamity. This, from the pen of a monastic historian, sheds a fearful light upon the ideas of the age. Well might the pyx fall from the high altar! Of course the burghal militia of Lincoln had fought on Stephen's side in the battle.

It is most unfortunate that there is a lacuna in the text of *Gesta Stephani* just at the point where information was given about the king's relations with the earl of Chester, which is perhaps not to be found in any other source.[70] What we read is:

... would diligently amend what he had done amiss. Consequently, the king was advised to allow the man (*viro* not *homini*) to renew the treaty, to make peace again, to see quietly whether he would keep his promise, and so he (the king) could go elsewhere to attend to other matters.

We are told nothing of the earl's seizure of Lincoln castle, but only of the townsmen's urgent messages to the king. It is made clear that after a considerable lapse of time the earl behaved no more loyally to the king. The siege and the battle are then recounted. We are told that the captured king, when they had disarmed him, kept on complaining humbly:

that indeed this mark of ignominy had come upon him by the vengeance of God for his offences; all the same those were not innocent of a very great crime who broke their faith and their oath, caring not at all that they had done him homage, and rebelling so criminally against him, whom of their own freewill they had made their king and lord. All were so moved by deep feelings of respect (*pietatis*) and pity that, not only did they break forth into tears and lamentations, but the deep penitence of their hearts was reflected in their faces.

That extremely significant passage is seldom quoted. The account of the whole affair which is given by Orderic Vitalis[71] is interesting mainly for the details it provides of the earls' seizure of Lincoln castle, in the best traditions of the cinema at its most athletic, and of the sack of Lincoln. He says, however, that the king's disaster

filled with grief the clergy and monks and common people; if his treacherous nobles had permitted, he would have stopped their nefarious enterprises and would have been a generous defender and benevolent friend of the country.

This is Orderic's last word on Stephen, for illness and infirmity obliged him to bring his work to an end very soon after this point.

Contemporary accounts become fewer as Stephen's reign goes on. By far the fullest account of the arrest of the earl of Chester in 1146 is given in *Gesta Stephani*. We are told how the earl, who 'by force of arms had acquired nearly a third part of the kingdom', came over to the king's side:

Yet though the earl, after the renewal of the peace pact, seemed a useful and loyal helper of the king, he was held suspect by him and by all the great men of his kingdom, both because he neglected to restore

the resources of the royal revenues and the castles which he had violently seized, and also because he had not given any surety in the form
of hostages or guarantors against his natural fickleness and inconstancy
of mind.[72]

So it was decided to wait and see what the earl would do and,
failing the restoration in full of all that belonged to the king, he
might be put under arrest when a suitable opportunity offered.
Eventually the earl, 'still craftily seeking the easiest way of
delivering the king into the hands of his enemies, without himself incurring the reputation for dishonour' came to court complaining of the depredations of the Welsh, and saying that he was
in danger of being driven out of his earldom by their attacks. He
invited Stephen to join him in an expedition against them, which
the king was very ready to do, when, lo and behold! all his leading
men (*primi omnes*) accused the earl of treachery. So when the king
reluctantly took their good advice, the earl was seized by the
barons, handed over to the king's guards and imprisoned. In all
this Stephen is represented as listening rather reluctantly to the
advice of his counsellors, and the actual arrest of the earl is represented as their doing. Stephen is also represented as taking advice
about the desirability of releasing the earl when his relatives and
friends offered terms on his behalf. Throughout his narrative the
author of *Gesta Stephani* assumes the guilt of earl Rannulf. He
represents the king as a guileless innocent and puts the onus for
the actions taken fairly and squarely upon the shoulders of the
king's advisers. This narrative of the arrival of Rannulf at the
king's court with a cock-and-bull story about a projected Welsh
campaign, designed to encompass the king's ruin, is over simpli-
fied. It omits any detailed account of the bargain which Stephen
made with the earl, the implementation of which on the king's
side is probably represented by the massive grant of lands and
castles in the charter already quoted.[73] It is highly probable that
this was issued in 1146, not as has sometimes been thought in
1140. The reference to Rannulf's tenure of Lincoln castle till such
time as his Norman lands could be recovered seems fairly conclusive on this point, for Stephen had not yet lost Normandy
irrevocably in 1140, as he had two years before 1146. We do not
know whether this agreement was the result of Stephen's initiative or that of the earl. Since the names of witnesses are not included in the abstract in which the terms of the charter have come

down to us, we do not know which, or how many, of Stephen's
supporters had cognizance of the agreement. It was in many
respects a rash and irresponsible grant, for many of the lands and
castles handed over to the earl belonged to or were claimed by
others. The castle of Tickhill, for example, had been granted to
the count of Eu, and William d'Aubigny (Brito) was apparently
disinherited. A royal grant of this kind to a most notorious rebel
was bound to cause deep resentment among those who were
liable to lose land or status by it and, furthermore, as John of
Hexham points out[74] there were a good many important barons,
such as William de Clerfai, count Alan of Richmond, William
Peverel of Nottingham and others, who were jealous of the favour
shown to earl Rannulf, or who had already suffered by his depredations on their lands. It is easy to account for the pressure that was
brought to bear upon Stephen to arrest the earl of Chester, but it
is not easy to excuse the extreme thoughtlessness and rashness of
the bargain which he had made with him and which was the cause
of a great deal of the trouble. It seems as though in this case
Stephen acted *inconsulte*. By 1153 the author of *Gesta* no longer
believed wholeheartedly in Stephen's cause and had come to see
duke Henry as the lawful heir and potential saviour of the country.
We find him taking a much more lenient view of earl Rannulf,
whom he describes as an Ishmael:

And it was with good cause that the earl, as long as he lived, exerted
all his efforts to attack the king's supporters . . . because the king, when
he had entered his court under safe conduct, gave orders for his arrest
and imprisonment, as has already been said.[75]

What reliance can we place upon the opinion of an historian who
is capable of such inconsistency?

Nonetheless, there is no better contemporary source to turn to
for an account of the arrest of Geoffrey de Mandeville in the
summer of 1143 at St Albans. Henry of Huntingdon merely in-
forms us of the event, which he describes as 'more by way of
retribution for the earl's wickedness than according to *jus gentium*,
more from necessity than honour. If he had not acted thus the
kingdom would have been spared the earl's perfidy'.[76] Let sleeping
dogs lie! It is difficult to see dispassionately this episode and
its sequel of bloody rebellion and devastation in eastern England. Geoffrey de Mandeville was, for this reason, the object of

contemporary obloquy and he died excommunicate. He has long been pictured like the villain of a more than usually bloodthirsty Wild Western drama – 'a proper fen tiger, all 'air and teeth, like a Ramsey man'. There is no question of trying to whitewash Geoffrey, but at least it has now been shown that he was just an ordinary kind of turncoat, deserting Stephen for the empress by the summer of 1141 and returning to Stephen, or rather his queen, soon after (for large bribes in each case), not a double traitor to both sides, as J.H.Round believed.[77] For our present purpose it is contemporary opinion of Stephen's behaviour that is important. We have seen Henry of Huntingdon's opinion; Gervase of Canterbury simply quotes it with the addition of a cautious 'as many people said'. Contemporary and later medieval historians were mainly preoccupied with the awful fate which overtook the oppressor and defiler of Ramsey Abbey, namely death while excommunicate. William of Newburgh devotes a chapter to him, headed 'Geoffrey de Mandeville's life of crime and well deserved death'.[78] He also refers to Geoffrey's arrest in terms similar to those of Henry of Huntingdon, as made, not indeed honourably and according to the *jus gentium*, but because of his deserts and the fear he aroused. Newburgh it is who provides the information about the insult offered to the king and queen by Geoffrey de Mandeville when he seized their daughter-in-law, Constance of France, and kept her in the Tower of London, and he speaks of Stephen's very just indignation, even after a considerable lapse of time, as some justification for arresting the earl.

The author of *Gesta Stephani* writes at some length of the wealth and power of Geoffrey de Mandeville and about his great ability and shrewdness. 'All that part of the kingdom that the king had subdued, he brought so completely under his control that everywhere he was the king's vicegerent' and was more readily heeded and obeyed than the king himself. This was particularly galling to the king's friends, especially as it was common talk that Geoffrey was going to hand the kingdom over to the countess of Anjou. For these reasons they advised the king to proclaim Geoffrey a traitor, arrest him and deprive him of his castles:

When the king had put this off for a long time, lest the royal majesty should be injured by the base reproach of betrayal, a dispute suddenly arose between Geoffrey and the barons, with insults and threats on both sides. And while the king was striving to calm down both parties and settle their disagreement, certain persons proceeded openly to accuse Geoffrey of laying a treasonable plot against him and his lieges. And since he did not trouble to clear himself of the crime he was accused of, but made light of the basest dishonour by joking about it, the king and the barons who were present suddenly arrested Geoffrey and his entourage. These things happened at St Albans as they have been related.[79]

In all these matters that we have considered it is right that Stephen should stand to judgment. Weak men in politics are frequently far more dangerous than wicked ones.

II. *The Empress*

Something must be said about the empress Maud, though her character does not call for such detailed treatment here as that of Stephen. The most favourable account of her was given by Oskar Rössler over seventy years ago.[80] Even he was obliged to admit her besetting sin of arrogance. Maud was born in 1102.[81] A proposal for her hand from the widowed emperor Henry v was accepted by king Henry i of England in 1109, and in 1110, as a little girl of eight years old, she was sent to Germany and was crowned, a magnificent ceremony for her at such an impressionable age. The emperor dismissed the English courtiers and servants who accompanied her, so that she might learn the German language and German manners and, above all, that she might be groomed for her exalted imperial station. This was probably not a difficult process for a princess of the Norman house, and it was thoroughly done; and so to her congenital hubris were added the stiffest kind of German etiquette and the imperiousness appropriate to an emperor's consort. Maud was married to the emperor early in 1114 and was crowned once more. In Germany she was an outstanding success, almost a Wagnerian figure. She was widowed on 22 May 1125, and the dying emperor placed his sceptre in her hands as though he were designating his heiress. Perhaps the weight of the sceptre irked the dying man and we ought not to read too much into the gesture. He gave the symbol of the imperial sway into hands worthy to hold it, but not necessarily to wield it. It is indeed difficult to believe that any people in that age would deliberately have chosen a woman as their ruler, but William of Malmesbury tells us that after Maud's return from Germany 'some princes of Lorraine and Lombardy came to England more than once in the following years to ask for her as their lady'.[82] By that time, however, Henry I's dynastic schemes required her to undertake a different, more realistic, rôle. All contemporaries are agreed about Maud's beauty, and there is no doubt that she was capable of inspiring the utmost devotion. Her half-brothers, Robert, earl of Gloucester, and Reginald, earl of Cornwall, and her devoted Brian fitz Count are perhaps the best known of her faithful adherents, but there were many more. *Virago* is a word often used of her by her contemporaries, meaning not necessarily a termagant but a woman of masculine spirit. Perhaps Arnulf of Lisieux provided the best gloss when he wrote of Maud as 'a woman who had nothing of the woman in her'; or the author of *Gesta Stephani*, who wrote of her in 1141, when her forces were routed at Winchester, as 'always superior to feminine softness and with a spirit steeled and unbroken in adversity'. Maud's personal courage and steady nerve were shown on more than one occasion: in her flight from the rout of Winchester and in her still more famous and dramatic escape from Oxford castle through the snow in December 1142. Her English career entailed a good many flights or hasty departures, which she must have found exceedingly disagreeable and humiliating.

Maud unquestionably had many of the qualities of a ruler, even a great ruler. She also had some of the characteristics of a tawdry dictator. The trappings and the minor techniques of dictatorship, the exaltation of the personality, were very much her genre. Maud's treatment of the bishop of Winchester, upon whose support and that of the church her success in 1141 so greatly depended, was arrogant and tactless in the extreme to a prince-bishop in whose veins ran the blood of the Conqueror. Her readiness to invest with ring and staff a Scottish intruder in the see of Durham showed clearly that she was prepared to treat the church with contempt and to renounce without a qualm the settlement of the Investiture Controversy which her father had reached with the papacy in 1107 (and which her first husband concluded at Worms in 1122). It displayed also an impenetrable stupidity. Again during her brief period of power in the summer of 1141, her contemptuous treatment of the citizens of London, so different from

Stephen's attitude, resulted in her ignominious flight from the capital city. The author of *Gesta Stephani* remarks that

> What was a sign of the utmost superciliousness and arrogance, when the king of Scotland and the bishop of Winchester and her own brother, the earl of Gloucester, the leading men of the whole realm, who were then her companions, came before her with bended knee to make some requests, she did not rise respectfully, as she ought, when they bowed before her, nor assent to their requests, but repeatedly sent them away, insultingly rebuffing them with an arrogant answer ... but ordained everything, as she herself saw fit, by her own will.

So might a German emperor have behaved, if he were unwise. It certainly was not the way to treat her cousin, the papal legate, her uncle, the king of Scots, and her brother, the earl of Gloucester, not to mention touchy Anglo-Norman feudatories, who considered it their right as well as their duty to proffer advice. In later life Maud's temperament seems to have mellowed a good deal, and she won a reputation for good works, though Walter Map, in his *De Nugis Curialium*, attributes the more unpleasant traits of Henry II's character to his mother's teaching. In some matters Maud gave her son very sound advice, as, for example, against the promotion to the see of Canterbury of Thomas Becket, who must have seemed to her the merest upstart. Yet she was prepared to act as a mediator in the quarrel between Henry and his archbishop. Maud ended her life in the habit, assumed on her deathbed, of a nun of Fontevrand. Her epitaph is said to have recorded that 'Here lies Henry's daughter, wife, mother; great by birth, greater by marriage, greatest by motherhood'. The authorship is unknown. This is the rival whom 'the mild man, soft and good' had first to face. She was a redoubtable antagonist.

4
Stephen, Henry of Blois and the Church

The decade of the 1130s began and continued with the church of Rome distraught by internal disagreements on many aspects of Christian faith, practice and policy. Powerful tensions and the working of disruptive forces in Rome resulted in open scandal when the death of pope Honorius II on 14 February 1130 was instantly followed by the schism of Anacletus. Among the most fundamental cleavages of opinion were those concerning the rights and wrongs of the possession by the church of landed resources and wealth, with its consequent involvement, and that of its clergy, in the secular relationships, cares and conflicts of this world. It was an issue that touched vital aspects of the church's position. To determine its place in the world and its function in a feudal society which was professedly Christian involved problems of the utmost importance and complexity – problems theological and ethical, intellectual problems and problems of the most practical, mundane kind, economic, legal, administrative and political problems. If the rôle of the church, by virtue of a divine mission and by means of a divine authority entrusted to it, was to unify human life in its every aspect and to mould human society in accordance with the teaching of Christianity, could it – dare it – seek to evade total involvement, even if this meant the possession of worldly wealth and authority and concern with worldly affairs? There was never a lack of churchmen to argue that from any practical point of view it would not be feasible for the church to restrain the powers of evil and fulfil its divine mission in the wicked world that resulted from the fall of man without resort to temporal means as instruments of good. Neither were there lacking saints and scholars, not usually the most orthodox and conformist, to urge that the involvement of the clergy in worldly affairs through their temporal possessions and connections and temporal authority must inevitably degrade them, bring discredit upon the church and stultify its mission. Total involvement might be achieved by other means, as St Francis was to show. This is to over-simplify almost ludicrously a fundamental and exceedingly complex issue which engaged the keenest intellects and stirred the most ardent spirits of Christendom in the Middle Ages. The history of the medieval church turns to a great extent upon it. In its medieval context this was an issue as vital as any that has confronted our own society, and as intractable.

Such an argument had its place in the well-known controversy between St Bernard and Peter the Venerable, representatives of the rising and declining powers, Cistercian and Cluniac respectively, in the western monastic world of the twelfth-century.[1] Basically, that controversy concerned the implementation of the Rule of St Benedict, to which both orders professed obedience, the Cistercians arguing with a good deal of cogency that Cluniac modifications had destroyed its efficacy. The two great abbots and the orders to which they belonged represented attitudes of mind by no means confined to monks, but which divided the whole church. Those who were not whole-heartedly for St Bernard and everything he stood for were, in his eyes, against him. Indeed his very vehemence often did make them active opponents. Whatever view be taken of the saint, it is undeniable that his uninhibited support of many a cause engendered bitter opposition, and as a result contestants received support, even in the Roman curia, which they might never have won solely on the merits of their cases. It is not to be imagined that the history of the church in England in Stephen's reign resolves itself simply into a dispute between the rival monastic empires of Cluny and Citeaux, but there are good reasons for considering the situation – in the first place from a Cluniac point of view.

Cluny was indeed vulnerable to criticism on the grounds of excessive wealth, grandeur and luxury and a way of monastic life that placed a disproportionate emphasis upon liturgical prayer; but in the 1130s Cluny was already moving in the direction of reform under the last of her remarkable succession of great abbots, Peter the Venerable. She continued, however, as she began, predisposed towards co-operation on a reciprocal basis with temporal rulers and secular magnates who were willing to support the ideals and further the interests of her order. Retrospectively Cluny can be seen as, deservedly, a waning power in the early twelfth century, but her decline was not, perhaps, quite so obvious to men of that age. At the time when Stephen became king of England, in the eyes of many Cluny's empire must still have represented a splendidly impressive and admirably conservative institution, a stabilising force in ecclesiastical and secular life in an age of change and uncertainty. Popes and prelates still sprang from the family of Cluny; devoted supporters and benefactors were to be found in the most exalted circles of the 'establishment' throughout the length and breadth of Christendom. Not least among these were king Stephen's uncle Henry I, his mother Adela, Henry's sister, who ended her days a nun in the Cluniac house of Marçigny-sur-Loire and his father-in-law, count Eustace of Boulogne, who also died in the Cluniac habit. In England during Stephen's reign, when the Cistercians and Augustinians were enjoying their most phenomenal success and expansion,[2] Cluniac influence was very far from negligible, though it is to be measured in terms of eminent Cluniac churchmen rather than in numbers of monasteries and religious. Some of the most important centres of Cluniac influence did not, in fact, belong to Cluny. Glastonbury, where Henry of Blois retained the abbacy after he became bishop of Winchester, and Gloucester, where Gilbert Foliot was abbot before he became bishop of Hereford, were both very ancient black monk houses. Henry I's splendid foundation at Reading, where Cluniac influence was very strong, was not affiliated and Faversham, described as Cluniac in Stephen's foundation charter, seems in fact to have been outside the order from the beginning.[3] Lewes Priory, the earliest of England's Cluniac houses, gave to Bath its bishop, Robert, probable author of *Gesta Stephani*, perhaps the most valuable of all the contemporary accounts of the reign. The eminent Cluniacs who have just been mentioned include the two greatest figures in the English church between Anselm and Becket (Henry of Blois and Gilbert Foliot), and these alone would have ensured that Cluny's attitude to the affairs of church and state was well represented.

Much had been gained by the Roman church during the half century which had elapsed since Gregory VII died in exile. If the righteousness he had loved had not wholly triumphed, neither had the iniquity prevailed that he had hated. The gains of the church had still to be consolidated and given full effect. In England in

5

1107, in a situation which lent itself to a compromise, Henry I, Anselm and Pascal II had recognised, however reluctantly, the need to achieve one. The king had formally abandoned the objectionable royal claim to exercise over clerics the right of investiture with the *spiritualia*, though the *temporalia* remained under effective royal control. Nominally, at least, freedom of election had been accorded to the church, so that it might hope to determine and control the personnel of its own hierarchy. Episcopal and abbatial election was compromised by the immense influence which the king could bring to bear to ensure compliance with his wishes. It is not always remembered that, besides the king, many other individuals and bodies, both lay and ecclesiastical, also interfered with the freedom of the church in countless ways, not necessarily out of malice, or even actively. In some cases their very existence constituted a potent influence, as in the case of the Cistercians in some regions, with St Bernard behind them. The personnel of capitular bodies was very mixed and likely to represent a variety of interests. Chapters were not always distinguished by a sense of solidarity or unanimity of purpose and action. When they were, this was as likely as not to take the form of opposition to their bishop. Minorities did not willingly give way to majorities, for the spirit of democracy was not abroad in Christendom in the twelfth century. There can have been few members of any chapter, monastic or otherwise, who were wholly uninfluenced by extraneous considerations of some kind, family connections, patronage or other interests both individual and collective. Freedom of ecclesiastical election, it should be remembered, could be jeopardised by the children of light no less than by the sons of Belial, by St Bernard or the papal legate just as much as by king or feudal dynast. Freedom from royal control was not likely, in practice, to simplify ecclesiastical elections; its absence was more likely to give increased scope to conflicting interests and crosscurrents within the chapters and to other kinds of external influence, even to physical violence, as before the elevation of Henry Murdac to the see of York. The cure might prove worse than the disease if royal control were not promptly and effectively replaced by that of higher ecclesiastical authority. This constituted a very vital problem for which a practicable solution needed to be found in England as in every part of Christendom. The supplanting of Henry I's authority over the church during his lifetime was not a practicable solution; but how would his successor react?

Not only ecclesiastical elections and control of temporalities were concerned, but other things no less vital to the church. Henry I had conceded in his coronation charter of liberties that the English church should be free (*sanctam Dei ecclesiam liberam facio*). Only a born passive resister like St Anselm could successfully insist upon his duty of obedience to the pope, and even he had to suffer exile for the maintenance of this fundamental ecclesiastical liberty. Again, although the Conqueror, in an impressive gesture, had separated the spiritual courts from the temporal, the line of demarcation had not been effectively drawn and jurisdiction continued to be exercised in secular courts in a great many cases over which the church would have liked to cast its mantle. In particular, the jurisdiction of the Roman curia was very much limited in English cases. Ever since the days of the Conqueror the English crown had claimed control over the country's recognition of the pope, the admission of papal legates and letters and the business of ecclesiastical synods. All in all, the situation of the church in England prior to the death of Henry I still left a great deal to be desired and a wide field of endeavour for Gregorian churchmen as well as for reformers of the new school.

A crisis in the affairs of the Anglo-Norman royal house was long expected but, in the actual course of events, a crisis supervened in the affairs of the Holy See. On 15 February 1130, the day after the death of Honorius II, a formal election was made by a majority of the cardinals. The man chosen as the successor of St Peter was a former Cluniac monk, cardinal Peter Pierleone, who assumed the papal name of Anacletus II. He was the grandson of a Jew who had been the financial adviser of pope Leo IX. This man had made a vast fortune, turned Christian and taken the name Pierleone in honour of his papal patron. His family, by virtue of its enormous wealth and its influence at the papal court, came to play an important part in Roman politics, arousing the bitter enmity of members of the Roman nobility, such as the Corsi and the Frangipani. There is little doubt that Peter Pierleone owed his election to the judicious application of his wealth and influence, that is to say that he was a very prince of simoniacs. His election therefore caused a scandal of the first magnitude and a protesting minority of sixteen cardinals was impelled to offer the papacy, on the same day on which Anacletus was elected, to Gregory, cardinal deacon of St Angelo, who took the name of Innocent II. Unable to maintain his position in Rome against his rival, Innocent retreated to Genoa and thence to Provence, Burgundy and France. Here, then, was a schism of the old, deplorable kind, which had occurred so often before the synod of Sutri in 1046. It began as a Roman affair, not as the outcome of conflict with the emperor and the setting up of an imperially-sponsored anti-pope. Both claimants to the chair of St Peter sought anxiously for allies. Anacletus won the militarily powerful, and for the moment decisive, support of the Normans of Sicily. Innocent II had behind him the tremendous, though sometimes embarrassing, spiritual support of St Bernard. This engendered, almost automatically, a not inconsiderable body of opposition in the church, but it counted for much in gaining for Innocent the adherence of France. England, Aragon and Castile were won to his side and Norbert of Xanten, the austere founder of the Premonstratensians, helped to secure the support of the emperor Lothair II. With imperial support Innocent returned briefly to Rome, but without the continued imperial presence he was unable to remain there, nor did he recover the imperial city till 1136, when Lothair returned with an army. Such was the situation of the papacy during the critical five years that preceded the death of Henry I. Stephen and his brother Henry must have followed its development with the closest attention, especially if, as I believe, they were already thinking of taking action in England and Normandy as soon as their uncle should die.

Henry of Blois was the fourth son of Stephen, count of Blois and Chartres, the Crusader, and of Adela, the Conqueror's daughter. His mother was, as became her birth, a woman of great capability and force of character, and Henry seems to have inherited some of her qualities. Adela was a firm churchwoman, who took the veil in later life. She was the friend of such distinguished figures as Ivo, bishop of Chartres, the great canonist, and Peter the Venerable. It is believed that she exercised some influence in bringing about the concordat between her brother, Henry I, and the papacy in 1107. It seems probable that her youngest son Henry was destined from an early age to be devoted to religion, and with the teaching of such a mother the boy may even have felt a genuine monastic vocation, though he may soon have lost it. He was sent to be brought up at Cluny, a worthy family for the fostering of a prince, and he remained deeply devoted to it throughout his life, becoming one of its most munificent benefactors. There, too, he formed a close friendship with his mother's friend, Peter the Venerable, which was marred only by one period of misunderstanding. Peter had a deep affection for the sons of his house, and even the most starkly literal translation cannot disguise this in many of his letters. Writing to Henry on behalf of Marçigny, where Adela had retired, he addressed the letter 'To our bishop of Winchester, brother Peter, his abbot of the Cluniacs, salvation and all the affection of his heart'. Henry of Blois was first and foremost a great Cluniac, nurtured in the traditions of that family and educated as one of the *corps d'élite* of young administrators whom the great abbots of Cluny were so adept at picking out and training. It was no accident that so many notable ecclesiastical administrators in all parts of Christendom were drawn from Cluny. It would be interesting to speculate upon what the history of England might have been had Henry of Blois been a son of Clairvaux instead of Cluny. Secondly, and hardly less important than his churchmanship, was Henry's descent. He was a grandson of William the Conqueror and, through his mother he must have inherited his generous portion of the masterfulness, determination and ability of his grandfather, qualities which were so lacking in the character of his elder brother, Stephen. Perhaps, too, he inherited qualities of vigour and shrewdness from his great-grandmother, Herleva.

Henry of Blois possessed outstanding talents as an administrator combined with a remarkable aptitude for finance and a capacity for dealing with landed property and the claims of greedy neighbours which would have done credit to the very greatest of secular magnates, or to the crown had he worn it instead of his brother. These gifts enabled him to restore the fortunes both of Glastonbury and of Cluny and to maintain the vast wealth that he enjoyed from his abbacy and his see. As a statesmen Henry was less impressive for he was perhaps too much of an opportunist, and as poor a judge of men as of political situations; too forthright, even naïve, in his approach; unable to recognise the limits of what was possible and unwilling ever to abandon his

purpose in the face of discouragement and rebuffs. He was believed capable of going to any lengths to achieve his ends and
thought to be devoid of scruples; hence the uncharitable suggestion of the Cistercian Eugenius III that, like the devil, he had
'trailed his tail through the English sea'. The grandson of the
Conqueror could hardly fail to possess some of the instincts of a
soldier. Henry was a builder of castles in his see on as great a
scale as Roger, bishop of Salisbury, and his nephews. Henry of
Huntingdon denounced him as 'that new kind of monster, com-
pounded of the sound and the corrupt, monk and knight in
one',[4] for the bishop was quite ready on occasion to take up
knightly arms in place of the episcopal staff. He even became
involved, whether or not he was immediately responsible for it,
in the burning of houses and monasteries in his own episcopal
city in the fighting there in 1141. There was an edge, a taunt, in
the closing sentence of a very remarkable letter written to the
bishop by Brian fitz Count, c. 1142-3:

> Know, therefore, all faithful of holy church that I, Brian fitz Count,
> whom good king Henry brought up and to whom he gave arms and an
> honour, am ready to prove what I assert in this letter against Henry,
> nephew of king Henry, bishop of Winchester and legate of the apos-
> tolic see, either by ordeal of combat (*bello*) or a judicial investigation
> (*judicio*), through one clerk or one layman.[5]

The monster referred to by Henry of Huntingdon was no new
phenomenon in Stephen's reign; it is depicted, not as Siamese
twins but as obverse and reverse, on the seal of Odo, bishop of
Bayeux and earl of Kent (bishop Henry's great uncle of the half
blood on his mother's side). No strain is put on the imagination
in discerning the mitre beneath the mail coif.[6] Henry was another
kind of monster too, a most uncanonical combination of abbot
(of Glastonbury), dean (of St Martin le Grand, London) and
bishop (of Winchester).

Henry of Blois was one of the most discerning lovers of
antiquity, of art and of architecture in his age. He was a builder
on a regal scale not only of castles but of cathedral and conven-
tual buildings at Cluny and Glastonbury and at Winchester and
of 'gorgeous palaces' (*palatia sumptuosissima*), with gardens,
ornamental waters, ingenious aqueducts, statues and menageries;
a man to delight the heart of the late Sir George Sitwell—very

likely he did.[7] He was a collector and the possessor of vast wealth to indulge his tastes, for he was by far the richest of all the English prelates and few, if any, nobles could rival him. John of Salisbury wrote maliciously of him buying 'old statues' in Rome (possibly some of the precious things he gave to Winchester cathedral), and quoted a satire of Horace where 'buying old statues sent Damasippus mad', and play is made with his need of a barber. For John such collector's pieces were silly heathen idols, and the venerable–looking buyer, whose cultivated taste probably owed a good deal to Cluny and perhaps something to Chartres, was a figure of fun, deluded, swindled and mean withal.[8] Henry certainly was not mean in any ordinary sense of the word, though it is quite possible that he disliked greasing notoriously itching palms in the papal curia. In a broader sense, he was a man of generous temperament, urbane and devoid of any real malice, so that his struggles with such opponents as Theobald, archbishop of Canterbury, seem to have been conducted with vigour but without personal rancour. There is no doubt that Henry of Blois was a man of outstanding ability and certain qualities of greatness which made him one of the most distinguished personages in the Anglo-Norman lands and if not the peer in Christendom of such as St Bernard, at least an actor not unworthy to appear on the same stage. There can be no doubt that he saw himself in a star part.

Henry came to England in 1126 as a young man of less than thirty and was given the abbacy of Glastonbury, recently vacant by the elevation of abbot Seffrid Pelochin to the see of Chichester. He was an absentee from his abbey during most of the forty-five years that he held it but, nonetheless, he achieved most impressive material restorations there and it seems that he arranged for the imposition of some disciplinary reforms on Cluniac lines.[9] After the death of William Giffard in January 1129 and a ten months' vacancy, Henry was given the rich see of Winchester, with which he continued to hold the abbacy of Glastonbury until his death in 1171.[10] Perhaps it is not without significance that the city of Winchester was also the home of the royal treasury and that Henry, with his marked financial and administrative flair, had an opportunity there of getting to know the chamberlains of the treasury and other royal officials who were concerned with financial and judicial business in the exchequer. They would have found him a fascinating and persuasive acquaintance. It is clear that by the time when Stephen made his bid for the throne in December 1135 Henry was pretty closely in touch with those who mattered most including such important officials as Roger, bishop of Salisbury, chief justiciar, and William Pontdelarche, chamberlain in charge of the treasury. As a Cluniac, a member of the English episcopal bench, a favoured nephew of Henry I and a son of the house of Blois, he had influential and wide-ranging contacts throughout western Christendom. He was likely to have been well-informed, and if it were a matter of pulling strings Henry was in a position to pull with the best.

As he surveyed his world in the early 1130s, certain considerations doubtless presented themselves with great clarity in Henry's mind. First and foremost he was a churchman and a reformer on Cluniac and Gregorian lines. He would certainly have hoped for the full implementation in England of the concordat of 1107 and for still further extension of the liberties and the authority of the church beyond what had then been conceded. Both as a Cluniac and as a member of the royal family circle, he would have hoped to achieve these aims, with the active assistance of the crown, or at least without arousing its fears or strenuous opposition. England offered great possibilities for a churchman of Henry's calibre and position. He might very reasonably hope for the see of Canterbury in the not too distant future and it would not be surprising if he even dreamed of the chair of St Peter. As far as the papal schism was concerned, he probably appreciated at an early stage that the future was more likely to lie with Innocent than with Anacletus. Innocent must strive for an early end to the damaging schism and in the situation in which he found himself he must be prepared to make some concessions to actual and potential supporters. His agreement with the emperor Lothair II in 1133 must have interested Henry a great deal. Innocent agreed that the German prelates should receive their regalian rights only from the emperor. Lothair, on his side, agreed to receive the fiefs of the countess Matilda of Tuscany (that bone of stubborn contention with the papacy) at the hands of Innocent, on the understanding that they should pass on Lothair's death to his son-in-law, Henry of Bavaria. These agreements pointed to interesting possibilities of an accommodation with pope Innocent in which political and dynastic adjustment might be linked with concessions of liberties to the church. Dom David Knowles has rightly stressed the view that, as a Cluniac who 'held the full Gregorian conception of church government', Henry was prepared to bargain.[11] In this as in other respects, he differed from the party of reform which St Bernard represented, in whose eyes he was 'that old seducer of Winchester' (*seductor ille vetus Wintoniensis*).

On the secular side, Henry must have been as acutely aware as anyone could be of the intense dislike of the Anglo-Norman baronage for the dynastic arrangements of Henry I and the imminent prospect if they were carried out of having Maud on the throne with an alien Angevin husband to share it. Henry himself, as a grandson of the Conqueror, was probably not immune, churchman though he was, from the stirrings of dynastic ambition for his own branch of the family. We know that with him family feeling went very deep. In at least half a dozen episcopal and several abbatial elections he used all his influence on behalf of his relatives or protégés.[12] William of Malmesbury tells us of his dispute with the empress in 1141, which he describes as the origin of all the evils that followed in England:

These counties (Boulogne and Mortain) the legate had intended to give to his nephew, Eustace, whom I have mentioned, as his of right while his father was held in captivity; the empress flatly refusing, whether or not she had actually promised them to others. He, offended by this affront, stayed away from her court for many days and, though he was often invited back, he persisted in refusing. Meanwhile he had a personal interview with the queen, his brother's wife, at Guildford . . .[13]

It was clear to an observer as perceptive as William of Malmesbury that this episode as much as the reactionary arrogance of the empress in the affairs of the church led bishop Henry to abandon her cause.

In the years immediately preceding the death of his uncle the king, it may well have seemed to Henry that he could fill the rôle of *deus ex machina* for church, state and family. The danger of Maud's succession, with all that it was likely to entail, might be averted if the crown could pass to a grandson of the Conqueror on the female side. After all, no inflexible rule of succession had been observed since the day when Edward the Confessor was alive and dead, and there were a good many objections to female succession. The church's consecration of the king was, in a churchman's eyes, more important than any other consideration, and a dynastic adjustment might be made with the approval of the church, in return for such concessions as reformers had long and earnestly desired. There was a fitting candidate for the throne in the person of Henry's elder brother, Stephen, a weaker and less able man than himself but, it might be hoped, manageable. Stephen was of the royal blood; he had been brought up as a highly favoured nephew at the court of Henry I, where he ought to have learned valuable lessons in the arts of kingship; he possessed wide lands and resources and he had shown admirable piety and generosity in his benefactions; he was skilled in the knightly arts and he was an amiable and widely popular prince. Here, surely, was an ideal alternative to Maud. Henry would expect, as part of the bargain for winning the church to Stephen's side, supreme control over ecclesiastical affairs in England, so that Gregorian reforms might be achieved and fully implemented there. The design would involve nothing less than the establishment of a new monarchy for the house of Blois. It would be based upon an intimate relationship with the church – a church reorganised and strengthened in England by the administrative genius of Henry himself. The realm should present a model of harmonious co-operation between the two swords, and a power should be established in western Christendom strong against schism and clerical abuses and against the enemies of the papacy. It was a prospect to entrance one whose motives, tainted though they might be by worldly considerations and dynastic ambition, were not wholly unworthy of a son of Cluny or of a descendant of the Norman rulers.

Such a design would have to be initiated in England rather than in Normandy, for Henry was best placed in England to influence in Stephen's interest many of the people who mattered most. In the sequel Normandy fell into line when Stephen won England. If the hypothesis which has been advanced bears any relation to reality, the measure of Henry's success is to be seen in the speed and relative smoothness with which Stephen's coup was carried through in December 1135. Not every danger had been foreseen, for in such movements a certain amount has to be played by ear, but all the more serious of the immediate difficulties had, it would seem, been anticipated and provided for. It is difficult otherwise to account for the swift and unimpeded sequence of events during the first three weeks of December 1135.

All that has been said here about the designs of Henry of Blois and his brother Stephen is, it must be emphasised, reasonable supposition at best and not established historical fact. We come to indisputable facts in the Oxford charter of liberties of early April 1136, in which are set down in detail the terms upon which Stephen's succession was secured.[14] The implementation of this charter was personally guaranteed by bishop Henry ('I made myself the guarantor between him and God that he would honour and exalt holy church and that he would maintain good laws and abrogate bad ones').[15] The terms are worth setting out in full so that the extent of Stephen's concessions to the church, which has often been exaggerated and accordingly denounced, may be correctly appreciated.

I, Stephen, by God's grace elected king of the English by the assent of the clergy and people and consecrated by William, archbishop of Canterbury and legate of the holy Roman church, and subsequently confirmed by Innocent, pontiff of the holy Roman see, concede out of respect and love of God that holy church be free and I confirm the reverence due to it. I promise that I will not do nor permit anything simoniacal in the church or in ecclesiastical affairs. I grant and confirm that jurisdiction and authority over the persons of ecclesiastics and all clerks and their property and the distribution of the goods of ecclesiastics are to be in the hands of the bishops. I decree and concede that the dignities of ecclesiastics, their confirmed privileges and the customs they have by right of ancient possession remain inviolate.

I concede that all the possessions and tenures of churches which they had on the day when William, king of the English, my grandfather, was alive and dead, be theirs quit, absolved and free from recovery by any claimant.

If a church have lost, by whatever means, anything that it had or possessed before the death of the said king, let it seek indulgence, and I reserve to myself the decision whether to restore it or take it away.

I confirm also whatever they have accumulated since the death of the said king by the liberality of kings, the largesse of princes or oblation, provision or transfer of whatever kind by the faithful.

I promise that I will give and preserve for them peace and justice in all things.

I reserve for myself the forests which king William, my grandfather, and the second William, my uncle, created and held. All the others which king Henry added, I restore and concede quit to the churches and to the kingdom.

While sees are vacant of their own pastor, they and all their possessions shall be committed to the hands and custody of the clergy or of worthy men of the church until a pastor be canonically appointed.

I abolish all exactions and injustices and miskennings evilly introduced, whether by sheriffs or by other persons. I will observe and I command and decree to be observed the good laws and ancient and just customs in murders, pleas and other causes.

All these I truly grant and confirm, saving my regal and just dignity.

Witnesses: William, archbishop of Canterbury, and Hugh, archbishop of Rouen, and Henry, bishop of Winchester, and Roger, bishop of Salisbury, and Alexander, bishop of Lincoln, and Nigel, bishop of Ely, and Everard, bishop of Norwich, and Simon, bishop of Worcester, and Bernard, bishop of St David's, and Auden, bishop of Évreux, and Richard, bishop of Avranches, and Robert, bishop of Hereford, and John, bishop of Rochester, and Adelulf, bishop of Carlisle, and Roger the chancellor, and Henry (de Sully) the king's nephew, and Robert, earl of Gloucester, and William, earl of Warenne, and Rannulf, earl of Chester, and Roger, earl of Warwick, and Robert de Ver and Miles of Gloucester and Robert d'Oilly and Brian fitz Count, constables; William Martel, Hugh Bigod and Humphrey de Bohun and Simon de Beauchamp, stewards; and William d'Aubigny and Eudes Martel, butlers; and Robert de Ferrers and William Peverel and Simon of Senlis and William d'Aubigny (*Brito*), and Payn fitz John and Hamo de St Clare and Ilbert de Lacy. At Oxford in the year of the Lord's incarnation MCXXXVI and the first of my reign.

The long list of witnesses shows the composition of the king's court on a great state occasion, or the more important personages who were present, and it indicates the support that Stephen appeared to have won.

The superscription of the charter, the terms in which Stephen's title to the throne are set out, is unexampled in England. It concedes to the church an influence which had not hitherto been recognised in England; but, whatever the implications might be, it blazons forth the fact, vitally important for Stephen, that he had been properly consecrated and crowned by the archbishop of Canterbury, whose right it was to perform this ceremony, and that he had been recognised by pope Innocent II. Innocent was now making some headway against his rival. Stephen or rather, it may be supposed, Henry, had backed the right horse.

Thus Stephen's rival, the empress, countess of Anjou, was placed at a disadvantage from which it would be very difficult for her ever to recover. A king consecrated and recognised as Stephen had been was not easily to be ousted. Such a guarantee must, from Stephen's point of view, have been worth many concessions.

The concessions which this charter made were important for the church and two of them, perhaps, were of outstanding significance. Jurisdiction and authority over clergy and their property was to be in the hands of the bishops. This was rather more explicit than the decree of the Conqueror which separated ecclesiastical from secular jurisdiction, and it undoubtedly strengthened the claim of the church to the benefit of clergy which so exacerbated the relations of Stephen's successor with Becket. Nonetheless, the concession was vague and ill-defined. It will be seen in a subsequent chapter relating to law and the administration of justice that a variety of cases concerning clergy came before the *curia regis* in Stephen's reign, and in a number of cases, such as that of the abbot of Abingdon in Stephen's last year, ecclesiastical authority was still powerless in the face of a royal writ relating to the tenure of lands belonging to the *temporalia*. It is, in fact, difficult to say precisely what this clause of the charter involved in practice. It probably depended upon what the crown on the one side or the church on the other could get away with in any particular case. The second significant grant, perhaps the most important single concession, is that relating to the guardianship of temporalities by clerics or by other lawful men of the church during vacancies. The intention was that the crown should no longer be able to abuse its control over *temporalia* in such circumstances as Rufus and Henry I had abused it for their own profit, but the right of the crown to designate guardians from among those eligible and to determine when the *temporalia* should be handed over to the elect does not seem to have been affected. Bishop Henry's idea undoubtedly was that he personally should exercise a guiding influence in such matters, and he did administer the see of Salisbury during the vacancy that followed the death of bishop Roger in December 1139, that of London between 1138 and 1141, and Canterbury after the death of William of Corbeil. It may be doubted whether this personal arrangement provided an entirely satisfactory remedy for what had long been a major grievance of the English church.

Henry, as 'the guarantor between Stephen and God', was bound to find himself sooner or later in an exceedingly uncomfortable situation.

The warranty by the crown of church possessions as they were before William I's death and the recognition of clerical control over the distribution of the goods of deceased clerks were concessions to which little objection could be raised. Stephen, however, retained his right to decide about any property that the church had lost since William I's death. The disafforestation of lands afforested since the time of the Conqueror, even though it was bound to cost the crown something in revenue, was well justified by the goodwill it might be expected to create. Churches and abbeys as well as laymen had suffered very considerable loss of amenity through the afforestations of Rufus and Henry I. Even thus early in the twelfth century there can be little doubt that the royal forests, with their oppressive legal and administrative arrangements, were run as much for the king's financial advantage as for his recreation. Other clauses concerning the maintenance of good laws, the doing of justice and the suppression of exactions and wrongs, probably amounted to no more than a reiteration of the coronation oath, though the explicit abolition of *miskenning* does mark a forward step in the evolution of legal procedure. Simony is renounced, but no explicit mention is made of ecclesiastical elections, or of investiture, except in the vaguest terms, or of the jurisdiction of the Roman curia, or indeed of anything that was widely recognised as embarassing for the crown. Benefit of clergy was not yet a burning issue. All would be well it was hoped, for these matters would be dealt with by the king's brother, the bishop of Winchester. It was an intensely personal arrangement in which everything really depended upon the ability of bishop Henry to handle each situation as it arose in a way agreeable both to the king and to the church. Altogether, provided that things went according to plan, Stephen was not paying an excessive price for the crown.

Ideally, Henry should in due course have been elevated to the see of Canterbury, and the brothers should have worked in close harmony in the best interests of church and state. All did not go well, and it is difficult to say precisely when and why things went wrong, but it would probably not be misleading to say that the ink was hardly dry on the numerous copies of the Oxford charter of liberties which must have been issued, before the honeymoon period was over. The coolness that has already been noted between Henry and Peter the Venerable was paralleled by a coolness between him and his royal brother. Stephen's most fatal weakness, a defect of his outstanding quality of amiability, lay in his susceptibility to persuasion. Already, by the time of the siege of Exeter castle in the hot summer of 1136, Henry was finding it difficult to manage his brother, though in a secular matter. He failed to prevent him from giving way to the persuasions of the earl of Gloucester and certain barons whose private interests would not have been served by the unconditional surrender of the Exeter garrison.[16] This was ominous. Then the see of Canterbury fell vacant by the death of William of Corbeil on 21 November 1136. Its administration was placed in Henry's hands, but there was no indecent haste in having him elected to fill the vacancy. On the contrary, a vacancy of over two years ensued. This, too, was ominous. There can be little doubt that Henry confidently expected to become archbishop of Canterbury; indeed Orderic Vitalis actually asserts that he was elected.[17] Bitter disappointment awaited him, for behind his back the electors, in the presence of the king and the legate, chose the undistinguished Theobald of Bec to fill the chair of St Augustine. Henry's subsequent appointment by Innocent II as his legate merely added a new complication to the situation in England. It seems probable that, even as early as 1136, Stephen had begun to place his confidence in count Waleran of Meulan and his brother Robert, earl of Leicester, first in Normandy and soon in England.[18] Stephen's growing reliance on the advice and support of the Beaumonts must have caused Henry many misgivings, since it seriously diminished his control of the situation. Also it may well be that the royal favour shown to the Beaumonts and the weakening of Henry's position, which resulted from the king's unreliability, shook the confidence of some of the leaders of the old royal administrative service, clerical and lay – of Roger, bishop of Salisbury and his family, of William Pontdelarche, the chamberlain of the treasury, of Miles of Gloucester, the constable, and of John, the marshal.

The events of 22 June 1139 at Oxford came as the culmination of a period of growing tension and insecurity. They shattered the old intimate relationship between the king and his brother so that things could never be quite the same again. For Henry it must have been the ultimate disillusionment, far worse than that which he later suffered at the hands of the empress, when he was merely struggling to make the best of a bad situation. The brother whose good conduct he had solemnly guaranteed before the whole church, had, by turning to rend four of its ministers, placed him in an impossible position. Stephen had wantonly destroyed the foundation upon which Henry had built the new kingship. Ironically, the men whom Stephen sought to destroy in June 1139 were key men, whose adherence to his cause had ensured his control of the administration; men whom Henry had in all probability taken endless pains to win over long before December 1135. This was the moment of high tragedy in Henry's career, when his dream was trodden under the feet of the feudal militants in Oxford in June.

Henry had no other course open to him in the circumstances than to take almost the strongest measure in his power against his brother – a hard decision. If the situation were to be retrieved Stephen must be brought under control. The bishop therefore produced his legatine commission, which he had refrained from making public since receiving it in March, thereby creating an excellent impression of restraint.[19] A legatine council was held at Winchester in August, to which Stephen was cited. The legate once again emphasised the vital part played by the church in Stephen's elevation to the throne and the duty of submission and atonement which he owed. Throughout the proceedings Henry seems to have acted with firmness, moderation and dignity. There was, however, no submission by the king, who, fortified it would seem by the support of archbishop Hugh of Rouen (a Cluniac), was firmly convinced of the rightness of his action. There was no settlement and no formal reconciliation. When the bishops prostrated themselves before him, begging him to submit formally to the censure of the church, Stephen rose respectfully, but showed no sign of putting his chartered promises into effect.[20] At this point of time Henry, if he had really had the heart to bring his brother to heel, should have ignored all dangers and threats and brought the strongest ecclesiastical sanctions to bear upon him. It is highly probable that family and personal feeling held him back from inflicting the ultimate humiliation upon Stephen; perhaps, too, hope of retrieving something of his grand design from the débâcle restrained him. A powerful pope might have taken a strong line, but Innocent II was not so free from embarrassments that he could afford to do so. It is true that Anacletus was dead and that his successor, Victor IV, had been but briefly schismatical. The Second Lateran Council of April 1139 had officially marked the end of the schism, but in the hard world of secular politics Roger of Sicily, the old ally of Anacletus, had still to be dealt with. When Innocent marched against him, he suffered a humiliating defeat and was obliged to concede to Roger everything that Anacletus had accorded him in return for Norman support. Innocent was striving manfully to cope with the difficulties that beset him, but even the now undisputed successor of St Peter was in no position to crow over a perjured monarch of the Norman stock.

It is doubtful whether the relationship between Stephen and Henry can ever have been fully restored on a basis of mutual trust. Things simmered down but slowly. Henry took over the custody of the see of Salisbury after the death of the broken Roger on 11 December 1139. He found himself, however, under the necessity of using his legatine influence against the election to the vacant see of Stephen's candidate, his chancellor Philip de Harcourt. Philip was a dependent of the Beaumonts whom Henry had every reason to distrust and to thwart when he could. By the time that the see of York fell vacant early in 1140, Stephen and Henry were in sufficiently close harmony to work for the promotion to the northern metropolitan see of their own nephews, first Henry de Sully and then William fitz Herbert. The handling of this protracted affair did nothing to enhance Henry's reputation, but ultimately involved him in dealings which bore the taint of simony and grave suspicion of the misuse of his legatine powers. Worse than all, it earned him the undying hostility of St Bernard.

For Henry the capture of Stephen at the battle of Lincoln must have come as an unpleasant shock, disastrously upsetting his designs at a time when Stephen seems to have been working fairly harmoniously with him once more in church affairs. Henry does not appear in a very creditable light in the events which immediately ensued. He found himself in a deeply embarassing position. This was perceived by the author of *Gesta Stephani* (probably his fellow Cluniac, Robert, bishop of Bath).[21] The excuses this writer offers are, first, that Henry was caught completely unawares, not having adequately munitioned and garrisoned his castles, so that he was in no position to resist; second, that Henry decided to make a temporary agreement with the king's enemies, hoping to assist his brother if more favourable circumstances should develop, as indeed they did. William of Malmesbury, a writer with much less sympathy for 'that idol of Winchester' (as St Bernard was to call him), and an eyewitness of the events, gives an account of the council of Winchester which does not conceal the more disingenuous parts of the legate's arguments or the embarrassment he suffered. Speaking of Stephen's election, Henry is made to say:

And so, because it appeared tedious to wait for the lady, who was taking her time about coming to England (*Moras . . . nectebat*), for she was living in Normandy, provision was made for the peace of the country and my brother was permitted to reign.[22]

A gloss so transparent cannot have been seriously intended to deceive. Henry passed on quickly to denounce, we may believe with genuine grief and indignation, the deplorable failure of his brother to keep the terms enshrined in the Oxford charter of liberties, which the bishop had personally guaranteed. William of Malmesbury makes the most of the scene in which a clerk arrives with a letter from the queen, which he hands to the legate, who reads it in silence and then bawls out (*uoce quantum potuit exaltata dixit*) that it is not lawful (*legitimam*) and ought not to be read out in such an assembly. 'While he was shuffling thus,' (*ita illo tricante*), the clerk did not fail in his mission, but with admirable assurance (*preclara fiducia*) read it out.[23] William of Malmesbury is obviously describing, not without a grain of malice, the conduct of a prelate who was profoundly embarrassed and shamed by the part he felt obliged to play, and who was hating every moment of his schizophrenic ordeal. Henry, it must be said, never lost sight of the all-important consideration, the interests of the church as he saw them. At his first meeting with the empress on the third Sunday of Lent, a day of ominously weeping skies, he obtained from her on oath an assurance that 'all the most important matters in England, in particular the bestowal of bishoprics and abbacies, should be under his control'.[24] This was desired by Henry, we may reasonably believe, not simply to exalt his personal authority, but because it was the best guarantee he could devise that the choice of the personnel of the ecclesiastical hierarchy in England should be made by the power spiritual rather than by the crown. Henry spoke with genuine conviction when he said that 'any right-thinking person must realise that while I ought to love any mortal brother, I must give infinitely greater weight to the cause of my immortal Father'.[25] At the council of Winchester everything was done to emphasise the decisive importance of the church. It was not the acclamation of the baronage of England that raised Maud to the position of lady of England, but the choice of the higher clergy, the bishops, abbots and archdeacons.[26]

All this was a desperate effort on the part of bishop Henry to make his original design viable in the new circumstances which had resulted from the capture and imprisonment of Stephen. It needs no hindsight to realise that it could not work; this was quite clear to contemporaries. The image of the all-powerful papal legate had been irreparably damaged. Henry's heroic efforts in the fighting at Winchester in the summer of 1141 certainly helped to vindicate him as a prince of the house of Blois, but as the dominating force in the English church he was no longer quite convincing after two changes of side in so short a time. The rest of his career in Stephen's reign, though by no means insignificant, for he was a man of wide-ranging influence, was 'bound in shallows and in miseries'. As soon as the news of Innocent II's death on 24 September 1143 reached England, Henry's legatine commission lapsed, never to be renewed. The man who had entertained so grand a design was reduced to striving unsuccessfully for the creation of a metropolitan see of Winchester, which should relieve him of the very disagreeable necessity of submitting to the superior ecclesiastical authority of Theobald, archbishop of Canterbury, Perhaps the drastic curtailment of Henry's authority eased his relationship with his brother and made him a less overbearing ally. His knowledge of the ecclesiastical world and his still extensive personal influence were placed at Stephen's service, especially in striving to promote the dynastic interests of the house of Blois. For such a man relegation to the second division must have been very hard to bear and it is not surprising that he sought solace in collecting 'old statues', in building and in laying out his gardens.

The career of bishop Henry during Stephen's reign cannot however be dismissed as ineffectually anti-climactic. As a result of his design for promoting Stephen's candidature for the English throne, the church achieved a recognition of its authority in the very highest affairs of state that was unparalleled in English history until king John made his surrender to Innocent III. Concessions were made to the church which had been sought in vain since the days of Gregory VII; and Henry, by the use of his influence and especially of his legatine authority, gave a great extension both to papal jurisdiction and to the independence and authority of ecclesiastical councils in England. This was not destined to be easily and peacefully maintained, but the church was given an opportunity in England which it would not otherwise have had. This, in its way – a very practical Gregorian and Cluniac way – was as effective as anything that St Bernard and the spreading Cistercians were able to achieve in the full flush of their vigour. The ultimate aim was the same, but the means were utterly different. Probably neither archbishop Theobald nor Eugenius III would have been able to act with as much firmness as they ultimately did in England, had not Henry of Blois prepared the way which he himself was unable to tread.

A detailed history of the church in England in all its aspects is outside the scope of this book. This does not mean that other persons and other aspects are unimportant. Much has been written, most outstandingly by Professor Knowles, about the great monastic revival.[27] The undistinguished but staunch Theobald, archbishop of Canterbury, is worthy of study for reasons which have been made clear by Professor Saltman.[28] Gilbert Foliot, if his influence was still somewhat local in Stephen's reign, has left us in his letters one of the most valuable of all the sources for the history of the period. Perhaps the most interesting problem that still remains to be discussed concerns the English episcopate as a whole. Why were the bishops still so ready to give their allegiance to the crown (even Foliot) and so very unwilling to support any firm archiepiscopal or papal line in opposition to the king? This requires a study in depth and detail which cannot be undertaken here.

5
The Aristocracy

When a royal charter was addressed for the realm as a whole those who were included were the archbishops, bishops, abbots, earls, justices, sheriffs, barons, officials (*ministri*) and all the king's faithful men (*fideles*), French and English. Here is one ready-made definition of the aristocracy of office and of birth. The higher clergy may be regarded as a separate class, as indeed they were, but it is important to remember that, being great landholders in respect of their temporalities, they had much in common with the lay aristocracy. Also many of them were sons of baronial, comital or even princely families, who thoroughly understood and in some important respects even shared the outlook of their lay kinsmen, which is not to say that they habitually condoned their sins and faults. The secular connections and sympathies of many churchmen, the religious feelings of many laymen and their relations with one another were in the long run probably of far greater significance in medieval society than the inflexibility of some churchmen, the violence of some laymen and the sharp practices of both. We have all too many examples of the latter in monastic chronicles, for often monks were still worldly enough to rub their hands over a smart piece of business on their own part and to resent the same on the part of others when they suffered by it. Some of the best illustrations of feudal customs and relationships, as of the organisation of manorial estates, have been found in ecclesiastical records, often simply because these have better survived the vicissitudes of time and change than those of secular lordships. All this is perhaps just to say that the church was part of the 'establishment'; but it was more than that. In studying the aristocratic, as with any other element in mid-twelfth-century society, it is essential to keep in one's mind the pervasive influence of the church not only as part of the 'establishment' but also as something apart from, above and even in a sense alien to the 'establishment'. It is not a simple, uncomplicated relationship explicable in the facile generalisations by which the history of the English church in Stephen's reign has suffered much distortion. Where the aristocracy are concerned, the intervention of a cleric in, for example, the matter of a ransom or a marriage within the wide prohibited degrees, or a man's taking the monastic habit, a church endowed or despoiled, a word spoken in haste about a 'low-born clerk', an excommunication – all these could affect a dynasty – royal or baronial – and profoundly influence a country's history.

It has been fashionable in recent years to deny that the Norman conquest of England was a revolutionary event. In various respects a strong case can be made for such a view, but in one at least there can be no doubt of its revolutionary nature. It established on the soil of England a foreign military aristocracy which brought with it a wide range of personal, family and tenurial relationships which had developed in Normandy, Brittany and Flanders. The transference of these to English soil brought profound changes for all concerned, conquerors and conquered alike. The class of thegns which, whether or not it be deemed feudal, had filled so important a rôle in Old English society had, within a short space of time after 1066, disintegrated and ceased to have any significance as a class. Individuals of thegnly descent did survive the cataclysm and even found a niche, usually a relatively humble one, in the new Anglo-Norman feudal society, but neither their Englishry (unless they were murdered) nor their thegnishness was of very much consequence. The family of Multon, whose representative in Stephen's reign was Lambert de Multon, affords an example of a feudal family of sub-tenant status descended from English thegns.[1] Among the conquerors themselves the utmost importance attaches both to their growingly complex feudal relationships and to their family connections and marriage alliances. I refer to these, for the sake of convenience, as 'feudo-dynastic' relations.[2]

In twelfth-century England towns were growing in numbers, size and importance, yet, if we are to believe some contemporary monastic chronicles, a contempt and even a hatred of the burgess class was shared by churchmen and lay aristocracy. The burgesses did indeed suffer horribly when towns were sacked, but they were

The distribution of power in the Midlands and the West, 1139–41.

not by any means a repressed class. It is customary to refer to the wealthiest and most important burgesses, if one refers to them at all in such terms, as a patriciate rather than an aristocracy. Some burgesses achieved a different status by reason of feudal tenures or other circumstances. At some date between 1139 and 1154 Gervase of Cornhill, a wealthy and important burgess, sometime justice and sheriff of London, acquired land in Berkesdon in Aspenden (Herts.) to be held for half a knight's service rendered annually in money.[3] From several points of view this is an interesting arrangement. The subsuming in this way of burgesses in the feudal hierarchy, not merely collectively, as in many continental communes, but as individuals, is very significant. The relations of burgesses with feudal aristocracies in different regions and differing circumstances and the whole question of intermarriage and the participation of feudal aristocrats in urban affairs still need closer investigation and wider comparative study than they have yet received.

Those who held offices in the royal household are considered separately. We are concerned here, first, with the men who held the most important and responsible offices in the shires. The earls provide the most obvious starting-point for a study of the Anglo-Norman aristocracy, for they were not only an aristocracy of office but also an aristocracy of birth and of tenure. Comital rank was not only a personal but a family distinction in France and Normandy. Several great men enjoyed this rank in England as members of comital families, such as Waleran, count of Meulan, who had succeeded to his father's honours in Normandy and France, Alan, lord of the Honour of Richmond, who was a count of Brittany, Aubrey III de Vere, husband of the heiress of the count of Guisnes, and others. This sometimes leads to confusion, since territorial appellations were used rather carelessly and since several men of comital status became English earls such as William of Aumâle, earl of York, and count Waleran, earl of Worcester. It is sometimes very difficult to discover when a specific English earldom was created. An English earldom was not by any means merely honorific, as many historians have supposed. An English earl received, from early times, the third penny (of the judicial profits) of his shire and this, in Stephen's reign, was not just a profitable survival from times when the earl had earned his pay; he still did. In actual fact, the great authority, influence and status which their office conferred probably counted with English earls for a good deal more than the money. Mr R.H.C.Davis has argued, with clarity and admirable logic, that the office of earl in Stephen's reign was one of great importance, both military and administrative.[4] He has also suggested that the fall in June 1139 of Roger, bishop of Salisbury, the old head of the administration, meant that Stephen 'would have to find a new set of local governors who could oversee the work of the sheriffs and suppress incipient rebellion'. Mr Davis sees in this the real explanation of Stephen's prolific creation of earldoms, a point of great importance, though there were signs, even before June 1139, of his increasing reliance on magnates of comital status. The great majority of royal writs relating to local affairs were addressed to the bishop, earl, justice, sheriff, barons, officials and faithful men of a specific shire, that is, in effect, to the shire court, but significant numbers of writs have survived in which only the earl and officials or the earl, sheriff and officials are addressed. This is a clear indication that earls were actively involved in the administration of their shires. It is impossible, or so it seems, to discern any distinctive pattern which would suggest that earls were more especially concerned with certain specialised aspects of administration. They seemed to have been called upon to attend to much the same range of affairs as the sheriff and justice and shire court, to protect peoples' rights, to give seisin and so on. There is no indication that these writs belong to a particular period such, for example, as that which immediately followed Stephen's release from captivity, when local administration might be expected to have been in such confusion that only the earls were able to give effect to the king's commands. Neither is there any indication of special circumstances when the authority of the earls had to be invoked. It is, however, clear that earls were not just figureheads in their shires.[5] Much probably depended upon the character and ability of individual earls. Geoffrey de Mandeville was obviously a most active administrator and so, probably, was earl Miles of Hereford.

To say that in Stephen's reign as a whole thirty-three earldoms were in existence is true enough but misleading. A further analysis is necessary. At the time of Stephen's accession there were seven: Buckinghamshire (Walter Giffard), Chester (Rannulf II de Gernon), Gloucester (Henry I's illegitimate son Robert),

Huntingdon (David, king of Scots), Leicester (Robert de Beaumont), Surrey (William de Warenne, half-brother of the earl of Leicester), and Warwick (Roger de Beaumont, cousin german of the earl of Leicester and brother-in-law of the earl of Surrey). It is impossible to date precisely all Stephen's creations, of which there were nineteen all told. Three of these were appointments of earls of Lincoln. The creations of the empress, eight in all, can be dated more closely, five to her period of power in 1141. Three of the eight were appointments of earls in shires where Stephen had already appointed earls, namely, in Cornwall, Herefordshire and Wiltshire. One of Stephen's appointments, that of his second son William, in Norfolk and Suffolk (1148–9), conflicted with Maud's appointment of Hugh Bigod (1141). There were also cases, such as that of William de Roumare, earl of Lincoln, and Gilbert de Gant, where rival earls were recognised by Stephen and the empress, though in fact Stephen had bestowed that earldom upon William, who forfeited it, as far as the king was concerned, by his involvement in the rebellion of his half-brother, Rannulf, earl of Chester. There are at least two examples of transfers from one earldom to another: William d'Aubigny (*pincerna*) from Lincoln to Sussex, a title which seems to have been synonymous with Chichester and Arundel, and William de Roumare from Cambridge to Lincoln. There were five shires which in Stephen's reign lacked an earl: Berkshire, Hampshire, Kent, Middlesex and Shropshire. Of these Berkshire was likely to have been dependent upon the royal castle of Windsor and Middlesex upon the Tower of London. It is probable that the bishop of Winchester exercised comital authority in Hampshire, and there is no doubt that William of Ypres was earl, in all but name, in Kent. The reason for the apparent vacancy of the earldom of Shrewsbury (or Shropshire) during Stephen's reign may be that (according to William of Malmesbury) it had been given to queen Adeliza by Henry I in 1126 (*HN* 3). Neither Stephen nor the empress would have interfered with this.

The Breton count Alan seems to have been referred to as an earl of Richmond as early as 1136. He is referred to in *Gesta Stephani* as a man of the utmost ferocity and guile. Apart from his flight from the battle of Lincoln, he seems to have remained loyal to Stephen till his death in 1146. He played a prominent part in the fracas which led to the arrest of the bishops at Oxford in

June 1139, and it seems that Stephen placed a good deal of trust in him in the early years of his reign. Simon II of Senlis was recognised as an earl soon after 1136, but, despite the king's goodwill his position was a difficult and embarrassing one for several years. Simon was the son, by her first marriage, of Maud, daughter of earl Waltheof, and as such he had a strong claim both to Northampton and to Huntingdon as belonging to his grandfather's earldom. Maud, however, married as her second husband David, king of Scots, who held Huntingdon in her right, as later did their son Henry. Although Huntingdon and Northampton belonged together, the latter seems to have been made into an earldom for Simon of Senlis, who acquired the whole earldom of Huntingdon when Henry, son of the king of Scots, lost it at the end of 1141. Simon was a constant adherent of Stephen – a hawk, it would appear, rather than a dove – until he died in 1153, and an ally of Robert, earl of Leicester, whose daughter Isabel he married.[6]

In 1137 Stephen granted the earldom of Bedfordshire to Hugh le Poer, younger brother of Waleran, count of Meulan, and Robert, earl of Leicester. This led immediately to the rebellion of Miles de Beauchamp, the sheriff, who refused to surrender Bedford castle for the new earl. Hugh lost his position, such as it was, in 1141. Several earls were created in 1138 for their services, as it was generally believed, in the battle of the Standard in August of that year. Of these one of the most important was William le Gros, count of Aumâle, who was of Stephen's kin, being a grandson of Eudo, the disinherited count of Champagne and his wife Adelaide, daughter of duke Richard I of Normandy and Herleva and therefore sister (of the whole blood) of William the Conqueror, whose daughter Adela was Stephen's mother. Earl William supported Stephen consistently in war and peace, in conflicts with the king of Scots and with the earl of Chester and in all the troubles which resulted from the disputed elections to the see of York. Count Waleran of Meulan, of whom more will be said, is believed to have become earl of Worcester in 1138 and certainly he held that earldom by the end of 1139. Robert de Ferrers became earl of Derbyshire and Nottinghamshire, dying in 1139. He was the son of Henry, seigneur of Ferrières-Saint-Hilaire and of Chambrais (modern Broglie), who was a Domesday commissioner and a very substantial landholder, with some two hundred and ten lordships or manors. More than half of these were in Derbyshire, but the *caput* of the Ferrers honour was Tutbury in Staffordshire. Earl Robert was Henry's third son and inherited most of his lands. Earl Robert II was less consistently loyal to Stephen than his father, for he is named as an ally of the rebel earl of Chester in his treaty with Robert earl of Leicester.[7] He married Margaret, daughter and heiress of William Peverel of Nottingham, and when duke Henry gave the Peverel lands to the earl of Chester in 1153 earl Robert naturally went into opposition to him. Another of the 1138 earls was a member of the great house of Clare, Gilbert fitz Gilbert, who became earl of Pembroke. Apart from the period of the ascendancy of the empress in 1141, he remained loyal to Stephen till 1147, when events connected with the rebellion of Rannulf, earl of Chester, and the seizure of his nephew, Gilbert fitz Richard de Clare, earl of Hertford, one of the earl of Chester's hostages, drove him into rebellion. He was reconciled with Stephen before his death in 1148. Gilbert fitz Richard de Clare was earl of Hertford by Christmas 1141, and in fact probably soon after 1138. After the events of 1147 he made peace with Stephen, like his uncle, the earl of Pembroke. These two earls of the house of Clare are difficult to distinguish because they are referred to indifferently as 'earl Gilbert'. They both opposed Stephen for a short time for personal and family reasons, not because of any particular attachment to the cause of the empress. Gilbert fitz Richard, earl of Hertford, was a nephew of Rannulf, earl of Chester, since his father, Richard fitz Gilbert, had married Rannulf's sister. It was this bond of close kinship that made the earl of Hertford a hostage for the earl of Chester in 1146; it was also the bond of kinship which impelled the earl of Pembroke to rebel when his nephew the earl of Hertford was seized.

In 1139, by the treaty of Durham between Stephen and David king of Scots, the earldom of Northumbria, once that of earl Waltheof, son of earl Siward, was revived for his grandson, Henry, son of David king of Scots and Waltheof's daughter, Matilda.[8] It was probably in 1139 that William d'Aubigny, son of William d'Aubigny (*Pincerna*), became earl of Lincoln. He married Adeliza of Louvain, the widow of Henry I, before September 1139, becoming in her right lord of the honour of Arundel. By Christmas 1141 he had become earl of Sussex or, as he was often called, earl of Arundel, or earl of Chichester – titles which were synonymous. William d'Aubigny was succeeded as earl of Lincoln by William de Roumare, seigneur of Roumare, near Rouen, and son of Roger fitz Gerold by Lucy, later countess of Chester and mother of earl Rannulf ii. William was one of those in charge of the defence of Normandy after the death of Henry i and he acted as justiciar there for Stephen.[9] He had been made earl of Cambridge as early as 1139, although he had no land there. Cambridge was in fact part of the old earldom of Huntingdon. It seems not unlikely that he received it when the Scots invaded England in 1138 and lost it again when Stephen made peace with king David in 1139. After this William de Roumare became earl of Lincoln. The date is uncertain but it may have been late in 1140, when Stephen had a meeting with him and his half-brother, the earl of Chester, and 'loaded them with honours'. William was a faithful ally of earl Rannulf and took part with him in the dramatic seizure of Lincoln castle before Christmas 1140. He married Hawise, sister of Baldwin de Redvers, first earl of Devonshire, which gave him a further connection with the irreconcilable opponents of king Stephen. William de Roumare's territorial interest in Lincolnshire, unlike that in Cambridgeshire, was considerable, for he inherited lands there from his mother. He also inherited the lands from his father's brother, Robert fitz Gerold. Earl William's rebellion in concert with the earl of Chester left Stephen free to appoint, if he would, another earl of Lincoln in his place, but he does not seem to have done so till 1149, perhaps as a result of his successful northern campaign in that year, when it seems most likely that he appointed Gilbert de Gant to the earldom. This Gilbert was a grandson of Gilbert de Gant, a Fleming from Alost, near Ghent, who according to Domesday Book possessed a large fee in Lincolnshire and lands in Yorkshire and eleven other shires. He was said to be the sixth in descent from King Alfred.[10] Earl Gilbert's uncle was Robert de Gant, who became Stephen's chancellor after the retirement from that office of Philip de Harcourt. The earl's father, Walter de Gant, fought in the battle of the Standard and Gilbert himself, as a very young man, was with Stephen at the battle of Lincoln. Captured by the earl of Chester, he was made to marry Rohese, daughter of Richard fitz Gilbert de Clare by earl Rannulf's sister, Adeliz.

In 1140 Stephen created Geoffrey de Mandeville earl of Essex.[11] He had previously been sheriff of the shire and was an experienced administrator. The author of *Gesta Stephani* says of him, at the time of his arrest in Stephen's court in 1143, that he was remarkable for the ability of his shrewd mind and that in all affairs he received more attention than the king and was better obeyed when he gave orders.[12] Geoffrey de Mandeville is one of the most notorious figures of Stephen's reign. This is partly because of the fantastically generous grants of lands, shrievalties and justiceships he received in successive bids from the empress and Stephen for his support,[13] and partly because of the dramatic circumstances of his arrest at St Albans, the extreme violence of his rebellion and his spectacular death, unshriven and excommunicate. Partly, too, his notoriety has been due to J.H.Round, who in his *Geoffrey de Mandeville*, as a result of the misdating of the charters of Stephen and the empress (which he would have savagely denounced had the error been committed by anyone else), represented Geoffrey as a double traitor to both sides, shamelessly selling his support to the highest bidder and turning his coat with chameleon-like rapidity when he received a still better offer. This has now been shown up for the misconception it is.[14] Geoffrey's record is no worse than that of many others, for he was just an ordinary traitor who deserted to the empress in her period of triumph in 1141, extracting all he could from her and subsequently returning to his allegiance to Stephen. He was a good deal more successful than most in securing rewards in the form of lands and offices. The author of *Gesta Stephani* says of him in 1143 that he

surpassed all the great men of the kingdom in the vastness of his wealth and the splendour of his dignity. He not only had the Tower of London in his hand but also castles of impregnable strength built round the city and all that part of the kingdom which had recognised the king he had so securely subjected to his control that throughout the kingdom he acted in the king's place . . . Those especially who were the closest familiars of the king could hardly bear this, because Geoffrey, so it seemed, had cleverly taken over all the royal rights and it was widely believed that he had arranged to bestow the kingdom upon the countess of Anjou.[15]

The outcome was the ruin of a man, an unscrupulous one and violent, whose very considerable talents might otherwise have been of the utmost value to the cause he embraced, if he had had any capacity for loyalty.

It was in 1140 that Alan of Richmond was created earl of Cornwall by Stephen. He signally failed to maintain his position there against the rival earl set up by the empress. This was one of her half-brothers, Reginald de Dunstanville, an illegitimate son of Henry 1 by Sibyl, daughter of Robert Corbet. It was also about 1140 that Stephen granted the borough and castle and the whole shire of Hereford to Robert earl of Leicester.[16] This must have been an attempt to counteract the growing power of Miles of Gloucester in Herefordshire. We may take it that the tenants-in-chief whose lands earl Robert was not authorised to take over, namely Hugh Mortimer, Osbert fitz Hugh and Gotso of Dinan, were the only royal supporters of this status in the shire at that time. In spite of arguments to the contrary, there can really be little doubt that this was in fact the grant of a second earldom to Robert earl of Leicester.[17] On 25 July 1141 the empress, to the satisfaction of all, as *Gesta Stephani* tells us, conferred the earldom of Hereford upon Miles of Gloucester, now one of the staunchest and strongest of her supporters. After his death in a shooting accident on Christmas Eve 1143, it passed to his son Roger.[18] In 1140 Stephen's son-in-law, Hervey Brito, lord of the honour of Eye, received the castle of Devizes and is referred to in a royal charter as earl of Wiltshire.[19] He lost it the following year. At some date between 1141 and 1147 the empress set up there Patrick, usually styled earl of Salisbury, which title seems to have been synonymous with earl of Wiltshire. Patrick was sheriff of Wiltshire and a constable in the household of the empress. His grandfather, Edward of Salisbury, sheriff of Wiltshire, was Domesday tenant-in-chief of some thirty-three manors in Wiltshire, Dorset, Somerset, Hampshire, Surrey, Buckinghamshire, Hertfordshire and Oxfordshire. Edward's son, Walter of Salisbury, sheriff of Wiltshire, lost his office late in the reign of Henry 1. He was an early supporter of Stephen. His son, William of Salisbury, Patrick's brother, fought for the empress at the siege of Winchester in 1141 and commanded in Salisbury on her behalf in 1142 and 1143.[20] On 1 July 1143 he took part in the attack on the nunnery at Wilton, winning for himself a very evil reputation and his place in John of Salisbury's short list. Earl Patrick seems to have avoided anything spectacular of that kind. Swereford's notes on the pipe role of 1155 show him accounting for Wiltshire as sheriff.[21] Unlike so many others at that time, he accounts for the whole year, not just nine or six months. His account ends with the entry *'Et habet de superplus, xxl, xviijs, ijd. blancos'*, which means that he had paid out on behalf of the crown that amount more than was due from him. He did, however, pay in over £30 in cash, which in 1155 was a creditable achievement, so we may suppose that earl Patrick was a competent administrator.

About the end of July 1141 the empress made Aubrey III de Vere, son of Stephen's chamberlain, earl of Oxford. He was already of comital rank by his marriage with the heiress of the count of Guisnes in 1139. The intention, expressed in Maud's charter, was that he should have Cambridge unless the king of Scots already had a title to it, as indeed he had, since it was part of the earldom of Huntingdon. Aubrey was given as an alternative a choice of the counties of Oxford, Berkshire, Dorset and Wilts, and he chose the first of them.[22] He had returned to Stephen's side by 1145, but whether Stephen recognised his earldom of Oxford is uncertain, since he is referred to simply as *Albericus comes*. In the pipe roll of 1155 earl Aubrey accounts in Essex for five hundred marks to have the chamberlainship which his father had.[23] In 1141 also it seems likely as we have already seen, that Hugh Bigod was given the earldom of East Anglia, or perhaps only Norfolk, by the empress as a reward for his adherence to her cause after the battle of Lincoln.[24] In 1141, not later than June, the earldom of Somerset, a somewhat shady and transient title, was conferred upon William de Mohun. A William, seigneur of Moion, near Saint Lo, had come to England after 1066, obtaining lands mainly in Somerset (of which county he became sheriff) forming the honour of Dunster, where he built a strong castle.[25] William II de Mohun, his heir, acquired a very ill reputation in 1139, when he was active on behalf of the empress. The author of *Gesta Stephani*, who knew his West Country thoroughly well, describes William's activities in terms exactly reminiscent of the Old English chronicler's lurid account of the anarchy.[26] Mohun seems to have been one of the genus 'castleman', regarded with fear and dislike by both sides, fierce, predatory and utterly unreliable. He was with the empress at Westminster in 1141 and also at the siege of Winchester, but soon deserted. This desertion gained him the bitter hostility of Brian fitz Count, that fanatical supporter of the empress.[27] There is no evidence that Stephen even recognised him as earl of Somerset and certainly Henry II never recognised his son and heir. The family continued as lords of Dunster and were perhaps lucky to survive as such. In 1141 Baldwin de Redvers was recognised by the empress as earl of Exeter, that is, of Devonshire.[28] Henry I had granted Plympton and the lands in the Isle of Wight to Richard I de Redvers, a trusted supporter. He was descended through count Gilbert de Brionne (ancestor of the house of Clare) from Richard I, duke of Normandy. Earl Baldwin was the grandson of Baldwin de Meules, seigneur of Riviers (Calvados) and the sheriff of Devonshire. Earl Baldwin himself was sheriff of Devonshire and castellan of Exeter. He refused to attend Stephen's Easter court in 1136 to do homage and swear allegiance. When later he proffered his homage on the understanding that his lands should be confirmed, Stephen declined to accept the condition. This led to Baldwin's rebellion and he was, thereafter, a consistent and active supporter of the empress.

Over the earldom of Norfolk there is some confusion. Stephen's second and ultimately surviving son and heir, William, in 1148/9 married Isabel, heiress of the house of Warenne, to whose honours he succeeded. This meant that he became earl of Surrey. A very large part of the Warenne lands lay in East Anglia and Stephen gave his son, probably on his marriage, an *incrementum*, consisting of Norwich and Norfolk, but excluding *inter alia* the third penny of Norfolk 'of which Hugh Bigod is earl'.[29] This leaves Hugh Bigod's position somewhat equivocal and his attestation of the treaty does nothing to elucidate it. In the list of witnesses he appears among a group called collectively earls, but, though the shires of most of them are specified, that of Hugh Bigod is not. Neither, for that matter, are the shires of Patrick of Salisbury and William of Aumâle.

Completing the roll of earldoms, in 1153 duke Henry granted the borough, shire and earldom of Stafford to Rannulf earl of Chester.[30] Finally, something must be said about William of Ypres, one of the leading men in Stephen's entourage. Although he never appears formally as earl of Kent, Gervase of Canterbury says that Stephen gave him custody of the shire.[31] He exercised effective control there, providing a refuge and a base for queen Matilda after Stephen's capture at Lincoln. William was a

6

consistently loyal supporter of Stephen both in Normandy till July 1139 and afterwards in England. He witnessed a charter of Stephen to Clairmarais Abbey, c. 1142–7, as a royal constable.[32] He must have been a tough character and he needed to be as the commander of Stephen's Flemish mercenaries. It was probably owing to his influence that this exceedingly dangerous military element never, as far as we know, got completely out of hand in England. William of Ypres, born in about 1090, was a grandson of Robert le Frison, count of Flanders. His father was count Philip of Ypres. William became burgrave or *vicecomes*, that is castellan, of that city. After the murder at Bruges on 2 March 1127 of his half-brother, Charles the Good, count of Flanders, William became a candidate for the county. Louis VI of France opposed his candidature 'on the ground that he is illegitimate, the son, that is, of a noble father and a base-born mother, who ceased not to card wool while she was alive'.[33] The French king's candidate was William Clito, heir of duke Robert II of Normandy and nephew of Henry I of England. William of Ypres was active against him and in this he had the support of Henry I who had every cause to fear the Clito's success, and he had also the aid of Stephen, count of Mortain. William had the misfortune to be captured by Louis VI and the Clito at Ypres, but the Clito died in July 1128 from a wound sustained at the siege of Alost. Another candidate, Thierry of Alsace, became count of Flanders, and although William of Ypres was released, he was banished in 1133 as a potentially dangerous rival. He found refuge in England, where his opposition to William Clito had won him the friendship of Henry I. He also enjoyed the trust of Stephen, and repaid it by his firm support. It is significant that he was given control of Kent, commanding as it did the sea-communications of England with Boulogne and Flanders. Perhaps the title of earl of Kent was not conferred upon him, nor does he ever appear even as count William, because it was feared that the count of Flanders might mistake this for a recognition of his Flemish claims. From Kent William drew considerable revenues right up until 1156.[34] Loyal though he was to Stephen and a most valiant supporter, he was widely regarded as a man of violence.[35] He and others are alleged to have threatened to burn St Albans at the time of Geoffrey de Mandeville's arrest there in 1143.[36] About the same time he is said to have broken open the treasure-chest of Abingdon Abbey and stolen fifty marks of gold and five hundred marks of silver, though figures of this kind are never reliable.[37] William cannot, however, be dismissed simply as a 'violent oppressor'. Diplomacy was not outside his scope, for we are told by Gervase of Canterbury that when Stephen exiled archbishop Theobald, William and the queen induced him to remain available for negotiations at Saint Omer.[38] William was the founder of the Cistercian abbey of Boxley, c. 1144–6, but Gervase seems to ascribe his good works to the hope of recovering failing sight.[39]

A survey could be made of the sheriffs and shire justices of Stephen's reign, though a complete list would be difficult, if not impossible, to compile. This cannot be undertaken here. Enough is known about them to discern the kind of men who occupied these offices.[40] A considerable number of sheriffs who held office in Stephen's reign were men who came of hereditary shrieval families, like Walter of Salisbury in Hampshire (1136–46), Miles of Gloucester in Gloucestershire, John and William de Chesney in East Anglia and Geoffrey de Mandeville in London and Middlesex, Essex and Hertfordshire. A number of men of this class were, as we have seen, made earls both by Stephen and by the empress. The same men were often hereditary castellans of important castles, which went with the office of sheriff. Others were *curiales*, like William Martel in Surrey, William de Pontdelarche in Hampshire and, again, Miles of Gloucester. In general the sheriffs belonged to families which were, at least in origin, of modest baronial status, often tenants-in-chief in a number of shires. The office was obviously a road to promotion and profit, especially under a king like Henry I, and the desire of men to hold shrieval office hereditarily is very obvious indeed in Stephen's reign.[41] The continuation in shrieval office after they became earls of those like Miles of Gloucester and his son Roger, Geoffrey de Mandeville and Patrick of Salisbury is noteworthy, especially in the first mentioned case when the earldom was that of one shire, Hereford, and the shrievalty of another, Gloucestershire. Much the same things can be said of the local justices. They were men of the same kind of origins as the sheriffs. The office was one of growing importance, which even so great a magnate as Geoffrey de Mandeville was anxious to hold. The second charter of the empress in his favour indicates what it meant to him in terms of local authority, since she undertook that no other justice should hear pleas in his

shires, though in her first charter she had reserved the right occasionally to send one of his peers (presumably it would have had
to be another justice, not necessarily another earl) to sit with him
and satisfy himself that the pleas of the crown were being properly
heard.[42] In a few cases, notably in Lincoln and Lincolnshire and
perhaps in Wiltshire, the justiciarship was held by the local bishops,
those of Lincoln and Salisbury.[43] The other class of men who held
the office of justice consisted of the important burgesses of
London. There is no indication that any other city in England had
similar justices of its own.

The garrison commanders on both sides would be worth a
short study. Some, like William de Chesney, Stephen's commander
in Oxford, belonged to mesne-tenant families of some importance.
The Chesneys, from le Quesnay (Seine-Inf) were tenants of the
honours of Arundel and Warenne. They produced a bishop of
Lincoln (Robert) and several sheriffs of East Anglia. William and
his brother Roger, *Gesta Stephani* tells us, were warriors (*viri
bellaces*) 'second to none in military skill or in any good quality'.
They remained faithful to Stephen when he was captured, and
their loyal support stands in strong contrast to that of the magnates who fled at the battle of Lincoln or who deserted afterwards.
A more recent generation would probably have called them
officers and gentlemen. Some other garrison commanders were
mere mercenaries, men of low birth, not always faithful to their
employers, and their conduct as soldiers was unchivalrous to a
degree, not to say bestial.

It must be emphasised again that the aristocracy of office considered above belongs also to the aristocracy of birth and tenure.
We are concerned here, not exactly with a nobility, but with all
those laymen who, holding land directly or indirectly from the
king, had dependent tenants under them, whether these were
feudal vassals or a manorial population or both. Since it was
essentially a landed aristocracy, this may seem a fairly realistic
definition, but there remains a lingering doubt whether it is quite
flexible enough. The class of knights was a miscellaneous one,
ranging from men of truly baronial status to those of near insignificance. Where is one to draw the line between the aristocracy
and the others? Every case needs to be treated on its merits. There
were still in Stephen's reign landless knights, some at least of whom
ought not to be excluded from our purview. Take the case of

Roger Foliot in the following letter written by Gilbert Foliot
when he was abbot of St Peter's, Gloucester, to Henry, bishop of
Winchester:

> Charity compels me, beloved father in Christ, humbly to implore you
> that, of your grace and at my petition, you cause to be ransomed a
> knight called Roger Foliot, whom your men are holding in captivity
> ... For your sanctity should know that his father never had more than
> half a hide of land; he himself had only what he acquired by his service
> as a knight. Till the present time he has served the lord Brian (fitz
> Count) as a stipendary (*ad donativum*) and now, despoiled of his horses
> and arms, he has lost all at once everything he had.[44]

For a landless knight the loss of his horses and arms, his expensive professional equipment, was a shattering blow. Roger Foliot
was indeed fortunate to have for a kinsman an eminent cleric who
was prepared to use his influence to secure his ransom. Although
the son of an insignificant landholder and himself a landless knight,
entirely dependent upon the generosity of the lord he served,
Roger might, in favourable circumstances, have looked forward
to obtaining a landed estate. Perhaps he did get his reward. In the
cartae of 1166 – returns to an inquiry addressed by Henry II to his
tenants-in-chief as to how many knights they had of the 'old
feoffment' (i.e. given their fees before the death of Henry I), how
many of the 'new feoffment' (i.e. after that date) and how many
knights were on their demesnes – we find in the lordship of
Wallingford a Walter Foliot, who held two knights fees.[45] It would
be pleasing to think that this was Roger's heir, though I know of
no evidence that he was. In the Odell, or Wahull, *carta* of 1166, in
Bedfordshire, a Roger Foliot holds three knights' fees, but there
is no ground whatsoever for assuming his identity with our
Roger.[46] Such a knight as Roger Foliot might, by the misfortune
of war or from other causes, be reduced to penury, and his
descendants, if he had any, might find themselves in circumstances
no better than those of the meanest peasants. On the other hand,
the opportunities in a warlike age for a tough and ambitious
young knight, upon whom fortune smiled, were boundless. The
fairy stories had a solid basis in fact. The classic example is the
career of William, son of John fitz Gilbert the marshal, the same
whom Stephen is said to have saved from the gallows in early
childhood. He rose to fame as a soldier and did extremely well for

himself as the most successful tourneyer of his day from the ransoms and the horses and arms of the knights he vanquished. His
military qualities and his loyalty won him the favour of Richard I
and John; in due course he married his (Pembroke) heiress and
ended an adventurous and colourful career in 1219 in the odour
almost of sanctity, certainly of the utmost respectability, as earl of
Pembroke and Strigul, lord of Leinster in Ireland and many lands
besides, and regent of England.[47] Roger Foliot belonged to a
family, or rather there was a group of families of the name, which
produced a more than average share of archdeacons, abbots and
bishops, and one of whose members, Robert, acquired by marriage, before 1161, the lordship of Chipping Warden (Northamptonshire).[48] A branch of the Foliot family held lands of the earl of
Devon.[49] The Foliots seem to have originated in Western
Normandy and the Cotentin, where they were landholders in the
eleventh century.[50] It might be argued that a mere household
knight, such as Roger clearly was, cannot properly be included
among the aristocracy. In the quarters of the household knights of
any twelfth-century baron there must have been very mixed company, but a follower of Brian, lord of Wallingford, the most un-
swervingly loyal of all the adherents of the empress, 'whom good
king Henry brought up and gave arms and honour' (and, it
should be added, an heiress, the widow of Miles Crispin), could
bear himself proudly.[51] Wallingford probably saw as much fighting as any other single place in England during Stephen's reign,
so it was a good centre for an ambitious knight. Roger qualifies,
at least by descent, as a member of the Anglo-Norman military
aristocracy, though we may regard him at the time when abbot
Gilbert's letter was written as representing its lowest stratum. The
structure of the knightly class, if indeed it can be called a class at
this time, requires close investigation.

At the top of the scale were the earls[52] and greater tenants-in-
chief of the crown. The class of tenants-in-chief was a large and
very miscellaneous one including, as well as the mighty, men who
were holders of a mere knight's fee and hard put to it to maintain
their status. There were several such petty tenants-in-chief in
Hertfordshire in 1166 and, in reply to Henry II's inquiry, one of
them wrote succinctly and poignantly as follows:

William, son of Robert, to his dearest lord, Henry, king of the English, greeting. Know that I hold of you one very poor knight's fee and

I have not enfeoffed anyone else in it, because it is hardly enough for myself; and my father held it likewise. Farewell.[53]

This, pretty certainly, takes us back to Stephen's reign.

There were barons far more substantial than this who straddled the tenant-in-chief and sub-tenant classes. Thus Hugh de Bolbec, who died *c.* 1164–5, held in chief a barony which owed the services of ten knights.[54] In addition he held twenty knights' fees of the old feoffment of the honour of Giffard in England.[55]

The number of men who were predominant in the class of tenants-in-chief was not large. It has been said that something like half the land in England that was held directly by laymen from William the Conqueror had been given by him to only eleven men. The list actually includes two bishops, but their position among prelates was quite exceptional. The eleven were Odo, bishop of Bayeux and earl of Kent, the Conqueror's half brother; William fitz Osbern; Robert, count of Mortain; Roger of Montgomery; William de Warenne; Hugh fitz Richard, *Vicomte* of the Avranchin (a grandson of the Conqueror's mother); Eustace, count of Boulogne; Alan le Roux, a count of Brittany; Richard fitz Gilbert de Brionne; Geoffrey, bishop of Coutances, and Geoffrey de Mandeville.[56] The existence of such a first eleven must not mislead us. It is not to be supposed that, to take quite random examples, the Giffards in Buckinghamshire, the Ferrers of Derbyshire, the Peverels of Nottinghamshire, or the Bigods of Norfolk were other than very great magnates indeed, even though their lands were not quite so widespread and extensive. Likewise Mortimers, Bruces and Percies (by no means in the top division in the twelfth century, but all great names in the later Middle Ages) did not lack status and strong influence in their localities. By Stephen's reign not quite so much land was held by so few tenants-in-chief as under the Conqueror, though the number of barons of the first magnitude was still fairly small. Gone, by then, were Odo, bishop of Bayeux, and William fitz Osbern, earl of Hereford, and gone, too, the Montgomery earls of Shrewsbury. There were men of another stamp in the western Marches now. The English lands of the count of Mortain were merged in the crown and likewise those of the county of Boulogne were in Stephen's hands in the right of his queen, Matilda. The lands of the Warennes, earls of Surrey, came eventually to Stephen's second but surviving son and heir, William, through his marriage with Isabel, the ultimate

heiress of the Domesday William de Warenne. William of Blois
lived only till 1159 and then Henry II married his illegitimate
brother Hamelin to the widow, thus conveniently providing him
with an earldom. In Stephen's reign a Mandeville was still on
the make and so was the successor of earl Hugh of Chester. A
descendant of the red-headed count Alan, the dark count Alan III,
held the great Yorkshire honour of Richmond. The heirs of
Gilbert fitz Richard de Brionne, descendant of an illegitimate son
of duke Richard of Normandy, still flourished in England, where
they were known by the name they derived from the honour of
Clare, in Suffolk. The earldoms of Hertfordshire and Pembroke
were bestowed by Stephen on members of the Clare family, and
Strongbow, from his Pembroke springboard, was soon to be
received in Ireland with mingled awe and execration.

Other great names too are found in the top division in Stephen's
England. Most lofty in status were David I, king of Scots, and his
son Henry, with their English earldoms of Huntingdon and
Northumberland, and the lordship of Carlisle which the earl of
Chester so acrimoniously claimed. Then there is Robert de Caen,
the favourite and by far the most distinguished of Henry I's nine
illegitimate sons,[57] earl of Gloucester, lord of Bristol and other
English lands and also of Glamorgan. A great family bloc in the
west Midlands is represented by members of the Beaumont family,
the twins Waleran, count of Meulan, and Robert 'le bossu', second
earl of Leicester. Roger, earl of Warwick, was their cousin
german. Robert de Ferrers, earl of Derbyshire, represented another
great feudal power. Yet other names are those of men whom
Henry I raised to greatness, if not 'from the dust', at least from
modest estates, like Miles of Gloucester, created earl of Hereford
by the empress in 1141, and his fellow justice, Payn fitz John.
These men, and Miles in particular, represented a new power in
the western shires, the Marches and Brycheiniog.

The Anglo-Norman aristocracy of Stephen's England included,
besides the very mixed bag of tenants-in-chief, another group of
men, some of them of baronial rank, who were mesne-tenants,
that is sub-tenants, of the greater tenants-in-chief. They, too, are a
rather heterogeneous group. Again a random dip into the *cartae* of
1166 will illustrate the point. In Norfolk earl Hugh (Bigod)
acknowledges one hundred and twenty-five knights of the old
enfeoffment and thirty-five of the new. Among the former we find

William de Wallibus with thirty knights' fees, Bartholomew de
Cric with eight, Osbert fitz William with four, Richard fitz
Maurice with two-and-a-half, Herbert Baliun (a name of some
distinction) half a knight's fee and Fulcher and the son of Ulger a
quarter of a knight's fee. The number of really important mesne-
tenants, like William de Wallibus, with his thirty knights' fees, or
men with even a third of that number, was small even in the very
largest honours; perhaps half a dozen or ten at the most. Their
importance, however, was great. These were men who held
estates of baronial magnitude from one or more lords and themselves were sometimes tenants-in-chief, men who were often akin
to great families, men of social standing and political importance,
possessors of vassals of their own and of considerable economic
and military resources. They were the equals in all but name,
often far more than the equals, of a good many tenants-in-chief,
the class of men whose loyalty the Conqueror had found it advis-
able to secure in 1086 by exacting from them the 'Oath of Salisbury'.[58] Their voices carried weight in the affairs of the honours of
which they were tenants and these honours were microcosms
of the kingdom. The influence of tenants-in-chief in the honours
of their fellows through their tenure of knights' fees might repay
investigation.

The rise of the great Anglo-Norman families, both in England
and in Normandy, was accompanied *pari-passu* by the rise of
lesser families dependent upon them as tenants. We find Har-
courts from Harcourt (dép Eure, arr. Bernay, cant. Brionne),
which they held of the honour of Beaumont in Normandy, as
tenants of the earls of Leicester and Warwick in England. Curzons
from Notre-Dame-de-Courson (dép. Calvados, arr. Lisieux, cant.
Livarot), a fief of the Norman barony of Ferrières, held knights'
fees of the honour of Ferrers in England. Members of the family
of Chandos from Candos (dép Eure, arr. Pont Audemer, cant.
Montfort-sur-Risle) were Montfort tenants in Suffolk and
Herefordshire. Sometimes a Norman family of sub-tenant status
hitched its wagon to the rising star of a lord other than its own.
Thus the Bagpuz, tenants of the count of Évreux in Bacquepuits
(dép Eure, arr. and cant. Évreux), became extensive tenants of the
Ferrers in Derbyshire and Berkshire. The lord of Ferrières-saint-
Hilaire (dép Eure, arr. Bernay, cant. Broglie) was a not very dis-
tant Norman neighbour, who was better endowed with English

6*

lands than the count of Évreux.[59] Feudal and family relationships of this kind profoundly affected the structure and the
stability of the Anglo-Norman aristocracy in the generations
after the conquest of England. Rebellions were fatal to some of
the great houses and their forfeitures must have drastically affected
the social structure within their honours. The activities of William
Rufus and of Henry 1 and his 'new men' were more insidious,
more widespread and no less disruptive of the old feudal order
than rebellions were, though their effects are not easy to trace in detail. The intrusion of a new lord and the uncertainty as to tenure
which this must often have caused were very disturbing for the
tenants of an honour. This was a state of affairs that was much
aggravated in Stephen's reign.

Anyone who attempts a study of the Anglo-Norman aristocracy
in the mid-twelfth century is confronted with a tangled skein of
infinite complexity. From John of Salisbury's short list of nobles
whom he regarded as public enemies let us first extract Miles of
Gloucester. He makes a good starting-point for an interesting
cross-section of the baronage, and, besides, his aims and those of
his family have recently been elucidated.[60] The first member of
this family known in English history was Roger de Pîtres,
Domesday tenant of lands in Gloucestershire, Herefordshire,
Wiltshire and Hampshire. The centre, however, of his interests
was in Gloucestershire, where he was sheriff early in the reign of
William the Conqueror. Roger was succeeded by his brother
Durand and his son Walter, hereditary sheriffs of Gloucestershire
and castellans of Gloucester castle. Walter of Gloucester obtained
one of the constableships in the royal household, that which was
forfeited by the Abetot family. He died about 1126 in the remote
Augustinian priory of Llanthony Prima and was succeeded by his
son Miles, who soon rose to greatness. He was hereditary sheriff
of Gloucestershire, and also held the shrievalty of Staffordshire in
1130. He held the castle of Gloucester as castellan under earl
Robert. Miles also succeeded his father as a royal constable and
served as a royal justice, often in association with Payn fitz John.
These two men are said to have 'raised their power to such
heights that, from the Severn to the sea, all along the border
between England and Wales, they involved everyone in pleas and
burdened them with forced services'.[61] Added to the lands which
Miles inherited from his father were those he acquired by his

marriage in 1121 to Sibyl, heiress of Bernard de Neufmarché, conqueror and lord of Brychan and Brycheiniog. At the time of Stephen's accession Miles was a baron and marcher lord of considerable power as well as an eminent servant of the crown. He was castellan of the important castle of Gloucester at a strategic point on the lower Severn and this, together with his lands in Herefordshire and Wales, made him a key man at a time of Welsh resurgence and possible civil war at the beginning of Stephen's reign. At the very outset, Miles adhered to Stephen and a very welcome adherent he must have been to a king who had little reason to depend upon the loyalty of the earl of Gloucester. If the continued adherence of Miles could be assured much would have been done to neutralise the power of the earl of Gloucester in the west and in south Wales. For similar reasons it was greatly in the interest of the Angevins to win him over if they could. Miles was rewarded by Stephen not merely with the confirmation of his existing English and Welsh honours and his offices, which was no more than he had a right to expect, but with the very significant undertaking that the king would never question his right to any tenure he had held at the time of king Henry's death. Furthermore, he was given custody of the tower and castle of Gloucester as his patrimony, for the same ferm as in the time of Henry 1 so that its tenure would no longer depend upon the goodwill of the earl of Gloucester, under whom it had hitherto been held.[62]

Roger, the son and heir of Miles of Gloucester, made an advantageous marriage. The bride was Cecilia, one of the two daughters and co-heiresses of Miles's old colleague, Payn fitz John, sheriff of Hereford and Shropshire, who was killed by the Welsh on 10 July 1137. Payn had attained wealth and importance under Henry 1, much as Miles had done. He had married Sibyl, daughter of Geoffrey Talbot 1 by Agnes, a daughter (probably) of Walter de Lacy of Weobley (Herefordshire). This Lacy fee came into the hands of Agnes's brother, Hugh de Lacy, who died without issue before 1121, leaving as his heirs his sisters Agnes Talbot and Emma. The latter's son Gilbert, by an unknown husband, took his mother's patronymic (probably for reasons connected with the Lacy inheritance). Here was one claimant to the large Lacy fee in Herefordshire and Shropshire. Meanwhile Payn fitz John, another claimant through his wife, a co-heiress, gave his daughter Cecilia a marriage portion from the honour of Hugh de Lacy and all the claims that Payn had in the lands of Hugh de Lacy passed to Cecilia's husband Roger even though his mother-in-law, through whom the claim had descended, was still alive and at odds with him.[63] The settling of the inheritance of the Lacy fee in favour of Cecilia and Roger was just the kind of thing that two ministers of Henry I might have cosily arranged with royal connivance, though it is unlikely that Henry I would have allowed Miles and his son to get away with anything like as much as Stephen did. At all events, the loyalty of Miles of Gloucester was of sufficient consequence to Stephen to ensure his confirmation to Roger fitz Miles in December 1137 not only of Cecilia's share of her father's lands but of all the right he claimed in the honour of Hugh de Lacy.[64] Whether or not this meant that Roger obtained the whole honour, as appears to be the case, the other claimant, Gilbert de Lacy, rebelled against Stephen and in the summer of 1138 was engaged together with his relative, Geoffrey Talbot II, in the Angevin attack on Bath.[65] The violence of this Geoffrey Talbot's behaviour might suggest that he was one of the 'disinherited', a disappointed claimant to the Lacy lands. There is no record of this and furthermore, if he were such a claimant, his alliance with Miles of Gloucester in the attack on Hereford in 1140 would be surprising. I have therefore assumed that he must have been a step-son of Agnes Talbot (née Lacy) and was not a claimant, since, if he had been, his claims should have overridden those of his nephew Gilbert de Lacy and his nieces, Cecilia and Agnes, daughters of his (half-) sister Sibyl and Payn fitz John. Geoffrey died in 1140 – another of the reckless violators of churches.[66]

Meanwhile, in September 1139, the empress landed in England with her brother, earl Robert, one of whose earliest moves was to travel to Gloucester to try to win Miles over to the Angevin cause. In this he was completely successful and Miles became one of the staunchest of Maud's adherents. His immediate reward was a grant from her of St Briavel's castle and the whole forest of Dean.[67] In a successful campaign in 1140 he secured Hereford, and this together with the Lacy fief made Herefordshire (and Shropshire) as important to him as Gloucestershire. One result of Miles's change of allegiance was that Stephen, somewhat prematurely perhaps, granted the Lacy fee in Herefordshire to Gotso de Dinan (Dinant or Dinham). Gilbert de Lacy, whom these events had deprived of any hope of obtaining the Lacy fief either from the empress or from Stephen, was left in a very unenviable position. Gotso's unexplained desertion to the empress left the way open for Gilbert to join Stephen and by 1146 he had recovered most of the Lacy lands.[68] The empress created Miles of Gloucester earl of Hereford on 25 July 1141, though Stephen had probably granted the borough, castle and county to Robert earl of Leicester in the previous year.[69] Miles was now a magnate of the first rank in the western shires and in the Marches of Wales and, in addition to what he had directly from the empress, he received from Brian fitz Count and his wife, Matilda of Wallingford, the castle and the whole honour of Abergavenny to hold by the service of three knights, thereby adding very substantially to his Welsh territories.[70]

Between 25 July 1141 and 24 December 1143, when Miles was killed by an arrow when hunting – probably in June 1142, when Robert earl of Gloucester took hostages of his supporters before crossing to Normandy – the position of Miles was further secured by a 'league of affection' or compromise (*confederatio amoris*) between them.[71] Earl Robert got his hostage and Miles was assured of his protection and assistance in defending his castles and his rights and hereditaments and tenements and the conquests he had made and should make in the future. Earl Robert further promised not to make peace with Miles's enemies except with his consent, especially in the war between the empress and king Stephen, or in any other conflict. A similar agreement was made, probably soon after earl Robert's death in 1147, between William, the new earl of Gloucester, and Roger, who had succeeded his father as earl of Hereford.[72] By this *confederatio amoris* earl Roger agreed to keep faith with earl William, as his lord, against all men save Henry fitz Empress. Earl William, on his side, agreed to support Roger as his man, especially in disinheriting Gilbert de Lacy. The feudal relationship of lord and man is stressed here, perhaps in respect of earl Roger's tenure of the castle and borough of Gloucester. The *confederatio* contains an incidental mention of another agreement (of which we have no other knowledge) between Roger and the earl of Leicester, in which earl William had acted as a guarantor for the former. Perhaps Roger found his agreement with the earl of Gloucester less satisfactory than he had hoped, especially in regard to the disinheriting of Gilbert de Lacy, or perhaps it was just that in 1152 the military situation seemed to be turning in Stephen's favour. At all events, in that year we learn of a complicated piece of double-crossing, in which the king and earl Roger were both engaged. It is clear that at the time Roger was regarded as the most powerful of Stephen's opponents. He approached the king with a proposal for 'a pact of inviolable peace and friendship' whereby the king should besiege with him and hand over to him the castle of Worcester, which the knights of the count of Meulan had seized by trickery from William de Beauchamp, who had sided with Roger against the Beaumonts. Stephen thought it wise to accept Roger's proposal, as his barons advised, and did accordingly attack Worcester castle. Roger, however, sent a message to duke Henry urging him to hasten over to England; and Stephen, who was aware of his treachery,

therefore abandoned the siege and departed from Worcester, but he left a considerable part of his army to help the earl, lest he should appear to be the first to break the agreement between them to the earl's prejudice. But when the king had gone, the earl obtained the castle by agreement with the besieged and, breaking the pact of peace and concord which he had pledged the king, he again flew to arms against him.[73]

There was probably a good deal more behind this episode than the author of *Gesta Stephani* was aware of and it seems likely that Roger had made larger claims in the western shires than Stephen was prepared to meet.

This complicated history of family and feudal relationships and territorial claims suggests that hostilities in Gloucestershire, Herefordshire and Worcestershire in Stephen's reign were as much an outcome of conflicting claims to the inheritance of the late Hugh de Lacy and of the far-reaching ambitions of Miles of Gloucester and his son and of the earl of Leicester as they were the outcome of the dynastic struggle between the daughter and the nephew of Henry i. It was all part of the evil legacy of king Henry. As Professor R.W.Southern so clearly demonstrated in his Raleigh lecture to the British Academy in 1962, Henry had habitually enabled his ministers to operate, in association with the work of royal government, to his own advantage and theirs. These beneficiaries of royal patronage obtained, as major prizes, marriages, wardships, the fruits of forfeitures and 'opportunities for cutting into the estates of magnates in difficulties of one kind or another'. Added to these were the many and various smaller

Table 1. Claimants to the Honour of Hugh de Lacy

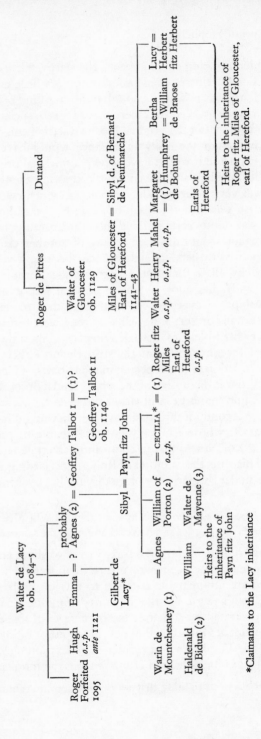

favours by which the king could enhance the status, facilitate the activities and line the purses of his minions at very little expense to himself.[74] Henry was powerful enough to do this kind of thing, and in the process he assisted the emergence of a new social order very different from that of the original Norman settlement. Under Henry I the matter of the Lacy inheritance would have been settled out of hand and it would have shown a financial profit for the crown. With Stephen and the empress contesting the throne, the situation was very different. The temptation, which neither of them could resist, was to outbid each other with rival claimant's; and nothing was more certain than that the meeting of one claimant's demands would make an enemy of another claimant. Such legerdemain with fiefs and inheritances became a very involved and tricky affair for all the participants. It must have played havoc with allegiance, a matter of vital importance in feudal relationships, at every level. What were men to do who could not be certain for very long whether they were tenants of, let us say, Roger fitz Miles or Gotso de Dinan or Gilbert de Lacy, and feared that the next move might strip them of their tenements? Such a situation as this repeated in many parts of England in Stephen's reign was disruptive of the whole feudal order. Lords did what they could to meet the situation and even the greatest of them had to take account of the possibility that they might have to recompense vassals whose tenures they were unable to protect. Thus Henry duke of Normandy, in confirming an estate to Nigel fitz Arthur and his wife, the daughter of Robert fitz Harding, as late as 1153-4, was under the necessity of qualifying his confirmation in these words:

If, however, I be not able to warrant it to them, I will give them ten librates of land from my demesne, in exchange, for the same service.

For this favour Nigel paid the duke forty marks of silver and his wife gave a golden ring, since it was a matter connected with her dower.[75] There are innumerable parallels to this in the baronial charters of Stephen's reign, but the insecurity of mesne-tenants is most vividly illustrated by a charter in about 1150 of Osbert de Wanci, a sub-tenant of Gilbert de Pinkney, in favour of Biddlesden Abbey, which Sir Frank Stenton printed a generation ago.[76] In return for his gift Gilbert secured *inter alia* from the monks that:

If there be such serious fighting that we cannot keep our animals in peace, they shall keep them with their own without cost (to themselves) and saving their order, that is, they shall not pledge their faith or take an oath if anyone wishes to take the animals away by force. If, indeed, they be stolen away or lost by any misfortune or if the beasts die or be killed or if they be taken they (the monks) shall not make good the loss. And if it should happen that I be captured, or my wife or son, they shall send one of their brethren to help us by their spiritual influence, not by money.

This refers to an area in the south-west corner of Northampton-shire, which, though it must have been very remote in those days, probably suffered a good deal in the private wars in which earl Simon was involved.

It is ironical that after such a determined struggle for a place in the sun the four sons of Miles of Gloucester, Roger, Walter, Henry and Mahel, all died without offspring. As in the case of so many great twelfth-century families, the inheritance of the Gloucester family was ultimately divided between the three daughters of Miles who were the co-heiresses. Consequently all the fruits of Miles's striving, intriguing and campaigning and of the no less determined endeavours of his son, Roger, passed into the hands of the Bohuns, Braozes and fitz Herberts. Earl Roger's widow, Cecilia, co-heiress of Payn fitz John and claimant to the Lacy lands, married William of Poitou and, after William's death, Walter of Mayenne; but, as she died childless, her estates eventually passed to her sister's children, the Mountchesneys.

From this point a number of interesting genealogical lines might be followed: that of Humphrey de Bohun, husband of Miles's elder daughter, Margaret, a royal steward and like his father-in-law an early deserter to the empress, ancestor of the medieval earls of Hereford of the third creation. Or we might trace the fortunes of Eustace, brother of Payn fitz John and like him a royal justice and administrator under Henry I, beneficiary of an advantageous marriage with the de Vesci heiress, friend and supporter of David king of Scots, and of his son Henry, to whom he was bound by reason of his (wife's) Northumbrian lordship of Alnwick and because of the grant to him of five valuable manors of the earldom of Huntingdon.[77] We may, however, find it more immediately profitable to pursue another clue provided by earl Roger's relations with the earl of Leicester, the count of Meulan and William de Beauchamp.

Table 2. The House of Beaumont

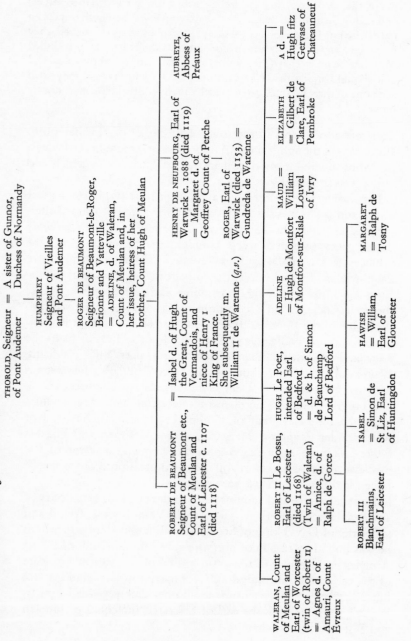

We now come to examine the position not of one of Henry I's 'new men', scion of a minor family of the Anglo-Norman aristocracy, but of one of the greatest houses of the old Norman baronage.[78] The representatives of this great house of Beaumont in Stephen's reign were Waleran, count of Meulan in the French Vexin, earl of Worcester and lord of Sturminster Royal (Dorsetshire); Robert 'le bossu', his twin brother, earl of Leicester and intended earl of Herefordshire; Hugh 'le poer', proposed earl of Bedfordshire; and their cousin Roger, earl of Warwick. Their common grandfather was Roger, seigneur of Beaumont-le-Roger, Brionne and Vatteville in Normandy, who had married Adeline, who became, in her issue, heir to the comté of Meulan in the French Vexin. Their son, Robert I, inherited the Norman lordships and the comté of Meulan and was created earl of Leicester, probably by Henry I. His eminence is indicated by his marriage to Isabel, daughter of Hugh 'the great', count of Vermandois, the Crusader, younger son of king Henry I of France. It was an interesting union in several respects. First, the twins were born in 1104, and when they were only three or four years old count Robert, a little prematurely as it turned out, obtained royal approval of a plan to divide his inheritance between them. Waleran, who was the first born, was to have the comté of Meulan, the Norman feifs and Sturminster in England (which had been held by his grandfather). Robert was to have the earldom of Leicester and the rest of the English lands. If the lands on either side of the Channel were lost, the twins were to share what remained; a measure of the uncertainty of Henry I's tenure of England and Normandy at that time. If count Robert had been banking on having no more children, he made the mistake of counting his chickens before they were all hatched. Isabel subsequently presented him with Hugh, known as 'the poor' because his elder brothers already had the whole inheritance, and several daughters. The mother of this brood seems to have been abducted by William II de Warenne, earl of Surrey, whom she married after Robert's death on 5 June 1118. She became the mother of William III de Warenne, earl of Surrey, and two daughters, of whom the elder, Gundred, married Isabel's nephew by (her first) marriage, Roger earl of Warwick. The younger, Ada, married Henry, son of king David, and became the mother of two kings of Scots, Malcolm 'the Maiden' and William 'the Lion'.

Table 3. The House of Warenne

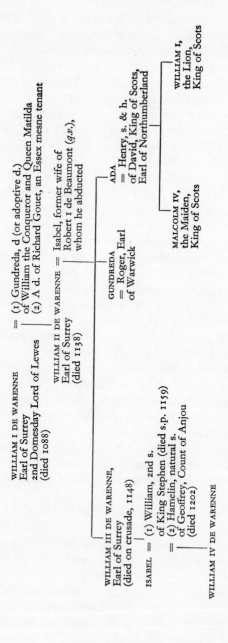

Since Robert I, count of Meulan and earl of Leicester, had been a close friend and adviser of Henry I, the king undertook the up-bringing of the twins after their father's death. At the royal court they must have been well acquainted with Henry's favourite nephew, Stephen of Blois, and friendly enough with him to account for their close relations with him after he became king. Waleran seems to have been the more active and adventurous of the twins. He was guilty of great ingratitude to Henry I for in 1123 he threw in his lot with William Clito, son of duke Robert Curthose and claimant to the duchy of Normandy. He was assisted in his treason by his three brothers-in-law, Hugh de Montfort, seigneur of Montfort-sur-Risle, Hugh fitz Gervase, seigneur of Chateauneuf and William Louvel, seigneur of Ivry, all of them important Norman barons. Reduced to subjection and imprisoned by Henry in 1124, he was released in 1129, recovering all his castles except Pont-Audemer. According to Orderic Vitalis, Waleran, his twin brother Robert, earl of Leicester, and their half-brother William III de Warenne, earl of Surrey, were present at Lyons-la-Forêt when the king died on 1 December 1135. None of them seems to have had anything to say on the subject of Henry I's alleged deathbed recognition of Stephen as his heir. Perhaps they were wise.

What kind of men were Waleran and his twin? They had an academic education which enabled them to sustain, even if it was carefully arranged, a philosophical discussion with the cardinals on the occasion when Henry I met pope Calixtus at Gisors in 1119. Waleran is described in an elegy by the author of *Draco Normannicus*, Stephen of Rouen, a monk of Bec, of which house the count was the lay patron (*advocatus*):

> In looks, a Paris; tall as Nestor; Ulysses
> In counsel; in warlike strength a Hector;
> A Croesus in riches; in lawsuits a Quintilian;
> A Cicero in eloquence; in verse a very Maro.[79]

If some of Waleran's Virgilian verses had survived we might be better able to assess the judgment of the monk Stephen. Henry of Huntingdon took a very different view of him as an adherent of Stephen at the battle of Lincoln. In the pre-battle oration which he puts into the mouth of the earl of Gloucester Henry describes Waleran as crafty, deceitful, vicious, slothful, boastful in speech and cowardly in act, the last to enter a fight and the first to retreat.[80] He was, in fact, one of the first to flee at Lincoln and the chronicler knew it when he composed the speech. We must judge count Waleran by his actions. It seems clear that from early manhood Waleran thought of himself in a leading rôle in the affairs of Normandy, for which his birth, his inheritance and his powerful connexions seemed to have cast him. For this he hardly possessed the talents; indeed one is greatly tempted to see him and Stephen as two of a kind. Mr G.H.White described Waleran as an 'arch-mediocrity', an antithesis of ideas which underlines the probable truth.[81]

Waleran backed the wrong horse in 1123, and in so doing gained a reputation for faithlessness and ingratitude. He was fortunate indeed in recovering his liberty, his estates and his castles from a king who was not wont to tolerate rivals or rebels. The castles of Brionne, Beaumont and Pont-Audomer (the last of which he did not immediately recover) in the valley of the Risle and those of Vatteville and Meulan (in the French Vexin) on the Seine, gave him a very strong military position in the duchy and on its eastern frontier. After Henry I's death Stephen hastened to secure the support of so important a personage. He gave Waleran the castle of Montfort-sur-Risle, which belonged to his still imprisoned brother-in-law, Hugh de Montfort. Waleran seems not to have had the slightest scruple about taking it in the circumstances. Further, Stephen betrothed his two-year-old daughter to Waleran and began to build up his position in England, as well as in Normandy, by giving him the town of Worcester. From the very beginning of his reign it seems clear, and subsequent events substantiate this, that Stephen was thinking like a typical feudatory in terms of 'feudo-dynastic' alliances. By this term I mean alliances, often arising from or fortified by marriages, whereby complexes of fiefs were built up and family territorial blocs created to the greater glory and enhanced political influence of their members. For the crown to enter into alliances with baronial families was to endanger the policy of Henry I, who had sought to restrain their power. One of his many means, and an effective one, was to encourage and enable his 'new men' (whose loyalty to him was stimulated by the bitter hostility of 'the disinherited') to eat away the resources of great baronial families. The 'new men' themselves were, as we have seen in the case of Miles of Gloucester, soon deeply involved in the old game of feudo-dynastic aggrandisement and Stephen was not strong enough to prevent them, so that some of them became as dangerously powerful as the greatest of the old baronage; more so because of their judicial and administrative expertise and their grip on local offices such as shrievalties, shire justiceships and castellanships. Some of the older baronage, very notably Geoffrey de Mandeville, were ready and able to emulate them.

Stephen, it must be remembered, had from the beginning of his reign, if not earlier, an alliance with his brother Henry, bishop of Winchester, and through him as guarantor a commitment to the church. It was this that secured him the throne, and if he were to remain there and establish a royal dynasty it was essential that Stephen and his episcopal brother should cleave to each other. Further, the efficiency of the administrative machine which Stephen had inherited owed much to the administrative family of which Roger, bishop of Salisbury, was the head. Things might have gone more smoothly had the king been able to retain their loyalty. It must be admitted that in the circumstances of Stephen's early years it would have been a courageous, perhaps a foolhardy, king who relied solely upon the church and upon Henry I's *curiales*, clerical and lay. Stephen could not but feel the need of military strength. To begin with, the enemies whom Stephen had most to fear were Maud and her husband Geoffrey of Anjou, who would certainly try to launch an attack on Normandy; Robert earl of Gloucester, who might assail him in England from the west; and the king of Scots, who threatened him in the north. The value in these circumstances of a feudo-dynastic alliance with the Beaumonts, providing a bulwark south of Trent, is obvious. Count Waleran, if he could be relied upon, would immensely strengthen Stephen's political and military position in Normandy. Closely bound to Stephen, he would have the strongest incentive to exert all his power to keep out the Angevins. If, however, things went wrong for Stephen in Normandy, as they soon did, and the Angevins gained the upper hand, Waleran's continued loyalty would entail the loss of his great Norman fiefs, a heavier sacrifice than could be expected of him. A feudo-dynastic alliance of this kind had, for a king who was committed to it, certain grave disadvantages, prominent among them the hostility of the allied family's enemies. The king was thus liable to become involved in feuds from which in the long run he was as likely as not to be the chief loser.

The year 1136 found Waleran and his twin, Robert earl of Leicester, very actively engaged not so much in protecting Stephen's interests in Normandy as in carrying on a vendetta with Roger de Tosny, their hereditary enemy. Roger was the head of one of the great baronial families of Normandy and no mean antagonist for the Beaumonts. He was seigneur of Conches, some twenty kilometres south-east of Beaumont-le-Roger, which, rather than Tosny itself, was the *caput* of the Honour of Tosny in Normandy. Such internecine strife did not contribute to uniting the Norman baronage under Stephen to meet the menace of Angevin attack, and the king's own ill-starred visit to Normandy in 1137 alienated numbers of them from his cause. Waleran was active as a soldier in these years. Early in 1138 he drove the king of Scots from the siege of Wark castle, but returned to Normandy with his twin and William of Ypres in May. While they repelled an Angevin attack they failed to scotch that danger and they failed, too, to deal effectively with the earl of Gloucester, who was established in Caen. What was accomplished was, surprisingly enough, the reconciliation of Roger de Tosny with the Beaumonts and shortly afterwards with Stephen. It is probable that Waleran received the earldom of Worcester for his services, past and future, perhaps as early as 1138. We cannot pause here to review the history of the loss of Normandy.

The outcome for Stephen of his alliance with the Beaumonts was a whole series of unfortunate, even disastrous, complications. There is little room to doubt that they, and most especially Waleran, aspired to a dominant position in the Anglo-Norman dominions. This brought them into conflict with a number of rival interests. In the first place, their influence with his brother was deeply resented by Henry bishop of Winchester as a threat to his own predominance and aims. If the election on 24 December to the vacant see of Canterbury of the relatively obscure Theobald of Bec (of whose house Waleran was *advocatus*) was indeed engineered by the Beaumonts, Henry's feelings are understandable. Not only did the circumstances make this a personal affront, not only was it a bitter disappointment for him, but it also undermined the close relationship between him and the king, upon which Stephen's initial success had been founded and upon which Henry's hopes for the future must largely depend. Next, Beaumont ambition was hostile to the old servants of Henry I, especially

Roger, bishop of Salisbury, and his family, who were still prominent under Stephen. The 'arrest of the bishops' in June 1139 was
often, then and since, attributed to Beaumont influence; certainly
it was a Beaumont dependent, Philip de Harcourt, who replaced
the fallen chancellor, Roger le Poer. It must have looked as if the
whole administration was about to be taken over by the Beaumonts. These events completed the breach between Stephen and
his brother and no subsequent reconciliation could ever quite
restore their old alliance; it was a disaster for both of them. The
same events, together with the threatening extension of the
Beaumont tentacles into Worcestershire, were a warning to Miles
of Gloucester. He was probably convinced that there was no
future for him in the service of a king who was abandoning the
ways of the Lion of Justice (so exceedingly profitable to his devoted servants) in favour of that feudo-dynasticism against which
the old king had so consistently and so successfully striven. It is
not difficult to imagine the arguments used so effectively by the
earl of Gloucester when he won Miles over to the side of the
empress soon after her landing in England at the end of September
1139. If this was true of Miles, it was probably true of the other
old servants of Henry I who joined the empress. It is tempting
and easy to make the Beaumonts the scapegoats for every disastrous blunder of Stephen's first five years, but the onus must lie on
the king himself. There is no doubt that Stephen's policy for
political and military reasons of strengthening the position of the
Beaumonts in England as well as in Normandy did greatly be-
devil the whole feudo-dynastic situation: the repercussions were
powerful and widespread.

Already, when Stephen became king, Robert le Bossu was earl
of Leicester and his and Waleran's cousin german, Roger, husband
of their half-sister, Gundreda de Warenne, was earl of Warwick.
There are innuendos in contemporary histories which suggest
that Roger was a homosexual and he was certainly very much
overawed by his wife. Neither earl possessed a solid block of
territory in his earldom, but each had many vassals and numerous
manors interspersed among those of other landholders. Thus,
more than a score of manors or lordships in Leicestershire belonged to the honour of Chester and gave the earl of Chester a
considerable stake and a powerful influence there.[82] This, as we
shall see, was a matter of the utmost consequence.

In 1138 two royal grants embroiled both the Beaumonts and the king himself with members of the Beauchamp family. One of these was the grant (never really effective) of the earldom of Bedfordshire to Hugh le Poer, younger brother of Waleran and Robert. More particularly perhaps, the cause of trouble was the feudo-dynastic provision made for the intended new earl. The king arranged for Hugh's marriage to the most important heiress in Bedfordshire, the daughter of Simon de Beauchamp, the greatest tenant-in-chief in the shire, and for the transfer to him of the whole honour of Beauchamp of Bedford. With this went the hereditary custody of Bedford castle and this was in the hands of Miles de Beauchamp, who flatly refused to give it up. The genealogy of the Beauchamps of Bedford is not clear at this point and it is difficult to say upon what ground Miles's claim to the inheritance rested; he may have been a nephew of Simon.[83] Whatever the rights and wrongs of the case, the result was that Stephen had another rebellion on his hands in a vintage year of wars and risings: the great Scottish invasion and the risings of Mohun and Lovel in Somerset, Talbot at Hereford, fitz Alan at Shrewsbury and Maminot at Dover. The Beaumont earldom of Bedfordshire foundered in 1141. The other grant, that of the earldom of Worcestershire to count Waleran, was no doubt intended to strengthen the position and extend the influence of Stephen's supporters in the western shires and towards the Marches of Wales. Had Miles of Gloucester remained loyal to Stephen, the position *vis-à-vis* the earl of Gloucester and the empress would have been strong indeed; with his desertion after September 1139, the balance of power in that region tipped markedly in favour of the Angevins. Furthermore, the extension of Beaumont power into Worcestershire aroused the bitter resentment of William de Beauchamp, lord of the barony of Salwarpe (Worcs.), part of the forfeited Abetot lands. His father, Walter de Beauchamp, who died in 1131, had been sheriff of Worcestershire and a royal constable and dispenser. Henry I seems to have given Walter's constableship to his favourite, Brian fitz Count, and since Brian was a staunch supporter of the empress this might have been expected to make William de Beauchamp an adherent of Stephen. He does not, in fact, witness a single charter of Stephen, so it is doubtful whether he ever supported the king. By the beginning of August 1141 we find him in the camp of the temporarily triumphant empress, who, as was her wont in such cases, bid excessively high for his support. Her charter in his favour *c.* 25 July – 1 August 1141 confirmed to him the castle of Worcester with its *motte*, to be held in chief, hereditarily, of Maud and her heirs, and also the shrievalty of Worcestershire and the forests of that heavily afforested region at the old ferm for which his father had held them.[84] Once again, it must be strongly emphasised, it is upon an hereditary castellanship and a shrievalty (the two very often went together) that such great store is set by a feudatory. The text of the charter continues as follows:

For this, William himself became my liege man against all mortals and expressly against Waleran, count of Meulan, in such wise that neither count Waleran not any of those aforesaid[85] may make a fine with me (i.e., in effect, pay for an arrangement) whereby William should not hold of me in chief, unless of his own freewill and consent he wish to hold of the aforesaid count.

This leaves no doubt as to whom William de Beauchamp regarded as his chief enemy, though it is interesting to note that already a change of allegiance by Waleran was in the air. The charter also includes various grants of land, of which the most important is the castle and honour of Tamworth (Staffs.), whose Domesday lord was Robert the dispenser, brother of Urse d'Abetot. This inheritance was claimed by William de Beauchamp, as it had been by his father, Walter, who had obtained Urse's constableship in the royal household and his shrievalty of Worcester through his marriage to Urse's daughter, Emmeline. But that part of the inheritance of Robert the dispenser which comprised the honour of Tamworth had passed to the family of Marmion, possibly because Roger Marmion, who died before Michaelmas 1129, had married a daughter of Urse d'Abetot. Cousins they might be, but William de Beauchamp and Robert Marmion, Roger's son and heir, were on opposite sides in the wars of Stephen's reign because of their rival claims to the inheritance of Robert the dispenser. Such a complication was typical of a feudo-dynastic situation which, in the circumstances of a disputed title to the crown itself, had got thoroughly out of hand. Numbers of individual and family claims and feuds of this kind were caught up in the struggle between Stephen and the empress. With very few exceptions, such as Brian fitz Count and William Martel, self interest rather than conviction determined men's allegiance. Count Waleran's desertion from Stephen before the end of 1141 did not by any means put an end to the feud between him and Walter de Beauchamp. As we have seen, it was still being actively pursued in the town and castle of Worcester in 1152.

These contretemps with the Beauchamps cannot be compared with the enormous strife to which the discontents and the ambitions of the earl of Chester gave rise. There can be no doubt that Rannulf II de Gernon, earl of Chester, with his numerous lordships in Nottinghamshire and Derbyshire, Leicestershire, Warwickshire, Staffordshire and Northamptonshire, was a restless and uncomfortable neighbour for the Ferrers, Peverils and Beaumonts. His possessions were not confined to these midland shires. The honour of Chester, apart from the palatinate itself, also included large fiefs in Yorkshire and Lincolnshire and lands in Berkshire, Bucks., Devon, Dorset, Essex, Gloucestershire, Hants., Oxfordshire, Rutland, Norfolk and Suffolk, Somerset and Wilts.[86] Earl Rannulf was one of the very greatest territorial magnates in England. He and his father, Rannulf le Meschin, were hereditary *vicomtes* of the Bessin (Calvados) and earls Hugh and Richard, whom they succeeded, were hereditary *vicomtes* of the Avranchin (Manche) where they had important military duties. It would be interesting, but not in the least profitable, to speculate upon what the outcome might have been had Stephen at the outset pinned his faith on the earl of Chester instead of on the Beaumonts. Rannulf's character is not drawn in flattering terms by contemporaries. He was, says Henry of Huntingdon in the pre-battle oration he puts into the mouth of Baldwin fitz Gilbert at Lincoln,

a man audacious but lacking in judgment; ready to plot treason but wavering in pursuit of it; ready to rush into battle and regardless of all danger; aiming beyond his reach; striving after the unattainable . . . for whatever he begins like a man he ends like a woman; unfortunate in all his undertakings, in his military engagements he has either been defeated or, if by chance he wins an occasional victory, it is with greater loss to himself than to the defeated.

Perhaps, writing some time after the battle of Lincoln, where Rannulf greatly distinguished himself, Henry of Huntingdon's intention in this passage was ironical. To judge from his actions, earl Rannulf was a man of enterprise and daring and determination. He was also arrogant, touchy and hot-headed and he was a man with a grievance. This was a legacy from Henry I, the result of a piece of manipulation that was very typical of him, especially after the loss of his heir in the *White Ship* in 1120, when he feared that all his achievements were endangered, and his dynasty certainly was imperilled. One of those who perished in the *White Ship* was Richard d'Avranches, earl of Chester and lord of the vast honour whose extent has been indicated. Henry granted the earldom of Chester to Richard's cousin, Rannulf I, le Meschin, *vicomte* of the Bessin and lord of the honour of Carlisle. While there is no good authority for the statement that in return for the earldom Rannulf was obliged to surrender Carlisle, this is really a quibble, for there is no possible manner of doubt that Carlisle was taken from him and other affronts and losses were inflicted upon him. Rannulf le Meschin had married Lucy, widow of Roger fitz Gerald de Roumare (and previously of Ivo de Taillebois), and her son and heir by her second marriage was William de Roumare. In the ordinary course of events Lucy's third husband, earl Rannulf I, might have expected to obtain control of her inheritance (the honour of Bolingbroke), her dower (a considerable holding in Lincolnshire) and the temporary guardianship of his step-son's inheritance. He may have hoped also to make good her hereditary claims in Lincoln castle. King Henry must certainly have considered, with every justification, that the earldom and honour of Chester already constituted a potential menace. He was clear-sighted enough to perceive what Horace Round perceived seven and a half centuries later, that an earl of Chester with bastions at Chester and Coventry and with lordships and castles scattered across the midland shires and with a large fee in Lincolnshire would hold a menacing strategic position astride the centre of the kingdom. In the north there was the large Chester fee in Yorkshire. These possessions must on no account be augmented by the acquisition of still more lands and strongholds in Lincolnshire and by the recovery of Carlisle, which would make the earl of Chester the dominant feudal power in central and northern England. Henry I saw to it that this did not occur. Furthermore, when William de Roumare asked for his paternal inheritance in 1122, Henry declined to give it to him. William, not unnaturally, rebelled and with others joined William Clito. In 1128, when the Clito menace had been removed, Henry found it expedient to pardon William de Roumare and restore him to high favour. But if

William de Roumare had been conciliated, his step-father, earl Rannulf I, and his half-brother Rannulf II, had not. They could not bring themselves to acquiesce in the permanent loss of Carlisle. Rannulf II de Gernon (or *aux Gernons*) succeeded his father in 1129 and, as may be seen in another context, this was the occasion for the extraction of large sums of money from him and his mother by the rapacious exchequer machine.[87]

If earl Rannulf II entered the new reign with bright and optimistic hopes of obtaining from the easy-going Stephen what Henry I had denied him, they were very quickly blighted. Stephen's friends the Beaumonts were probably anxious enough to see the menacing power of their neighbour, the earl of Chester, curbed, but the greatest hindrance to the realisation of Rannulf's hopes was, at first, the king of Scots. Shortly after Christmas, 1135, David II crossed the border, nominally at least in support of his niece, the empress, whom he had, in his capacity as an English earl, taken the oath to acknowledge as Henry I's successor.[88] He took the castles of Carlisle, Wark, Alnwick, Norham and Newcastle, but any further advance was prevented by the arrival of king Stephen early in February 1136. A temporary settlement was negotiated whereby David's son, Henry, did homage to Stephen at York (an act which David was careful not to countenance by his presence) and received Carlisle and Doncaster besides his mother's earldom of Huntingdon. Stephen also promised that his claim to the earldom of Northumbria should receive first consideration if he should see his way to re-create it. The grant of his father's old honour of Carlisle to the Scots was taken very ill indeed by the earl of Chester. When Henry of Scots attended Stephen's Easter court in 1136 and was placed at the king's right hand, the insulting behaviour of archbishop William of Canterbury, who considered the place his by right, and of the exasperated earl of Chester, bereft of Carlisle, obliged him to withdraw. After further Anglo-Scottish wars, culminating in the battle of the Standard, generous terms of peace were arranged, despite Scottish reverses, by the instrumentality of the papal legate and Stephen's queen. These were embodied in the treaty of Durham in April 1139, and they included not only the grant of the earldom of Northumbria to the prince of Scots but also the confirmation to him of Carlisle. This was a settlement in which the earl of Chester could not be expected to acquiesce meekly, and Stephen very soon made matters worse. The grant of the earldom of Lincoln to William II d'Aubigny (*pincerna*) was undoubtedly resented by earl Rannulf's half-brother and constant ally, William de Roumare, who had considerable possessions and hereditary claims in Lincolnshire. The grant to him of the earldom of Cambridgeshire not a very satisfactory consolation prize, even if it did encroach on Scottish rights in the earldom of Huntingdon. Worse still from Rannulf's point of view was the marriage which Stephen arranged for the detested prince of Scots, the usurper of Carlisle. He was given as his bride Ada de Warenne, half-sister of Waleran, Robert and Hugh de Beaumont. At a time when Beaumont influence was predominant at Stephen's court, this must have appeared to the earl of Chester as a very sinister move. The Scot, now firmly entrenched in Northumbria, Carlisle and Huntingdonshire, was allied by marriage with a family group whose power in the Midlands already constituted a dangerous threat to Rannulf's position and ambitions there. Stephen and his advisers may have thought that at one blow they had pacified the Scots and cleverly curbed the dangerous power of the earl of Chester. If so, they deceived themselves. The first reaction of earl Rannulf was to attempt to waylay and capture Henry of Scots and his bride.[89] It seems clear that late in 1140 Stephen made a serious effort at conciliation. He met Rannulf and William de Roumare in Lincolnshire and 'increased the honours' of the former[90] and probably gave the earldom of Lincoln to the latter. Earl Rannulf seems to have given in return some kind of undertaking of good behaviour. In making concessions at this time, Stephen showed his weakness and earned the contempt of earl Rannulf. There followed the seizure of Lincoln castle by Rannulf and William, Stephen's arrival in the Christmas holiday to bring them to book, the battle of Lincoln on 2 February 1141, and all that ensued from that disaster to royal arms. These and later events have already been mentioned and need not be traced again in detail.[91]

One fact stands out starkly in the whole history of earl Rannulf's career. At every critical juncture, and not only then but consistently and continuously, he was moved solely by consideration of his own interests – not always his best interests, hot-head that he was. The fact that he sought military aid from earl Robert of Gloucester for the operation which led to the battle of Lincoln does not necessarily mean that he had gone over to the side of the empress. Earl Robert was his father-in-law. For Rannulf the battle of Lincoln was a battle between Stephen and himself. A charter of Simon Tuschet, a tenant of the honour of Chester, in favour of the nuns of Haverholme (Lincs.) is dated 'in the year when the battle occurred between king Stephen and the earl of Chester',[92] which shows that at least one of the earl's vassals saw the event as a personal affair. The arrogant behaviour of the empress in her hour of victory must have caused earl Rannulf some misgivings. This led him to join the queen when she summoned the royalist adherents for an attack on Winchester; but his good faith was naturally suspect and such was his reception that he then joined the empress 'late and ineffectively'.[93] Stephen might be the Lord's Anointed and the empress not so, at least in England, but earl Rannulf did not conduct his concerns with any regard for such considerations. His approach to public business was that of a feudatory and one who, as earl of Chester, was untrammelled by any vestige of royal control in the administration of his palatinate.

Nothing could be more revealing than the *détente* between him and Robert earl of Leicester at some date between 19 December 1148 and 16 December 1153, which seems to have ended a period of warfare between them, about which we have no details.[94] This agreement is in the form of a chirograph, that is to say that duplicate texts were written on a sheet of parchment which was then cut in two leaving one copy for each party. When the document begins by saying that this is the final peace and concord which was accepted and divided by the two earls (*concessa et divisa*), it means precisely that. This was done in the presence of Robert de Chesney, bishop of Lincoln, and the earls' own men, three being named on each side. The agreement is very strictly a feudal and military affair. There are detailed arrangements about castles. The two earls undertake in two separate clauses almost identically worded to keep faith with each other saving the faith that each owes to his liege lord. There is no indication of who the liege lords were, whether Stephen or duke Henry (and since there is no mention of a liege lady, presumably the empress was not involved, which suggests a date after the early part of 1148 if not after 1150). No explicit reference is made to the king; the royal authority as such is ignored. If either earl should be obliged to march against the other with his liege lord he may not bring more than twenty knights and any captured property is to be restored.

Neither earl may seek to entrap the other (*impedire corpus*) unless he has defied him a fortnight in advance. This is reminiscent of the *Consuetudines et Justicie* of William the Conqueror. The earl of Leicester undertakes to aid the earl of Chester against all men except his liege lord and earl Simon of Northampton, his son-in-law. If earl Simon attacks (or injures) the earl of Chester and refuses to make amends at the request of the earl of Leicester, he is not to receive assistance; if however the earl of Chester should injure earl Simon and refuse to make amends at the request of the earl of Leicester, then the latter may assist Simon. A precisely similar arrangement is made in respect of the earl of Chester's ally, earl Robert de Ferrers. This last mentioned alliance is a little surprising. The earls of Chester and Leicester have pledged their faith in the hand of Robert, bishop of Lincoln, to keep this agreement, the bishop standing surety for its enforcement and if either party fails to keep it within fifteen days after he has been requested to do so, the bishop of Lincoln and the bishop of Chester are to do justice upon him, as for broken faith.

This episcopal guarantee is most interesting. The whole implication of the document is that the king, who is never mentioned, is powerless to keep the peace and these two great feudal magnates, who clearly do not trust each other, but are earnestly anxious to put an end to the state of war between them, are obliged to look for an ecclesiastical guarantee. Respect is paid to the liege lord (or lords) but he is conceived of as a nominal overlord, who seems to know no other way of dealing with the internecine feuds of his vassals than taking part in them himself. One other clause of the agreement is of such peculiar interest that it must be given in full:

And, if earl Rannulf make a complaint against William de Alneto, the earl of Leicester shall hold him to right in his court, so long as the said William shall remain the man of the earl of Leicester and hold land of him. And provided that, if William and his men shall have withdrawn from the fealty of the earl of Leicester by reason of the destruction of his castle or because he is unwilling to do right in the earl of Leicester's court, neither William nor his men shall be received into the power of the earl of Chester to work evil against the earl of Leicester.

If the king was unable to restrain his recalcitrant earls, they in turn found themselves in a very uncomfortable position. Clearly, neither the earl of Chester nor the earl of Leicester was entirely

7

confident of his ability to control his own vassals. William de
Alneto, a sub-tenant of the earl of Leicester, seems to have been a
castleman, whose castle had been destroyed and who, on that
account, had a grievance. It was hoped that if a complaint arose
feudal justice would take its ordinary course in the overlord's
court, as custom required.[95] If the vassal refused to stand to right,
then it was devoutly to be hoped that he would not seek the protection of one of his lord's enemies, and this must be prevented, if
possible, by agreements such as the present one. The whole structure of feudal society in the worst afflicted parts of England was
very severely shaken by the wars of Stephen's reign. Treaties such
as those which the earl of Leicester made with his powerful
neighbours, the earl of Chester and the earl of Hereford, and such
as the successive earls of Gloucester and Hereford made with each
other, seemed the only way of preventing anarchy. This state of
affairs was made possible by the disputed title to the throne, by the
weakness both of Stephen and the empress and by their readiness
to give enormous bribes. But for the feudo-dynastic self-interest of
numbers of the aristocracy, who kept wars and disturbances going,
the Angevins might not have been able to maintain their position
in England after the death of the earl of Gloucester in 1147. As it
was, Stephen never succeeded in making himself unquestioned
master in his whole kingdom, and effective control only became
possible after he had reached a final agreement with duke Henry
in 1153.

There is need for further and more detailed studies of the
aristocracy in Stephen's reign. One of the most interesting and
illuminating would be a study of the Yorkshire baronage, based
upon the splendid series of volumes of *Early Yorkshire Charters*
edited, with such erudition and such intimate knowledge of the
family relationships and feudal structure of the region, by the late
William Farrer and by Sir Charles Clay. There is much that is interesting and illuminating in the history of such families as the
Bruces, who skilfully kept a foot on each of two tightropes and a
fief on each side of the Scottish border. The family probably came
from Brix (dép. Manche, cant. Valognes) and the indications are
that Robert 1 de Brus was given his Yorkshire fee soon after the
battle of Tinchebrai (28 September 1106).[96] This Robert was a
close friend of David 1, king of Scots, by whom he was given the
fee of Annandale soon after 1124. English barons had gone to

David's aid on at least one occasion when rebellion threatened
him,[97] and a number of them held Scottish fiefs. We may accept
the spirit of the speech which Aelred of Rievaulx put into the
mouth of Robert Brus before the battle of the Standard, when he
told the king of Scots roundly that he owed to the barons of
northern England both his kingdom and the security of his position there. Robert I de Brus was an adherent of king David and
witnessed a good many of his charters during the years after 1134
and he supported him as staunchly as he could till his death in
1142. When, however, in 1138 David pushed with his army right
into Yorkshire, Brus with his fellow barons of the north, having
done everything in his power and yet having failed to persuade
the king of Scots that his best interests would be served by withdrawal, renounced his allegiance and fought against him. In this
affair the influence of the venerable Thurstan, archbishop of
York, played a decisive part. Robert II de Brus (le Meschin) sided
with his father, but his younger brother, Adam, was on the
Scottish side in the battle of the Standard. Thus the continuance of
the fee of Annandale in Brus hands was assured. It is an interesting
fact that the English army after its victory over the Scots at
Northallerton did not follow it up and turn the Scottish flight into
an utter *débâcle*. It was not in the interests of the northern barons
to do so; they had too much at stake in Scotland. After the treaty
of Durham in 1139, those who held fiefs of the Scots quickly returned to their allegiance to the king of Scots and to his son,
Henry, earl of Northumbria. It was in the north that plurality of
homage and conflicting allegiances made themselves most acutely
felt, but these men were extraordinarily successful in avoiding the
unpleasant consequences which might be expected to result from
this state of affairs.

Interesting and valuable as the study of such family groups
would be, we need even more to learn about those who sought no
more than the enjoyment of what they had and such protection
from injury and loss as was available in this age of violence, of
men like Osbert de Wanci, the Pinkney tenant, whom we have
seen so concerned about the safety of his cattle. The Pinkneys
(from Picquiqny) were small tenants-in-chief in Northamptonshire and others were mesne-tenants of the honours of Chokes and
Warenne. A Walter de Pinkney was Stephen's garrison commander
at Malmesbury in 1145, a man well versed in the arts of war; and

again in 1147, after being captured and handed over to the empress, he was engaged in violent hostilities on the Hampshire-Wiltshire borders, pillage of church property and savage oppression in the manner so often described by contemporary historians. He met a spectacular end at the hands of a local man who 'boldly swung a very sharp axe at his neck'.[98] If Gilbert de Pinkney was closely related to Walter, his sub-tenant, Osbert de Wanci, may well have had cause to fear reprisals. The history of many families may seem about as exciting as the 'begats' in the Book of Genesis. That, indeed, is very largely how we see them in surviving muniments and monuments, together, of course, with their lands. Yet these lesser men are the very stuff of feudal society, no less important, if only we could see them clearly in their real environment, than the great families whose history can be written in terms so much more dramatic.

It is often said or implied that the *tempus werre*, as contemaries so often called it, taught the English baronage a very severe lesson about the drawbacks for themselves of a weak monarchy and made them the more willing to acquiesce in, if not positively to welcome, the firm rule of Henry II. Let us, however, beware of exaggeration. The barons respected a strong king, but only because he obliged them to do so. They did not want another Lion of Justice. There is little indication of any widespread belief among them that a powerful monarchy would be preferable to the prevailing conditions. For the great barons that was probably not the best alternative. In 1152 and 1153, when the war between Stephen and Henry began to be waged with a new determination on both sides, the barons became thoroughly alarmed by the possibility of a decisive victory for one or other of the contenders. When, as a result of operations connected with the siege of Crowmarsh in 1153, a pitched battle between the king and the duke seemed imminent, barons on both sides busied themselves frantically to arrange a truce. They feared, as Henry of Huntingdon so ingenuously puts it, lest the defeat of the one should enable the other to dominate them the more easily, whereas a continued state of mutual apprehension would prevent either Stephen or Henry from subjecting them effectually to royal authority.[99] Perhaps the greater magnates were still content to limit their feuds and private wars by such treaties as the earl of Leicester made with the earls of Chester and Hereford. This was not a practical alternative to an effective central government, for obviously such local agreements were likely to ensure only a precarious stability in limited areas for limited times. It is clear, too, from the terms of the treaty between the earls of Chester and Leicester that the mesne tenants were getting out of hand, jibbing at honorial justice and reluctant to hold their castles entirely at the service of their lords. Adulterine castles were as much a menace to the barons as they were to the crown. It is clear enough from every contemporary history that these represented gangsterdom through the length and breadth of the land. The continued warfare, in which armies invariably lived off the country, wasted the substance of a great many barons. However extortionately they might treat their peasants, landlords were bound to feel severely the effects of such conditions as *Gesta Stephani* describes (with certain inconsistencies) in 1143:

Some, through lack of food (for a dire famine prevailed all over England), ate the forbidden and unaccustomed flesh of dogs and horses to relieve their hunger; others fed unsatisfied on raw and filthy herbs and roots. Some in every region . . . wasted away and died in droves, others voluntarily took themselves off with their families into sad exile. You could have seen vills with very well-known names standing solitary and almost empty, the peasants of either sex and every age dead, the fields growing white with a fine harvest, for autumn had arrived, but their cultivators taken away from them by the dreadful famine, and all England bearing everywhere the look of grief and calamity, the aspect of misery and oppression.

The historian continues with a description of the savage depredations of the mercenary troops. This account does not altogether hang together; it is in fact a very recognisable variant of a more or less standard description of the effects of warfare and famine. We cannot, however, ignore it; men, women and children suffered horribly, whatever form the author's description may take and, beyond a doubt, the agrarian economy of parts of England must have been seriously, if only very temporarily, affected. If the barons in 1153 were not very anxious to see either Stephen or Henry victorious, they had very good reasons to wish and to work for the ending of hostilities. The continuation, if only for another year or two, of the intensified warfare of 1153 would have brought widespread ruin: it would not be confined mainly to the old campaigning grounds in the middle and upper Thames valley and the western shires, for it had already spread to the Midlands and east and might engulf any part of the country. The English baronage was sensible enough to see that, on balance, its own interests required the ending of the war. Private wars regulated by private treaties were no longer tolerable.

6

The Royal Household

The nuclei of central government in the kingdoms of medieval Christendom are to be sought in the courts and in the households of their kings. They are to be found in the assemblies of magnates whose duty it was and whose right it was in feudal monarchies to advise the king, to declare the law which it was his duty to enforce, and to act, under his presidency, as a supreme court of justice. But such assemblies were, in the nature of things, occasional. It was the custom of the Norman kings to hold high festival and to wear their crown in state at the three principal feasts of the year. Under the Conqueror these crown-wearings were said to take place in Gloucester at Christmas, in Winchester at Easter and in Westminster at Whitsuntide,[1] but the locations soon varied, since it was not easy for an itinerant court, especially one that was often in Normandy, to maintain so strict a schedule. On these occasions great matters might be discussed and determined but obviously many important things had to be decided when the king had not got all his tenants-in-chief around him. Then he would be advised by such magnates as happened to be in attendance and by the officials of his household. There are few detailed descriptions of the meetings of the *magnum concilium*. We learn a little about its activities from contemporary accounts of the arrests of Geoffrey de Mandeville, earl of Essex, and of the earl of Chester. The author of *Gesta Stephani* gives some account of the great council of churchmen and laymen which Stephen summoned in London at Easter 1136 and, in one respect at least, this is of considerable interest. The metaphor used is highly uncomplimentary and coarse and the meaning is not entirely clear. What the author seems to say is that 'flowing together there as if into a single bilge, or sewer (*sentinam*), the pillars of the church sitting ranged in order, the ordinary members (*vulgo*) also as usual pushing themselves in everywhere in disorderly confusion, many matters for the profit of the kingdom and the church were usefully brought up and beneficially discussed'. It does not seem likely that the word *vulgo* here refers to the rabble of London. More probably it means the main body of councillors, who did not trouble to seat themselves according to rank and precedence, as the clergy did. The proceedings were apparently quite uninhibited by the presence of the king. Vigorous speeches were made denouncing Henry I's treatment of the church as well as his immorality. The king listened patiently and made the necessary concessions, which were shortly afterwards embodied in his 'Oxford charter of liberties'.[2] The work of the *magnum concilium* as a court is discussed in connection with the administration of justice.[3]

For the ordinary business of administration the king relied upon a small group of trusted supporters and upon the great officers of his household. The greatest of all the royal ministers, though not as such a member of the household, was the chief justiciar, whose office came into prominence under Henry I, because his frequent absences in Normandy made it necessary to have someone to deputise for him at such times not merely at the head of the judiciary but to supervise the whole English administration.[4] The functions of chief justiciar seem to have been performed during the greater part of Henry I's reign by Roger, bishop of Salisbury. He denied that he had ever been in Stephen's service, for he had taken the oath to Maud; but, if he hoped that he might not seem to have broken it, he deceived himself. The observant William of Malmesbury reports:

I have often heard Roger, bishop of Salisbury, saying that he was released from the oath he had sworn to the empress: for he had taken the oath on the understanding (*eo pacto*) that the king would not give his daughter in marriage to anyone outside the kingdom without consulting him and the other magnates. No one advised that marriage, or knew that it would take place, except Robert earl of Gloucester, and Brian fitz Count and the bishop of Lisieux. I would not say, on this account, that I would believe the word of a man who knew how to adapt himself to every situation according to the changeability of fortune; but, like a true historian, I put down in my writing the opinion of the people of the realm (*opinionem provincialium*).[5]

In any case, one of Roger's own *acta* gives him the lie. This is a writ of about 1138 addressed to Sibyl, widow of Payn fitz John,

one of Henry 1's sheriffs and justices. It begins: 'I command you
on the king's behalf and on my own' and ends: 'as the king ordered
in his writ'.[6] Another writ of bishop Roger, issued about 1137–8,
addressed to the sheriff of Herefordshire on behalf of St Guthlac's
Priory, Hereford, a dependency of Gloucester Abbey, must also
have been issued by him in his capacity as chief justiciar, but the
appropriate formula (quoted above) is not used.[7] This writ opens
with a most peremptory injunction: 'Cause the monks of Gloucester to have . . .' it ends: 'And unless you do so Miles of Gloucester
shall cause it to be done'. No subject, other than the chief
justiciar, could write with such impressive authority. There can
be no doubt that despite his denial bishop Roger continued to act
as Stephen's chief justiciar perhaps until 24 June 1139, when he
was arrested, together with his son Roger the chancellor and his
nephew Alexander, bishop of Lincoln, at Oxford.[8] It was said by
Aubrey de Vere, the king's spokesman at the legatine council of
Winchester in that year, that bishop Roger did not often come to
court, and this was held against him by his enemies, so he may not
have been a very active chief justiciar during the early years of
Stephen's reign.

The need for such an officer became, in one respect, less urgent
after Henry 1's death. Stephen is only known to have been out of
England once in the whole course of his reign (apart from one very
brief Scottish campaign); that was between mid-March and late
November 1137, when he was in Normandy. Stephen was by no
means inactive or incompetent in judicial and administrative business. Nonetheless there was still need for a capable and experienced
official at the head of the administration for, as Richardson and
Sayles have observed, the system made enormous demands upon
the king, such as few men were capable of sustaining, and they
consider that there is no more melancholy reading than the lives of
the kings of England.[9] One may disagree with the latter part of the
generalisation, that is, about the melancholy reading of royal lives,
but the assessment of the burden which kings had to bear is just.
On few kings can it have pressed more heavily than upon Stephen.
The rigours of his travels alone, apart from the business transacted
and the fighting in which he was so constantly engaged, must have
been uncommonly severe. He performed great cross-country
marches at all seasons and in all weathers by abominable roads and
tracks. Stephen's stamina, like that of most medieval kings, must

7*

have been remarkable. For example, in the year 1139 even the bare skeleton itinerary that it is possible to construct for him gives at least thirty-four journeys from place to place, ranging from Leominster in the west to London in the east, from Newark in the north to Arundel in the south. There were five major sieges of places as far apart as Ludlow, Corfe, Marlborough, Arundel and Trowbridge. There occurred the arrest of the bishops at Oxford and the pursuit of bishop Nigel to Devizes and the landing of the empress and her brother Robert, which entailed Stephen's presence at Arundel, and the death of the bishop of Salisbury which brought Stephen to that town. These are only the events and the movements which were important enough to be recorded. For the king there can hardly have been a day out of the saddle; and yet medieval kings were as likely as not to employ their few hours of leisure in the chase.

After the fall of bishop Roger the office of chief justiciar does not seem to have been filled. Queen Matilda acted bravely and vigorously on her husband's behalf during his captivity, between 2 February and 1 November 1141, but this was quite a different matter. It was expected of a lady, especially of a queen, so to act in such circumstances and the expectation was usually justified. The claim that Richard de Lucy was chief justiciar during the latter part of Stephen's reign is not borne out by the charters cited, all of which seem to refer to his position as a local justice in London and Essex.[10] Similarly the suggestion of Dr West that duke Henry acted as chief justiciar for Stephen after their treaty in 1153 is not sustained. The charters cited cannot with certainty, or even probability, be dated after the treaty.[11] That the royal administration did not ostensibly suffer a complete and disastrous breakdown as soon as the guiding hands of bishop Roger and his family were so forcibly removed is a remarkable tribute both to the efficiency and stability of the administrative machine that had been established under Henry 1 and to the ability of Stephen and his officials to keep it functioning, however imperfectly. Amid all the justifiable denunciations of Stephen for feebleness and futility, this ought to be remembered.

Much was due, in all probability, to the efficiency of the royal household and to the strength which enabled it to survive not only a spate of desertions to the empress in and after 1139 but also more remarkable still, to survive, however weakened, the disaster which must have overtaken it when the king was captured at Lincoln. This is an aspect of medieval government which deserves more attention than it has ever received. It is easy to attribute the survival of a government in times of stress to a bishop Roger or a Hubert Walter, but what could they have achieved without a governmental machine capable of withstanding exceptional stresses?

The organisation of the royal household in Stephen's reign is revealed to us primarily by a document of unknown authorship called *Constitutio Domus Regis*, which may be translated as 'the establishment of the royal household'.[12] It has been suggested that this document was drawn up either by or for Nigel, bishop of Ely, who had been Henry I's treasurer. It survives not in the original manuscript but in two later compilations *The Red Book of the Exchequer* and *The Little Black Book of the Exchequer*. The *Constitutio* shows how the royal household was organised at the end of Henry I's reign. It is clear from internal evidence that it was drawn up after his death, which is explicitly mentioned, and before John fitz Gilbert, who appears in it as master marshal, went over to the empress. These facts give us the extreme limits of date for the document, namely 1 December 1135 and some time in September 1139 (for Stephen was besieging John Marshal's castle of Marlborough when the empress landed in England at the end of September 1139).[13] The *Constitutio* is generally believed to have been prepared for the new king very soon after his accession, probably early in 1136. In it are set out in order the officers of the royal household and their subordinate staffs with their scales of pay and allowances. Implicit in this are the limitations of the *Constitutio* as a source of information about the royal household. It was not primarily concerned with the details of the duties of individuals or groups of officials, but only with the establishment and its liveries or payments and allowances. It gives us no more than a bare framework round which we may build, to a limited extent, with materials from other sources. One of the most useful of such sources is the *Dialogus de Scaccario*, or 'Dialogue concerning the Exchequer', which dates from a generation later than the *Constitutio*, in the next reign, and it is not easy to determine whether or how far it may legitimately be used for our purpose. Additional contemporary material is by no means negligible. It is possible to discover from the witness-lists of important royal charters issued on state occasions, such as the 'Oxford charter of liberties' of April 1136, who the holders of the great household offices were. This information can be supplemented from other charters and from histories and chronicles. In this way a reasonably clear idea may be formed of the personnel of the royal household and of its fluctuations during the reign. An examination of the family connections and recorded actions of individual officers provides some additional information about the tenure of their offices and the nature of their administrative and other functions. This is of the utmost importance because it was upon the members of his household that a twelfth-century king had to rely for the performance of many of the judicial, administrative and financial functions of central and of local government. In one other way we may enlarge our knowledge, namely by a careful examination of the official products of the activities of the household officers and their staffs. In the mid-twelfth century the household was not yet as far as we know so fully departmentalised that each department had its own secretarial staff and records. Such invaluable records of departmental activities as wardrobe books and the like are not yet available, and without them the functioning of the household cannot be observed in detail. The products of one department, however, are available in plenty – the charters and writs which emanated from what is often loosely referred to as the Chancery. It is doubtful whether we can properly talk of a Chancery but there is no doubt whatever of the existence of a royal scriptorium in which royal documents were written, and its activities will in due course be examined.

One of the first things which must strike even the most casual reader of the *Constitutio* is the immense importance that attached to status. This was the case throughout society, not simply in the royal household. Status in the household is reflected in the liveries of the officers, that is to say in their rates of pay and allowances of simnels, wine and those peculiar status-symbols, candles and even candle-ends. So, for example, the chancellor was allowed one large wax candle and forty candle-ends daily, while one of his chief subordinates, the master of the writing-office (*magister scriptorii*), even at the increased rate of pay and allowances given by Henry 1 to Robert De Sigillo, keeper of the royal seal 1131–5, when there was no chancellor,[14] had only one small wax candle and twenty-four candle-ends. The seneschals, stewards or sewers (*dapiferi*), who acted in turn as (formally) head of the kitchen, pantry and larder and were officers of the first rank like the chancellor, had as many candles as they wanted (*plenarie candelam*). Their subordinate, the clerk of the spence of bread and wine, an officer of the second rank like the master of the scriptorium had, when living in the household, the same livery as the latter but when he did not eat in he had an additional 10*d* a day. Even candle-ends represented a degree of amenity which only officials of some importance enjoyed. The rush-dip, which less important people may have had to make do with, was a dim and malodorous affair, but good enough for the illiterate rank-and-file. Amenity, also apportioned in accordance with status, was represented by the simnels of finest quality and the spiced wine enjoyed by the chancellor and by William fitz Odo, one of the constables. The chancellor, however, had these in addition to the allowance of salted simnels and *vin ordinaire* appropriate to an officer of his rank. These issues were quite apart from the meals eaten in the household by officers on duty. A chamberlain 'without livery', that is, in effect, not on duty, might eat in the household if he wished. Stewards, being officers of the first rank, were paid 5*s* a day, like the chancellor, when they ate out but only 3*s* 6*d* a day when they ate in, together with two salted simnels, one sextary[15] of *vin ordinaire* and their candles at discretion. Some of the ushers who were not of knightly rank ate in the household but had no livery. Certain subordinate officials, like the cook of the upper kitchen, were expected to eat in; others, like the royal tailor, ate out. Most of the lower servants had a customary, or standard, food ration, but some whose duties were probably regarded as strenuous, like the watchmen, who were under the marshal's control, were allowed a double ration. Such evidence as this may seem trivial, but it shows that status was very important and that protocol was very strict in the royal household. Conditions of a similar kind undoubtedly obtained in the households of the great magnates, clerical as well as lay.

An office in the royal household conferred great dignity, importance and influence upon its holder, whatever his rank. The holders of some of the highest offices in the royal household held great estates. Thus the honour of Haughley (Suffolk) came later to be known as the honour of the constabulary (*honor constabularie*). This was held in Stephen's reign, together with a royal constableship, by Robert de Vere, a 'new man'. He obtained the estate and the office through his marriage to Alice de Montfort, heiress of Robert de Montfort, a constable of Henry I who was banished in 1107. There is no proof, however, that at this time the lands went with the office as a grand serjeanty instead of being held in fee by the family. It is clear that when in 1133 Aubrey II de Vere received from Henry I the master chamberlainship of England (as distinct from Normandy), he was given the office itself 'in gross', hereditarily, not lands to be held in grand serjeanty by performing the service of master chamberlain.[16] Much confusion has arisen over such household offices and the lands which may appear to go with them; but where the original royal grant has survived, as in the case of Aubrey II de Vere's chamberlainship, all doubt is removed. An ecclesiastic occupying a household office of the first rank like the chancellorship, or one of the second rank such as the mastership of the scriptorium, or indeed any fortunate chaplain or clerk who won the royal favour, if only by his quick way with a mass, might look forward to high ecclesiastical preferment. Not a few bishops, deans and canons with well endowed prebends reached their thrones and comfortable stalls by this avenue. Other emoluments were not lacking. A clerk, named Adam, who was in Stephen's service, had received from Henry I a considerable amount of land in the royal soke of Hintlesham (Suffolk) hereditarily in fee for a rent of 16s and burgage land in Norwich in return for the services it owed. Stephen augmented this estate by giving Adam the land and service of one Halden, in Samford Hundred, for a rent of 2s 5½d in lieu of all services.[17] It is perhaps an unwarranted assumption that these grants represent royal generosity to a servant. Charters do not always reveal the financial transactions, the inheritances and so forth which underlie them, so that what has the appearance of a royal gift may, in fact, be something very different. Two royal scribes, Peter (about whose career more will be said) and Gisolf, held some property close to the city wall in Gloucester.[18] All that we can safely conclude is that the royal clerk, Adam, and the two scribes, Peter and Gisolf, held landed property, however they came by it, and were men of some little substance. For royal servants of every grade there must have been perquisites and opportunities, legitimate and otherwise, of enrichment and advancement. It is not beyond the bounds of possibility that even quite humble members of the household could invest in land or other property.

The great officers of the royal household in Stephen's reign played an important part in the work of government. It is easier to find out a little about them as individuals than to discover how the household itself functioned. Its vital importance as a central administrative machine, especially the importance of the chamber and the wardrobe, in the thirteenth century and later has been fully demonstrated by T.F.Tout in a famous work.[19] While it is a dangerous method to read history backwards, we must not dismiss the household as unimportant in the first half of the twelfth century simply because no household records have survived from so early a date. There is plenty of evidence that some of its functions were already significant. It will be convenient to sketch first the organisation of the household as a whole and then to consider the position of both individuals and groups of its officials.

The officers and servants of the household can be classified according to their liveries and their rations but, more important for the present purpose, they are divided according to their functions into five main groups. At the head of the first group is the chancellor, an official of the highest rank, paid at the top rate of 5s a day and having his allowances of simnels, wine and candles on the most generous scale. This strongly suggests, if the liveries of other first-grade officers of the household are any guide, that he did not live in, though the *Constitutio* does not actually say so. The chancellor was formally the custodian of the king's seal, though its actual custodian in Stephen's reign may have been Baldric de Sigillo.[20] The chancellor was also formally the head of the whole clerical establishment of the household. By this is meant the royal clerks (*clerici*) and chaplains (*capellani*), terms which were apparently synonymous and used, so far as one can see, without any distinction. Apart from the chaplain in charge of the chapel and relics, and the clerk of the spence of bread and wine, who appears in the *Constitutio* as a second-grade officer under the stewards, and the clerk of the constabulary, of whom we hear in the later *Dialogus de Scaccario*, there is no indication of a clerical staff or evidence (apart from what will be considered in connection with the Chancery) that there were separate scribal staffs in the scriptorium and under the chief officers of the household.

The *Constitutio* shows us two officials subordinate to the chancellor. One was the master of the scriptorium, or writing-office (*magister scriptorii*). Henry I, during the last two years of his reign, did not employ a chancellor, but used a keeper of the seal who was also master of the scriptorium. This was Robert de Sigillo, whose livery was raised to the level appropriate to a second-grade household officer, namely 2s a day, one sextary of *vin ordinaire*, one salt simnel, one small wax candle and twenty-four candle-ends. The name *de Sigillo* is in fact a title denoting the office of keeper of the seal, not in origin a family name. There is reason to believe, as we shall see, that during Stephen's reign successive chancellors concerned themselves less and less with the routine work of the scriptorium (and possibly of the exchequer also) leaving this to the master of the scriptorium, keeper of the seal. There is no mention in the *Constitutio* of a scribal staff under the master of the scriptorium, though we know that there was such a staff and it would have been very interesting to learn about its status in terms of livery. The other chief subordinate of the chancellor was the chaplain in charge of the chapel and relics, whose livery is not mentioned. A Christian name followed by *de Capella* usually denotes a holder of this office. The *Constitutio* lists four serjeants, or servants, of the chapel, each with double rations. Two sumpter-horses to carry the chapel furniture as the household moved about the country each had an allowance of 1d a day and 1d a month for shoeing, which was the standard rate for household transport.

The next group of officers in the *Constitutio* are the sewers, stewards or seneschals (*dapiferi*). These were officers of the first rank with the same pay as the chancellor, viz. 5s, when they ate out, though 1s 6d a day less and no special allowance of superior simnels and spiced wine when they were living in the household. Under the stewards, as officers of the second grade, with a basic salary of 2s a day in court, are the clerk of the spence of bread and wine, the master dispenser of bread and the master dispenser of the larder. In the third grade, at an indoors salary of 10d a day and allowances of bread and wine, are dispensers in the pantry (bread) and the larder. Since they serve in turn and are not constantly on duty, their outdoors pay of 1s 7d a day and slightly larger allowances of bread and wine are also specified in the same way as those of their superiors. The outdoors pay differentials are in fact 1s 6d a day for officers of the first rank, 10d a day for those of the second rank (who come off relatively badly) and 9d a day for those of the third rank. Other officials in the kitchen, pantry, larder and hall are naperers, an accountant (really a checker of bread issues),

ushers of the spence larder and kitchen, bakers, waferer, keeper of
the tables, bearer of the alms dish, cooks, slaughtermen, scullion
and serjeants, with the sumpter-horses necessary for transport.

Next we are told of the buttery. At its head is the master butler
(*magister pincerna*), an officer of the first rank. Then, the master
dispensers of the buttery serving in turn, who were of the third
rank. Usher, cup-bearers serving four together in turn, cellarmen,
cooper, serjeant, mazer-keeper, fruiterers, labourers and carter
complete the staff receiving liveries or rations. Persons who did
not receive these, or else a money allowance through their
superiors, were not the concern of the *Constitutio*. Various officers
in the buttery, as elsewhere in the household, have their men or
mates, for whom money allowances are made. We are probably
to understand that office-holders in the household, even those of
relatively lowly rank, did not perform in person any menial duties.
That must be what the men were for. The cellarmen, for example,
had three halfpence for each of their men and so were probably
cellar superintendents rather than rollers and tappers of casks.

After the buttery comes the chamber (*camera*), which was in
origin (and still formally) the staff of the royal bedchamber. This
was of immense importance in the household, especially as the
privy purse department, and it was destined for further development in the future. It is a pity that the *Constitutio* tells us so very
little about it, but when the administrative functions of the
chamberlains are discussed it will be possible to enlarge a little
upon what we learn there. The chief officers are two, the master
chamberlain and the treasurer. William Mauduit is mentioned by
name as having a salary of 1s 2d and being permanently on duty. His
office will be discussed below. His livery seems to equate him with
the assistant constables and the marshal when on duty. Chamberlains serving in turn were paid 2s a day, with the appropriate allowances of simnels, wine and candles, as officers of the second rank.
When they were not on duty, and were therefore 'without livery',
they might eat in the household. There was a bearer of the king's
bed, a tailor (*tallator*),[21] a chamberlain of the chandlery and an
ewer (*aquarius*) who rated a double food ration like the serjeants of
the chapel, carters of the kitchen and larder, watchmen and, interestingly enough, the mazer-keeper. The ewer had 1d for drying the
king's clothes when he travelled – a telling side-light on the
rigours of an itinerant court. He also had 4d when the king bathed,

except on the three great feasts of the year. What conclusion is to be drawn from this is not clear, unless it be that a much more exalted functionary officiated at the bath on great state occasions, least common hands might wash the balm from an anointed king.

The fifth main group of household officers includes the constables and the master marshal. The constables (no number is mentioned) are of the first rank. Three men, William fitz Odo, Henry de la Pomerai and Roger d'Oilly, are mentioned by name, presumably as assistant constables. No salary is mentioned for William fitz Odo but he has the rather exceptional allowance of superior simnel-bread and spiced wine, one small wax candle and twenty-four candle-ends, which is far more luxurious than second-grade officers usually received. The other two have the status of ordinary second-grade officers with an indoors salary of 1s 2d a day.

In 1136 Henry de la Pomerai was one of Stephen's commanders in Normandy. He married, not later than 1146, Rohese, illegitimate daughter of Henry 1 by Sibyl Corbet. The master-marshal is of the same status. Some of his special duties are mentioned, which is unique in the *Constitutio*, and these will be considered below. Four under-marshals served the household in making billeting arrangements and so on. The marshal's ushers, knightly and non-knightly, serjeants, watchmen, furnaceman and his menials, for whom a money allowance is made, complete the establishment under the constables.

At the end of the *Constitutio* comes the outdoors staff. First there is an usher of the chamber for the royal bed with an allowance of 4d a day when the king is on a journey. There is also a tent keeper with a man and a sumpter-horse. These officials must be regarded, in spite of their position in the *Constitutio*, as part of the establishment of the chamber, whose responsibilities would extend to caring for the king's comfort when he travelled; and travelling, it must be remembered, occupied a very large proportion of his time. Finally there is an elaborate hunting establishment, fully equipped for all kinds of ground game, whether beasts of the chase or of the warren; but, strangely, nothing is said of provision for the sport of hawking, which must be an oversight. There were knightly huntsmen who received the standard knight's wage of 8d a day and non-knightly huntsmen who were paid 5d, the same as the archers. There were men to take charge of each kind of hounds,

whether on leash or in the pack. The wolfhunters had an allowance of 1s 8d a day for men, horses and hounds. They should have
a pack of twenty-four hounds (*canes currentes*) and eight grey-
hounds; and they should have £6 a year for buying horses, 'but
they say £8'.

This vast household at full strength is suggestive of great occasions, such as the crown-wearings at Christmas, Easter and
Whitsuntide. It is possible, indeed very likely, that the household
functions of the greatest of its officers were more and more confined to such state occasions and that the practical day-to-day
household duties were carried out by their subordinates. This does
not mean that the great officers ceased to be in attendance on the
king except on state occasions, but rather that they were employed
on other and more important duties of state. We can hardly imagine that a king so constantly on campaign as Stephen was all
through his reign progressed with such a huge household entourage. Something more like a skeleton staff, together with his
chief advisers, several of whom in fact held the highest positions
in the household, must have accompanied him on many of his
journeys. There would also have been a strong bodyguard of
knights and soldiers. The arrival of the king with such a *meinie* in
any town, castle, manor or religious house must have been almost
as bad as the arrival of an occupying army. We need to remember
that the king's great officers and his earls and barons had their own
personal entourages, which swelled the host. Many magnates,
both laymen and prelates, were also constantly on the move about
the country with followings suited to, or designed to enhance,
their dignity and to display their power. What all this meant in the
life of town and countryside it is difficult now to understand. Consider the following witness-list of a charter of Theobald, archbishop of Canterbury, for the priory of Stoke-by-Clare (Suffolk)
about 1150–3. It gives some idea of his household, clerical and lay,
but certainly does not include anything like its complete personnel, since only men of some dignity would witness a charter for the
Lord Archbishop.[22]

Roger, archdeacon of Canterbury[23]; Thomas, clerk of London[24];
master John of Salisbury[25]; John of Canterbury[26]; Philip de Sal'; master
Guy de Pressenni; master John of Tilbury; master Roger Species; (and
the following added in a later hand in the cartulary) Osbert, clerk, the
cross-bearer; William, Gilbert, Roger and Lechard, nephews of the lord

archbishop; Thomas, clerk of Évreux, their tutor; Elinand the chancellor; Richard of Clare and (Walter) of Gloucester, monks, archiepiscopal chaplains; Robert the butler; Richard the dispenser; Gilbert the chamberlain; Odo the seneschal; William the master-cook; Laurence the usher; William son of Payn the porter; Baylehache the marshal[27] and many others.

Even a royal charter seldom produces a more elaborate or more distinguished household. Small wonder that the followings of bishops making visitations of their dioceses had to be limited by conciliar decree, to avoid over-taxing the enforced hospitality of their clergy.

We must now consider in some detail the higher ranks of the household officers and the work done by them and their subordinates. It is clear from this brief account of the establishment of the royal household that some very important members of the central administration find no place in the *Constitutio Domus Regis*. The most important of all the king's servants, the chief justiciar, was not in that capacity a member of the household. Also, one of the most important departments of state, the treasury and exchequer, is not mentioned by name, though the existence of a treasurer as a household officer and of chamberlains whom we know from other sources to have been chamberlains of the treasury, does point to a very important link between the royal chamber and its great financial offshoot.

Since there is much to say about the chancellor and the scriptorium and about the exchequer and the financial side of the administration, these will be reserved for separate chapters. We will first consider the other great office-holders of the household.

After the chancellor and his subordinate in the *Constitutio* there come the stewards (*dapiferi*). At the beginning of Stephen's reign we find no less than six men described as stewards. They were Simon de Beauchamp, Hugh Bigod, Humphrey de Bohun, Robert fitz Richard de Clare, Robert Malet and William Martel. By 1141 all but one of them had died or transferred their allegiance to the empress. For the rest of Stephen's reign we hear only of William Martel as steward, though Robert fitz Richard had a son, Walter, who might have been expected to succeed to his father's office.[28] William Martel had been a butler in Henry I's household; now he was the lay head of Stephen's household and a constant and most loyal supporter. The author of *Gesta Stephani* refers to him as an

illustrious man who 'was very closely bound to the king by
fealty and friendship'.[29] The fact that he witnessed no less than 181
of Stephen's surviving charters shows that he must have been
constantly in attendance. It was his rearguard action at the battle of
Wilton in 1143 that saved Stephen from the disgrace and disaster
of being captured a second time. He himself was taken prisoner,
but so valuable was he that his castle of Sherborne, a very important south-western outpost, was sacrificed to secure his release. It
is surprising that his captors let him go even at that price. J.H.
Round suggested that William Martel, together with William of
Ypres and the earls of Warenne and Arundel, was deeply involved
in the events connected with the arrest of Geoffrey de Mandeville
in 1143 and in some violation at that time of the sanctuary of St
Albans Abbey.[30] Again, a letter of pope Eugenius III dated 23
July 1147 to the archbishop of Canterbury and the bishops of
Lincoln, Salisbury and Worcester, recorded in the cartulary of
Abingdon Abbey, contains the following:

We have received a grave complaint from the monks of Abingdon
that William Martel, Hugh de Bolbec, William de Beauchamp, John
Marshal and their men and also many other members of your flocks
violently invade their property, seize their goods and take them away
and exact from them castle-works that they do not owe.[31]

It is significant that the monks of Abingdon appealed to the pope
for protection and redress. What hope had they from the king, if
his seneschal and close friend and supporter was one of their
oppressors! William Martel must have been campaigning vigorously in the upper Thames valley area at this time. We do not
know very much about the king's own movements in 1147 and we
have no record of his presence in that region. But it was a time of
much military activity, with the earls of Chester, Lincoln (William
de Roumare), Hertford, Pembroke and other magnates in rebellion, the first of these in particular, with his kinsmen and supporters, acting with the utmost violence and savagery; and there was
an irresponsible and unorganised, but nonetheless disturbing, invasion by the youthful Henry. It was a year of constant alarms and
excursions for the king and his adherents and forced labour on
castle-works was bound to be widespread. William Martel's
activity in this respect is evidence of his military zeal in the king's
cause rather than of any animus against the monks of Abingdon,

but, like most of his contemporaries, he probably considered that military necessity must override ecclesiastical liberties and religious scruples. Few indeed are the records of religious houses spared in the wars of Stephen's reign. One exception is the immunity granted by David, king of Scots, to Hexham Priory, which is all the more remarkable because it was respected in spite of the extreme savagery of the Scottish incursions.[32] William Martel presided as a royal justice at a joint assembly of the shires of Norfolk and Suffolk, when the jurisdictional privileges of St Edmunds Abbey were vindicated.[33] He also acted as a justice on other occasions and it is probable that he was a justice on eyre early in the reign.[34] Indeed, if Richardson and Sayles are right in their view that a body of justices known as *justiciarii totius Anglie* existed in the reign of Henry I, then it seems pretty certain that William Martel was one under Stephen.[35] This very active and loyal friend and supporter may well have been the linchpin of Stephen's household establishment and, in so far as it effectively functioned after the fall of bishop Roger, of the central government. The subordinates of the steward are not of great interest, for we know little about them as individuals or about their functions as administrative officers.

Next in order in the household establishment comes the master-butler. At the beginning of Stephen's reign there seem to have been two, William d'Aubigny and Eudo Martel. The former died in 1139 and his son and heir of the same name succeeded him and became earl first of Lincoln for a short time *c.* 1139–41 and then of Sussex (often called earl of Arundel).[36] He married the dowager queen Adelaide. Perhaps he had become too grand to attach a great deal of importance to his high office in the royal household, though this is most unlikely. He never used the title *pincerna* or butler in any charter he witnessed after he became an earl; but at least as earl he did not need to be distinguished from the other William d'Aubigny (*Brito*). Earl William d'Aubigny did not play any very prominent part in public affairs, or at all events his activities did not attract the attention of the chroniclers. We have no information about Eudo Martel, a younger brother of William Martel, after 1139.

The establishment of the royal chamber (*camera*) is of great interest and importance both intrinsically and because of its continued connection with its old offshoot, the treasury, which had long since gone out of court, and with the exchequer. The chamberlainship of Normandy need not concern us here, since Stephen held the duchy for so short a time and since the hereditary chamberlain of Normandy, Rabel de Tancarville, did not support him, nor did his heir. The office of master-chamberlain of England may have been held by Robert Malet until he was banished and his estates forfeited some time before the battle of Tinchebrai (28 September 1106). There is no indication that the office of Robert Malet, if this was the master-chamberlainship, was filled until July 1133, when Henry I granted the hereditary master-chamberlainship of England to Aubrey II de Vere.[37] This grant was the foundation of all later claims to the office.[38] It was, as has already been said, a grant of the office itself, not of lands to be held by the performance of the master-chamberlain's service. Aubrey II de Vere, the chamberlain, inherited from his father Aubrey I[39] lands in Essex, Suffolk, Cambridge, Middlesex, Northants and Huntingdonshire. By his marriage to Alice, daughter of Gilbert fitz Richard, he was connected with the great Anglo-Norman house of Clare and with the earls of Hertfordshire and Pembroke, who were members of that house. In feudal and dynastic terms Aubrey II de Vere was a magnate of considerable importance and his position was vastly enhanced by the offices he held. He held office as sheriff of London and Middlesex in 1121 or 1122, was joint-sheriff there in 1125 and was sheriff of Essex at various times. From Michaelmas 1129 he was joint-sheriff (with Richard Basset) of Bedfordshire, Buckinghamshire, Cambridgeshire, Huntingdonshire, Norfolk, Suffolk and Surrey, and by Easter 1130 Essex, Hertfordshire, Leicestershire and Northamptonshire were added to these. Aubrey II also acted as a justice for Henry I. According to his son William, he was a justice of all England (*totius anglie justiciarius*),[40] a member, it would seem, of a group of royal justices whose activities were not confined, like those of shire justices, to a single county but who were available for service anywhere. Possibly they supervised groups of shires or acted as justices-on-eyre, that is, itinerant justices.[41] That Aubrey de Vere was well suited for such duties we need not doubt, for his experience was wide and unless he had been a man of great acumen he would never have been given so many important offices by Henry I. William of Malmesbury, in his account of the legatine council of Winchester in 1139, where Aubrey was king Stephen's spokesman, refers to him as 'experienced in many kinds of cases' and as *causidicus*, a not very easily translatable but certainly uncomplimentary term for a professional advocate, though Aubrey was never that as far as our information goes. He was an experienced judge and administrator, acted as a justice for Stephen and remained in office as master-chamberlain till his death in a London riot in May 1140.[42] His death meant a grievous loss to Stephen's administration. His son Aubrey III de Vere, who had become count of Guisnes in or before 1139 in the right of his wife Beatrice, the heiress, joined the empress in 1141. She created him earl of Oxford and conceded to him his hereditary master-chamberlainship of England, which was confirmed by her son Henry.[43] Aubrey III was arrested with his brother-in-law Geoffrey de Mandeville in 1143. He returned to Stephen in about 1145,[44] and although he probably retained the chamberlain's office he never witnessed a surviving charter of Stephen explicitly in that capacity. Probably the routine, as distinct from the ceremonial, duties of the office had already passed in Henry I's reign to the chamberlains of the treasury.[45] The information supplied in the *Constitutio Domus Regis* would at least permit, if not positively dictate, the conclusion that the chamberlains of the treasury had a head in the person of the treasurer, who, since he was an officer of the first rank, was probably not subordinate to the master-chamberlain.

The office of treasurer had been held by Nigel, bishop of Ely, towards the end of Henry I's reign; and under Stephen, at least in 1137, it was occupied by Athelhelm, another of bishop Roger's family. He had become dean of Lincoln by 1145.[46] At the time of Henry I's death William de Pontdelarche held a chamberlainship which was clearly a chamberlainship of the treasury. This office had belonged to the elder Robert Mauduit and William acquired it together with Robert's daughter, as his second wife, for 1,000 marks.[47] At the same time he paid twelve marks and one ounce of gold for the office of receiver in the royal chamber (*camera curie*) and two ounces of gold for the same office for his brother, Osbert. He appears in the pipe roll of 1130 as sheriff of Hampshire and Berkshire. William de Pontdelarche was in charge of the treasury at Winchester at Henry I's death and he joined with Roger, bishop of Salisbury, in handing the treasure over to Stephen.[48] According to the *Gesta* story, he resisted the blandishments of the bishop of Winchester, waiting cautiously to see which way the cat would jump. It was a tricky situation for a man in William's position and a miscalculation could have been fatal for him. When Stephen arrived at Winchester he could hardly hope to resist, and he handed over without fuss 'whether moved by fear of him or affection for him'. William went over to the empress in 1141. Again he could have had little choice in the matter with the bishop of Winchester temporarily on the side of the empress and all power in the hands of her supporters. This unfortunate official, caught in the web of circumstance, reaped little benefit from his change of allegiance. The *Gesta* story is that in pursuit of a quarrel with the bishop of Winchester he asked the empress for military aid. She sent one Robert fitz Hildebrand, who seduced (or was seduced by) William's young wife and took over his castle. Robert fitz Hildebrand was, inevitably, overtaken by divine retribution in the shape of a worm which slowly gnawed his vitals (*vermis quidam intra vitalia illius innatus irrepsit, lentoque morsu interiora exedens*; it might be a description of cancer). The position of William Mauduit under Stephen is left obscure in the *Constitutio Domus Regis*. His father had held a chamberlainship of the treasury and he himself appears in the pipe roll of 1130 as a receiver of payments in *camera curie*, so he seems then to have been treasurer of the chamber.[49]

The last groups of officers mentioned in the *Constitutio* consist of those of the constabulary and marshalsea. In 1136 Stephen had four constables: Robert de Vere, Miles of Gloucester, Robert d'Oilly and Brian fitz Count.[50] All of them are interesting and important men but changes of allegiance soon reduced the number to one, Robert de Vere, who was in constant attendance on Stephen, as is shown by his attestation of over one hundred and forty surviving charters. He died about 1151 and was succeeded by Henry de Essex, who had married his daughter; so for the second time this office descended through the female line. The hereditary master-marshal was John fitz Gilbert,[51] castellan of Marlborough. He rebelled against Stephen before the arrival in 1139 of the empress, whom he thereupon joined, and he was not, as far as can be discovered, replaced by Stephen: his duties may have been left to his former subordinates. In the royal household the constables seem originally to have been concerned with the stables, kennels and everything to do with sport; the marshal likewise had once been concerned with horses. He had the duty of maintaining order in the household and of finding billets for its members when the court was travelling. By the time that the *Dialogus de Scaccario* was written the constables and the marshal had other more important duties. The constable, like the chancellor, was *ex officio* a baron of the exchequer even if, also like the chancellor, he did not always attend in person at exchequer sessions. He had a clerk of the constabulary, whose duty it was to produce at the exchequer the counterparts of all the writs of *computate*, *liberate* and *perdono* issued by the crown, that is, writs which had a direct financial implication for the exchequer, in respect of credits, payments out and pardons. The constable and the marshal were responsible at this later date for paying the wages of the king's troops and of the members of the royal hunting establishment. The marshal also had the special duty of keeping the wooden tallies and other vouchers relating to payments out of the treasury and the chamber.[52] In this respect the *Constitutio* says of him that 'he ought to keep the tallies against all the king's officers, as a universal witness (*ut testis per omnia*)'. It seems that John Marshal, when in office, carried out in person his duties in the exchequer, for fitz Stephen, the biographer of Becket, describes him as sitting 'with the treasurers and other receivers of revenue and public money in London, at the rectangular board which is called . . . exchequer, where pleas of the crown are also heard'.[53]

Stephen, like his predecessor, greatly relied upon the leading members of his household for the performance of administrative and judicial duties, both at the centre of rule and locally as barons of the exchequer and justices. We have no evidence of household officials acting as sheriffs of large groups of shires, as Aubrey II de Vere had in Henry I's reign, but if a pipe roll had been available for Stephen's reign we might have found that it was still the case. Geoffrey de Mandeville was sheriff of London and at least three shires. The king must also have relied a good deal for advice and discussion of affairs upon the household officials who were his constant companions. There were others who were not members of the household who were his intimates, such as William of Ypres, the commander of his Flemish mercenaries. Stephen's brother, Henry of Blois, bishop of Winchester, was also prominent in his counsels, though not in 1139, after the arrest of the bishops or indeed for some time before, and not, of course, during the greater part of 1141. How far Stephen ever trusted him, especially after

June 1139, is open to question. Other counsellors also swayed him at times, as the Beaumont twins, count Waleran of Meulan and Robert earl of Leicester, did in and before 1139. It seems possible that Stephen was on terms of some intimacy with the house of Warenne, whose heiress eventually married his younger son, William. Stephen's queen, Matilda, countess of Boulogne, seems to have been a woman of great spirit, determination and force of character, as is shown by her courageous behaviour during the king's captivity, and she may have influenced him as strongly as any of his advisers. She was prominent in peace negotiations with the Scots and with the Angevins.

7
The Chancery

The heading of this chapter is used as a matter of convenience. It begs a question: was there in Stephen's reign anything that could strictly be called a chancery? Certainly it had not yet 'gone out of court' like the treasury. There did not exist then, or until well into the thirteenth century, a chancery with a separate staff and independent organisation of its own. The chancellor and his subordinates were still essentially a part of the royal household. Well and good; but there *was* a chancellor and subordinate to him were the establishments of the chapel and the scriptorium. The chancellor was formally the custodian of the king's seal, and royal documents were prepared in the scriptorium and authenticated by having the royal seal appended. It is this aspect of the organisation with which we are concerned and it is to this that for the sake of convenience the name chancery is given. When we refer to chancery practice, we mean in particular the formal methods of drafting, writing, authenticating, issuing and preserving those royal documents for which the chancellor and his subordinates were responsible.

Stephen had three chancellors in the course of his reign. The first was Roger, called 'le Poer', who according to Orderic Vitalis was the son of Roger, bishop of Salisbury, and Maud of Ramsbury.[1] His poverty was relieved, if William of Malmesbury's story and its implications are true, when his father obtained the chancellorship for him at the beginning of the reign, perhaps as part of the price of recognising Stephen as king. At the same time he obtained the treasureship for his nephew Athelhelm.[2] Bishop Roger was certainly giving hostages to fortune. Roger the chancellor, then, came of a most distinguished, if not, for Stephen, a very reliable, administrative family. It must have been essential for either the chancellor in person or a trusted subordinate to be in constant attendance upon the king when business was being transacted, so that arrangements could be made for drawing up any documents that should be involved. An active and efficient chancellor might be expected to be in attendance as constantly as possible, while a less conscientious dignitary, or one occupied with other duties, might be inclined more often to leave the conduct of secretarial functions to his subordinates. In fact the more competent and experienced the subordinates the more likely were they, in any case, to do the real work. The experience of Henry I's last years, when he had not employed a chancellor, had shown that the functions could be undertaken without any obvious loss of efficiency by a keeper of the seal and master of the scriptorium, who was a less expensive official to maintain. There was probably the same strong tendency in the English court that we find in other royal courts, and in the Roman curia itself, for the technical duties of great officials to be taken over by their subordinates, leaving them in a position of dignity which a great man, such as Thomas Becket, could still make immensely influential and powerful. The chancellor was a dignitary of such standing that if he were constantly in personal attendance on the king, he would almost inevitably be a frequent witness of royal charters. It may consequently be supposed that the frequency of a chancellor's attestations provides an index of his activity. Roger le Poer during the period of three and a half years when he was chancellor witnessed sixty-one of the royal charters that have survived, and these survivals can only be a fraction of the documents, many of them of a more ephemeral nature, that were actually issued.[3] On this basis it may be said that Roger le Poer was probably an active chancellor. With the ink of administration in his blood, this is indeed likely. Anyone who has a mind to do so may work out many statistics from the witness-lists of charters, but human beings are not to be judged thus. It is a pity that we know nothing about Roger as a person, or about Stephen's other two chancellors. On his fall on 24 June 1139, and the fall of his family, Roger was succeeded in office by Philip de Harcourt, dean of the collegiate church of Beaumont-le-Roger, a member of a family taking its name from Harcourt (dép. Eure) who were tenants of the honour of Beaumont in Normandy and of the Beaumont earls of Leicester and Warwick in England. Philip de Harcourt was probably recommended to Stephen by his patron, Waleran count of Meulan, upon whom, together with his twin brother Robert earl of Leicester, the king greatly depended at this time. Philip's dozen attestations of royal charters are consonant with his taking office as chancellor soon after 24 June 1139.[4] He did not remain chancellor for very long, for he undoubtedly resigned when in March 1140 he was nominated for election to the see of Salisbury, vacant by the death of bishop Roger in December 1139. Philip de Harcourt was not destined to step from the son's shoes into the father's. Bishop Henry of Winchester saw to that, using all his legatine influence to prevent it. Behind this must have lain bitter hostility between the king's brother and the Beaumonts, greatly exacerbated, though perhaps not first engendered, by the events of 24 June 1139 and their sequel. It seems that Philip de Harcourt followed his patron into the camp of the empress, though as he was no longer chancellor this did not matter very much. The close adherence of Norman mesne-tenants to their feudal lords – of lesser families to greater – is very noticeable at the time of the conquest of England and for several generations thereafter. Loyalty in the case of Philip de Harcourt was handsomely rewarded when in 1142 he received the see of Bayeux. He was succeeded as Stephen's chancellor by Robert de Gant, a member of a large and important family of Flemish origin, connected through his mother with the distinguished house of Montfort. He was an uncle of Gilbert de Gant, whom Stephen created earl of Lincoln about 1149. Robert became dean of York at least as early as 1147. There is some reason to believe that he may not have been on very good terms with his sovereign during the last months of the reign because of the losses suffered by his kin in the treaty between Stephen and duke Henry.[5] The number of Gilbert's attestations of surviving royal charters during his chancellorship of fourteen-and-a-half years (March 1140 to 25 October 1154) is no more than nineteen. In the absence of any other evidence it might be inferred from this that Gilbert de Gant was not a very assiduous chancellor. Perhaps as a member of an important noble family he was not inclined to take his duties too seriously, or perhaps, for reasons unknown to us, he was not required to do so. It would be unfair to write down an elderly chancellor, about whose character we are ignorant, as lazy and inefficient on the basis simply of his infrequent appearance as a witness of royal charters. Apart from other considerations it is well to remember the strain involved in following an itinerant court.

It would not be surprising if some royal officials were unable to keep up, for the mileage expected of them to the sextary of *vin ordinaire* was very considerable.

The most interesting and important of the chancellor's clerical subordinates, from an historical if not from a contemporary point of view, were those whose special duty lay in the royal scriptorium. The head of this writing office at the end of Henry I's reign was, as we have seen, Robert de Sigillo. Since he witnesses none of Stephen's charters, it seems obvious that he was not retained in office. According to a northern chronicler, John of Hexham, he became a monk in Henry I's highly privileged foundation, Reading abbey.[6] He obtained the see of London in 1141 under the aegis of the empress, who seems to have had a considerable regard for her father's old servants, as so many of them had for her. Robert de Sigillo died on 29 September 1150. The name 'de Sigillo' was, at least in origin, that of the keeper of the king's seal. Baldric de Sigillo, who is described by king Stephen as 'my clerk' (*clericus meus*), was given a prebend in Lincoln cathedral, to the endowment of which the king subscribed in 1139–40.[7] It seems probable that he was master of the scriptorium as well as keeper of the seal. He appears as a witness of sixteen of Stephen's surviving charters with a wide range of dates, one certainly as late as 1154[8] and two others which must fall between November 1153 and the end of the reign. In a number of cases he occupies a high place in the witness-list, such as the chancellor himself might have occupied had he attested,[9] which suggests that he may have been deputising; and in one case he witnesses immediately after the chancellor.[10] Baldric undoubtedly occupied a high position among the royal chaplains and clerks and his responsibilities must have been all the heavier if Robert de Gant, for whatever reason, was not a very active chancellor. It is just possible, though unlikely, that Baldric's place was taken at the very end of Stephen's reign by Nicholas de Sigillo, who was in office in Henry II's second year.[11] Finally there is an interesting clerk called Reginald, who became abbot of Reading about 1151–4, was deposed in 1158 and subsequently became abbot of Walden. According to the Walden chronicle 'in the time of king Stephen he sometimes acted as *bajulus* (i.e. bearer or keeper) of the royal seal in place of (*vice*) the chancellor'.[12] It would be interesting to know more about him, especially as Stephen's surviving charters have not revealed any royal clerk or chaplain called Reginald.

The *Constitutio Domus Regis* does not list an establishment of clerks or scribes under the master of the scriptorium or of chaplains under the chaplain in charge of the chapel and the relics. Seventeen or eighteen individuals have been identified from their attestations of royal charters as clerks or chaplains of the king and four as clerks or chaplains of the queen (who also had her own chancellor, Ralph, and later, probably, Thomas).[13] No distinction appears to be drawn between clerks and chaplains and perhaps the clerks of the household acted as chaplains and said mass in turn. Stephen's clerical household, while it had not the brilliance of archbishop Theobald's, did not lack men of substance and importance. Adam the clerk has already been noted as a property-holder in Suffolk and in Norwich town, as have been Baldric de Sigillo as a cannon of Lincoln cathedral and Reginald as subsequently abbot of Reading and of Walden. Gilbert de Cimmay, a relative of Gilbert de Clare, earl of Hertford, was presented to the church of Luton. Gilbert d'Évreux, who must have died early in Stephen's reign, had served Henry I for a time as treasurer of Normandy and he was precentor of Rouen cathedral. Roger de Fécamp, who may also have served Henry I as treasurer of Normandy, became an archdeacon. William fitz Herbert, son of Herbert the chamberlain and Stephen's illegitimate sister Emma, was a royal chaplain at the beginning of Stephen's reign.[14] Treasurer of York since soon after 1114, he was elected archbishop of York in 1141.[15] Chequered though his career was as archbishop, he was the only royal chaplain to be canonised (1227).[16] It is possible that Hugh the chaplain was Hugh Pudsey or du Puiset, also Stephen's nephew, who succeeded William fitz Herbert as treasurer of York and became bishop of Durham in 1153.[17] There is no indication that the office of a royal clerk or chaplain carried any livery, but probably the king's clerks were beneficed, absentees and pluralists very often; certainly the royal service gave great opportunities of ecclesiastical advancement for its clerical personnel.

It has always been believed that until the Chancery eventually acquired a separate staff of its own, the clerks of the royal chapel were responsible for writing the king's documents. There is no need entirely to reject this idea, for every royal scribe was undoubtedly a *clericus* and would have been properly so described, but not every royal clerk was employed as a scribe. That is perfectly clear if only from the respective numbers of scribes and clerks, for the known *clerici* outnumbered the known *scriptores* by nearly two to one. It seems clear that numbers of clerks were employed in the royal household not because they were needed as chaplains but because they were skilled professional scribes. This does not simply mean that they were able to write. The Scottish Writers to the Signet, whose origin was exactly similar, perhaps give a better idea of the kind of professional status which royal scribes enjoyed. Very illuminating too is the description which Becket's biographer, William fitz Stephen, gives of his own position in the archbishop's service:

I was his fellow citizen, his clerk and a member of his household . . . I was a draftsman in his chancery, subdeacon in his chapel when he celebrated, reader of letters and instruments when he sat to hear suits, and in some of these, when he himself ordered, advocate . . .

This scribe in Becket's chancery was no mere writer, nor, we may be very sure, were the scribes in the royal service. We may note also the proud bearing of queen Matilda's clerk, Christian, who was the bearer of her letter to the council of Winchester in 1141 demanding the release of the king, her husband. The legate tried to prevent Christian from reading this letter to the council but, as William of Malmesbury tells us, 'the clerk did not fail to perform his commission but, with admirable assurance (*preclara fiducia*), read the letter before that audience . . .' It needed considerable courage and confidence for a clerk thus to defy the papal legate. Such men had the training and possessed the knowledge necessary for drafting documents of every kind; not merely the etiquette of correspondence in exalted circles, but understanding of the form which various administrative documents should take, of the correct drafting of charters, writs and legal instruments of every variety to meet the requirements of the numerous law courts, royal and ecclesiastical, public and private. Probably they also required a knowledge of accounting and related matters, as then practised. If one studies with attention a charter drafted by a royal or any professional scribe and a similar document written by a cathedral or monastic scribe, accustomed mainly to writing or copying liturgical, historical and theological books, the differences between the two will be seen to be very marked, both in external appearance and in formulation. The ease, conciseness and efficiency of the professional's work are striking. These professional scribes were certainly drawn from among the educated young men

8

of the day, who had perhaps attended famous schools, such as those of Paris or Bologna, or provincial centres like Chartres, Tours, Orleans or Oxford. The learning of the schools had a profound effect upon the systematic study and understanding both of subjects like law, which had an academic as well as a practical side, and of arts like that of administration. Such educated men when employed as scribes were no mere quill-drivers, though indeed they began to drive their quills faster than had previously been done: they were invaluable auxiliaries of prelates and princes in the government of church and state, the nucleus of a civil service. An attractive career beckoned able and ambitious young graduates of the schools. Those who were fortunate enough to enter the service of a king like Henry I or a prelate like Roger bishop of Salisbury, or Theobald archbishop of Canterbury, might hope for the highest preferment, such as was achieved by Thomas Becket and his rival, Roger de Pont l'Evêque, two of the brightest stars of Theobald's household. A third great luminary of that remarkable household was Master John of Salisbury, otherwise John Little (*Parvus*), pupil of Abelard, papal curialist, secretary of arbishop Theobald, political thinker, historian, and bishop of Chartres. Another good example of the career of an outstanding administrator and literary figure of the twelfth century is to be found in the life of Peter of Blois whose English career began some thirteen years after Stephen's death and well repays study.[18] These men achieved and surpassed in their upward progress the heights of an administrative profession[19] whose lower ranks included humble clerks and scribes and even vagabonds, who might turn their needy hands to forgery, that commonest of crimes among the literate of the twelfth century. It was not only, or most frequently, the needy who practised it.

A man who undertook employment as a scribe needed to be able to compose correctly as well as to write out any kind of document required of him and to do so not only in accordance with the nature and purpose of the document itself, but in a style nicely appropriate to the status and authority of his employer. Charters in which grants of land were made by a king, a bishop and a baronial magnate would necessarily have much in common. Because of their legal import and the requirements of the law courts their vocabularies and the terms in which their texts were formulated would be basically the same. On the other hand, their superscriptions and addresses and the precise wording of their component clauses and their external appearance would differ considerably. The regal style and formulae, deriving directly from the royal authority, were obviously not appropriate to an episcopal charter, nor those of an episcopal charter to a royal one; neither would be fitting in a baronial charter. Nonetheless the degree of similarity between such documents is often, at least on first sight, more striking than the dissimilarities if they have been professionally drafted. A scribe who spent some time in one kind of employment and then moved to another was likely to bring with him his acquired tricks of draftsmanship, and these can sometimes be detected in the documents he wrote for his new employer. Some royal scribes occasionally display characteristics suggestive of previous ecclesiastical employment.

Eleven scribes who were in Stephen's service in the course of his reign have been identified by their handwriting. We owe this to the work of Mr T.A.M.Bishop, who has also identified the scribes employed by Henry I and Henry II.[20] Broadly speaking, given a number of original royal charters or writs,[21] even if only two, in the same handwriting, issued at different times and places for different beneficiaries, and provided that there are no suspicious features, Mr Bishop assumes that they are the work of a royal scribe. If we accept this it is not unreasonable to assume that any other royal charters in the same handwriting which may be found are genuine also. This is not, however, an entirely safe deduction first, because forgery rings, including several religious houses, have been found, so that it would not be surprising if the same scribe forged charters for several different beneficiaries;[22] and secondly, because the handwriting of two of Stephen's scribes has been found in two charters bearing impressions of the same forged seal.[23] These scribes may in fact have been quite innocent of forgery, but the circumstances in one of the cases are very suspicious.[24] Scribes other than royal scribes can, naturally, be identified in the same way and it must be admitted that the method employed represents in the main as high an order of probability as a worker in the difficult field of early charters can very well expect. It was a perfectly normal practice in the twelfth century for recipients of royal grants to employ their own scribes to write the necessary charters and to get these properly authenticated by having the royal seal officially appended to them. A group of charters all in the same handwriting and all in favour of the same beneficiary suggests that the scribe was employed by that beneficiary. They also tend to arouse suspicion and so they must be examined with great care.

The authenticity of these and of every other charter, without exception, must be rigorously tested. First, attention must be given to the external appearance of an original charter or writ or deed. The seal, if it survives, even as a mere fragment, must be examined in detail to determine whether it is a genuine seal or whether there are any signs of tampering which might indicate that it had been transferred from another document.[25] Similarly the parchment must be scrutinised for any signs of scraping and rewriting, and the ink and the handwriting must be congruous with the date to which the document ostensibly belongs. The internal evidence of the charter must also be considered: are there any anachronisms in its formulation or incompatibility of witnesses with each other or with persons or events mentioned in the document, or does it contain any statements or claims which can be shown historically to be false?

The vast majority of royal charters and writs survived not in the form of original documents but as transcripts of originals preserved in the chancery rolls, in cartularies, chronicles and histories, and in the collections of antiquaries made at various times. If we can establish the diplomatic, that is the form of technical composition, which genuine original charters and writs ordinarily took at a given time, this provides a valuable standard of comparison for those which we know only from transcripts. It must be remembered, however, that charters written by beneficiaries' scribes may not conform with contemporary chancery practice, but may still be perfectly genuine. The total number of original English and Norman royal and quasi-royal charters and writs surviving from Stephen's reign is 197.[26] Of these, 139 are genuine or pretended charters and writs of Stephen himself and two are procuratorial writs of Roger, bishop of Salisbury.[27] There are likewise twenty-two original charters and writs of the empress and the same number of her son Henry from the time when he became duke of Normandy in 1150 until his succession to the English throne in 1154. Others are charters of Stephen's queen, Matilda, of Geoffrey of Anjou as duke of Normandy 1144–50, of the empress and Henry jointly, and of Geoffrey and Henry jointly.[28]

The eleven scribes employed by Stephen are identified only by numbers, except in the case of scribe xiv, whom Mr Bishop has shown to be Peter the Scribe.[29] Their numbers, as assigned by Mr Bishop, are x, xi, xiii, xiv, xvi, xvii, xviii, xix, xx, xxi and xxii. It is a pity that we have to see these men as ciphers, not as persons, but when one has studied their handwriting, their characteristic tricks of style and their quirks of draftsmanship, one gets the feeling (doubtless an illusion) that one has acquired some very slight insight into their characters. Thus scribe xiii seems to me rather careless, pretentious, flamboyant, artistic, conceited perhaps; while scribe xxii appears dull, industrious, precise and meticulous, a little man with, metaphorically, a bowler hat and a neatly rolled umbrella, the model private secretary.[30]

The first four of the scribes listed above had been in the service of Henry I and scribes x and xi each wrote only one of Stephen's surviving original charters.[31] The dates assigned to the two latter would be consonant with their leaving the royal scriptorium at the time of the fall of Roger the chancellor in June 1139 or earlier. It would be interesting to know how scribes obtained employment in the royal service. The patronage of great men, especially great household officials, is one probable means. It is not unlikely that a change of chancellor involved changes in the personnel of the chapel and of the scriptorium, but unfortunately it is impossible to date Stephen's charters closely enough to see whether or not this occurred. None of the surviving originals written for Stephen by scribe xiii is of a later date than 1140 and it may well be that he was thrown out of employment by the disintegration of the royal household which undoubtedly followed the battle of Lincoln (2 February 1141). Soon, apparently, this scribe found a post with his old superior in the scriptorium, Robert de Sigillo, bishop of London, for he wrote a charter for him in 1142.[32] Another interesting thing about this scribe is that his is the handwriting of a (pretended) charter for Reading abbey which bears an unmistakable fragment of a forged seal resembling Stephen's first seal, which was used until the fall of Roger the chancellor, but which can easily be distinguished from this by detailed comparison.[33] It is, however, possible, though in my view unlikely, that this seal was a genuine seal of king Stephen which was used for a short time after the fall of Roger the chancellor. It has survived whole or in fragmentary form on five charters, for Oseney, Reading, Rochester cathedral (one each) and Worcester (two). All of these have suspicious features. Robert de Sigillo, it may be remembered, became a monk of Reading after he ceased to be keeper of the seal and master of the royal scriptorium. Reginald, dismissed from the abbacy of Reading in 1158, was supposed to have been in Stephen's service and to have acted as keeper of the royal seal. Reading abbey did not lack experts in the drafting of royal charters who knew exactly what the royal seal looked like. Scribe XIII is interesting for yet another reason. His style in the composition of charters is often excessively elaborate. So much is this the case that if his products were compared with other genuine royal charters without the knowledge that he wrote twenty-one surviving original charters of Henry I and twelve of Stephen for different beneficiaries on different occasions and was undoubtedly a royal scribe, a number of them would certainly be held suspect. Interestingly enough, his Reading charter with the forged seal is not written in his inflated style. His dating of charters, and he dates them more often than most scribes, is nearly always confused and inaccurate.

Scribe XIV is perhaps the most interesting of all, not only because we know he was Peter the Scribe, a property-holder in Gloucester, but because his varied career can be traced over some thirty years (c. 1130–60).[34] He wrote charters for Henry I, Stephen, the empress, and as many as all these put together for archbishop Theobald. He almost certainly went over to the empress after the battle of Lincoln, for he wrote a charter for her in favour of Oseney abbey which can be dated about 30 March 1141,[35] and continued in her employment till 1144, when he seems to have entered the priory of St Martin le Grand, London, either as a canon or as a scribal employee, or possibly even as a teacher in its school. Next, he took service with archbishop Theobald about 1147 or 1148. He is also known to have written a letter for Nigel, bishop of Ely, and a charter for the prior of Christchurch, Canterbury, in favour of Peter himself, and he became a member of the community.

Scribe XVI is known to have written only two charters for Stephen, neither of them later than 1136. Scribe XVII is known to have written four at the beginning of the reign. Scribe XVIII's activities date from, at the latest, December 1137, if not from two years earlier. It seems as though he, too, left Stephen's service

after the battle of Lincoln. This scribe's handwriting is found in
a charter for Worcester cathedral priory about 1136–9, the text of
which has been tampered with, and which once bore a forged seal
of Stephen from the same matrix as the Reading abbey forgery.[36]
There is no reason to believe that this scribe was concerned in that
fraud, for the 'improvement' is not in his hand. Scribe XIX occurs
within the date limits 1137–40; scribe XX within the years 1138
(before August) and 1145 or later; scribe XXI before 1143 and at
least as late as 1149 or possibly 1153. Scribe XXII occurs between
about 1146 and 1154. He is of some special interest because of the
strong tendency towards standardisation in the charters and writs
he wrote, both in external appearance and in the formulation of
their texts, especially their vital injunctive clauses, which formally
express the royal will.

From this summary of information about the scribes in king
Stephen's service some conclusions may be attempted. At the end
of Henry I's reign and the beginning of Stephen's the royal
scriptorium seems to have employed at least six scribes (X, XI,
XIII, XIV, XVI, XVII), and possibly two more (XVIII and XIX) whom
we know to have been at work at least as early as 1137. It is possible that X, XI, XVI and XVII had left the scriptorium by 1137 and
that XVIII and XIX were then brought in. On the other hand, the
first mentioned four of these scribes, or any of them, may have
remained till the fall of Roger the chancellor in 1139. Between 24
June 1139 and 2 February 1141, scribes XIII, XIV, XVIII, XX, and
perhaps also XIX, were functioning. Then, inevitably, the team
broke up. Scribes XIII and XIV found new employment, the
former with his old chief when he became bishop of London, the
latter with the empress; probably they counted themselves very
fortunate to do so. Of XVIII and XIX we know no more, but their
handwriting may eventually be detected in some other employment. Scribe XX, who was employed before August 1138, was
still writing charters for Stephen till 1144–5 or later. Scribe XXI
seems to have joined the royal scriptorium after Stephen's release
from captivity (1 November 1141) and before 1143. Consequently,
after the reconstitution of Stephen's household towards the end of
1141, it seems as though to begin with there may have been only
one scribe, later two, XX and XXI. This is a good index of the
disarray of the royal administration at that time. Did scribe XX
leave Stephen's service about 1145–6, being replaced by that

treasure, scribe xxii? If so, there would have been two royal scribes on the establishment between about 1145–6 and about 1153 and perhaps one only, scribe xxii, in the last year of Stephen's reign.

The disastrous effects of the battle of Lincoln are very clearly reflected in the history of the royal scriptorium. The question which immediately arises is whether the reduction of the staff reflects a proportionate diminution in its output of documents and so a falling off in administrative activity. It is hard to avoid the conclusion that this must have been so. If we could date Stephen's charters and writs more narrowly this might be demonstrated to be the case. For what the crude statistics are worth (there are reservations about using them in this way), if we take the charters and writs which can be dated pretty definitely before the battle of Lincoln and those that can be dated after, there are approximately 450 in all. Of these 273 are before and 177 are after that crucial date. This (making all kinds of reservations) points towards a diminution of activity in Stephen's scriptorium.

Mr Bishop has drawn attention to the advanced cursive forms which are a feature of the handwriting of the scribes of Henry i and Stephen.[37] He attributes them, and rightly, to the increasing pressure of urgent official business. Their surviving original charters, he says, point to:

A formidable activity in the written work of government, an output of writing in ephemeral business vastly greater than the permanently valuable records that have survived. And it is remarkable that their cursive script, an index of this activity, reaches its most advanced development in the early years of Stephen.

This is very much more important than a minor revolution in the history of handwriting. A revolution in the whole process of administration was in train, which was of immense significance for the future. How much of this was due to the work of Roger bishop of Salisbury and his family, we can only guess.[38] In Dr A.L.Poole's view our guess probably ought not to err on the modest side. I am inclined to think that they were not so much brilliant innovators as highly competent administrators. There are many small indications of the existence even before Henry i's reign (and probably before the Norman Conquest), of a more elaborate administrative system, both centrally and in the shires,

than we know about. Roger and his family must have had some
basis to work upon. This is not to devalue their achievement.
They were, I believe, under Henry I, the real moulders of the
highly organised royal household administration and the financial
machine, whose development we can only begin to trace in any
detail after the middle of the twelfth century. But already, at the
time of Stephen's accession, it was an organisation with a very
vigorous life of its own, which even the fall of its great ministers in 1139 and all the disturbances of Stephen's unquiet reign
could not destroy.

The growth in the volume of royal business dealt with in writing
can be clearly illustrated by some quite crude statistics. From the
twenty-one-year reign of the Conqueror there have survived (in
round figures) the texts of some three hundred charters and writs;
from the thirteen-year reign of Rufus, two hundred. We have
fifteen hundred charters and writs dating from Henry I's thirty-five
years – an impressive increase – and from Stephen's 'nineteen
winters' well over seven hundred of his own, apart from those of
his rivals. This does not seem to represent a very great overall
downward trend during Stephen's reign, in spite of the probable
diminution in the output of the royal scriptorium after 2 February
1141.

The documents produced by Stephen's scribes do not differ very
markedly from those issued by Henry I's scriptorium; the traditions and the trends were continued. One might venture the
generalisation that there was a steady tendency throughout both
reigns towards the simplification and gradual elimination of age-
old mnemonic formulae, which were ceasing to serve any vital
legal purpose. New legal processes were being tentatively tried by
the crown, and the people at whose expense this was done did not
easily find effective means of countering them.[39] There was growing emphasis upon matters such as *seisin* (possession), hereditary
tenure, and lack or default of justice, in which the crown was
tending more and more to intervene by the issue of writs in favour
of one party, disobedience to which involved a plea of the crown. In
all this Stephen's scribes played their part, not least the last of them,
scribe XXII, with his tidy mind and perception, however limited,
of the value and importance of the standardisation of royal writs.
The continued existence under Stephen of a skilled secretarial
staff, with even a modest degree of development in the techniques

8*

it employed, and the survival of this embryonic chancery, whose professional expertise might permeate the whole royal household and government, were of fundamental and vital importance for the future development of England's central administration.

8

The Royal Revenue and the Coinage

I. *The Royal Revenue and Financial Administration*

It is heartily to be wished that more could be known about the
financial side of Stephen's government. We can only observe
reflections in a glass very darkly and the little that can be said on
the subject is bound to raise far more questions than it is possible
to answer on the basis of the available evidence. We tend to think
of the exchequer as springing like an Athene from the head of Zeus
in the reign of Henry I. If this was so, Roger bishop of Salisbury
and Nigel bishop of Ely must have been innovators of quite remarkable originality. Able administrators they unquestionably
were, but it is instinctive to believe that 'The Tallies', as the exchequer was first called, probably provided a basis for them to
work upon which was very much older and more elaborate and
sophisticated than we know. This is also quite likely to be true of
the local administration of the shire. It is a consideration of very
great importance for, if true, it would help to account for the
extraordinary vitality of an administrative system which proved
capable of surviving the disturbances of Stephen's reign.

The chamber, in its capacity as the treasury of the royal household, must have been far more important than any surviving
records reveal. Later, under Henry II and his successors the
chamber and its offshoot, the wardrobe, grew in importance and
became at times very powerful financial organs whose scope extended far beyond the domestic needs of the royal household. No
distinction was drawn between the king's public and private
positions, and his revenue could be received and disbursed through
whichever organisation best suited his convenience, the treasury
at Winchester or the treasury of the household. It is in no way
surprising that royal convenience in the thirteenth century should
have dictated the use of the household department of the wardrobe
for war finance. There is very little evidence about the activities of

the *camera curie* under Henry I and Stephen, but Mr Richardson and Professor Sayles have remarked that to recognise the great and far-reaching activities of the wardrobe in the thirteenth century and fail to look for a counterpart in the twelfth is a failure in historical imagination.[1] They, in fact, see the early development of the chamber as due, like that of the chief justiciarship, to Henry I's frequent travelling between England and Normandy and to the consequent need for a separate financial department in the royal household – a single chamber, be it noted, not separate chambers for England and Normandy. It is quite clear from the pipe roll of 1130 that the chamber was already well established by that time, and it would seem from the *Constitutio Domus Regis* that the liveries of members of the household might be paid either from the treasury or from the chamber, the marshal, in either case, keeping the tallies. Unfortunately no exchequer record has survived from Stephen's reign, so there is no extant pipe roll between 31 Henry I (September, 1129–30) and 2 Henry II (September, 1155–6). This is a very difficult gap to attempt to bridge. Alexander Swereford included some extracts from the then surviving pipe roll of 1 Henry II when, sometime before 1231, he compiled the information contained in *The Red Book of the Exchequer*. The fact that this conscientious and interested official did not note any pipe rolls of Stephen's reign probably means that none had survived. The roll of 1 Henry II would have included the last month of Stephen's reign, since he died on 25 October 1154 and exchequer years ran from Michaelmas till Michaelmas.[2] This roll also included the further two months which elapsed before Henry II's formal accession on 19 December 1154. Some items of the accounts might be expected to have dated from earlier years, as is the case in all early pipe rolls. Swereford's extracts from this roll include several significant references to the chamber. For example, Richard de Lucy, a loyal supporter of Stephen, accounting for the ferm of Essex, is credited with the following payments: *In camera curie xx* l, *Item xx* l. *Item xli* l, 15 s. *per breve regis. Item l* l. Similarly, the bishop of Chichester, accounting in Sussex for nine months, is credited with a payment of twenty marks into the chamber and a further twenty marks from (the ferm of) Boseham. The surviving pipe roll of the following year, 2 Henry II (1155–6) shows a few relatively small payments into the chamber in the Yorkshire, Staffordshire and Kent accounts. Whether the payments into the chamber recorded in the now missing pipe roll of 1 Henry II are due simply to the immediate financial needs of the new king, or whether they were carried over from Stephen's reign, it is impossible on the available evidence to say.

Did the exchequer function at all in Stephen's reign and, if so, did it function throughout the reign? If we are to believe the author of *Dialogus de Scaccario*, Richard fitz Neal, the son of bishop Nigel of Ely and a great admirer of his father,

he (Nigel) also, at the repeated request of the illustrious king Henry II, restored the knowledge of the exchequer, which had almost entirely perished during the long years of war and, like another Ezra, the sedulous restorer of the scriptures, revived its form in all its details.

This statement must not be misinterpreted. Richard fitz Neal does not say that the exchequer had ceased to function but only that detailed knowledge (or understanding) of it had been lost. We can be pretty certain that at the beginning of his reign Stephen inherited, as well as a rich treasury, an exchequer in working order, even though there are no pipe rolls for Henry I's last years. In 1155 we find the exchequer functioning, but judging from Swereford's extracts from the pipe roll of that year, the royal revenues were in a state of very considerable disorder. In the pipe roll of 1156 the sheriffs of London are credited with (that is, they had a writ of *computate* for) 66s 8d which is five marks, for the repair of the exchequer buildings (*in reparatione domorum scaccarii*). It is not a large sum so we need not picture the buildings in a state of complete dilapidation; but nonetheless the fact is indicative of previous lack of care or funds, or both. More significant than this is the note which concludes Swereford's extracts from the pipe roll of 1155: 'And here ends the first year of king Henry, since the accounts of the other shires, which are not noted here, were not heard this year.' Here is chaos and confusion. The shires of Bedford, Bucks. Derby, Hants, Rutland and Warwick are missing, besides the shires in Scottish hands. Swereford's notes, scant as they are, show that a number of sheriffs or custodians accounted for the ferms of their shires for only nine or six months, that is, either from after Henry II's coronation in December 1154 or from the Easter session of the exchequer in 1155. Swereford's notes, however, are of such a nature that when the period of account is not explicitly stated we cannot be quite sure whether or not it was a whole year. We note, too, in a number of cases, such as that of earl Patrick, who accounted for Wiltshire, the significant phrase at the end of his account: *Et habet de superplus xx* l. *xviij* s. *ij* d *blancos*. This does not mean that the sheriff had a surplus which went into the treasury or into his own pocket, however capacious. He had legitimately disbursed on behalf of the crown, or perhaps had even paid into the chamber, more money than he had collected. Probably no great significance should be attached to such entries at this time, because they were not uncommon in perfectly normal circumstances. However, such scanty evidence as there is indicates unmistakably that the royal revenues were in a very bad state at the end of Stephen's reign. To see the situation in some sort of proportion one ought really to compare the state of the revenue after other prolonged periods of warfare.

Much significance has sometimes been attached to the allowances for waste in the Danegeld assessments of many shires and the equivalent in boroughs in the early pipe rolls of Henry II. The late H.W.C.Davis argued that the proportion of waste to the assessed Danegeld ought to provide an index of the extent of the devastation which shires and boroughs had suffered in Stephen's reign.[3] Various other factors must, of course, be taken into account, such as the time which had elapsed in different regions since serious devastation occurred. The whole argument was rejected by Dr A.L.Poole on the ground that these statistics showed the highest proportion of waste in the most unlikely places, such as Warwickshire.[4] But even if we cannot fully explain the plight of this county (duke Henry was there with his army in June 1153 and it may well have suffered severely in the wars of the earl of Chester with the Beaumonts) it would be wrong on this account to reject the Danegeld figures out of hand.

The kind of result that emerges from Davis's suggestion is shown in the table on the following page, which comprises an arbitrary selection of shires.

In the boroughs, no waste is recorded in Canterbury or in York. The proportion of waste to assessed Danegeld is over one-third in Oxford and nearly five-twelfths in Lincoln. Kent was not the scene of much serious fighting during Stephen's reign and the relatively low proportion of waste in Sussex and Yorkshire may probably be accounted for by their having experienced their worst troubles in the earlier years of Stephen's reign and so having had

Shire	Danegeld Assessed	Waste Allowed	Proportion of Waste
Kent	£105 16 10	£ 0 8 0	about $\frac{1}{264}$
Sussex	£216 10 6	£ 9 2 0	over $\frac{1}{24}$
Yorkshire	£165 9 5	£11 1 8	over $\frac{1}{15}$
Gloucestershire	£194 1 6	£59 3 6	nearly $\frac{1}{3}$
Lincolnshire	£225 19 8	£70 14 10	nearly $\frac{1}{3}$
Northants	£119 10 9	£38 12 1	nearly $\frac{1}{3}$
Oxfordshire	£249 6 5	£96 2 10	nearly $\frac{2}{5}$
Notts and Derby	£112 1 11	£58 11 6	over $\frac{1}{2}$

some chance of recovery. Oxfordshire and Gloucestershire were the scene of constant campaigning. Lincoln and Lincolnshire must have suffered severely both in 1140–1 and in 1146, and afterwards from the violence of Rannulf, earl of Chester. His strife with such enemies as the Peverels would help to account for the plight of Nottinghamshire and Derbyshire. The town of Nottingham was sacked and burned by the earl of Gloucester in 1140, and burned again in the summer of 1153 when duke Henry attacked it. Northamptonshire, too, suffered from private warfare. In short, in the sample chosen the degree of devastation indicated by the proportion allowed for waste in the Danegeld assessments is in no case incompatible with what is known about local conditions during Stephen's reign. There seems to be some substance in Davis's argument and such conditions as those that have just been mentioned would, in themselves, sufficiently account for the bad state of the royal revenues from the shires at the end of the reign. This kind of statistic, however, could only become really meaningful if local conditions could be compared in some detail and if the condition of individual estates and the situation of their owners could be adequately assessed. An immense amount of work remains to be done on private charters if local conditions are to be elucidated. The material is in its nature limited, but there is a great deal to be found in such collections as the monumental *Early Yorkshire Charters*, so admirably edited by the late William Farrer and by Sir Charles Clay, and in the numerous cartularies and so forth, both edited and unedited, in which this country is so rich.[5] We still badly need scholars with the skill, time and perseverance to use them.

Henry II's early pipe rolls reflect a considerable amount of dis-organisation in the royal finances; they also show quite clearly the survival in some sort of working order of an exchequer machine which quickly recovered its rhythm and brought the royal revenues into relatively good shape in a comparatively short span of years. The indications are that the exchequer had continued to function, at least after a fashion, in Stephen's reign, though its working must at times have been seriously interrupted and the range of its activities circumscribed. The task of getting in such revenues as might be collected must have been formidable. We ought not, however, to underestimate the abilities of royal officers in this respect. The sheriff, even under king Stephen, was locally a very formidable person,[6] and the detailed nature of the sheriffs' accounts in the earliest surviving pipe roll would suggest that they had at their command in the shires a more highly organised administrative machine than we have any detailed knowledge of. The mere survival of the exchequer machine provides evidence, which is perhaps even more striking than the survival of an organised royal scriptorium, of the strength of the administrative system that had been developed in the reign of Henry I; evidence, too, of the ability and remarkable tenacity of the personnel who ran it.

Clear evidence of the continuity of exchequer work during the reign of Stephen is not easy to find. A very careful correlation of his charter grants with later pipe roll entries corresponding to them might provide some useful evidence – a wearisome task. One example may be given by way of illustration. In 1136 Stephen granted to Cluny his manor of Letcombe Regis (Berks.) in lieu of an annual pension of one hundred marks of silver which the abbey had from Henry I 'out of his own pocket' (*de proprio thesauro suo*), Letcombe bringing in the same amount.[7] The account of the sheriff of Berkshire in the pipe roll of 1156 shows, among the sums deducted from his ferm for lands in the shire granted away by the king, the following item: 'And to the monks of Cluny £66 13s 4d by tale in Letcombe', that is, one hundred marks of silver. This may have been a standing item in the Berkshire accounts since 1136, or the monks of Cluny may have sued out a fresh grant from Henry II. A series of such coincidences would probably indicate some continuity of exchequer activity.

Explicit references to the exchequer and the treasury in Stephen's reign are few. A notable example comes from Oseney abbey. Stephen granted the canons remission of 5s 5¾d payable by them in respect of land known as 'the king's eight virgates'.[8] During Maud's period of power, on about 30 March 1141 Oseney obtained from her the same concession. Her writ of *computate* has survived as an original and it is addressed in proper form to the barons of the exchequer.[9] That is to say, it assumes that the exchequer was functioning normally just about the time when it should have been holding its Easter session. If it was functioning then, so very soon after the capture of Stephen, it was a remarkable achievement by the administration of the empress. One of the witnesses of the writ was bishop Nigel of Ely, and if anyone was capable of organising an exchequer session, he was. The writ of *computate* is essentially an intra-departmental exchequer writ and, at least in later times, would have emanated from the exchequer rather than from the crown in person. This Oseney writ of the empress technically concerns not the canons but the sheriff of Oxfordshire and the reeve of Oxford, who were accounting for the ferm from which the 5s 5¾d was deducted, and the barons of the exchequer whose business it was to hear the account. According to the later *Dialogus de Scaccario*, such an original writ of *computate* should have been put away in the marshal's forels, or pouches, and not produced again unless some question arose concerning it.[10] This Oseney original, however, has survived not in the exchequer records but in the muniments of Oseney abbey, which seems highly irregular. How this occurred is not known, but the fact suggests that it was not used, perhaps because the exchequer was not functioning either at Easter 1141 or at Michaelmas, when the empress was not in control of London. We may note another charter of the empress by which she restored to the abbey of Tiron the pension of fifteen marks granted by Henry I from the treasury of Winchester, adding five marks thereto and arranging for the whole sum to be paid in future by the fermor of Winchester.[11] There is a rather similar charter of Stephen, belonging to 1137, when he was in Normandy, restoring to the abbey of Fontevrault and granting in perpetuity the pension of one hundred marks of silver charged on the ferms of London and Winchester, which Henry I had granted from his treasury.[12] Other examples are Stephen's grant to Lincoln cathedral and to Baldric, his chaplain, of the tithe of the ferm of the city of Lincoln *in prebendam*, about 1140–41 or 1146–54,[13] and his grant to St Peter's hospital, York, in the summer of 1154, of 40*s* annually from the ferm of the city of York.[14] Other royal grants of this kind exist in plenty and although precise dating is seldom possible they spread widely over the reign. They all assume the regular collection of the royal revenues and imply the functioning of the exchequer, whether or not the assumption was justified. On the whole, princes and magnates did not make grants which they could not implement, without offering compensation in that event. Two examples will serve to illustrate this. One has already been cited in another context. In Stephen's fabulous grant to the earl of Chester in 1146 there was included Greetham, 'but if it happen that the heirs of Greetham make a concord with the king, the said honour shall nonetheless remain in earl Rannulf's possession and the king will give them an exchange' (that is to say, an equivalent estate).[15] The other example occurs in a charter (1153–4) by which duke Henry confirmed to Nigel fitz Arthur certain land which the latter had received from the earl of Gloucester and had given to his wife in dower. 'If', continues the ducal charter, 'I be not able to guarantee it to them I will give them ten librates of land from my demesne in exchange for it for the same service' (one quarter of a knight's service).[16] It is to be assumed that royal grants were worth more than the parchment they were written on, though it may be argued that lands and pensions chargeable upon royal ferms are two very different things. Perhaps no king dare ever admit that he might not be able to implement a grant from his revenues.

No charters are more significant in the context of the royal finances than those granted by Stephen and the empress to Geoffrey de Mandeville, earl of Essex, in 1141.[17] These show us grants of the hereditary tenure of the sheriff's office in London, Middlesex, Essex and Hertfordshire for the ancient ferms at which the earl's grandfather had held them; lavish alienations of lands, escheats etc. to be held free of any ferm payable in the exchequer, a practice which, on any scale, would play havoc with the royal revenues. These grants to earl Geoffrey are neither unprecedented nor unparalleled. Those made by Stephen to Miles of Gloucester between 1136 and 1139 are similarly lavish,[18] and that to the earl of Chester in 1146 is quite staggering in its generosity. These throw no direct light on the treasury or the exchequer, but they must have considerably diminished the receipts of the former and the labours of the latter.

Stephen's charters and writs provide much more information about potential sources of royal revenue than about its extent and collection. This is equally true of the charters of his predecessors and successors. Without additional sources of information of a financial kind we cannot hope for a clear picture. Many of his charters include quittances of Danegeld and confirm earlier grants of this kind. These are mainly charters in favour of religious houses and ecclesiastics, but these have had a much better chance of survival in ecclesiastical muniments than had the muniments of private individuals which were subject to more hazards. Such quittances of Danegeld ought to have corresponded with those recorded in the pipe roll under the heading of 'pardons by royal writ'. It is well known that the pipe roll of 1130 records in each shire the exemptions from Danegeld which tenants-in-chief were allowed on their demesne lands. Since the tax was levied at two shillings on the hide, it is easy to discover how many hides each tenant-in-chief had in demesne. Mr R.H.C.Davis has made on this basis a most illuminating calculation of the amount of land which Stephen himself held in England in 1130.[19] He arrived at a total of 1,339 hides of demesne land. Assuming the conventional figure of one hundred and twenty acres to the hide (which was really a fiscal unit of assessment rather than a fixed acreage) this would amount to well over 160,000 acres in demesne. Again, assuming that a tenant-in-chief's demesne land was not likely to be more than one third of his total holding, it would seem that at a very modest estimate Stephen, before he became king, may have held something of the order of half a million acres in England, quite apart from his Norman fiefs, and the county of Boulogne which he held in the right of his wife. Add to all this, after he became king, the still very extensive lands of the royal demesne and it is obvious that Stephen possessed enormous resources in land. Even such lavish bribes as he was compelled to bestow, at least temporarily, on the earls of Chester and Essex and others. especially as escheated and forfeited lands formed a considerable proportion of such grants, would not have impoverished him disastrously, though they made considerable inroads on his resources.

Quittance of Danegeld for a piece of land was a valuable concession to any landowner, and if quittances were being granted we may believe that the crown was at least trying to impose and collect the levy. How frequent the levy of Danegeld was in Stephen's reign and how productive there is no means of knowing. Some of his writs relating to Danegeld are of special interest and would be even more valuable if they could be dated precisely. Take for example a writ from the muniments of Westminster abbey, to which only the limit dates of the reign (1135–54) can be assigned.[20] This is a precept addressed to William Martel (as sheriff of Surrey) ordering him to bring to justice the abbot of Chertsey and other tenants of the abbot of Westminster, who deprive him of his rights and have not acquitted their tenements, which they hold from him, of the Danegeld due to the king. This is to be done without delay and, meanwhile, the abbot of Westminster is to have respite for the extra hidage (*superplus hidagii*) imposed upon his land. Here is explicit evidence both of the imposition of Danegeld and of some of the difficulties involved in its collection. The meaning of *superplus hidagii* is not quite clear, but in this context it seems to mean that the abbot of Westminster was being required to pay Danegeld on the hidage at which his tenants' lands were rated. He was technically responsible for it but his tenants were withholding their payment. An interesting document in the archives of the Dean and Chapter of Canterbury records a judgment of the shire court of Kent in 1153 in a case involving liability for Danegeld and other dues.[21] This is considered below in connection with the administration of justice, but it needs to be mentioned here because it shows Ralph Picot, sheriff of Kent, active and rather over-zealous in the collection of the king's revenues towards the end of the reign. Kent was less affected than any other shire by the wars of Stephen's reign and even during the time of the king's captivity it remained under the control of the queen and William of Ypres. Probably the royal officials, the sheriff and justice and their subordinates, were more effectively in control in Kent than elsewhere.

References to scutage (the commutation for money payment of the military obligations of tenants-in-chief in respect of their knights' service) are as rare in Stephen's reign as in that of Henry I. The early history of scutage is, in fact, still very obscure. It has generally been held that its real development was just beginning under Henry I, but some, like Warren Hollister, Bruce Lyon and J. O. Prestwich, have suggested a possible pre-Conquest origin.[22]

Such uncertainty about the stage of development that scutage had reached by Stephen's reign makes it difficult to draw inferences from the few references that occur.[23] One would guess that since Stephen made constant and extensive use of mercenaries, the levy of scutage may have been resorted to as often as he dared risk it, or as often as he was able to make bargains with his tenants-in-chief. Grants to religious houses of exemption from military service are common enough, but exemptions from scutage are extremely rare.[24] Quittances of gelds, scots,[25] customs[26] and tolls in general are numerous; freedom from payments like lastage[27] and landing-dues is much less so.

The feudal resources of the crown in the hands of a powerful, thrifty and not over-scrupulous monarch like Henry I were considerable.[28] The whole range of feudal incidents, forfeitures and escheats, reliefs, aids, sale of wardships and marriages and the like, fully exploited, could produce a not inconsiderable revenue, as the pipe roll of 1130 shows on every membrane. Fines, too, were a very lucrative source of money. These are to be distinguished from amercements, which, together with murdrum fines, forfeitures of felons' goods, pecuniary and territorial forfeitures and the like, made up the profits of justice. A 'fine' on the other hand was a final arrangement, bargain or agreement with the crown involving, usually, a money payment. A fine, resulting in the boon of royal favour, might relate to anything from the expediting of litigation to the acquisition of an office of dignity and profit, the marriage of an heiress or a wardship or just the remission of the king's ill-will or the exercise of his good offices. There was little that the crown could not sell. A random glance at the pipe roll of 1130 will show how these sources of revenue were exploited by Henry I. In Lincolnshire the earl of Chester owed one thousand pounds of his father's debt for the land of earl Hugh. This in itself is interesting, since the palatine earldom of Chester did not come within the sphere of the exchequer and the earl's debts could only be dealt with (presumably) in another shire where he was a substantial tenant-in-chief. The earl also owed five hundred marks (£333 6s 8d) for the agreement which the king made between him and his mother about her dower; and four hundred marks (£266 13s 4d) for his share of a debt of his father's (total amount unspecified) for the payment of which the crown had advanced the money. The earl's mother, countess Lucy, no chicken in 1130, accounted

for £266 13s 4d for the land of her father and five hundred marks
for the privilege of remaining unmarried for five years and – a
refinement of extortion – a further forty-five marks for the making
of this agreement, to be paid to whomsoever the king wished (a
disappointed suitor?) and twenty marks to the queen, who customarily had her percentage on private bargains made with the king.
Countess Lucy also owed one hundred marks for the right to hold
her feudal court. Altogether, in Lincolnshire alone, Henry I was
exacting a total of at least some £2,300 from the earl of Chester
and his mother. In the same shire Baldwin fitz Gilbert owed £301
16s 4d for the land of William de Rullos and the hand of his niece;
Robert Marmion accounted for £176 13s 4d for the relief of his
father's land; Osbert son of Adam accounted for ten pounds for
the doing of justice (*pro recto*) concerning land he claimed – and so
it goes on. How Stephen manipulated this source of revenue we
have no means of knowing in the absence of any pipe rolls; less
successfully than his uncle, we may be pretty sure, but the source
was there if he could exploit it. We have records of such things as
his grants of wardships,[29] but not of the financial transactions and
the profits accruing to the crown.

The royal forests provided yet another source of revenue.[30]
Forests, it should be remembered, were not just woodland, moor
and heath, but included agricultural land and villages, where
forest restrictions and penalties bore severely on the inhabitants.
The economy of the royal forests was of course exploited. In
addition there were very heavy physical penalties, amercements and
forfeitures for breaches of the oppressive forest law, especially for
offences against the *venison*, or protected beasts of the chase, and
against the *vert*, or cover and pasture for this game. *Assarts*, or
clearings, and *purprestures*, or encroachments, however small, incurred a pecuniary penalty and further annual payments if they
were retained. Stephen announced in his 'Oxford charter of
liberties' of April 1136 that he would retain the forests created by
William I and William II, but would disafforest the additions made
by Henry I. This showed some appreciation of the widespread
hatred of Henry I's grasping and oppressive forest system which
was violently manifested in the indiscriminate slaughter of the
beasts of the forest which occurred in England immediately after
king Henry's death.[31] Stephen nonetheless began his régime in stern
Norman fashion by holding a forest assize at the royal hunting

lodge of Brampton, near Huntingdon, in 1136, to the unconcealed annoyance of the barons who were impleaded for forest
offences.[32] Henry I would certainly have done the same in similar
circumstances, if these are imaginable in his reign, but Stephen
lacked his uncle's presence, his thunderous voice and his authority;
his action did him a great deal of harm politically. It would be
difficult to say how far he was able thereafter to maintain the
forest administration and enforce the forest law. In the circumstances of his reign the task must have been a very difficult one. A
fair, but by no means excessive, number of grants of forest
privileges and exemptions is to be found among his charters,
which would imply, if not an actively operative forest system, at
least one which was liable to be revived. Two charters of about
1153-4[33] in favour of St John's abbey, Colchester, grant exemption from forest pleas, as does one in favour of St Paul's cathedral.[34]
All three refer to land in Tendring (Essex). There are grants of the
office of forester-in-fee to Alvric de Brochelia and William
Spileman[35] and to Humphrey de Barrington of the forest office of
his father, Eustace.[36]

The great question regarding Stephen's finances is how and
where he raised the money not only to maintain the government
but to pay his large force of mercenaries, and generally to finance
his endless campaigns. He inherited a full treasury from Henry I
and he had the lands of the royal demesne besides his own personal lands in England (so far as he did not alienate them) and
the resources of the county of Boulogne. Temporalities held by the
crown during ecclesiastical vacancies may have contributed to the
revenue from time to time and the forfeitures of deserters, in so
far as they could be exacted, may have helped. The arrest of the
bishops in 1139 is said to have produced quantities of treasure,
and prelates and ecclesiastical bodies were probably laid under
contribution from time to time. All these were in the nature of
occasional bonuses and they do not represent a regular or reliable
revenue.

Did Stephen resort to borrowing on a large scale? Chance has
provided a few crumbs of evidence about royal debts. A charter of
Stephen, which can be dated no more closely than between
December 1142 and April 1146, grants to the abbey of St Augustine, Canterbury, a mill near the east bridge in repayment of a loan
of one hundred marks.[37] A mill was a valuable capital asset and

the monks probably had the best of the bargain in the long run. We have also a record of a loan of unspecified amount raised by Stephen's queen, Matilda, from Gervase of Cornhill, justice of London, on the security of land in the vill of Gamlingay (Cambridgeshire).[38] This is not necessarily connected with the period of Stephen's captivity and may be dated within the years 1136–47. Gamlingay belonged to queen Matilda in her own right. There may have been more and bigger transactions of this kind of which no record has survived. Borrowing merely on the scale revealed by these two charters could hardly have met the royal needs.

Mr R.Holmes, in his edition of the cartulary of St John of Pontefract,[39] refers to a small group of charters in the following terms: '(it) helps naturally to illustrate the fortunes of the widespread family of the descendants of Asulf, probably a monied trader, who aided king Stephen in some of the financial difficulties of the earlier part of his reign, and who received in payment, or perhaps bought by his action, a vast tract of country in the middle of Yorkshire'. The charters may illustrate the fortunes of Asulf's descendants, but since Mr Holmes did not reveal the source of his information about Asulf's own financial dealings with Stephen, we are left very much in the dark about them. It does however raise the possibility of large-scale moneylending in Stephen's reign. The king need not, indeed probably did not, confine his borrowing to English merchants or moneylenders. It is not impossible that the Flemish mercenaries were paid with Flemish money, for Stephen's relations with Flemings were close. William of Ypres, illegitimate son of count Philip of Ypres and grandson of Robert le Frison, count of Flanders, leader of Stephen's mercenaries, was one of his most consistent supporters throughout his reign. Flemish interests in England after the Conquest were second only to those of the Normans themselves and Flemings were prominent among the aristocracy. Their prosperous fortunes can be illustrated in, for example, the history of the family of Ghent, or Gant, which produced an earl of Lincoln, and a dean of York and royal chancellor, and which was allied by marriage with the houses of Montfort, Clare, Senlis and the counts of Brittany.[40] Flemish merchants, too, had profitable connections with England and it may be that they contributed, along with English and perhaps Boulogne merchants, to the financing of king Stephen's wars.

We are not without some evidence about the activities of Flemish financiers, and although it does not belong strictly to Stephen's reign it is close enough to suggest that they were operating in England at that time. If the risks were great, the profits must have made them well worth taking. The pipe roll of 2 Henry II (1156) contains 51 references to the activities of William Cade, a Fleming. These activities were brilliantly illuminated by the late Sir Hilary Jenkinson in two articles.[41] Cade was a usurer who probably died in 1166, and he left property, including debts owing to him, amounting to some five thousand pounds. His debtors included such eminent public servants as Nigel, bishop of Ely, and his son Richard (the author of *Dialogus de Scaccario*), a justice, two royal chamberlains and several bishops, earls and sheriffs; religious houses, also, owed him money. The crown took over this property and a roll of the debts was compiled which has survived among the exchequer (K.R.) records. It appears from this roll and from the original bonds, which have also survived, that William Cade lent money not only to private persons but to the king, enabling him to anticipate his revenue, for the crown in many cases ordered its debtors to pay their debt to Cade. Not only so, but Cade's private loans seem often to have been connected with exchequer business. He had official business at the exchequer for some years, for both Swereford's extracts from the lost pipe roll of 1155 and subsequent surviving rolls show that he had some responsibility for the ferm of Dover. If later practice were a safe guide, one would guess that Cade was given the concession of farming royal dues and the opportunity of making a profit from this in lieu of the payment of a royal debt. It seems probable that he also conducted his own private business at the times of exchequer sessions, where he would find many clients, and that he increased his usurious profits by taking bonds instead of cash from the royal debtors whose debts had been assigned to him. A moneylender on this scale must have made a very good thing of his opportunities, and so notorious was William Cade that he was portrayed as the typical usurer in Robert de Courçon's treatise on the subject of usury half a century later. The indications are that Cade came from St Omer. He witnessed, about 1140, a charter by which Hugh of Chilham, son of Fulbert of Dover, granted the church of Chilham to the abbey of St Bertin,[42] which suggests that early in Stephen's reign he was already a man of some local standing in quiet Kent, and that in a place (Chilham) where William of Ypres had rights. It would not, in all probability, have been difficult for him to be brought to the notice of king Stephen as an obliging financier, if he was not already known to Stephen in Boulogne. It is highly unlikely that William Cade sprang suddenly into prominence as a financier in 1155; the probability is that he had been operating in England for some time and that the foundation of his fortune had been laid in Stephen's reign. All this suggests possibilities in connection with Stephen's finances about which it would be interesting to know more. English towns and merchants are also likely to have contributed their quota to the royal finances in the form of loans, voluntary and otherwise, and accommodations. Stephen's relations with the citizens of London, Lincoln, York and other towns seem to have been cordial and the circumstances of his reign must have made possible arrangements of mutual advantage to the king and the citizens.

II. The Coinage

This discussion of Stephen's finances, so largely guesswork, cannot be concluded without some reference to the coinage. The quality of its coinage is an index of the solvency and stability of a régime and in coins we have concrete evidence which can be examined and weighed. Here, it might be thought, we are on sure ground; but the coinage of Stephen's reign presents some very intractable problems.

William of Malmesbury writes, under the year 1140, that:

Everything was getting worse because of the lack of justice (*pro justitie penuria*) and now the cost of living was gradually increasing because of conterfeiting (*pro falsitate*). Such had become the difficulty about money that scarcely twelve pennies could be accepted out of ten shillings or more. It was said that the king himself had ordered the weight of pennies to be reduced from what it had been in king Henry's time because, having exhausted his predecessor's immense treasure, he could not meet the expense of so many troops. So everything in England was for sale and now churches and abbeys were knocked down in lots, not secretly but openly.[43]

These remarks about the prevalence of counterfeiting and the rising cost of living are closely paralleled by an entry in the E

version of the Old English Chronicle for the year 1124. It speaks
of the inclement season and the high price of corn, 'and', it continues, 'the penny was so bad that, if a man had a pound at market,
he could not by any means get the value of twelve pence for it.'
The Peterborough chronicler and William of Malmesbury are
using well-worn clichés. Malmesbury regarded the bad state of
affairs in 1140 as the result of *iustitie penuria*, a thing which it was
a prime duty of the king to prevent. Counterfeiting or debasement was obviously considered symptomatic of the times; it was
bound to occur, like so many other evils, if justice were not enforced by the strong hand. Falsification was a major crime, and
probably Henry 1's ruthless and brutal punishment of the moneyers
at Christmas 1124 was still remembered. The Peterborough
chronicler recorded the proceedings with relish and approval.
This, he says, was necessary because 'a man who had a pound
could not get a pennyworth at market' and the savage mutilations
of the moneyers, castration and loss of the right hand, were in his
view 'very justly done because they had ruined all the land with
their great false dealing and they all paid for it'. Legislation against
falsification was severe. Henry 1 had pronounced against it in his
coronation charter of 5 August 1100 and at the following Christmas he sent very stringent regulations about the coinage to all the
shires. Further measures are recorded in 1107 and 1108, but in
spite of these efforts the king still had to make an example of the
moneyers in 1124.

Minting of coin was carried out locally in boroughs, but the
minting dies and the moneyers were under strict royal control. It
is difficult to find much detailed information about the moneyers,
but there are a few crumbs in the pipe roll of 1130. In Hampshire,
Saietus the moneyer owed 278 marks of silver, a considerable sum,
for a plea concerning two dies. Probably he had tampered with
them or misused them. Brand the moneyer in the honour of
Arundel paid twenty pounds to escape castration with the other
moneyers (it was probably, to a great extent, an hereditary craft).
These two moneyers must have been men of some means. Early
in Stephen's reign coins were struck at York, perhaps for Eustace
fitz John, and the moneyer responsible was Thomas fitz Ulf.
Probably we may identify him with the *Thomas de Everwic' filius
Ulvieti* who, in the pipe roll of 1130, owed a horse (a hunter, not a
war-horse) for the privilege of being alderman in the merchants'

gild of York. It is significant, but not surprising, that the craft of a moneyer should be exercised by so prominent a citizen. Probably it was necessary for a moneyer to be a goldsmith or silversmith, and such men were likely to be relatively wealthy. That moneyers had subordinates is obvious from the pipe roll of 1130, where in the honour of Arundel the sheriff accounts for one mark of silver from the men of the moneyers of Chichester. More interesting by far is a London entry in this pipe roll, where William son of Otto accounts for £36 0s 10d so that he may no longer have a master over him. This William must have been the grandson of Otto the goldsmith, Domesday tenant of Hawstead. The office of cutter of the dies for minting was apparently hereditary in his family. Otto was succeeded in 1098 by his son, Otto, who received various grants of land from Henry 1. The younger Otto was followed in turn by his son William, who at some date between 1116 and 1127 (perhaps nearer the latter year) had from Henry 1 a confirmation of all his father's lands and the craft of the dies, to be held by the same service which his father used to render.[44] The entry in the pipe roll of 1130 would not be inconsistent with William's having incurred a debt to the crown for liberation from apprenticeship several years earlier. He appears in the *Constitutio Domus Regis* in a position which appears to be that of an assistant constable with an unusual allowance of simnels and spiced wine. Probably he continued to serve Stephen for a time though he appears as a witness only in a peculiar pretended charter for Exeter cathedral.[45] He had joined the empress by midsummer 1141, when she ordered him to be seized at Benfleet (Essex). A writ, of perhaps 1154, in favour of Ely cathedral is addressed to Radulfus de Halstede (Hawstead) and his brothers Roger and William.[46] These were presumably the heirs of William fitz Otto.

The office of cutter of the dies was a very important one, for there is reason to believe that all the official dies for the minting of the king's coin were cut by him, or under his supervision, and distributed to the local moneyers. A further precaution for the maintenance of the coinage was of pre-Conquest origin. This was the withdrawal from circulation of each issue of coinage, probably following a periodical assay, after a fairly short period of years. Silver pennies, the only coins in circulation (since pounds, shillings and marks, whether of gold or silver, were notional coins of account), suffered from wear and from the common practices of clipping and sweating. The intervals between the issues of coinage do not seem to have been strictly regular. William the Conqueror had eight issues during his reign, William II five, Henry I fifteen and Stephen seven.

Tradition has it that the standard weight of a silver penny was $22\frac{1}{2}$ grains, but with so many mints and moneyers scattered throughout the country and with the techniques then known, the maintenance of an absolute standard could hardly be expected. It is difficult for numismatists dealing with these coins to make appropriate allowance in each example for loss of weight. Nonetheless the available evidence points to some quite considerable variations even in well-preserved specimens of the same issue. A few, in a good issue, are commonly found to be slightly over-weight, but perhaps the largest proportion falls between twenty-one and twenty-two grains and some may be found of as little as fourteen or fifteen grains. These are genuine coins, so we must assume that the moneyers struck a proportion of their coins light, the proceeds going into their pockets or to the crown, or both. The crown strove to pin down responsibility for the coinage upon the moneyers by insisting that their names and those of their mints should appear on the reverse of the coins they struck. Quite a few coins show attempts to make this obligatory information indecipherable. Coins might be deficient in the fineness of their metal. This was tested in the exchequer by a smelting process of pre-Conquest origin, known as 'blanching the ferm', whereby a random poundsworth of pence was melted down, the dross removed (a delicate operation) and the remaining bullion weighed against a standard pound.[47]

William of Malmesbury said it was rumoured (in 1140) that Stephen had caused the weight of the penny to be reduced from what it was in king Henry's time. Perhaps we ought not to insist upon the precise date, but be prepared to give or take a year or two. Such a rumour would have suited the king's enemies as well as the falsifiers of coin and the utterers of the products. Any implications which William's statement may carry that Henry I's coinage was impeccable will not bear examination. Numismatists have detected a distinct and progressive decadence in the coins of the fifth to the eleventh of Henry's issues, followed by an improvement in the twelfth issue, which is believed to have come after the dire events of Christmas 1124. Six or eight years later Henry I's fourteenth issue shows a higher proportion of lightweight coins than any Norman issue since the second of William the Conqueror. Furthermore, many of the coins of this issue contained excessive alloy. In Henry 1's last issue the proportion of lightweight coins had fallen again to a fairly normal level and blatant examples of fourteen- or fifteen-grain pennies are absent.

Compared with Henry 1's issues, the standard of Stephen's coins is not as bad as might be expected. His first issue is said to have remained in circulation till about 1141, which is the year after William of Malmesbury's date for the debasement. The quality of this first issue, compared with the issues since 1066 as a whole, was good. As far as the second issue is concerned, it is difficult to say whether or not it bore out William of Malmesbury's allegation, because the number of surviving coins is so very small. A fair proportion of the few surviving pennies of this issue approximates to the traditional weight. To sustain William's allegation, therefore, it would be necessary to postulate that only a few good coins survived because they alone were worth hoarding. Very little is known about Stephen's third, fourth, fifth and sixth issues because examples are so scarce, but the surviving coins of the fourth and fifth issues, which may belong to about 1145–9, are of very light weight. Stephen's seventh and last issue was in the main good and remained in circulation for the first year or two of Henry 11's reign.[48] Here we must take into consideration statements made by two nearly contemporary historians. William of Newburgh refers to the tyrant lords of castles striking their own coin, which may be a generalisation from the fact that coins were struck for Eustace fitz John, a prominent lord of William's native region.[49] Roger of Hoveden says that Henry, when he came to England in 1149, struck a new coin which came to be known as 'the duke's money', but when he came (which is obscure, but may refer to 1153 or to his succession in 1154) he put down the coins of the greater part of the magnates.[50] It is tempting to believe that after the treaty between Stephen and Henry, there was a new issue of coin for which the duke bore joint responsibility. He could therefore afford to allow it to continue in circulation, as it seems to have done, for some time after his accession.

Several charters have survived by which Stephen made grants of dies for minting to the bishop of Chester, Coventry and Lichfield for a mint at Lichfield after 1149; to the bishop of Lincoln for a mint at his vill of Newark *c.* 1153–4; and a second and third die to the abbot of Bury St Edmund's probably after 1141.[51] He also confirmed to Reading abbey Henry I's grant of a mint and moneyer in London.[52] It is not clear what significance attaches to such grants beyond the local demand for coin and its obvious implications of trade. Stephen cannot be accused of reckless improvidence in making them, for he simply followed the practice of his three predecessors and his grants were just as sparing as theirs. All official local mints, as far as we know, received their dies from the royal die-cutter and were expected to issue standard royal pennies.

A striking feature of Stephen's reign, however, and clear testimony to the unsettled conditions is the relatively large number of surviving coins of irregular types. These are not forgeries but specimens of the issues of William of Newburgh's 'tyrant lords of castles', for they bear the titles of magnates, lay and ecclesiastical. Such coins have been attributed to Henry, bishop of Winchester, Henry, prince of Scots, earl of Northumberland, Eustace fitz John, lord of Knaresborough and Alnwick, Robert de Stuteville, lord of Cottingham, Brian fitz Count, lord of Wallingford and possibly Robert, earl of Leicester. There are others whose attribution is even more uncertain. It is highly improbable that such coins were issued by virtue of royal grants which have not survived. It seems more likely that magnates, such as those who have been mentioned, were powerful enough to put their own coin into circulation locally at times and in places when and where royal authority was not effectual, as it never was in Northumberland, for example, during all the time that Henry of Scots was earl. The empress and duke Henry also issued coin from Oxford and west country mints, inferior in weight to Stephen's better issues.

Numbers of pennies of Stephen's first issue were struck with erased (i.e. mutilated) obverse dies. It is perfectly obvious from the impressions that the marks of erasure were cut in the dies, and they take different forms.[53] The commonest mark of erasure is a plain cross from edge to edge of the coin, but sometimes these were parellel cuts from top to bottom, sometimes a small cross on the king's face or shoulder and in some cases an additional (symbolic?) stroke through the sceptre. The usual reason for such mutilation of minting-dies, as of seal matrices, is that they are no longer to be used officially and, if preserved, must be marked in such a way as to prevent unauthorised use or at least to indicate it as such. This is more likely to have been the reason for the mutilation of Stephen's coins than, as has been suggested, that they were struck by officials or partisans of the empress, who needed to use his coins but did not wish to appear to recognise his title. Such a suggestion must be rejected because some of the erased coins are from mints that were never under Angevin control. The probability is that minting-dies were mutilated at times of imminent danger, when they might fall into the hands of the king's enemies. Erased specimens were struck at various mints, including Bristol, Nottingham, Norwich, Thetford and York. Circumstances may well have justified mutilation at Bristol in 1138, in Nottingham in 1138 or 1140-1, at York in 1138, and at Norwich and Thetford, perhaps during Hugh Bigod's rebellion in 1136 or 1140. It is impossible to say why the dies, having been erased, were brought into use again, but obviously this could only have occurred in times of the utmost confusion.

Another intriguing problem is presented by coins which are of Stephen's first type but bear an unintelligible obverse superscription, + PERERIC or PERERICM. They bear the names of moneyers and mints on the reverse and specimens are known from the mints at Bristol, Canterbury, Lincoln, London, Stamford and Winchester (probably), which represents a very wide distribution. This was no hole-and-corner issue. These coins, especially of the London minting, are of very good quality and weight. Clearly they were intended to pass as good and acceptable currency. It is usually assumed that they were issued during the period of Stephen's captivity and it is difficult to suggest any other time when such an eccentric series could have been issued. One suggestion is that PERERIC is a shortened and blundered version of IMPERATRIX. Whether these dies were cut by the royal die-cutter or by some other craftsman in the service of the empress, neither is likely to have made such an illiterate and blundering shot at her title. Die-cutters were skilled craftsmen. Known coins of the empress minted in England bear legends, more or less abbreviated, of IMPERTRIX, MATILDIS COMITISSA and MATILDIS. Some of these PERERIC coins are from mints such as Canterbury, Lincoln and Stamford, where the empress was never effectively in control, though the authority of archbishop Theobald in Canterbury and that of the earl of Chester in Lincoln might have ensured their issue. An alternative suggestion by Dr Brooke was ingenious but not wholly convincing. He argued that in 1141 the moneyers were in a very awkward predicament. Their names and mints had to appear on the reverse of the coins they struck, but with a clearly intelligible obverse superscription either of the empress or of Stephen, this would have been tantamount to a declaration of allegiance which, after Maud's flight from London on 24 June 1141, it would have been rash to make. Consequently, Dr Brooke suggested, a garbled superscription was deliberately used. In support of this idea he quoted the example of Danish coins of the years 1044–7, when Swein and Magnus were fighting for the crown, which bore the inscription IOANSTREX. The argument is not an impossible one but it is clear that the local moneyers were not in a position to agree upon and execute a garbled inscription. They received their dies for a new issue of coin from the royal die-cutter and it would presumably be he, whether on his own initiative or not, who was responsible for the PERERIC inscription. William fitz Otto, who held the office and who was with the empress at Westminster at midsummer 1141,[54] had good reason very soon afterwards to equivocate if the empress had ordered a new issue of coin, for her continued ascendancy was in some doubt after her flight from London and still more after the rout of her forces at Winchester a month later. This may indeed be the solution of the problem, but it is well to remember that it would have been a very bold die-cutter who was prepared to confront the empress or even king Stephen with a new issue of coin with the inscription PERERIC. No good purpose is served by adding yet more conjectures; the problem seems insoluble on the basis of the evidence at present available.

The numismatic evidence as a whole indicates that Stephen's coinage was quite good in the early years of his reign, that lack of control led to confusion and difficulty and unauthorised and irregular issues of coinage in or after 1141, if not earlier, but that there were distinct signs of recovery by the early 1150s. There can be no doubt that marked fluctuations in the quality of the coinage are a good index of conditions in the country. We should probably not be far wrong in believing that the marked improvement of the coinage at the end of the reign was accompanied by an improvement in administration and by the beginnings of financial and economic recovery. The very fact that there were seven official issues of the king's coinage during Stephen's reign is evidence of an attempt at regulation in the customary manner. It supports all the other evidence we have of the extraordinary power of survival shown by the royal administrative machine during nineteen years of disturbance.

9
Law and the Administration of Justice

Every organised society possesses rules which regulate the behaviour of its members both in relation to the community as a whole and in their dealings with one another as individuals. Some of these are customs and conventions but nonetheless effectual because they are unwritten and not formally prescribed. Others are rules prescribed by competent authority. The situation in England up to and including the score of years with which we are specifically concerned was, to a modern mind, much complicated and confused because there did not yet exist a single and universal English law prescribed by the state which as a matter of course, overrode, the force of local custom and the dictates of external authority such as the Roman church. There was of course a corpus of royal law which it was the king's duty to proclaim and to enforce, but law, by deep-rooted tradition, was also good and approved custom, and custom and its application could vary a great deal in different areas and localities and in different kinds of courts. The law was in effect modified in its application by the customs of these different courts and one of the most important developments was the gradual spread of the custom of the king's court. There were whole areas of law administered in feudal and manorial courts where the custom of the honour or of the manor was all-important. Most significant of all, perhaps, is the fact that the courts Christian, the courts of the church governed by canon law, embraced so wide a sphere of justice and jurisdiction, including a great deal which now comes within the purview of the secular courts. In short, different, and even to a considerable extent conflicting, systems of law and jurisdictional organisation are found in early twelfth-century England. That this state of affairs was not wholly incompatible with strong royal government was convincingly demonstrated by the rule of Henry I. The aggressive rôle of royal justice, closely linked with a new and efficient financial machine, is one of the most striking features of his reign. 'Justice', as Richard fitz Neal, author of the *Dialogue of the Exchequer* was careful to point out in the reign of Henry I's grandson, 'is exceedingly profitable.' There is no doubt that this profit motive had a great deal to do with the development and extension of royal justice, but it would be a mistake to regard it as the sole motive. The great and growing interest in the study of law in the twelfth century is well known. Kings had a practical concern in its administration since tradition and duty, as well as self-interest, obliged them to spend a good deal of their time in hearing cases. Many of them unquestionably took pride in the performance of this function and were genuinely interested in it.

In any study of the law and the administration of justice in the twelfth century one still turns back with admiration and gratitude to the work of F. W. Maitland. A sentence of his provides, in effect, the theme of this chapter: 'In the woeful days of Stephen the future of English law looks very uncertain; if English law sur-survives at all, it may break into a hundred local customs, and if it does so, the ultimate triumph of Roman law is assured.' English law did survive. Why and how did it do so? Three quarters of a century after Maitland wrote these words, the methodical collection of royal charters and writs has provided us with a good deal more information about the administration of justice under Henry I and Stephen than was easily available to him. For most of us, who lack Maitland's encyclopaedic knowledge and clear insight into the medieval history of English law, the subject is still wrapped in obscurity, especially in the age before that of Glanvill and the reforms of Henry II.

'He (Henry I) was a good man and people were in great awe of him. No one dared injure another in his time. He made peace for man and beast. Whoever carried his burden of gold and silver, nobody dared say anything but good to him. . . .[1] When the traitors understood that he (Stephen) was a mild man, gentle and good, who did not exact the full penalties of the law, they perpetrated every enormity.'[2] The Old English chronicler's dramatic contrast represents in black and white what ought to be shown in varying shades of grey. However powerful a medieval king, his executive authority was not always and everywhere wholly effectual. The control even of a Henry I, a Henry II or an Edward I over the administration of justice sometimes fell far short of his intentions. Under Henry I there were some rebellions and some acts of lawlessness and savagery comparable with those that occurred much more frequently in Stephen's reign. Under Stephen, on the other hand, we have a good deal of evidence of the continued functioning of royal administration and of the law courts at all levels, though probably not all the time in every region, on the lines laid down in his predecessor's reign. It is indeed an important and impressive fact that these never broke down completely but however shaken by the vicissitudes of Stephen's reign survived it in some sort of working order. Henry II could profess to ignore the nineteen years of usurpation and look back to the rule and the precedents of his grandfather, only because indestructible foundations were then laid upon which his own genius, or that of his ministers, or a combination of royal drive and ministerial expertise, could build anew. But Stephen must have a little share of the credit for keeping the traditions alive and the institutions functioning well enough to be quickly revived.

Henry I was remembered as the 'Lion of Justice', but it is well to remember that the lion is a beast of prey. It can be seen with the utmost clarity in almost every membrane of the one surviving pipe roll of Henry's reign that justice was exploited as a source of profit.[3] There is nothing remarkable in the fact that many individuals should account, often in very substantial sums, for amercements which they had incurred in the recent judicial eyres, both general and relating to the royal forests. Thus, in Nottinghamshire and Derbyshire, Robert, son of Tol, owes thirty marks of silver of the pleas of Geoffrey de Clinton and Suen de Porta owes one hundred shillings 'of the pleas of Ralph Basset'.[4] In Yorkshire and Northumberland Walter Espec (a royal justice) accounts for two hundred marks 'for a plea of a stag', that is, for a forest offence which attracted a very heavy penalty.[5] Such random examples could be multiplied many times and the sums involved are by no means trifling. '*De minimis*,' one might say, '*non curat rex.*' But there are payments of another kind for the favour of royal intervention as for example in Nottinghamshire and Derbyshire, where William de Luvetot, who also pays heavily in connection with the pleas of Geoffrey de Clinton (a royal justice on eyre), accounts for the large sum of two hundred marks of silver for the king to condone the plea on which he was impleaded at Blyth.[6] Again, in the same shires, Nigel de Rameton accounts for ten marks of silver so as not to answer the plea of Morcard concerning his father's land. Likewise Richard de Davidville accounts for ten marks of silver in order that he may not have to plead concerning his land of Weston.[7] An even more illuminating case occurs in Dorsetshire and Wiltshire, where William of St Edward and his son, Jordan, are recorded as paying ten marks of silver for 'right' (i.e. the hearing of their case) concerning the land of Jordan's uncle. If they succeed in proving their claim they are to give twenty marks of silver.[8] Such entries as these occur very frequently throughout the roll. It is likely, as Maitland suggests, that what these men were really paying for were evocatory writs, that is, writs removing their cases from other courts for hearing in the king's court, or, one may add by way of caution, writs which in practice, though not in form, had that effect. 'Evocatory writs must be paid for and they were not to be had as matters of course . . . the king's justice was still extraordinary.'[9] The examples which have been quoted might even tend to suggest a minimum ten-mark tariff for a writ of this kind, though the case of William of St Edward and his son reveals that a successful litigant might be expected to pay the king a good deal more, perhaps for the further favour of a royal confirmation and the royal warranty that went with it. It is only fair to suppose that the crown, even if it drove a hard bargain, gave value for money – at least so long as the other party to the suit did did not offer more. This looks like the sale of right or justice which Magna Carta later sought to prevent.[10] In circumstances where royal intervention could be procured for a money payment and in an age when writs connected with the processes of law had not yet been standardised, it is not surprising that many royal writs of Henry 1 and Stephen give a strong impression of arbitrary, even irresponsible, intervention in law suits. Nonetheless it was in just this way that royal justice began to be made more widely available. One now begins better to understand the meaning of the author of the legal treatise called, somewhat misleadingly, *Leges Henrici Primi*. He tells us that 'the certain truth of law and the remedy established by settled provision are rarely to be found but, to the great confusion of all, a new method of pleading is sought . . . Legal process is involved in so many and so great anxieties and deceits that men avoid these actions and the uncertain dice of pleas.'

The element of conservatism in law is most clearly to be perceived in the most formal legal and official pronouncements.
Revolutions apart, the state generally finds it expedient to recognise the strength of traditionalism in public opinion and to try
to maintain at least a façade which will satisfy it. Medieval coronation charters are monuments of conservatism. Stephen's first
charter of liberties issued in December 1135 is very brief and
expressed in broad general terms: 'Know that I have granted . . .
to all my barons and men of England all the liberties and good
laws which Henry, king of the English . . . granted and conceded
to them. I also grant them all the good laws and good customs
which they enjoyed in the time of king Edward.' That is all. His
so-called 'Oxford charter of liberties', issued in April 1136, is
much more detailed in respect of concessions to the church, but
as regards the law in general it is hardly more specific than the first
charter. 'I wholly annul', it runs, 'all exactions, injustices and
"miskennings", whether wrongfully imposed by sheriffs or by any
other person. I will observe the good laws and the ancient and
lawful customs in respect of "murdrum" and other causes and I
command that they be observed and established.' What was the
law of king Edward, which successive kings swore to maintain,
and what were the 'good laws and ancient and lawful customs'?
Can any precise meaning be attached to these in the second
generation after the Norman Conquest, or are they mere
verbiage?

In studying such a question a number of considerations must be
kept in mind. In the first place, the maintenance, at least formally,
of the old laws gave the Conqueror and his successors a useful
hold, not only over their English subjects, but over their Norman,
Flemish, Breton and other French barons as well. Secondly, in
spite of the retention of much that was English, the settlement on
the land of England of an alien military aristocracy amounted to a
social revolution that no argument for continuity can disguise. In
any case, quite apart from this, the later eleventh and the twelfth
centuries saw considerable changes and rapid development in the
structure of society everywhere in Christendom. Consequently
'the good laws and ancient customs' of pre-Conquest England
could not long continue, unaltered, to meet the needs of the new
age, though some of the old methods of procedure (when
anachronisms like 'miskenning' had been eliminated) proved

capable of development which was really revolutionary.[11] Change and development were necessary and inevitable. These processes can be seen at work far back in English history; as far, indeed, as the earliest surviving law codes. We can see the attempts of successive kings to adapt old laws to changing needs and more complex conditions, in spite of the strong restraint of custom hallowed by tradition. Such efforts were at first tentative, for as king Alfred said about his own code, 'I dared not write much of my own'. The later tenth century saw an outburst of legislation and re-codification, but the most important milestone in the development of pre-Conquest law was undoubtedly the code of Cnut. It is probably true to say that this was the real basis of the so-called *laga Edwardi*, and it is to this code that early post-Conquest legal writers constantly hark back.

It is well known that at the time of the Norman conquest there were three main codes of law, those of Wessex, Mercia and the Danelaw, but what is not always sufficiently emphasised is that, whatever their differences, they had a good deal in common in the form of legal assumptions and legal processes. A very important feature of old English procedure was the manifest desire to restrict the scope of violence. There was a marked preference for settlement between litigants, under the auspices of a court, in which there was an element of give and take on both sides, rather than the fighting out of cases in court to the point of no return – a final judgment which was almost certain to leave one of the parties dissatisfied, embittered and in consequence likely to resort to force. The jury method, which it has often been argued was derived through the Normans from the Frankish 'inquest', by which royal rights were determined, has some claim to an independent origin in pre-Conquest England. Lady Stenton has recently argued with eloquence, learning and cogency that 'there is no longer any inherent improbability in the suggestion that the jury, common to the Scandinavian peoples on either side of the North Sea, rising to the surface for a moment under Æthelred II, may have persisted in England to become incorporated in the fabric of the Anglo-Norman state.'[12] The reference is, of course, to the twelve senior thegns of Æthelred's 'Wantage Code', who in every wapentake were to take an oath that they would not wrongfully accuse any innocent man or conceal any guilty one. The actual establishment of the sworn inquest as a vital part of civil procedure belongs to Norman rather than to pre-Conquest times. But, to quote Lady Stenton again, 'it would have been impossible without the Anglo-Saxon invention of the sealed writ by which the king's commands could be carried in a stereotyped phraseology throughout the land'.

Of all the results of the Norman Conquest the most important was probably the establishment of a very strong kingship and, with it, the opportunity of extending the scope of royal justice and of making it more effectual. At the same time, with the settlement in the country of a foreign military aristocracy, whose culture and feudal relationships were derived from Frankish sources, there were bound to be new and powerful influences at work in the sphere of law. These lords brought with them the customs which governed their feudal courts, the honour courts and barony courts, which regulated the relations of lords with their vassals and of their vassals with one another. We are told in *Leges Henrici Primi* that a vassal residing in the remotest manor of an honour was obliged to attend its court at the summons of his lord. In that court the custom of the honour was the law which was enforced, and while such courts (where they existed) throughout the country had a great deal in common in the custom they maintained, there was room for much local diversity. Again, a few powerful feudal lords, or their representatives, in a shire or a hundred court could exercise an influence upon its procedure and proceedings out of all proportion to their numbers. This was why the maintenance by the Conqueror and his successors of the *laga Edwardi* was so important as a brake upon the extension of Norman feudal custom to the public, as distinct from the private, courts. It is probably true that the most immediate effect of the Norman Conquest in the sphere of law was the introduction of these new complications. Yet, as Maitland so rightly warned his readers, we shall be deceived if we think, simply and crudely, in terms of two streams of law, one French, the other English, meeting to form a single river. He found the idea of a chemical compound equally misleading. Had Maitland been acquainted with the modern science of genetics, he might have found in it a more appropriate pattern of thought and certainly an intriguing one. His point is relentlessly, and correctly, driven home. 'The law which prevailed in England in the twelfth century can not be called a mixture of the law which prevailed in England on the day when the Confessor was alive and

9*

dead and the law which prevailed in Normandy on the day when William set sail from St Valery.'[13]

The *laga Edwardi*, as amended and confirmed by the Conqueror and his sons, was proclaimed to be the law of the land, but where exactly was it all to be found and what did a great deal of it mean to the king's subjects, whether of English or Norman descent or both, in the twelfth century? Something, perhaps a great deal, survived in the memory of the public courts of shire and hundred, that is in the memory of their suitors, especially the most ancient and venerable of them. The testimony of venerable Englishmen had been much relied upon in a number of great disputes as to rights which came to trial in the years after the Conquest, as on the famous occasion at Pinnenden Heath. This continued participation in the work of the public courts is shown by the fact that all the Norman kings, when they addressed writs to shire courts or charters generally for the realm, habitually included 'all their faithful men, French and English'. In the twelfth century this may have been no more than a stereotyped formula used by the royal scriptorium, but it is not without historical significance.

The state of the law before the reign of Henry I may best be judged from a number of legal treatises produced in the early decades of the twelfth century. The *Quadripartitus* is a work which belies its name, since the last two of the projected four books do not exist and it is doubtful whether they ever were written. What has survived is little more than a not very good Latin translation of old English 'dooms', with the code of Cnut in the forefront as the latest authoritative statement of English law. The *Leges Henrici Primi* may have been written, as Felix Liebermann long ago suggested, by a royal justice.[14] It is a difficult book, partly because the author's Latin is so peculiar, partly because he lacked clarity of mind and seemed incapable of devising an orderly plan for his work, so that he was overwhelmed by his material. Obviously he was attempting to set forth the law as it was administered in Henry I's reign, and he tricked out his work with a meretricious erudition by dipping into the works of Isidore and Burchard of Worms, the *Lex Salica*, the Frankish capitularies and the Visigothic version of the Theodosian code. While it is remarkable that so ambitious a treatise should have been attempted at so early a date (*c.* 1118), we are left with the impression that the author neither understood very clearly nor much approved of the developments which were taking place in the England of his day in law and the administration of justice. The treatise as a whole is not one greatly to commend itself to historians and lawyers nowadays, but parts of it are undeniably useful. Another treatise of this same age is the bilingual *Leges Willelmi* in French and Latin. Such value as it possesses lies particularly in its statement of some of the rules of Old English law as interpreted in Norman times. The part which shows the influence of Roman law is, in Maitland's view, significant because 'it shows us how men were helplessly looking about for some general principles of jurisprudence which would deliver them from their practical and intellectual difficulties'. Like the other two authors, this writer also makes considerable use of the code of Cnut. A fourth treatise called *Leges Edwardi Confessoris* professes to set out the laws of king Edward as stated to the Conqueror by juries from various parts of England. It carried much weight in the Middle Ages but seems in fact thoroughly unreliable.

In the early twelfth century men in England had every reason to be bewildered by the law. Those who thought themselves skilled in it, like the authors of the treatises just mentioned, sought in earlier codes, especially that of Cnut, for authoritative statements of law and in a welter of legal muddle they strove for some kind of clarification. Law indeed varied through the shires and the hundred courts and the honour courts and all the other secular courts, each guided by the memory of its suitors as to the custom to be observed. But already the very slow and painful process of simplification, or rather consolidation, was beginning. This is not to say that the law became simpler, but rather that, in process of time, through the working and extension of the custom of the king's court, a single common law would gradually develop, overriding the dictates of provincial and local custom and applying to all the king's free subjects. We can see it emerging fairly clearly in the thirteenth century; we can just see it beginning to take shape in the later twelfth century, especially in the reforms of Henry II. Those reforms were, beyond question, a work of genius, but they represent not so much innovation as remarkable insight and organising ability, which enabled the old laws and legal processes to be seen in a clear light, firmly developed and utilised with a new efficiency. The difference is that between the confusion of *Leges Henrici Primi* and the orderliness and clarity of Glanvill's *De Legibus et Consuetudinibus Anglie*. The reign of Henry I is a crucial period in the whole development of English law, for he worked empirically, effectively and without the deterrent of scruples. Stephen's reign is hardly less important, for the astonishing fact is that the judicial system, as Henry I left it, continued like his administrative and financial systems to function sufficiently to survive in some kind of working order the nineteen winters when Christ and his saints slept.

Maitland remarked that, as regards the malefactor, the community may assume one of four attitudes: it may make war upon him (outlawry); it may leave him exposed to the vengeance of those whom he has wronged (blood-feud); it may allow him to make amendment; it may inflict upon him a determinate punishment.[15] Long before the Norman Conquest, the blood-feud and outlawry were giving way to a system of reparation, as more offences became emendable by payment to the injured party or his kin, to his lord and, not least, to the king. In particular, offences which were regarded as in a peculiar sense offences against society and the state, rather than against individuals, are important. Jurisdiction over crimes of this nature came to be regarded as the king's prerogative and the profits of justice accrued to him. These were the pleas of the crown.

The fact that so many offences were emendable, many even of those that were pleas of the crown, meant that a strong financial interest was early and deeply entrenched in the administration of justice. Consequently, apart from the status and influence it conferred, the possession of jurisdictional rights with profits from amercements and forfeitures was eagerly sought by churchmen no less than by laymen. Both before and after the Conquest great numbers of estates, large and small, all over the country had annexed to them rights of sake and soke, that is, the right of holding a court and drawing the profits. Furthermore, rights not merely of private but of public jurisdiction, or the profits thereof, particularly in hundred courts, were granted to individuals, perhaps even more frequently to churches and monasteries than to laymen. Add to these franchises the post-Conquest feudal courts and it is easy to see that they constituted innumerable impediments to the spread of royal justice and the growth of common law.

The growth of pleas of the crown is highly significant but even in Cnut's code, where there is a concise list of rights which the king enjoys over all men, the phrase is added: 'unless he wishes to honour any man more highly'. That is to say that even the pleas of the crown could be alienated. Indeed the only royal rights which never seem to have been alienated by pre-Conquest kings are those comprised in the *trimoda necessitas*. These were the royal right to exact service in the fyrd and the building and repair of fortifications and bridges. Time and again these were explicitly reserved in royal charters. Cnut's list of pleas of the crown is brief. In Wessex and Mercia they were *mundbryce*, or breach of the king's protection; *hamsocn*, or attack upon a homestead and injury of persons therein; *forstal*, or lying in wait; the fine for harbouring fugitives and the fine for neglect of military service. In the Danelaw the king had the fines for fighting and for neglecting military service, *grithbryce*, or breach of the king's peace and *hamsocn*. There were also certain offences, such as a wrong judgment owing to malice or bribery, which involved a heavy payment to the king. Some offences, such as breach of the king's special protection, could have very wide implications and might be involved automatically in some trivial offence committed at a time or place over which this royal protection extended. By the time of Henry I the pleas of the crown had become a long and disorderly list. The disorder may be due to the author of *Leges Henrici Primi*, from whose treatise this information is derived. There is, however, no reason to doubt the expansion of the pleas of the crown to include such offences as contempt of the king's writs or orders, injury or slaying of his servants, outlawry, *murdrum*, coining false money, arson, treasure-trove, wreck, forest offences, unjust judgments, default of justice and the wide, undefined category of transgressions of royal law (*prevaricatio legis regie*).[16] There is not a great deal else to go upon until the reign of Henry II, when the assizes of Clarendon and Northampton and Glanvill's treatise reveal to us the working of a highly organised system of royal justice.

In the earlier half of the twelfth century the existence of this miscellaneous category of pleas of the crown is important; so is the supreme justice inherent in the crown, which could override the justice administered at lower levels and was available to the king's subjects – at a price. No less significant are the channels through which this royal justice was made available. The king could exercise it in his *curia*, or court, in its widest from as the great council, with the assistance of his tenants-in-chief. No king could afford to neglect this method in dealing with cases concerning his realm and his earls and barons, collectively and individually. There was another court or another aspect of the court, called *curia regis*, which emerged with the evolution of a financial system centering in the exchequer, where the king's great household officers played an important part. This court could treat the whole process of exchequer accounting as a judicial operation and could deal with cases arising out of the royal revenues, a widely ranging category, and came to deal with pleas of land and criminal matters too.

For monarchs who like the first three Norman kings, and especially Henry I, spent a great deal of their time across the Channel, it was necessary to have a vicegerent to take charge of the administration during their absences. Sometimes the queen acted in such a capacity, and sometimes a subject carried on the king's business in his name. Information about the early history of this office, which came to be known as that of the Procurator or Chief Justiciar, is not very copious, but its existence and great importance are not open to question.[17] In the earlier years of Henry I's reign, about 1106, Roger, bishop of Salisbury, seems to have been doing work of this kind.[18] In 1111 and 1119 he was present at judicial sessions in the exchequer, taking precedence over the other judges.[19] Not only did he function during the king's absences in Normandy but in 1127 and 1132 when Henry I was in England, he was presiding at the exchequer, presumably as chief justiciar.[20] Roger probably continued in this office under Stephen until his arrest in June 1139.[21] Stephen's queen, Matilda, issued at least one writ in a viceregal capacity, which probably belongs to the time when she valiantly maintained his cause during his captivity.[22] It is addressed to the justice and John, the sheriff, and the barons, officials etc. of London and begins: 'I order and command you on my lord the king's part and on my own' (*mando vobis et precipio ex parte regis domini mei et mea*). The suggestion made by Mr Richardson and Professor Sayles that Richard de Lucy held the office of chief justiciar towards the end of Stephen's reign is hardly borne out by the writs upon which it is based. These seem to refer rather to his position as a justice of London and Essex.[23] There is no ground for the suggestion that duke Henry acted as chief justiciar after his treaty with Stephen.

There was certainly in the reign of Henry I a powerful judicial body at the centre of rule, often if not always presided over by a great royal official of procuratorial status, the chief justiciar. Members of this body, or other trusted royal servants, could be sent as royal justices to any locality, either to deal *ad hoc* with some particularly important case or with a general commission to hear pleas of the crown. Mr Richardson and Professor Sayles argue convincingly for the existence in Henry I's reign of a body of about a dozen 'justices of all England', prominent members of the king's court. These were not professional lawyers, but they were experienced royal administrators, well versed in the hearing of cases.[24] We know from the evidence of the pipe roll of 1130 supplemented by that of a number of royal writs that judicial eyres, or visitations by royal justices throughout the land, were held between 1120 and 1130, and there is some evidence of eyres much earlier in Henry I's reign.[25] The eyres reflected in the pipe roll seem to have been more extensive and systematic than anything that had previously been organised. This impression, however, may be due simply to the fact that, for the first and last time for a quarter of a century, we have a pipe roll to provide the vital evidence. Judicial eyres, even when they were eventually organised on a more regular footing, were still occasional events, whereas there was a need to keep an eye upon pleas of the crown and to provide for the administration of royal justice locally at all times. It seems likely that at one time royal as distinct from ordinary public justice was administered by the sheriff in each shire. This was an arrangement which placed too great and too varied power, financial, administrative and judicial, in the hands of a single man. To safeguard the jurisdictional rights of the crown, and to provide for the hearing of the pleas which belonged exclusively to it, there developed under the Norman kings the office of shire justice.[26] It is enough to say that well before the close of Henry I's reign, this was a well established and responsible office, which must have provided a useful check upon the powers of the sheriff. How important it had become is shown in Stephen's reign by the eagerness of great magnates like Geoffrey de Mandeville to acquire the office in their shires. Geoffrey acquired, in successive charters from the empress and Stephen, the justiceships of London and Middlesex, Essex and Hertfordshire.[27] The importance he attached to the office is well illustrated in the arrogant superscription and address of his charter of restitution to the canons of St Martin-le-Grand, London; 'Geoffrey, by God's grace earl of Essex and justice of London, to Robert, by the same grace bishop of London . . .'[28] Since Geoffrey was given the office of justice hereditarily and, also hereditarily, the office of sheriff in the same places, this represented a concentration of power in the hands of a subject which the crown could not long continue to tolerate, unless it were prepared to acquiesce in the complete abrogation of any royal authority in the region. The shire justice was indeed a man of all work, in many respects the predecessor of the coroner. By Stephen's reign he was almost invariably included in every writ addressed to a shire court and in charters and writs addressed for the whole realm. It is obvious that he had a very active part to play in judicial affairs, especially as the policy of the crown was to draw cases from private courts to the king's courts by writs which were evocatory in practice, if not in form.

In cases other than routine matters, in which the king's shire justices would automatically take some action, because pleas of the crown were involved in them or because a previous royal writ had already authorised certain action by them in certain circumstances, royal justice was activated by a royal writ authenticated by the king's seal. Here it is perhaps well to draw attention to the difference between a purely administrative writ, which had no judicial significance unless it were neglected (such e.g. as a command to a royal servant to repair a castle), and a legal writ, which had such significance. The distinction is not always absolutely clear in practice so long as the royal chancery has not learned that multi-purpose writs lead to confusion. By the time when Glanvill wrote his treatise, the legal reforms of Henry II were in operation and the chancery already had a considerable repertory of writs, each designed for a specific type of action. Earlier, however, under Henry I and Stephen, the issue of writs was much less highly organised and rationalised. The royal scribes were already becoming increasingly expert in the drafting of writs and were even feeling their way tentatively towards some degree of standardisation. To read our history backwards by taking the stereotyped writs we find in Glanvill and seeking their earlier prototypes among the writs of Henry II's predecessors is a dangerous historical method. This is not to say that examples strikingly similar to Henry II's writs are not to be found, but rather that an attempt to judge the intention of the earlier by the later writs may lead to false conclusions. One obvious difficulty which arises, if we attempt to place earlier writs in the categories we find in Glanvill, is due to the multi-purpose nature of many early writs, which has already been referred to. To take but one example, let us examine a writ of Stephen in favour of Reading abbey, which can only be dated within very wide limits (1140–54). Translated, it reads as follows:

Stephen, king of the English, to the earl of Warenne, greeting. I order you to allow the monks of Reading to hold their land of Catshill, which Geoffrey Purcel gave them with my permission, well and in peace and freely, as my charter concerning it, which they have, testifies that they should hold it. And anything you have taken therefrom you must justly return to them in full. And, if you claim anything therein, you must come to my court and I will fully deal with your case (*tenebo inde tibi plenum rectum*) as a matter pertaining to my crown. And know that I marvel at your troubling the monks in this matter. Witness Robert, the chancellor, at Oxford.[29]

Professor van Caenegem classifies this as a *Writ Praecipe of debt and entry*, but he is also obliged to classify it as a writ ordering reseisin before pleading, based upon the principle that when a case concerning seisin (possession) is pending, the *status quo ante* must be maintained until it is decided.

It is not at all difficult to find in Stephen's reign and in those of his three Norman predecessors royal writs which seem to adumbrate some of the famous writs of Henry II's time. But they are not, in fact, quite the same and it is not at all clear that they were put into effect in the same way. It cannot too often be emphasised that, in the spheres of English law and administration, genius was at work in the decades after 1154. Earlier, the king could intervene in law suits, usually at the request of a party who was willing to pay for the favour, by issuing a writ which was in effect, though never specifically in form, an evocatory writ. As a case in point, here is a writ of Stephen in favour of the Cathedral priory of Durham, which must have been issued either early in 1136 or early in 1138.

Stephen, king of the English, to Rainald de Muscamp and his sister C., greeting. I command that you return to St Cuthbert his land of Hetherslaw as well and as fully as your brother, Thomas de Muscamp, whose heirs you are, gave it in his lifetime and offered it upon the altar when he became a monk. And, unless you do so, Eustace fitz John (probably still the royal justice) shall do it, lest I hear any complaint about it, for I am unwilling that St Cuthbert should lose anything that belongs to him. Witness, William Martel, at Durham.[30]

This is typical of a fairly common kind of writ, though the final clause more usually runs: 'lest I hear any complaint about it on the ground of lack of a proper hearing (*penuria recti*) or default of justice (*defectus justitie*)', which, like disobedience to a royal writ, were pleas of the crown. This kind of writ assumes that the person addressed (the alleged disseisors in the case quoted) has acted wrongfully. He is ordered to restore the property in question to the demandant without delay, and if he fails to do so the royal justice of the shire or some other specified person is required to do it. The respondent is not ostensibly offered the alternative, as for example in the *Writ Praecipe*, of coming before the king's justice and showing cause why he should not comply with the royal writ. In practice, in many instances the respondent must have continued the dispute in the king's court and he might even get a writ in his turn. Certainly, by one means or another, cases of this kind could be protracted for years, even for generations. Perhaps the best outcome for both parties, in the end, was a *finalis concordia*, in which, after the old English fashion, agreement was reached by means of a little give and take on both sides. It is probably true that the mere possession by one party of a royal writ in his favour sometimes acted as a strong deterrent to the other party. No litigant dared lightly run counter to the express will of Henry I and even a king as weak as Stephen was not to be flouted with complete impunity.

Many writs of Henry I and Stephen convey to us the impression almost that they were issued irresponsibly. Indeed Stephen confessed explicitly to nothing less than this in a charter for Worcester cathedral, issued *c.* 1144–52. The vital clause reads as follows:

Know that I have restored to God and St Mary and the prior and monks of Worcester, for the soul of my uncle, king Henry, the church of Wolverhampton, which I previously gave without taking advice (*inconsulte*) to Roger, bishop of Chester. For I have learned from many people that it belonged to them of old and ought so to belong. And therefore it is my will that they should not suffer loss or disturbance in anything because of any writ which the bishop had for it.[31]

Such royal writs, by assuming that the persons in whose favour they were issued had right on their side, not infrequently overrode, or indeed ignored, the legitimate jurisdiction of other courts, especially private barony or honour courts. The man who received a royal writ of this kind and failed to implement it would be liable to appear before royal justice on a crown plea of neglect of the king's writ. There presumably he would plead his justification, if any, and the case at issue would thus have been evoked to the royal court. Here it may be that we have the 'new methods of pleading' referred to with such obvious distaste by the author of *Leges Henrici Primi*.

We have at least one account, obviously coloured and quite likely garbled, of the effect of the royal intervention by means of a writ.[32] The events, recorded in the Abingdon chronicle, took place in 1153. Turstin, son of Simon, the royal dispenser, complained to the king that the abbot of Abingdon had for a long time fraudulently retained possession of certain hereditary lands of his. According to the chronicle Turstin gave gifts to the king in order to secure the return of the property he claimed. This probably means in fact that he paid for a writ, which the king thereupon issued, requiring the abbot to give Turstin possession of what he claimed. The procedure seems quite typical. Then, we are told, the abbot, in view of the serious loss involved, did not lightly comply (*non leviter consensit*), but fixed a day to take the advice of his court about the course to be pursued. Even after a second meeting he was still in doubt how to act. Turstin seeing, it is said, his chance of enrichment postponed, approached the king again, falsely representing that the abbot had refused to obey the king's writ and once more he plied the king and those about him (*collaterales*) with gifts. Quite likely he thought it well worth while to pay for another writ. The king, taking the view that Turstin's complaint was reasonable, ordered Henry of Oxford, the sheriff (of Berkshire) to hear the case immediately according to royal law (*jus regium*), presumably as a plea of the crown. The sheriff, seduced by bribery (according to the Abingdon chronicler), deprived the proper owners and Turstin, as though by the king's command and dictation, was unjustly, as he afterwards confessed, given possession of what did not belong to him. Divine Providence, however, stepped in to punish the impious despoiler of the abbey and king Stephen consequently died within a year. There is a strong feeling in this account that the royal writs deprived the abbot of Abingdon not only of property but of his lawful jurisdictional rights, which had to give way to the *jus regium* administered by the sheriff, acting *ad hoc*, it would seem, as a royal justice. The abbot obviously could not find any way of preventing this. By such means the expansion and development of royal justice was promoted, to the incidental profit of the crown. The real importance, from the viewpoint of legal history, of writs of this kind issued by Henry I and Stephen is not so much that some of them bore a certain resemblance, in content and formulation, to the writs of Henry II: it is rather that these earlier writs helped enormously by their practical effects to establish the foundations and create the assumptions upon which later evocatory procedure could be firmly based.

It is important to see, as far as available sources permit, how the law was actually administered in various courts. It will be best to begin at the summit with cases heard *coram rege*, not least because there is most information about those which, in their day, were considered important or created some sensation. It would be difficult to find a more sensational case than that which Thomas of Monmouth, the monk of Norwich cathedral priory, described in his *Life and Miracles of St William of Norwich*.[33] It contains an account of the first alleged ritual murder by the Jews of a Christian boy in England. What is interesting and illuminating is the kind of assumptions that are made about the administration of justice in Stephen's reign. A priest named Godwin, a relative of the murdered William, laid a complaint against the Jews in a Norwich diocesan synod presided over by bishop Everard about 10 April 1144. Godwin betook himself to this ecclesiastical body as 'my one and only protection' and undertook to 'prove the truth of my words at such time and place and by such proof as is allowed me by Christian law'. It was decided that the Jews should be summoned to answer the accusation. They sought and obtained the protection of the sheriff, John de Chesney, and refused to appear before the synod. They absolutely denied the accusation against them and eventually the sheriff gave them shelter in the castle and, it was said, the bishop feared openly to oppose the king and his officers. Actually it is to be doubted whether bishop Everard was at all convinced of the truth of the accusation against the Jews. Matters were further complicated by the murder, probably in 1146, of the wealthy Jew, Eleazar, in whose house the murder of St William was alleged to have been done. This seems to have been the work of the men of a knight called Simon de Novers, who was being pressed by Eleazar for the repayment of a debt. Some time afterwards, king Stephen came to Norwich (*c.* 1148) and the Jews laid before him a complaint about this murder. Thomas of Monmouth gives what he calls an imaginary account of the trial (*In iudiciali genere coniecturalis causa*). 'We', they are represented as saying to the king, 'are thy Jews; we pay thee tribute yearly; we are continually necessary to thee in thy needs, since we are always faithful to thee and useful to thy realm.' They set forth their case with admirable logic and stressed the danger for the Jewish community if the murderer of a Jew should be allowed to go unpunished.

Simon de Novers denied the accusation and since he was a tenant of the new bishop of Norwich, William Turbe, the latter, by the king's permission, went to take charge of Simon's defence. The bishop made an eloquent plea for him, embodying a counter-charge against the Jews of the murder of St William. In view of the importance of the case, the king ordered that it should be postponed until the impending general council of clergy and barons should meet in London. In the interval, the Jews are alleged to have given the king a large bribe and to have tried but failed to corrupt the bishop of Norwich also. When, after a three days' session of the council, the bishop rose to reopen the case, king Stephen is alleged to have made the following reply:

My Lord bishop, we have been fatigued by a good deal of discourse today, and there is still business to detain us; we are unable, therefore, to give proper attention to so important a matter. But wait, meanwhile, with patience until we have cleared away these briars, as I may call them, and so be freer to whet the axe of our justice for felling the noxious tree. And inasmuch as this case is a very difficult one, it is not fitting that we should approach it rashly or hastily. For the more pressing the matter and the crime, the more warily must justice be applied. Let us therefore defer this case until another time, and thus reserved for greater convenience, when we are able and it is our pleasure, we will reconsider it with the aid of our common council.

If this account by Thomas of Monmouth bears the slightest relation to truth, it is clear that Stephen behaved, in this case, with good sense in refusing to be stampeded by the pressure of religious fanaticism. We are left with the feeling that it was possible for justice to be done *coram rege Stephano*, even in the face of public clamour.

Another very illuminating case is recorded in considerable (and much more factual) detail by the chronicler of Battle abbey, and with a good deal of satisfaction, since the outcome was so very gratifying for that highly privileged house.[34] This was a suit brought by the archbishop of Canterbury, at some date between 1139 and 1154, against the abbot of Battle, in respect of a trespass by his men of Dunge Marsh in taking a Romney ship as wreck. The archbishop pleaded the ordinance of Henry I to the effect that no right of wreck could be claimed if one member of the ship's crew survived. The abbot, on the other hand, relied upon the old law that the survivors must save their ship within a limited time. He argued, significantly, that the new law enacted by Henry I was not binding after his death, unless re-enacted by consent of the barons. Significantly, too, the assembled barons upheld this contention. The case was one between two prelates, who were tenants-in-chief of the crown, and it was therefore one for the king's court. Further, a plea concerning wreck was a royal plea unless jurisdiction over it had been alienated. The king, we are told, favoured the archbishop. The barons with one accord took a contrary view, swayed by the abbot's argument that 'though king Henry was able at his pleasure to change the ancient laws of the country during his own lifetime, he could not bind posterity to such a change without the consent of the barons of the realm. But, if those his (the abbot's) equals in rank (the barons present), with the consent of the royal court then sitting, agree to waive their own claim to that right which was now challenged in him, he himself would willingly relinquish his claim'. It was a clever appeal to men little disposed to relinquish anything profitable that they could contrive to retain. A vital point of law having thus been established *coram rege*, by the advice of the barons present, the case was remitted to the abbot's court of Dunge Marsh, where the offence occurred, since Battle abbey claimed wreck and other regalian rights as within its jurisdiction. The men of the archbishop of Canterbury were to appear in that court on the day fixed for hearing the case, but failed to do so. The matter was again brought before the king's court by the archbishop, who was nonsuited by common consent. This case provides a very useful example of how cases were dealt with *coram rege*. The law, where this was in dispute, was determined, and since the matter concerned one of the pleas of the crown this could not have been done in any inferior court. This done, the case was remitted to be heard in the local court whose claim to jurisdiction was recognised. In cases of this kind, care seems to have been taken not to interfere with the legitimate jurisdiction of other courts, and not to allow anyone to flout such jurisdiction. It was quite natural that barons, who themselves held jurisdictional rights, should avoid any action which might imperil them. This makes the king's intervention in lawsuits and the development of evocatory procedure appear all the more remarkable, even though a case such as the one we have just considered throws into relief the latent conflict of interest between royal and private justice.

The record of another suit *coram rege*, which took place late in December 1136, or early in 1137, shows a similar respect for the jurisdiction of other courts. This was a suit brought by the prior and canons of Holy Trinity, Aldgate, against Aschuill, keeper of the Tower of London.[35] Some time back, in Henry I's reign, his predecessor in the post, whose name was Other, had forcibly deprived the priory of a large part of the soke of the English cnihtengild, which had come into its possession.[36] The prior had sought justice from the king and a royal writ had been issued for the hearing of the case. The keeper of the Tower had done everything in his power to delay or prevent this, so that the case was still outstanding at the death of Henry I. Then, in the second year of Stephen's reign, prior Norman took advantage of the king's presence in Westminister to put forward his claim once more, with the assistance, we are told, of queen Matilda, Algar bishop of Coutances, Roger the chancellor, Arunlf archdeacon of Séez, William Martel the steward, Robert de Curcy, Aubrey de Vere, Geoffrey de Mandeville, Hugh Bigod, Adam de Belnai, Andrew Buchuinte (justice of London) and many London burgesses. This looks, in fact, extraordinarily like the witness-list of an important charter issued on a formal occasion, such as a Christmas court. Probably all that is meant by the assistance of these people is their presence on this occasion and perhaps their witnessing of the charter of confirmation which must eventually have been issued for the priory. When Aschuill was summoned before the king and asked what exactly his claim to the property was, he replied, perfectly reasonably, that he did not make any claim for, said he 'I have held it' (*tenui*). Possession, he submitted, was all that mattered, as far as he was concerned, for he had simply taken the land over, together with his post of keeper of the Tower, from his predecessor, Other. Then the king verbally commanded Andrew, the justice, and the other London burgesses who were present (probably in case their testimony should be required in the king's court), and he also issued them and others with a writ, to fix a day to meet on the land in question and discover what the situation had been at and since the Confessor's time. This is exactly in accordance with the terms of Stephen's Oxford charter of liberties. If the prior should establish his claim he was to be re-seised without delay. This procedure was duly followed and the prior's right was proved by the oath of twenty-one men, all important burgesses who are named in the document. 'Many more,' we are told, 'were prepared to take oath, but these were deemed sufficient. And so, by this means and by this mode and procedure, all that land and soke was adjudged to the aforesaid church. And this king Stephen confirms it to the said church, as the following charter shows.' In actual fact, the next charter in the cartulary shows nothing of the kind, but this merely points to a slip by the compiler. In this case, when it was first heard before Stephen, we are given the impression that he himself acted as the judge, but all the other circumstances suggest that he was sitting in his great council. The business of the court was, obviously, to establish the broad facts so that it might decide where, having regard to the nature of the case, jurisdiction properly lay. This case was duly remitted to the appropriate London court, it being no part of the king's duty to interfere with this jurisdiction so long as there was no complaint of *penuria recti* or *defectus justicie*. The London court proceeded to establish the facts of the possession of the soke of the English cnihtengild, from the time of king Edward to date, by setting up a sworn inquest. The recognition was made by the oath of twenty-one suitors of court, establishing the justice of prior Norman's claim.

Cases heard *coram rege* were not invariably referred to other courts for a decision. An item from the cartulary of St Frideswide's, Oxford, will serve as an example of another kind of procedure.[37] This can properly be described as a writ of Stephen for execution of judgment in a suit determined *coram rege*. It is addressed for Oxfordshire and records the grant to St Frideswide's probably *c.* 1138–9, of the island of Medley, in perpetual alms, 'concerning which my burgesses of Oxford recognised before me and my earls and barons that they had given the rent of that island, to wit, half a mark of silver, to restore the lighting of the said church', which the canons lost because of the stalls which were removed by the burgesses. The king frees the island from all service. The rent or profit of the stalls in question must have paid for the lighting of the church of St Frideswide's. Another writ in favour of the same house, confirming its right to its gate in the city wall and its right to build on the wall, also resulted from a formal recognition by the burgesses of Oxford before the king and his earls and barons that the property and easements belonged to the priory. This writ was issued at Oxford *c.* 1136–40.[38]

Another interesting case concerns Battle abbey.[39] Its date is precise: 7 December 1148. Here a suit is recorded of Walter, abbot of Battle, against the bishop of Chichester. The bishop having threatened the abbot with suspension for failure to attend a synod at Chichester, the latter appealed to the king at St. Albans. He obtained a writ forbidding the bishop to interfere with Battle abbey, which had the status of a royal chapel. Both parties were summoned to appear before the king in London on the octave of St Andrew, by a message delivered by Robert de Cornuville, the king's clerk. Both appeared, but the bishop, having other urgent business, defaulted. Stephen allowed the charters of William I and ordered them to be observed. It would be very interesting to know if the charters so allowed were genuine, because the surviving original foundation charter of William I is a blatant forgery.[40] It purports to make Battle abbey as free of bishops and others as Christchurch, Canterbury, was. Other examples of proceedings *coram rege* are to be found, but although such proceedings must have been frequent surviving records of them are not very numerous. If such proceedings are not ostensibly the subject of royal writs, it may be thought that they may, nonetheless, be inferred from certain writs. The utmost caution must be used in making such inferences for when a case had been heard and determined *coram rege*, any writ directly connected with the judgment was likely to mention the fact. The following may be taken as typical of a formal writ for execution of judgment in a case determined *coram rege*:

Stephen, king of the English, to his justice, sheriff, barons and all his officials and faithful men, French and English, of Lincolnshire, greeting. Be it known to you that the abbot and monks of Peterborough deraigned before me, against the canons of Lincoln, at Lincoln, their land of Northope.[41] Wherefore it is my will and firm command that those monks hold it well and in peace and freely and quit as they deraigned it before me in my court, and so that they be not impleaded upon this writ about the deraignment. Witnesses: Ralph fitz Gilbert, Turgis d'Avranches and Robert Gelle and Alan de Creon. At Stamford (1136–41).[42]

Sometimes a favoured beneficiary obtained the privilege of pleading only before the king himself in any plea of the crown. A concise little writ addressed for Oxfordshire and Berkshire (that is, for their shire courts) at some time between 1139 and 1154 guarantees the privilege to the abbot of Abingdon and his men, who are to plead only before the king in person, when he is at Oxford.[43] This was a very important concession because, had not Oxford been specified, the abbot and his men would have been liable to plead wherever the king chose to summon them and even, perhaps, to follow the court in its peregrinations until the case was heard. Perhaps we ought not to assume too readily that the crown gratuitously put people to inconvenience in such matters, for there is a good deal of evidence to suggest that local business was in fact dealt with locally when the king visited a region. The address of this writ to the two shires where the abbot of Abingdon and his men were most likely to become involved in pleas of the crown suggests that these were usually held in the shire court assembly, though under the presidency of a royal justice, not of the sheriff in his shrieval capacity. The rights of the Augustinian house of Holy Trinity, Ipswich (founded in 1133), illustrate a special kind of case. About 1135–9, Stephen issued in its favour a general confirmation and protection.[44] It is addressed in an unusual, if not unique, form to the bishop of Norwich and his archdeacons and to Hugh Bigod, presumably as sheriff, and his officials, thus including the representatives both of ecclesiastical and of secular justice. If anyone claims against the canons anything given to their house in alms, they are not to plead except before the bishop of Norwich and before the king's demesne justice (*coram mea justicia dominica*), since they are the king's canons and claim to hold of him. The demesne justice, unless this is another name for the shire justice, which seems unlikely, suggests that there were special arrangements for the administration of justice in the lands of the royal demesne. Further elucidation of this is greatly to be desired.

There does not seem to be any evidence that would enable us to say with complete certainty that judicial eyres were held in Stephen's reign. We have to depend solely upon the evidence of charters and writs, since there has not survived a single pipe roll in which the amercements arising from eyres are accounted for in each shire, as they are in the pipe roll of 1130. We know the names of a number of men who served Henry 1 as justices both at the centre of rule and on judicial eyres. Apart from Roger, bishop of Salisbury, who was chief justiciar, Ralph Basset and after him his son Richard were important members of this body. Other notable members were Aubrey 11 de Vere, Miles of Gloucester and Eustace and Payn fitz John. The latter was killed by the Welsh in July 1137. At the beginning of his reign, Stephen referred to Miles in a charter in his favour as 'my baron and justice', which makes it clear that he remained in office for a time, probably until he joined the empress in 1139.[45] Eustace, brother of Payn fitz John, also a justice, deserted Stephen in 1138 and fought on the Scottish side in the battle of the Standard in August of that year. Robert Arundel and Geoffrey de Clinton joined the empress by 1141 and Richard Basset soon followed suit. Walter d'Espec, a venerable and greatly respected figure in the north of England, did not transfer his allegiance; but after playing a leading part in the battle of the Standard he seems to have taken no further active part in affairs. Another of Henry 1's justices, William d'Aubigny (*Brito*),[46] must have forfeited his lands by 1146, because they were included in Stephen's grant to the earl of Chester in that year.[47] Most, in fact, of the body of 'justices of all England' who served Henry 1 deserted Stephen sooner or later. This, however, ought not to be interpreted as representing a majority opinion on their part that Stephen's title was invalid. They may indeed have thought so but in many cases motives of self interest are all too easy to discern.

That Stephen had shire justices is certain; that one or more of his great officers held pleas in various places is obvious. Such, however, is the difficulty of dating Stephen's charters and writs within narrow limits that we cannot be quite sure whether or not the examples afforded are sufficiently close together in point of time to suggest that the cases involved had been heard in the course of general eyres. Take for example, the following writ issued between Stephen's coronation and 1141:

> Stephen, king of the English, to the sheriff and his officials of Huntingdonshire, greeting. I order that the abbot of Thorney have his market and all his customs of Yaxley as well and peacefully and honourably as ever he best and most freely had them in the time of king William and of king Henry on the day when he was alive and dead, and as it was decided before Aubrey de Vere and William Martel at Huntingdon. And the burgesses of Huntingdon may take their customs where they were wont to take them in the time of King Henry. Witness, Aubrey de Vere. At Westminster.[48]

The abbot of Thorney had charters from William II and Henry I which set Yaxley market free of custom and conferred the royal protection upon it and those attending, with the standard £10 penalty for infringement.[49] The abbot also obtained writs from Stephen to enforce the same protection and exemption.[50] Grants of the right to levy toll and custom and grants of exemption from all such levies were so common that they must have caused the utmost confusion with innumerable law suits arising from conflicting claims. Since Yaxley market enjoyed royal protection, any case concerning rights there would be a matter for royal justice. It may be that Aubrey de Vere and William Martel, both very important *curiales*, were sent to deal with this case, where owing to the claims of the Scottish royal house and of Simon of Senlis eminent toes might easily be trodden upon. Perhaps in such circumstances it was thought wise to entrust the hearing of the case to two of the king's greatest judicial officers. It is, nonetheless, tempting to believe that the Yaxley evidence does point, not just to the hearing of a single case, but to a general eyre between 1136 and 1141, conducted in the traditional way by royal justices; but this evidence can hardly be called conclusive.

Another interesting case occurred in Suffolk during approximately the same period of years (1136–40). A writ of Stephen, issued at Oxford, orders Alice Bigod to restore to the religious of Belvoir priory their tithes of Bradley. If she does not comply the bishop of Norwich is to see to it, and failing action by him Aubrey de Vere is charged with the duty.[51] Aubrey actually witnessed the writ. It looks as though a royal justice from the king's court has been deputed to attend to this specific case, where difficulty seems to have been anticipated. Alice Bigod seems to have proved re-calcitrant, for another writ, issued at Stamford (i.e. on another occasion), addressed to the bishop of Norwich, orders him to cause the religious of Belvoir to have their tithes of Bradley, which Alice Bigod is unjustly withholding.[52] There is no mention of Aubrey de Vere here but the writ is witnessed by another house-hold officer and royal justice, William Martel. There is no further evidence which might clarify the situation, which is quite typical of the difficulties encountered in dealing with the problems of the administration of justice in Stephen's reign.

Another case of about the same period refers to the lands of Canterbury Cathedral priory.[53] A writ is addressed to the justices and sheriffs within whose jurisdiction the prior and convent of Christchurch hold lands and orders them to ensure that they enjoy all the liberties they had under the king's predecessors. 'And unless you do so, Aubrey de Vere and my justice shall do it.'[54] Here the shire justices as well as the sheriffs are subject to super-vision by a justice from the central body.

There is no reason why an eyre should not have been held within the first five years of Stephen's reign. The disorder which had arisen in the country immediately after Henry I's death and other subsequent disturbances would certainly have provided plenty of business for the king's justices. While the association of men like William Martel and Aubrey de Vere in a judicial capacity is suggestive of an eyre, we have in fact but very slender and scrappy evidence upon which to base its existence. Mr Richardson and Professor Sayles have pointed out the absence in the early years of Henry II of anything like the general eyres of Henry I, and argue that, if such eyres had been frequently and systematically held in Stephen's reign, it is unlikely that they would have fallen into desuetude.[55] There does, however, seem to be a good deal of evidence, at least during the first five years of the reign, that royal justices from the central body, often former justices of Henry I, were exercising a supervisory authority in various regions, and were often instructed to give named individuals or churches possession of land adjudged to them if the sheriff and shire justice failed to do so. Under Henry I royal justices seem to have been assigned to specific areas for the purposes of the general eyre. Is it possible that they still exercised a supervisory authority in these areas when they were not actually engaged in the conduct of a general eyre? If so, the system evolved under Henry 1 was more elaborate than has yet been recognised. It also appears that, even in Stephen's early years, as members of the old body of justices drifted away from his allegiance, an increasingly heavy burden was falling upon the shoulders of a small number of loyal *curiales* – Aubrey de Vere, William Martel, Henry of Essex, Adam de Belnai and others.

By far the larger proportion of Stephen's writ-charters and writs are addressed to shire courts, namely, to the bishop to whose diocese the shire belonged, the earl where there was one, the justice, the sheriff, barons, officials, and all the king's lieges (*fideles*) of the shire. There was in fact a convention, well established from pre-Conquest days, that a new individual grant should bear a particular address, that is, to the persons or bodies most likely to be concerned, while a confirmation bore a more general address. As time went on and business became more complex, it is obvious from reading such documents, especially when they were multi-purpose documents, that even the royal scribes were sometimes puzzled as to what the correct address ought to be. Surviving charters and writs addressed to shires and shire officials almost invariably concern possession of land and dues of various kinds, liberties, franchises (i.e. judicial rights exercised by virtue of royal grant) and the like. Of these matters, not only the shire court, but the bishop, the justice and the sheriff, or some of them, needed to have cognizance in their individual capacities. A great deal of business of this kind came to every shire, but we have relatively little information dating specifically from Stephen's reign as to how the shire court functioned. It is not the intention here to discuss the early twelfth-century shire court in general terms, but rather to give a glimpse of it in action.

There is extant a judgment of the shire court of Kent to the effect that 'Ailwarditune' (Elmstone?) 'belonged to the table' of the monks of Canterbury and rendered £4 10s for their maintenance and 3s to the high altar in lieu of all services and customs due from the land. Ralph Picot, the sheriff, unjustly used to exact from that land scot and Danegeld and other dues. After many discussions the case was taken to the shire court, which Ralph Picot held at 'Castamers' (Studmarsh?). There by the judgment of the whole shire court, it was proved that none of those dues ought to be exacted from this land by the justices and officials of the king and that no one except the monks had any authority over it. 'This,' the record continues, 'occurred in the time of king Stephen and archbishop Theobald at 'Castamers' in 1153 before the following.'[56] Thirty-one names are listed, including Ralph Picot, the sheriff, Turstin, the archiepiscopal steward and Heielnoth, reeve of Hollingbourne. The list obviously includes the representatives of several important persons. Not the least interesting aspect of the case is that it was tried in the shire court under the presidency (it is to be presumed) of the very sheriff whose actions were complained of by the Christchurch monks. The outcome is indeed a tribute to the justice meted out by a shire court.

A writ of about 1136 relating to Hereford cathedral is of some interest. It is addressed to Miles of Gloucester and Payn fitz John, probably as shire justice and sheriff respectively of Herefordshire. They are instructed to cause a 'recognition' to be made by twelve lawful men of Herefordshire as to what woods of the bishop of Hereford Henry I afforested during his lifetime. All these are to be returned to the bishop and are placed under the protection of the royal forfeiture.[57] The fact is that we have very few records of ordinary proceedings in shire courts during Stephen's reign. We tend to learn of proceedings only when they are unusual or notorious, and most of those that have commonly been quoted as shire court proceedings are discovered, on closer examination, to be something quite different. The case of Turstin *v.* the abbot of Abingdon, discussed above, was finally settled under the presidency of the sheriff of Berkshire, but he was acting not in his ordinary capacity as president of the shire court but as a royal justice appointed *ad hoc* to deal with a case which arose from neglect of a royal writ, and was therefore a plea of the crown. Similarly, the famous case concerning the jurisdictional rights claimed by abbot Ording of Bury St Edmund's was not, technically, dealt with in a shire court, as we shall see.

We learn most about hundred courts when they are in private hands.[58] Cases concerning the property of St Martin-le-Grand, London, provide several examples of hundredal jurisdiction. So Richard de Lucy, the justice of Essex, and Maurice, the sheriff, were ordered by a royal writ, about 1147–52, to cause a sworn recognition to be made by good men of the three hundreds of Maldon, Dengie and Thurstable as to whether the canons of St

Martin's were seised of the marsh of Maldon up to the time when Walter fitz Gilbert went on crusade. If the inquest found in favour of the canons, they were to be given possession at once.[59] The crown could indirectly evoke cases from other courts to the royal courts. Also, as is clearly shown in this writ, the crown could if it wished order a case to be settled forthwith in a public court. A subsequent writ ordered the same justice and sheriff to give the canons of St Martin's seisin of the marsh of Maldon as the hundred court recognised and testified that it belonged to them. The writ ends as follows: 'And they are not to be impleaded unjustly (*sic*) in this matter till Walter, of whom they hold the marsh, returns to England; and do them full right for the force and injury they have suffered, but so that my right therein, if I have any, be not lost sight of.'[60] There are clear indications here of the kind of procedure with which legal historians are so familiar in the reign of Henry II, under the possessory assizes.

Another writ of about 1139 in favour of Worcester cathedral deserves more than a passing mention.[61] The original, which has survived, is in the hand of an identified royal scribe, but the text has been slightly 'improved' and the seal it once bore, now detached, is a forged seal. Nonetheless, as far as the main point to be made here is concerned, we may accept its evidence.[62] Among other things, the justices and sheriffs of Herefordshire and Shropshire are informed that the cathedral's land of Boraston (Salop) owes suit only to the hall moot of Burford (Salop). This is one of the interesting cases where a manorial court is not exactly identical with a hundred court, but is certainly the place selected for the meeting of the public court. Already, it seems, the distinction between the two is beginning to be blurred. This kind of arrangement was not nearly so uncommon as might be supposed and it involved the inherent danger of a confusion both of the suit and of the jurisdiction pertaining to different courts which met in the same place.

It is necessary, at this point, to take a quick look at the jungle of private jurisdiction. To penetrate its recesses in the first half of the twelfth century is out of the question (though, ironically enough, this is always regarded as the great age of franchisal, barony and honorial jurisdiction), for no adequate source material is available until the second half of the thirteenth century.[63] Care must be taken not to argue back from the later age to the earlier.

In principle, three kinds of 'private' jurisdiction may be distinguished: franchisal jurisdiction, frequently a hundred court in private hands; the feudal type of barony or honour jurisdiction, arising from the relationship of lord and vassals; and the manorial or domainal type of jurisdiction which a lord exercised over his manorial tenants. In later times, when records provide us with information, it appears that, in some cases, the distinctions between these different kinds of jurisdiction were kept quite clear, while in others they were not. It was very easy for distinctions of this kind to become blurred when the mere convenience of the lord and the suitors of his various courts dictated their meeting, and the exercise of what ought to have been distinct functions, in the same place, as in the case of the hundredal jurisdiction exercised in the hall moot of Burford (Salop) which has just been mentioned.

In the first half of the twelfth century we are confronted with a situation in which numerous grants of public jurisdiction were still being made by the crown, and at the same time the process was beginning whereby a considerable amount of litigation was being evoked from private to royal courts. The judicial reforms of Henry ii greatly accelerated this process, which in the course of time was to strip private courts of all significant public jurisdiction. In Stephen's reign, as in that of Henry i, there is more information about public courts in private hands than about honour, barony and manor jurisdiction. It is only a very rare charter that throws light on these private courts, and then only a fitful gleam. The suit of Turstin against the abbot of Abingdon, which has already been quoted, is a very interesting case in point. Confronted with a royal writ which ordered him to hand over certain property to Turstin, the abbot assembled his court and fixed a day when, after deliberation therein, he should decide how to deal with the situation (*Adunata tamen curia sua, diem statuit qua, habita deliberatione, excogitaret quid super hoc responderet*). This is a clear case of an (ecclesiastical) lord consulting his barony court, where his vassals had the right and the duty of advising him. In a sense it was almost tantamount to a trial of Turstin's case in the court where it ought properly to be heard, but already a royal writ had overridden it. The abbot was obviously furious and desperately anxious to find a way out of his dilemma, but none suggested itself. Another example, though not ostensibly a distressing one, is to be found in a charter issued by Anselm, abbot of St Edmund's. Here, after the

10

usual superscription, address and greeting to all the men, French and English, of St Edmund's, the abbot says: 'I notify you that, by the concession of the whole convent of St Edmund's and by the council of my barons, I have conceded and restored to William, son of Ailbold' and his heirs certain lands specified.[64] There is quite enough evidence of this nature to substantiate the active existence of barony and honour courts, but little or nothing to show exactly how they functioned in Stephen's reign. In connection with the cartels of 1166 the earl of Arundel refers to an inquest, held possibly in the time of Henry I, to determine the liability of knights of the honour to serve in an army raised for a campaign in Wales. Four knights of the honour of Arundel were elected and made a sworn recognition about the service due.[65] They were elected from among 'the best most law-worthy and most ancient' and, characteristically, their verdict was accepted without question. The procedure was probably that which any court, public or private, would have followed in similar circumstances.

One of the best-known legal decisions of Stephen's reign concerns the franchisal jurisdiction of the abbey of Bury St Edmund's.[66] The circumstances have been much misunderstood and the case has often been quoted as an example of shire court procedure. This it certainly was not. We are told that in Stephen's reign, in the year after the siege of Bedford (the first siege of which began at Christmas 1137), the two shires of Norfolk and Suffolk were summoned to appear before the king at Norwich. They duly met in the bishop's garden and William Martel, the king's steward, presided. These two shires were generally farmed together, that is, they had the same sheriff and they also had the same shire justice. It is unlikely, however, that they were regarded as forming a single shire court. The joint assembly of the two shires was clearly exceptional, though not surprising. On this occasion they were presided over, not by the sheriff, who was the ordinary president of the shire court, but by William Martel acting as a royal justice. He was hearing what unquestionably was, unless it had been alienated, a plea of the crown which particularly concerned the two shires. It seems to have been customary for pleas of the crown, when these were heard locally, to be taken in the assembly of the shire sitting not as a shire court under the presidency of the sheriff but as a royal court under the presidency of a royal justice. In the account we have the importance attached to this assembly in

Norwich is underlined by the inclusion of a list of the great men, clerical and lay, who attended. The king himself must have been in Norwich at the time, for although he took no direct part in the proceedings he was available for consultation at the crucial moment. The business before the court was the 'appealing' of two knights, tenants of St Edmund's abbey, who were accused of treason against the king.[67] Treason against the king was a plea of the crown; certainly it was no matter for a sheriff to meddle with in a shire court, but only a royal justice. Abbot Ording promptly objected to the hearing of the case by the court that had been assembled, on the ground that jurisdiction over its own men, even in a plea of the crown, belonged to the abbey 'as the privileges and muniments of our church testify'. He then went to the king to show him these evidences and was told to take them back and have them read to the royal justice and the assembly of the two shires. Whatsoever rights the barons (significantly) of the shires testified as belonging to St Edmunds the abbey should have. When this had been done, an old man, named Hervé de Glanvyle, stood up and spoke as follows:

Law-worthy and most prudent men! It is a long time since I first heard the charters of St Edmund's which were read here just now and they have always been authoritative unto this day. I would have you know, then, that I am a very old man, as you can see, and I remember many things that happened in the time of king Henry and before it, when justice and right, peace and fidelity flourished in England, whereas now, under pressure of war, justice has fled and laws have fallen silent and the liberties of churches, like other good things, have been lost in many places; nonetheless I say for certain, testify and affirm that fifty years have passed since I first began to attend the hundred and shire courts with my father, before I had an estate of my own, and I have done so ever since.[68] And every time a case arose in the shire courts involving any man of the eight-and-a-half hundreds (of Bury St Edmunds abbey), whosesoever man he was, the abbot of St Edmunds or his steward and officials took the case with them for hearing in the court of St Edmunds and, whatsoever the suit or accusation, with the exception of treasure trove and 'murdrum', it was dealt with there.

The bishops and great men approved. Many others, including the sheriffs and the men of the honours of Warenne, earl Hugh Bigod and Eye (the largest feudal complexes in the two shires) testified to the same effect. 'The barons therefore made presentation to

William Martel, the king's justice, that this belonged of right to the liberty of St Edmunds.' What followed is even more significant. William Martel took some of the barons with him formally to notify the king of the testimony of the assembly. When Stephen heard this he ordered that it should be ratified and confirmed and he commanded the abbot of St Edmunds to fix a day in his court to 'do him right' concerning the men accused of treason. This the abbot did. On the same occasion a case of trespass on a warren was similarly removed to the abbey's court. A few days later the king came in person to St Edmunds where the abbot managed to reconcile him with the men accused of treason.

And so this account has been written in order that posterity may not be ignorant of the magnitude of the liberty of the church of St Edmund and how constantly and strenuously the abbots and good men thereof have laboured to maintain the liberty. And let it be known that this chronicle shall lie open to view in the psalter which customarily lies before the lord abbot in his chapel.[69]

No successor of abbot Ording must ever be allowed to forget what was expected of an abbot of St Edmunds.

This account is doubtless dramatised to some extent, but there is no reason to doubt its essential truth. Surviving charters authenticate the abbey's jurisdictional claims. The case is of great interest because of the light it throws upon procedure before a royal justice in a court with the same personnel as the shire court. It is of interest also because of the weight attached to the memory of one of the 'wise and ancient' of the assembly and because it emphasises the extent to which regalian rights have been alienated long before Stephen's reign. Perhaps most striking of all is the willingness of king Stephen to submit himself to the judgment of the court of St Edmunds in a case of treason against him. His conduct was 'correct' but it is easy to see why the Old English chronicler wrote of him as 'a mild man, soft and good'. The Lion of Justice would hardly have acted thus, not indeed his grandson. Several of the cases *coram rege* which have been considered underline the king's respect for the lawful jurisdiction of other courts, whether public or private, provided that there was no default of justice or lack of right there. This is shown formally in a writ in favour of the abbot of Burton, *c.* 1136–38:

Stephen, king of the English, to his justices, sheriffs and barons and all within whose jurisdiction the abbot of Burton has land, greeting. I command that the abbot of Burton have his court as well and in peace as king Henry ordered by his writ; and he is not to be obliged to go outside the court to plead in any other court so long as he makes no default of right there. Witness, Robert de Ferrers. At Nottingham.[70]

To all appearance this affords the fullest protection, yet Stephen does not seem to have had any greater scruples than Henry I in issuing writs, such as that to the abbot of Abingdon, which had the effect of overriding the jurisdiction of private courts.

The crown seems to have been concerning itself increasingly with matters involving seisin, that is possession, which probably gave rise to more litigation than any other single cause, and ensuring at least nominally that such cases were given a proper hearing and that justice was done. A considerable number of writs such as the following was issued during Stephen's reign:

Stephen, king of the English, to Maurice de Haia and Hugh fitz Stephen, greeting. I command that the church and the canons of St Botulph of Colchester hold those lands in Tendring Hundred (co. Essex) which Hugh fitz Stephen gave them in alms. And they are to have them as well and peacefully and freely and quit and justly as they were given in alms and as the chirograph drawn up about this testifies. Let no one offer them injury or insult. And, unless you do this, my justice shall cause it to be done lest I hear any complaint from them in this matter about lack of a hearing or of justice (*ne super hoc pro penuria recti vel justicie clamorem inde audiam*). Witness, Jordan de Blosseville. At London. (*c.* 1135–54.)[71]

The final clause of such a writ is a formal indication that neglect of the royal order or any complaint about default of justice from the beneficiaries of the writ will have to be answered for before the king's court. Means of evasion were often found, as can be seen from the repetition of the same writ on one or more occasions. Postponement on various pretexts was obviously not difficult. It can be seen clearly from the kind of evidence that has been examined that the process of eroding the jurisdiction of private courts and evoking cases to the royal courts was in full swing under Stephen, as it had been under Henry I. The reforms of Henry II merely gave the process greater force and precision.

Whatever was happening to English law in Stephen's reign, it seems that, unless his writs were not worth the small pieces of parchment they were written on, royal justice and the custom of the king's court managed to survive. Cases such as that of Turstin *v.* the abbot of Abingdon would indicate that, towards the very end of Stephen's reign at any rate, a royal writ was not lightly to be disregarded nor was it ineffectual. It is not unreasonable to argue that Stephen's long experience at the court of Henry I had given him some grasp, if not of the principles – such as they were – of Anglo-Norman jurisprudence, at least of legal practice. He followed the precedents of his uncle in respect of pleas of the crown and the use made of royal justice and royal justices. At the same time he showed a greater respect than Henry I for the juris-diction of private courts and public courts in private hands, where this could be shown lawfully to exist. The few surviving accounts of cases *coram rege* show king Stephen behaving with propriety and good sense in his judicial capacity; and he respected the views of his barons, even when he disagreed with them.

Did Maitland underestimate the strength of English law and English courts, especially the king's court, when he referred to the danger of the ultimate triumph of Roman Law if during Stephen's reign English Law should 'break into a hundred local customs'? It is of course perfectly true that just at this time the serious study of Roman Law was beginning in England. Most eminent in this sphere was the Mantuan civilian, Master Vacarius, who joined the household of archbishop Theobald during Stephen's reign. Whether or not Vacarius, a canonist as well as a civilian, was brought over to assist Theobald in litigation against Henry, bishop of Winchester, there is no doubt that he power-fully reinforced the archbishop's legal advisers in that struggle. He was in close touch with the other distinguished members of the archiepiscopal household, Becket the future martyr, Roger of Pont l'Evêque, future archbishop of York, John Belmeis, future bishop of Poitiers and archbishop of Lyons and John of Salisbury, future bishop of Chartres. Vacarius was highly distinguished both as a legal writer and as a teacher in the archiepiscopal household and in Oxford.[72] He was, temporarily at least, silenced by Stephen about 1152. It would be rash to attribute this action on the king's part simply to disapproval and fear of Roman Law and Canon Law or to the reactionary feudal outlook of his baronial advisers. Probably it is a tribute, rather, to the distinction of Master Vacarius among the adherents of the archbishop at a time when Stephen's relations with the church were still strained. He must have appeared a formidable opponent and trainer of young men as potential opponents of the crown and the dynasty. There were several alleged cases of poisoning about this time, but we are not told that the hemlock was proffered to Vacarius!

One other kind of secular law and jurisdiction remains to be mentioned, that of the royal forest. The administration of the royal forest was already highly organised in the reign of Henry I[73] and the pipe roll of 1130 provides clear evidence of a forest eyre in the recent past. The king himself sometimes heard pleas of the forest. One of the things that happened in England immediately after Henry I's death was, as we learn in the opening chapter of *Gesta Stephani*, that:

> Game also, which had previously been most stringently preserved throughout the realm, as though in a park, was now put up, scattered and shot without fear by all and sundry. And this, though less of a blow (than the civil commotion) and not greatly to be complained of, was still very remarkable, that so many thousands of wild beasts, which had once roamed in great herds all over the land, were so suddenly exterminated that, from such an innumerable multitude, you could scarcely find two together ...[74]

In his Oxford charter of liberties of April 1136, Stephen retained for the crown the forests created by William I and William II but restored 'to the churches and to the realm' those which Henry I had added.[75] In earnest of his good intentions a writ of about 1136, addressed to Miles of Gloucester and Payn fitz John, orders them to cause recognition to be made by the oaths of twelve lawful men of Herefordshire of the woods of the bishop which king Henry had afforested. All these are to be restored to the bishop.[76] Considering the havoc that had been wrought among the king's deer it is not surprising that in 1136, when Stephen was trying to restore order in the country, he impleaded numbers of barons for trespass to the venison and the vert[77] in his court at the royal hunting-lodge of Brampton. This was very bitterly resented and did a good deal of harm to his cause. There had been very strong feeling about the additions which Henry I had made to the royal forests and the extreme stringency with which he preserved them. There is room for more than a suspicion that, already, the royal forests were preserved and the forest law was enforced not simply for the sake of the king's hunting but even more for his financial profit.

Stephen made quite a few grants to religious houses of freedom from the financial penalties for assarting (clearing land) and of rights and easements of various kinds in the royal forests. A few grants of the custody of forests have survived[78] and also some grants of the office of forester hereditarily in fee.[79] Freedom from pleas of the forest is rarely accorded; in fact, all three examples here refer to the same place, although two religious houses are involved.[80] The extreme scarcity of forest quittances of this kind suggests that, in principle, the forest law was intended to be strictly enforced. A charter in favour of Peterborough abbey grants to it all assarts made up to a specified date. The injunctive clause orders that these shall be held 'quit and absolved from every secular exaction and every "reguard" of the forest (*quiete et absolute ab omni seculari exactione et ab omni rewardo foreste*)'.[81] Such an explicit reference to the forest 'reguard' is rare before the Assize of the Forest (1184) and we have no evidence about how it functioned. When in that assize, thirty years after his accession, Henry II stated the severity of his intentions towards offenders he said: 'For if anyone henceforth offend and be convicted, he (the king) intends to exact the full penalty from him, as was done in the time of king Henry, his grandfather.' This does not necessarily imply leniency in the intervening half-century, but may indicate no more than Henry II's habit of ignoring Stephen's reign and of regarding himself in all things as the direct successor of his grandfather. The probability, however, is that in Stephen's reign many people got away with forest offences who would not have escaped under his predecessor or his successor.

Abbreviations

The following abbreviations are used in the footnotes:

CSHR.   *Chronicles of the Reigns of Stephen, Henry II and Richard I* (RS. 4 vols, 1884 etc) ed. R. Howlett.

DB.   *Domesday Book* (2 vols., transcribed by Abraham Farley, 1783, and subsequent vols).

EHR.   *The English Historical Review.*

G de M.   J. H. Round, *Geoffrey de Mandeville* (London, 1892).

GEC.   G. E. C(okayne) *The Complete Peerage.* New edn. by Vicary Gibbs, H. A. Doubleday, Lord Howard de Walden and G. H. White (London, 1910 etc.).

Gesta.   *Gesta Stephani. The Deeds of Stephen.* ed. with trans. by K. R. Potter (Nelson's Medieval Texts, 1955).

Gov.   H. G. Richardson and G. O. Sayles, *The Governance of Medieval England from the Conquest to Magna Carta* (Edinburgh, 1963).

HEL.   Sir Frederick Pollock and Frederick William Maitland, *The History of English Law Before the Time of Edward I*, 2 vols. (Cambridge, 1895 edn. is referred to here).

HH.   *Henrici Archidiaconi Huntingdonensis Historia Anglorum. The History of the English by Henry, Archdeacon of Huntingdon* (RS) 1879, ed. T. Arnold.

HKF.   William Farrer, *Honours and Knights' Fees* (3 vols. Manchester, 1923–5).

HN.   *Willelmi Malmesbiriensis Historia Novella. The Historia Novella of William of Malmesbury*, ed. with trans. by K. R. Potter (Nelson's Medieval Texts, 1955).

HP   *Johannis Saresberiensis Historia Pontificalis. John of Salisbury's Memoirs of the Papal Court*, ed. with trans. by Marjorie Chibnall (*Nelson's Medieval Texts*, 1956).

KS.   R. H. C. Davis, *King Stephen*, 1135–54 (London, 1967).

MO.   M. D. Knowles, *The Monastic Order in England* (Cambridge, 1949).

MPL.   J. P. Migne, *Patrologiae Cursus Completus, Series Latina.*

NI.   C. H. Haskins, *Norman Institutions* (Harvard Historical Series XXIV, 1925).

OV.

Orderici Vitalis Historia Ecclesiastica ed. A. le Prévost and L.Delisle (Societé de l'Histoire de France, 5 vols. 1840–55); Translation by T.Forester, *The Ecclesiastical History of Orderic Vitalis* (1854).

PR.

Pipe Roll (PR 31 Hen.1. ed. Joseph Hunter, 1833).

RBE.

The Red Book of the Exchequer, ed. Hubert Hall (3 vols. London, 1896).

Reg.

Regesta Regum Anglo-Normannorum 1066–1154 (4 vols. Oxford 1913–69) Vol. I *Regesta Willelmi Conquestoris et Willelmi Rufi 1066–1100,* ed. H.W.C.Davis and R.J Whitwell. Vol. II *Regesta Henrici Primi 1100–1135,* ed. Charles Johnson and H.A.Cronne. Vol. III *Regesta Stephani etc. 1135–1154* ed. H.A.Cronne and R.H.C.Davis. Vol. IV. *Facsimilies of Original Charters and Writs of Stephen etc.* ed. H.A.Cronne and R.H.C.Davis.

RS

Rolls Series.

TRHS.

Transactions of the Royal Historical Society.

VCH.

The Victoria History of the Counties of England (in progress).

Voss.

Lena Voss, *Heinrich von Blois* (Berlin, 1932).

WN.

Historia Rerum Anglicarum. The History of English Affairs by William of Newburgh (RS) in *CSHR* I and II, ed. R.Howlett.

Notes

Chapter 1. 'The Anarchy of Stephen's Reign'

1. See p. 72.
2. *Gesta*, 92, 72.
3. 'Charters of the Earldom of Hereford' ed. David Walker, in *Camden Miscellany* XXII (Camden 4th Ser. I, 1964).
4. *OV* iii, 277 ff.
5. I am happy to find that, in this position, I am in the company of Professor V.H.Galbraith, though our arguments are not identical. See his *1066 and All That. Norman Conquest Commemoration Lecture*, 1966, (Leicestershire Archaeol. and Hist. Soc., 1967).
6. See D.C.Douglas, *English Scholars 1660–1730* (2nd. ed. 1951); H.A.Cronne, 'Charter scholarship in England', in *Univ. of Birmingham Historical Journal* VIII (1961).
7. F.M.Page, *The Estates of Crowland Abbey*, (Cambridge, 1934) 72.
8. British Museum MS Cotton Nero C iv, f.39.
9. See H.W.C.Davis in *EHR*, XXV, 297 ff; *MPL*, CXC, 799, No. 79.
10. *NI.* App.D, 283.
11. See p. 78.
12. See map p. 137.
13. R.W.Southern, 'The Place of Henry 1 in English History', in *Proceedings of the British Academy* XLVIII, 1962.

Chapter 2. A Chronicle of Events 1135–54

1. The history of Stephen's reign has been recounted most recently and authoritatively by R.H.C.Davis in *King Stephen 1135–54* (London, 1967). The fifth chapter of *England under the Normans and Angevins* (first published London, 1905) by this author's distinguished father, H.W.C.Davis, is still very useful, as are chapter V and the relevant portion of chapter VI in A.L.Pool's *From Domesday Book to Magna Carta* (Oxford History of England, 1951). The two latter books show Stephen's reign in a longer perspective of English history.

2. See *GEC*, XI, App.D.
3. *Gesta* 3–4.
4. *Reg.* III, **270**.
5. *HN*, 18.
6. *Reg.* III, **271**.
7. See p. 147.
8. See p. 141.
9. Chronicle of Richard of Hexham in *CSHR*, III, 176.
10. 1 January 1140 is meant here, though other styles of dating were used, such as those which began the year on Christmas Day, Easter Day and Lady Day (Annunciation, 25 March).
11. *HN*, 46. This almost certainly means that Stephen had given them honours in the sense of fiefs, not merely 'conferred distinctions' upon them, as Mr Potter has translated it.
12. See ch. 5.
13. *Gesta*, 78.
14. *Reg.* III, **274–5**; R.H.C.Davis, 'Geoffrey de Mandeville reconsidered', in *EHR*, LXXIX (1964) 299 ff.
15. *Gesta*, 81–2.
16. *Gervase of Canterbury, Historical Works* (RS) ed. W. Stubbs, 1879–80, I, 125, dates this 1 July, though the *Gesta* narrative (undated throughout) would suggest a date sooner after the capture of Oxford castle.
17. *Gesta*, 99.
18. On the whole issue see M.D.Knowles, 'The case of St William of York', in *The Historian and Character*, (Cambridge, 1963) pp. 76–97.
19. Much detailed information about bishop Nigel is to be found in *Liber Eliensis* (Camden 3rd Series, XCII, 1962), ed. E.O.Blake.
20. This is discussed in ch. 3.
21. See *KS*, 91–2 for an account of the conflicting interests and loyalties involved in this affair.
22. *Reg.* III, **178**, and see ch. 3.
23. *Gesta*, 148.
24. See *HP*, 83.
25. *Gesta*, 142.
26. *Gesta*, 154.
27. *de proditione procerum suorum anxie conquerentes uterque* – *HH*, 228.
28. *Reg.* III, **272**.
29. *KS*, 123.
30. *Reg.* III, **180**. This was granted 'unless he be able to prove in my court that he is not guilty of crime and treason'.
31. *WN*, 80–1.

Chapter 3. The King and the Empress

1. See D.C.Douglas, *William the Conqueror* (London, 1964) App. C.
2. Ed. Paul Meyer (Soc. de l'hist. de France, 3 vols. 1891–1901) ll. 509–650.
3. *HH*, 284 for date.
4. *KS*, 10–11.
5. *OV*, XII, cxvi.
6. *HN*, 16.
7. *Anglo Saxon Chronicle E* sub ann. 1137. There is a revised translation by D.Whitelock and others (London, 1961). Cf. a very factual account of anarchy in Normandy in *NI*, 62–4.
8. *HN*, 36, 43.
9. *Epistola ad Walterum* in *HH*, 309*n*.
10. *Inferno*, xii, 102.
11. *KS*.
12. *OV*. XIII c.xliii.
13. So called from his office of butler (*pincerna*) in the royal household and so distinguished from his namesake, William d'Aubigny (*Brito*), who was of Breton descent.
14. *Gesta*, 137.
15. See R.H.C.Davis, '*The authorship of Gesta Stephani*', in *EHR*, LXXVII (1952), 209 ff.
16. *Reg.* III, **178**.
17. *Reg.* III, **276**.
18. The meaning is not quite clear in the Latin text.
19. Alice de Condet was a sister of earl Rannulf. Horncaster is probably a copyist's error for Thornhill.
20. See *HKF*, II (The Chester Fee) and map at p. 137 below.
21. *Reg.* III, **274–5**.
22. See R.W.Southern in *Proc. Brit. Acad.* XLVIII (1962), 127 ff.
23. *HN*, 21–2.
24. Ibid.
25. *Gesta*, 7.
26. *HN*, 40 ff.
27. *Reg.* III, **969**.
28. In the closing words of his *Constitutional History*, vol. III.
29. *HN*, 4, 65.
30. *Gesta*, 7.
31. *HN*, 15.
32. *Reg.* III, **271**, for the text of this charter. *HN* says that the solemn oath which William, archbishop of Canterbury, exacted from Stephen, and which was guaranteed by the bishop of Winchester, was afterwards put into writing; obviously in this charter.

33. Various dates have been given, but *HN*, 15–16 states explicitly, repeatedly and most emphatically that it was 22 Dec.
34. *HH*, 259.
35. *Annales Monastici*, (RS) II, 228.
36. *HH*, 270.
37. *KS*, 141–2. This is contrary to the hitherto accepted view, but it makes sense, as that view does not.
38. *Gervase of Canterbury* (RS) I, 136–7.
39. *Reg.* III, **272**. It seems clear that Stephen only now recognised him as of comital status.
40. *G.deM.* App.B; R.L.Poole ed. *Historia Pontificalis*, App. vi; Marjorie Chibnall in *HP*, xliii, who follows Poole. Innocent II's bull of 1136 confirming Stephen's title (text in *MPL* vol. 179, p. 301, No. CCL) makes no reference to a hearing in the papal curia.
41. That is, within the prohibited degrees.
42. This was doubted – See *HN*, 3.
43. *Radulfi de Diceto Decani Lundoniensis Opera Historica. The Historical Works of Master Ralph de Diceto, Dean of London* (RS) ed. W.Stubbs (1876) 253 ff.
44. John of Salisbury enjoyed telling anecdotes of this kind – cf. his stories about Henry, bishop of Winchester.
45. See *The Letters of Arnulf of Lisieux* (Camden 3rd Series LXI) ed. Frank Barlow, xi ff.
46. *MPL* vol. 190, 796–801; H.W.C.Davis, 'Henry of Blois and Brian fitz Count' in *EHR*, XXV, 297–303.
47. Theobald of Bec was elected when the bishop of Winchester was out of the way, conducting ordinations of deacons at St Pauls. He was consecrated on 8 Jan, 1139. The see had been vacant for over two years.
48. *Gesta*, 39–40.
49. Ibid, 48.
50. *HH*, 3, 1.
51. His narrative was, however, used a good deal by later writers, such as Gervase of Canterbury and William of Newburgh.
52. *HH*, 265.
53. *HN*, 25.
54. e.g. H.Böhmer, *Kirche und Staat in England* (Leipzig, 1899); Z.N.Brooke, *The English Church and the Papacy from the Conquest to the Reign of John* (Cambridge, 1931); Lena Voss, *Heinrich von Blois* (Berlin, 1932).
55. See Isabel Megaw, 'Stephen's ecclesiastical policy', in *Essays in British and Irish History in Honour of James Eadie Todd*, ed. H.A.Cronne, T.W.Moody and D.B.Quinn (London, 1949) 24 ff.

56. *OV*, XIII. xi.
57. *WN*, I, 37.
58. See Norman F. Cantor, *Church, Kingship and Lay Investiture in England 1089–1135* (Princeton Studies in History, vol 10. 1958).
59. Knowles, 'The case of St William of York', loc. cit. 76 ff.
60. Ibid.
61. *HP*, 86.
62. *Gervase of Canterbury*, I, 47.
63. *HP*, 78.
64. *HP*, 79.
65. See Knowles, 'Cluniacs and Cistercians', in *The Historian and Character*.
66. See *The Works of Giraldus Cambrensis* (RS) vols I–IV, ed. V. S. Brewer and V–VII, ed. J. F. Dimock. 1861–77, VII, 46.
67. See R. H. C. Davis in *EHR*, LXXV (1960) and LXXIX (1964).
68. *HH*, 268.
69. *HN*, 46–7.
70. *Gesta*, 73.
71. *OV*, XIII, xliii.
72. *Gesta*, 122.
73. See p. 78.
74. John of Hexham in *The Historical Works of Symeon of Durham* (RS) ed. T. Arnold, 1882–5, II, 308–9.
75. *Gesta*, 156.
76. *HH*, 276.
77. See R. H. C. Davis in *EHR* LXXIX (1964).
78. *WN*, 44 ff.
79. *Gesta*, 107.
80. O. Rössler, *Kaiserin Mathilde* (Berlin, 1897).
81. *Gervase of Canterbury*, I, 91–2. According to Fitz Stephen she was born in London.
82. *HN*, 2.

Chapter 4. Stephen, Henry of Blois and the Church

1. See Knowles, 'Cistercians and Cluniacs, the controversy between St Bernard and Peter the Venerable', in *The Historian and Character* 50 ff. This, together with the second, third and fifth essays in the same volume and Dom Knowles's *Monastic Order in England*, is valuable for an understanding of the English church in Stephen's reign.
2. See *MO*, chs. xi–xiv; J. C. Dickinson, *The Origins of the Austin Canons* (London, 1950).

3. *Reg.* III, **300**; M.D.Knowles and R.N.Hadcock, *Medieval Religious Houses. England and Wales*, (London etc., 1953) 66, 96.

4. *HH*, 315. The fullest and most enthusiastic account of Henry, bishop of Winchester, is that by Voss.

5. See H.W.C.Davis, 'Henry of Blois and Brian fitz Count' in *EHR* XXV, 300–3.

6. *Sir Christopher Hatton's Book of Seals* (Oxford, 1950) ed. L.C.Loyd and D.M.Stenton, 304.

7. See *Adami de Domerham de rebus gestis Glastoniensibus* (London, 1727) ed. T.Hearne, II, 316; *Giraldus Cambrensis* VII, 45; *WN*, I, 41; Edmund Bishop, *Liturgica Historica* (Oxford, 1918) 396, 400; *MO*, 290–1; Voss, 188.

8. Horace, *Satires* II, iii, 16, 17; *HP*, 79–80.

9. *MO*, 282–3.

10. *Symeon of Durham*, II, 283, seems to have thought that he merely held 'the honour of Glastonbury' *ad procurationem*, but this is not borne out by other evidence.

11. *MO*, 290.

12. Voss, 42 ff.

13. *HN*, 57–8.

14. *Reg.* III, **271**. The translation which follows is of the Salisbury version of the charter, one of the three surviving original exemplifications. The others derive from Exeter and Hereford, and the latter is in the handwriting of royal scribe xiii (see ch. 7).

15. *HN*, 53.

16. *Gesta*, 27 ff.

17. *OV*, v, 79.

18. See ch. 5 and Avrom Saltman, *Theobald Archbishop of Canterbury* (London, 1956), 7ff. Orderic may have been mistaken.

19. *HN*, 29.

20. *HN*, 34.

21. *Gesta*, 78.

22. *HN*, 53.

23. *HN*, 55.

24. *HN*, 50.

25. *HN*, 53.

26. *HN*, 52.

27. *MO*, chapters xi–xvi.

28. Avrom Saltman, op. cit.

Chapter 5. The Aristocracy

1. See *Lincolnshire Domesday* (Lincolnshire Record Soc.) 132, 201; *VCH. Lincs*, II, 107 *n.*2; *RBE*, 377. Thurkell of Arden and

Colswein of Lincoln were exceptional survivals in the magnate class.

2. F.M.Stenton's *First Century of English Feudalism* (2nd ed. Oxford, 1961), after nearly forty years, is still one of the best works on English feudal society between 1066 and 1166; it is admirably documented. See also C.Warren Hollister, *The Military Organization of Norman England* (Oxford, 1965); D.C.Douglas, *The Domesday Monachorum of Christ Church Canterbury* (London, 1944) for English knights on Canterbury lands.

3. *Reg.* III, **244**; cf. *Sir C.Hatton's Book of Seals*, No. 105. See also *G. de M*, App. K, and 'London under Stephen' in Round's *Commune of London* (London, 1899) 97 ff; F.M.Stenton, *Norman London* (Historical Assoc. leaflet, 1934).

4. *KS*, App. i and 32–3. Reference should also be made to G.H.White, 'King Stephen's Earldoms' in *TRHS*, 4th series, XIII (1930).

5. *Reg.* III, **101, 124, 210, 316a, 344, 411, 414, 533, 597, 671, 689, 966–7, 991–2.**

6. On the earldom of Huntingdon see G.W.S.Barrow ed., *Regesta Regum Scottorum* I (*Malcolm IV, 1153–65*) (Edinburgh, 1960) I, 102.

7. Text and translation in F.M.Stenton's *First Century*.

8. See Barrow, loc. cit.

9. *NI*, 91–2.

10. A.S.Ellis in *Yorkshire Archaeological Journal*, IV, 230.

11. *Reg.* III, **273.**

12. *Gesta*, 106–7.

13. *Reg.* III, **274–6.**

14. R.H.C.Davis, 'Geoffrey de Mandeville reconsidered' in *EHR* LXXIX (1964) 299–307.

15. *Gesta*, 16–17.

16. *Reg.* III, **437.**

17. For the contrary view see G.H.White in *TRHS* 4th ser. XIII, 72–7.

18. *Reg.* III, **393** and see p. 161.

19. *Reg.* III, **16.**

20. *Gesta*, 98 and *n*; *Reg.* III, **791.**

21. *RBE*, 649.

22. *Reg.* III, **634.**

23. *RBE*, 651. The charter of the empress granting Aubrey his earldom and his father's chamberlainship is printed in *Reg.* III, **634.**

24. See above p. 88–9.

25. *VCH Somerset*, I, 501; *Dunster*, in Somerset Record Society vol. XXXIII; H.Maxwell Lyte, *A History of Dunster*, 1–58.

26. *Gesta*, 54.
27. See *EHR* XXV (1910), 301.
28. *Reg*. III, **274**.
29. *Reg*. III, **272**, treaty between king Stephen and duke Henry.
30. *Reg*. III, **180**.
31. *Gervase of Canterbury*, II, 73.
32. *Reg*. III, **197**.
33. Life of Charles the Good by Galbert the Notary, in *Acta Sanctorum* 2 March, cap. 11.
34. *RBE*, 658; *PR 2 Hen II*, 65.
35. *Gervase of Canterbury*, I, 121; William fitz Stephen in his 'Vita Sancti Thomae' – *Materials for the History of Thomas Becket, Archbishop of Canterbury* (RS) III, 19 – calls him *violentus incubator Cantiae* at the time when Henry 11 sent him and the Flemish mercenaries packing.
36. See *Gesta Abbatum S. Albani* (RS) I, 194.
37. *Chronicon Monasterii de Abingdon* (RS) II, 292.
38. *Gervase of Canterbury* I, 135–6.
39. Ibid. II, 77.
40. See *Reg*. III, xxiv-xxv.
41. See e.g. the grants to Geoffrey de Mandeville in *Reg*. III **274–6** and to William de Beauchamp in *Reg*. III, **68**. Also see, in general, Stenton, *First Century*, ch. vii.
42. *Reg*. III, **274–5**.
43. *Reg*. III, **490, 885, 887, 351**.
44. *Gilberti Foliot Epistolae* ed. J.A.Giles (1845) in *MPL* vol. CXC, no. lviii.
45. *RBE*, 309.
46. *RBE*, 323.
47. See S.Painter, *William Marshal*.
48. See I.J.Sanders, *English Baronies* (Oxford, 1960), 33; *VCH Northants*; I, 242, 289; *Chronicon Abbatiae Ramesiensis* (RS) I, index.
49. *Book of Fees*, 447.
50. See L.C.Loyd, *Origins of Some Anglo-Norman Families* (Harleian Soc., 1951) 43. This is commonly known as 'Loyd's Address Book'.
51. See H.W.C.Davis in *EHR* XXV, 300–3.
52. See *Reg*. III, xxiii-xxvi and G.H.White in *TRHS* 4th series XIII (1930).
53. *RBE*, 363–4.
54. *RBE*, 317.
55. *RBE*, 312.

56. D.C.Douglas, *William the Conqueror*, 269.
57. *GEC* XII pt i, Appendix.
58. Stenton, *First Century*, (1932 ed.) 111 ff.
59. On these family and territorial relationships consult 'Loyd's Address Book'.
60. David Walker, loc. cit. and also his 'Miles of Gloucester, earl of Hereford', in *Transactions of the Bristol and Gloucestershire Archaeol. Soc.* LXXVII, 66–84; 'The "honours" of the earls of Hereford in the twelfth century', ibid. LXXIX, 174–211. R.H.C.Davis, 'Treaty between William, earl of Gloucester and Roger, earl of Hereford', in *Early Medieval Miscellany for Doris Mary Stenton* (Pipe Roll Soc., New Series XXXVI (1960), 139–46).
61. *Gesta*, 16. The pleas referred to were probably pleas of the crown, which were taken by royal justices, as distinct from matters within the jurisdiction of the courts of shire and hundred.
62. *Reg.* III, 386–8. Other lands were also confirmed: 389–90.
63. *Reg.* III 313.
64. *Reg.* III, 312.
65. *Gesta*, 37 ff.
66. *Gesta*, 72.
67. *Reg.* III, 391.
68. R.W.Eyton, *Antiquities of Shropshire* (1854–60) V, 248–52.
69. *Reg.* III, 437.
70. *Reg.* III, 394.
71. Printed in *G. de M.* with a note; also in *Sir C.Hatton's Book of Seals*, 212.
72. R.H.C.Davis, in *Early Med. Miscellany for D.M.Stenton*.
73. *Gesta*, 150–1.
74. Southern, in *Proc. Brit. Acad* XLVIII.
75. *Reg.* III, 306.
76. Stenton, *First Century* (1932 ed.) 246–7, 284–5.
77. Barrow, *Reg. Scottorum* I, 103.
78. See G.H.White, 'The career of Waleran, count of Meulan and earl of Worcester', in *TRHS*, 4th ser xvii (1934) 19 ff; H.W.C. Davis, 'Some documents of the anarchy' in *Essays in History presented to Reginald Lane Poole*, ed. Davis, (Oxford, 1927), 172–6. See the genealogical table at p. 164.
79. *CSHR*, II, 767.
80. *HH*, 269–70.
81. White, 'Career of Waleran', 46.
82. See *HKF*, II.
83. Stenton, *First Century* (1932) 235 ff. and references given there.

84. *Reg.* III, **68**.
85. There are in fact none 'aforesaid' except Waleran.
86. See *HKF* II, 1–293. On the career of Rannulf II, earl of Chester, see J.H.Round, 'Stephen and the earl of Chester', in *EHR*, X, 87 ff; H.A.Cronne, 'Rannulf de Gernons, earl of Chester', in *TRHS* 4th ser. XX (1937) 103 ff; R.H.C.Davis, 'King Stephen and the earl of Chester revised', in *EHR* (1960) corrects Round and Cronne on some important points, thus changing the interpretation of the earl's career.
87. See p. 231–2.
88. David was also the uncle of Stephen's queen, Matilda of Boulogne.
89. *John of Hexham*, 306.
90. *HN*, 46; *Gesta* 73.
91. See above p. 42 ff.
92. *Lincolnshire Notes and Queries*, XVII, 37–8.
93. *John of Hexham*, 310; *HN*, 59.
94. This is most conveniently accessible, with a translation and a commentary, in Stenton, *First Century*.
95. *Leges Henrici Primi* lv, 1.
96. *HKF*, II, 11 ff.
97. *Aelred of Rievaulx*, *Relatio de Standardo*, 193.
98. *Gesta*, 118, 140.
99. *HH*, 287.

Chapter 6. The Royal Household

1. *Willelmi Monachi Malmesbiriensis Opera* (RS) III, 275.
2. *Reg.* III, **271**.
3. See p. 262 ff.
4. See *Gov.* ch. viii.
5. *HN*, 15, 32.
6. *Reg.* III, **313**.
7. *Reg.* III, **397**.
8. See p. 37–8.
9. *Gov.* 155.
10. *Gov.* 166. cf. *Reg.* III, **534, 546–50, 552, 559**.
11. F.J.West, *The Justiciarship in England 1066–1232*, 26–7; *Gov.* 254–5 refutes the suggestion.
12. *Dialogus de Scaccario. The Course of the Exchequer*, ed. Charles Johnson (Nelson's Medieval Texts, 1950), xliv and the references given there; 129 ff. See also G.H.White, 'The household of the Norman kings' in *TRHS* 4th ser. XXX (1948).
13. *Chronicle of John of Worcester*, ed. J.R.H.Weaver (*Anecdota Oxoniensia*, 1908) 55 *n.* 4.

14. He was also master of the royal scriptorium and he became bishop of London (1141–50).
15. A *sextary* was probably four gallons.
16. *Reg.* II, **1777**, *Reg.* III, **634-5**, *GEC*, X, App.
17. *Reg.* III, **15**.
18. Camden 4th Series IV (1964) 3, 14.
19. T.F.Tout, *Chapters in the Administrative History of Medieval England* (Manchester, 1923–35).
20. See below, p. 209.
21. More probably a tailor than a tally-cutter.
22. Avrom Saltman, *Theobald Archbishop of Canterbury* (London, 1956) 482.
23. Roger de Pont l'Évêque, later archbishop of York and a rival of Becket.
24. Thomas Becket, later royal chancellor, archbishop of Canterbury and martyr.
25. Pupil of Abelard, scholar, historian, teacher, secretary to archbishop Theobald, bishop of Chartres (died 1180).
26. Treasurer of York.
27. The lowly place which this querulous or queasy-sounding functionary occupied is surprising. It is doubtful, however, whether the added names of witnesses are in the correct order of precedence.
28. *Reg.* III, **239***C*.
29. *Gesta*, 97.
30. *Gesta Abbatum S.Albani* (RS) I, 194; *G. de M.* 206 *n* 3. It is worth noting that William Martel's father, Geoffrey, was a tenant of Geoffrey de Mandeville's grandfather in Abbess Roding (Essex) – DB II, 57b. He came from Boucqueville-en-Caux near Manneville (Seine-inf.) which probably explains the Mandeville-Martel connection.
31. *Cartularium Monasterii de Abingdon* (RS) II, 200, 543.
32. *Richard of Hexham* (RS), 151.
33. See below p. 276.
34. See below p. 270–1.
35. *Gov.* omits.
36. *Reg.* III, xviii.
37. The point is that this grant did not include the chamberlainship of Normandy, which was held hereditarily in the Tancarville family.
38. See G.H.White, in *GEC*, X, App F.
39. He came from Ver (dép. Manche) near Coutances and appears in *DB* as a tenant of Geoffrey, bishop of Coutances. He was the father-in-law of Geoffrey de Mandeville, earl of Essex.

40. William de Vere in *De miraculis Osithe*, cited in John Leland's *Itinerary*, ed Lucy Toulmin-Smith, V, 172.
41. *Gov.* 174 ff; also below in ch. 9, pp. 256–7.
42. For his judicial activities see below ch. 9. The date of his death has been disputed; see G.H.White in *Notes and Queries*, CLXIII, 10; E.O.Blake (ed.) in *Liber Eliensis* (Camden 3rd ser., XCII, 1962); *Reg.* III, xix and **46, 945–9**.
43. *Reg.* III, **634–5**.
44. *Reg.* III, xix and **460**; cf. *GEC*, X, 202.
45. *Gov.* App. iii, 422 ff.
46. See *Reg.* III, xix *n*.6.
47. *PR* 31 *Hen. 1* ed. Joseph Hunter (1833).
48. *HH*, 15; *Gesta*, 5.
49. *PR* 31 *Hen. 1*, 134. See also *Gov.* 221–3, 421–37.
50. *Reg.* III, xix-xx.
51. See G.H.White in *GEC*, X, App. G.
52. See 'Constitutio Domus Regis' in *Dialogus de Scaccario*, ed. C. Johnson, 134.
53. *Materials for the History of Thomas Becket* (RS) III, **51**.

Chapter 7. The Chancery

1. *OV*. xiii, xl.
2. *HN*, 39.
3. See *Reg.* III, x.
4. Ibid.
5. *KS*, 125–6; *Reg.* III, **272**.
6. *Simeonis Monachi Opera* (RS) II, 309.
7. *Reg.* III, **478–80**.
8. *Reg.* III, **489**.
9. *Reg.* III, **199–200**.
10. *Reg.* III, **489**.
11. See Saltman, *Theobald Archbishop of Canterbury*, no. 209.
12. British Museum, Arundel MS 29, f45v.
13. Since chaplains and clerks are usually mentioned only by their Christian names, it is often difficult to identify individuals with any certainty. See *Reg.* III, x-xiii.
14. *Reg.* III, **979**.
15. See Knowles 'The case of St William of York', in *The Historian and Character*, 76–97.
16. Becket was never a mere chaplain in the royal household.
17. See *Reg.* III, **246**. He was Stephen's nephew, the son of his sister Agnes.
18. See J.A.Robinson, *Somerset Historical Essays* (1921), 100–140;

R.W.Southern, *The Making of the Middle Ages* (London, 1953) 210 ff.

19. Note Becket's agreement with Roger de Pont l'Évêque and John of Poitiers for mutual assistance in obtaining benefices, mentioned by Becket's biographer, William of Canterbury, *Materials* I, 4.

20. See T.A.M.Bishop, *Scriptores Regis* (Oxford, 1961).

21. 'Original' is used here in the archival sense, not in the legal sense of a writ which initiates an action at law.

22. See *Reg*. IV, 5 and references there.

23. *Reg*. IV, plates viiia and xxvii.

24. See below p. 215.

25. A detailed comparison of the genuine and forged first seals of Stephen is made in *Reg*. IV, plates i and ii.

26. This figure is subject to correction, since known originals can still be lost or destroyed and unknown or lost originals still, happily, turn up.

27. See p. 256 *n*. 21.

28. A list of surviving originals with their scribes (when identified) is given in *Reg*. IV, 25 ff.

29. Bishop, op. cit. 24–25.

30. Examples of the work of these scribes are given in *Reg*. IV.

31. *Reg*. III, **786** and **521** respectively.

32. London, St Paul's Cathedral Dean and Chapter Muniments, A40/1443; Facsimile in *Reg*. IV plate xi.

33. See *Reg*. IV, plates i, ii and viiib.

34. Bishop, op. cit.

35. *Reg*. III, **628**.

36. *Reg*. III, **963**; *Reg*. IV, plates i, ii, x, xxiii. The same forged seal is found on a Rochester Cathedral charter and also on an Oseney abbey charter.

37. Bishop, op. cit. 13.

38. See A.L.Poole, *From Domesday Book to Magna Carta*.

39. See chapter 9.

Chapter 8. The Royal Revenue and the Coinage

1. *Gov*. 229 and, in general, ch. xii of that work.

2. For this reason the regnal and exchequer years of English kings do not coincide.

3. H.W.C.Davis. 'The Anarchy of Stephen's Reign', in *EHR* XVIII, (1903), 630.

4. A.L.Poole, *From Domesday Book to Magna Carta*, 151.

5. See G.R.C.Davis, *Medieval Cartularies of Great Britain, A Short Catalogue* (London, 1958); E.L.C.Mullins, *Texts and Calendars, and Analytical Guide to Serial Publications* (R. Hist. Soc., 1958).
6. W.A.Morris, *The Medieval English Sheriff to 1300* (Manchester, 1927) is still a very useful guide.
7. *Reg.* III, 204.
8. *Reg.* III, 626.
9. *Reg.* III, 628.
10. *Dialogus de Scaccario*, 33.
11. *Reg.* III, 899.
12. *Reg.* III, 327.
13. *Reg.* III, 480.
14. *Reg.* III, 993.
15. *Reg.* III, 178. For a translation of the whole document see above, p. 78.
16. *Reg.* III, 306.
17. *Reg.* III, 274–6; R.H.C.Davis in *EHR* LXXIX, (1964), 299.
18. *Reg.* III, 386–94.
19. *KS*, 8–9.
20. *Reg.* III, 934.
21. Canterbury Cathedral Dean and Chapter muniments, Reg. B.f. 431; see below p. 272.
22. Warren Hollister 'The significance of scutage rates in 11th and 12th century England', in *EHR*, LXXV (1960), 577 ff.
23. See *Reg.* III, 919, 961, for examples of exemption from scutage.
24. On this subject see Helena M. Chew, *The English Ecclesiastical Tenants-in-Chief and Knight Service* (London, 1932).
25. *Scot*, assessment on a community; *Lot*, the contribution of the individual member.
26. *Consuetudines*, customary exactions, *custuma*, fixed dues.
27. *Lestagium*, lastage, due levied on a ship's lading.
28. See R.W.Southern in *Proc. Brit. Acad.* XLVIII.
29. *Reg.* III, 201, 489.
30. H.A.Cronne 'The royal forest in the reign of Henry I' in *Essays ... in Honour of J.E.Todd.*
31. *Gesta*, 1, 2.
32. See *HH*, 260.
33. *Reg.* III, 239–239*a*.
34. *Reg.* III, 566.
35. *Reg.* III, 129–131.
36. *Reg.* III, 41.
37. *Reg.* III, 163, 38.
38. *Reg.* III, 243.

39. R.Holmes, *The Cartulary of St John of Pontefract* (Yorkshire Archaeol. Soc. Record Series, 1902) II, 395.
40. See William Farrer, *Early Yorkshire Charters*, II, 432 ff.
41. 'William Cade, a financier of the twelfth century', in *EHR* XXVIII (1913) and additional notes in ibid., 522; 731. 'A moneylender's bonds', in *Essays Presented to R.L.Poole*, 190 ff.
42. Haigneré, *Chartes de S. Bertin*, 1, no. 215; *Archaeologia Cantiana*, IV, 206; J.H.Round, *Calendar of Documents Preserved in France, 1327*.
43. *HN*, 42.
44. *Reg.* II, **1524**.
45. *Reg.* III, **284**.
46. *Reg.* III, **316**.
47. On coinage see G.C.Brooke, *Catalogue of Coins in the British Museum. Norman Kings*, (2nd ed. with supplement, 1950); R.H.Dolley's chapter in *Medieval England*, ed. A.L.Poole (1958), I.
48. For coins of the 'Awbridge' type see F.Elmore Jones, in *The British Numismatic Journal*, 537–54.
49. *WN*, 70.
50. *Chronica Magistri Rogeri de Houdene* (RS. 4 vols. 1868–71) ed. W. Stubbs, I, 211.
51. *Reg.* III, **457, 489, 762–3**.
52. *Reg.* III, **675**.
53. See illustrations of these coins in Brooke's *Catalogue*.
54. *Reg.* III, **316**.

Chapter 9. Law and the Administration of Justice

1. Anglo Saxon Chronicle E.Version, sub ann. 1135.
2. Ibid. sub ann. 1137.
3. *PR 31 Hen. I.*
4. Ibid. 9.
5. Ibid. 32.
6. Ibid. 10. This must have been a plea of the Crown.
7. Ibid. 11.
8. Ibid. 13.
9. *HEL*, I, 86 *n.* 3. The reservation is mine.
10. Magna Carta cap. 40.
11. *Miskenning or stultiloquium* in a lawsuit was a verbal error in repeating the set formulae in which the litigants were obliged to plead. Every such mistake brought an amercement, if the pleading was to be retrieved and an adverse judgment for *miskenning* avoided.
12. Doris M.Stenton, *English Justice 1066–1215* – The Jayne Lectures for 1963 (Philadelphia, The American Philosophical Society, 1964).

See also R. van Caenegem, *Royal Writs in England from the Conquest to Glanvill* (Selden Soc. vol 77, 1959).

13. *HEL*, I, 58.
14. F.Liebermann, *Die Gesetze der Angelsachsen* (Halle, 1898 etc).
15. *HEL*, II, 447.
16. Leges Henrici Primi, x, 1.
17. *Gov.* ch. ix for an account of this and other judicial offices.
18. *Reg.* II, 1538.
19. *Reg.* II, 1000, 1211.
20. *Reg.* II, 1514, 1741.
21. *Reg.* III, 31, 313, 397.
22. *Reg.* III, 530.
23. *Reg.* III, 534, 546–50, 552, 559.
24. *Gov.* 174 ff.
25. Ibid; *Reg.* II, xix.
26. See H.A.Cronne, 'The office of local justiciar in England under the Norman kings', in *Univ. of Birmingham Hist. Journ.*, VI (1957) 18–38.
27. *Reg.* III, 274–6.
28. *G. de M.* 118.
29. *Reg.* III, 692.
30. *Reg.* III, 257.
31. *Reg.* III, 969.
32. *Chron. Mon. de Abingdon* (RS) II, 184; M.M.Bigelow, *Placita Anglo-Normannica* (Boston, 1879), 168; see also his *History of Procedure in England from the Norman Conquest. The Norman Period 1066–1204* (London 1880).
33. A.Jessopp and M.R.James ed. *The Life and Miracles of St William of Norwich by Thomas of Monmouth* (Cambridge, 1896). Latin text with full translation and an introduction (though the historical note on Norwich by Hudson is not reliable).
34. *Chron. Mon. de Bello* (RS) 72; Bigelow, *Placita*, 143.
35. *Reg.* III, 506; J.H.Round, *The Commune of London*, 99.
36. The *English Cnihtengild* was a pre-Conquest association of burgesses, possessing land and jurisdiction in London known as their *soke*.
37. *Reg.* III, 639.
38. *Reg.* III, 637.
39. *Chron. Mon. de Bello*, 70; Bigelow, *Placita*, 157.
40. British Museum, Harleian charter 83A, 12; *Reg.* I, 62.
41. *Deraigned*, proved their title.
42. *Reg.* III, 656.
43. *Reg.* III, 3.

44. *Reg.* III, 416.
45. *Reg.* III, 386.
46. William de Albini or d'Aubigny (Brito) of Belvoir. The family had connections with Dol and Rennes in Brittany. See 'Loyd's Address Book'.
47. See above p. 78.
48. *Reg.* III, 883. The customs referred to are, in this instance, customary levies.
49. *Reg.* I, 477; *Reg.* II, 1666.
50. *Reg.* III, 881–2.
51. *Reg.* III, 82.
52. *Reg.* III, 83.
53. *Reg.* III, 143, 54.
54. The word *et* here is probably a scribal error.
55. *Gov.* 192.
56. Canterbury Cathedral Dean and Chapter muniments, Reg. B. f. 431.
57. *Reg.* III, 382.
58. *Reg.* III, xxviii for information.
59. *Reg.* III, 546.
60 *Reg.* III, 547. Westminster Abbey muniments, 8113 (original).
61. *Reg.* III, 963. Univ. of Keele, Hatton Wood MS 708 (original).
62. See p. 217.
63. See F.M.Stenton, *First Century* 43 ff; W.O.Ault, *Private Jurisdiction in England* (Yale Historical Publications, 1923); N.Denholm Young, *Seigneurial Administration in England* (Oxford, 1937), ch. iii.
64. D.C.Douglas, *Feudal Documents from the Abbey of Bury St Edmunds* (London, Brit. Acad., 1932), 127, no. 133.
65. *RBE*, 200.
66. The year may have been 1138, since Stephen first besieged Bedford castle before Christmas, 1137. Rannulf, earl of Chester, helped him to take Bedford in 1146. Hugh Bigod is referred to in this account as earl, which he was not in 1138, but this is not decisive, as it may have been written some years after the event.
67. To appeal anyone involved an accusation of crime, in which the accuser (not infrequently a former associate in crime of the accused) offered the *duellum* or judicial ordeal by combat.
68. His recollection probably went back as far as Domesday.
69. *Pinchbeck Register*, ed. Lord Francis Hervey (Brighton, 1925) II, 297–9.
70. *Reg.* III, 133.
71. *Reg.* III, 212.

72. See F. de Zulueta ed., *Liber Pauperum* (Selden Soc. vol. 44, 1927), Introduction, for the life and work of Master Vacarius.

73. See H.A.Cronne, 'The royal forest in the reign of Henry I' in *Essays . . . in Honour of J.E.Todd.*

74. *Gesta*, 2.

75. *Reg.* III, 271.

76. *Reg.* III, 382.

77. The *vert* included everything that provided cover and feeding for the beasts of the forest.

78. *Reg.* III, 574.

79. *Reg.* III, 41, 129.

80. *Reg.* III, 239, 239a, 566.

81. *Reg.* III, 655.

Index